Caribbean Literature
and the Public Sphere

8/6

NEW WORLD STUDIES

J. Michael Dash, *Editor*

Frank Moya Pons and
Sandra Pouchet Paquet,
Associate Editors

Caribbean Literature and the Public Sphere

From the Plantation to the Postcolonial

Raphael Dalleo

University of Virginia Press

Charlottesville and London

University of Virginia Press
© 2011 by the Rector and Visitors of the University of Virginia
All rights reserved
Printed in the United States of America on acid-free paper
First published 2011

9 8 7 6 5 4 3 2 1

Library of Congress Cataloging-in-Publication Data
Dalleo, Raphael.
  Caribbean literature and the public sphere : from the plantation to the
postcolonial / Raphael Dalleo.
     p. cm. — (New world studies)
  Includes bibliographical references and index.
  ISBN 978-0-8139-3198-2 (cloth : alk. paper)
  ISBN 978-0-8139-3199-9 (pbk. : alk. paper)
  ISBN 978-0-8139-3202-6 (e-book)
  1. Caribbean literature—History and criticism. 2. Postcolonialism—
Caribbean Area. 3. Politics and literature—Caribbean Area. 4. Caribbean
Area—Intellectual life. 5. Public opinion—Caribbean Area. I. Title.
PN849.C3D35 2011
809'.89729—dc23

                                                          2011022865

THE
AMERICAN
LITERATURES
INITIATIVE

A book in the American Literatures Initiative (ALI), a collaborative
publishing project of NYU Press, Fordham University Press, Rutgers
University Press, Temple University Press, and the University of Virginia
Press. The Initiative is supported by The Andrew W. Mellon Foundation.
For more information, please visit www.americanliteratures.org.

Contents

Preface

PERIODIZATION IS AN ACTIVITY FRAUGHT with pitfalls, and the Caribbean context—with its multiple histories and temporalities—presents special challenges. My introduction addresses specific concerns that arise in periodizing comparatively across national and linguistic boundaries and traditions. Before asking how Caribbean literature might be periodized, however, it is worth asking if this endeavor is even worth attempting. Peter Hulme describes "historical periodization" as one of "the most resistant categories of Eurocentrism" ("Beyond the Straits" 42), because of its tendency to narrate world history via stages in European development as well as its reintroduction of the modernist teleology that drove Enlightenment and colonization alike. Alison Donnell's *Twentieth-Century Caribbean Literature* has mounted a powerful critique of attempts to construct a progressive narrative of Caribbean literary history. Donnell seeks to emphasize how "all histories and traditions are based on acts of selection, exclusion and preference" (4). Calling attention to canon building as an ideological process allows Donnell to deconstruct the present canon of Caribbean writing as the product of choices and selections made in the 1960s and 1970s that still exert influence on understandings of the field. The account of Caribbean literary history that develops from this moment, Donnell shows, became canonized because it resonated forcefully in the field's "nationalist moment of canon making" (42). I want to keep in mind Hulme's warning about the temptations of seeing history as a series of progressive stages, as well as Donnell's insight that every reconstruction of literary history is a story about the past informed by the present.

As much as Donnell's critique calls into question the kind of periodizing moves I am interested in making, her destabilizing of existing understandings of the Caribbean canon also opens up possibilities for telling different stories about the literary past like the one I tell in *Caribbean Literature and the Public Sphere*. Donnell's work makes visible how writers from the 1960s and 1970s like George Lamming and Kamau Brathwaite were able to project their own experiences and desires as the unifying logic of Caribbean writing in general. Donnell focuses especially on the teleological rise of nationalism in Caribbean literature, from its "awakening" in the 1930s to its full-blown emergence in the post–World War II era, as the most compelling of these stories. There are a number of other assumptions about the essential truth of Caribbean literature that come from the powerful histories constructed by what Donnell describes as the nationalist generation, few as enduring as the idea of "exile" as an organizing logic for Caribbean literature. Donnell's intervention clears space for an investigation like mine, where exile is viewed not as a transcendental trope of Caribbean experience but rather the reflection of a specific historical moment in the region's literary history: in the second half of this project, I argue for understanding this focus on exile as a product of the uncertainty about the social place of the writer brought about by the end of the modern colonial public sphere. Once these sorts of paradigms and critical assumptions are seen to be historical, the potential for looking at writers in a more dialectical relationship with society becomes possible.

Donnell's ability to call into question received tellings of Caribbean literary history comes in large part from her openness to the archive: as she puts it, "in order to deliver us to . . . the 'real' beginning of West Indian writing, these studies [by the nationalist generation] cut a narrow pathway through what I want to argue was a complex and densely populated literary scene" (42). Michael Dash points to a similar dynamic in Francophone literary history, where "the movements of the 1930s saw themselves as the beginning of Caribbean writing," and therefore "any effort at a periodization of francophone Caribbean writing must face head on the received ideas that have become entrenched about the origins of 'authentic' or 'true' Caribbean writing" (Dash, Introduction to Literary Genres 407). The 1930s functions as a myth of origins throughout the region by combining major events in anticolonial politics, such as the labor unrest in Jamaica and Trinidad and Tobago, Jacques Roumain's founding of Parti Communiste Haïtien in 1934, or the arrest of Pedro Albizu Campos in Puerto Rico in 1936, with literary events like the publication of Claude McKay's *Banana Bottom* in 1933 and the return of Aimé Césaire to Martinique in 1939.

My project seeks to resituate these events not as origins but as part of a moment of anticolonial consolidation made possible by a specific relationship between literature and the public sphere. In successfully crafting a heroic public role for the writer, these anticolonial men have made convenient founding fathers. But a wealth of new archival work has appeared in the past few decades to show just how much literary work from before this period exists. Moira Ferguson's 1987 reissue of the slave narrative *The History of Mary Prince* and her 1993 collection of writings by the Hart sisters sparked a veritable boom in republication of literary texts from the early British colonies. Nonfiction work from Jamaica followed, like Mary Seacole's 1857 *Wonderful Adventures*, republished in 1988, and Diana Paton's 2001 publication of *A Narrative of Events, since the First of August, 1834, by James Williams*. The presence of a number of early novels from Trinidad has especially changed the literary landscape, beginning with Selwyn Cudjoe's edited version of the 1854 novel *Emmanuel Appadocca* by Michel Maxwell Philip published in 1997 and continuing with a series of early Trinidadian novels, including *Warner Arundell, Adolphus, The Slave Son*, and *Rupert Gray*, all originally published between 1838 and 1907 and reissued from 2001 to 2006. Claims that Caribbean literature is a twentieth-century phenomenon can no longer be made in the face of this new material.

Along with these newly available texts, other forms of archival work have shed light on the range of this early writing. The opening up of the archive has shown the transnational routes that enmeshed the Francophone and Hispanophone Caribbean during the nineteenth and early twentieth centuries, in texts like Julio Ramos's *Divergent Modernities*, Kirsten Silva Gruesz's *Ambassadors of Culture*, Brent Hayes Edwards's *The Practice of Diaspora*, Anna Brickhouse's *Transamerican Literary Relations and the Nineteenth-Century Public Sphere*, Rodrigo Lazo's *Writing to Cuba*, and Laura Lomas's *Translating Empire*. New histories of the diverse forms of writing to emerge in the English colonies in this period have been assembled in Faith Smith's *Creole Recitations*, Cudjoe's *Beyond Boundaries*, Evelyn O'Callaghan's *Women Writing the West Indies, 1804–1939*, Leah Rosenberg's *Nationalism and the Formation of Caribbean Literature*, and Belinda Edmondson's *Caribbean Middlebrow*. Taken together, these new approaches to the archive make it possible to reconceptualize the literary history of the entire region.[1]

In attempting to tell my own story about Caribbean literature, to periodize it, and to draw broad conclusions about different moments in its development, I want to remain aware that overgeneralizing, leaving things out, and silencing are part of all literary history. But just as I do not want to lose sight of Donnell's argument for the ways this activity yields blindness, I also want to keep in mind the insights that Lamming, Brathwaite, and the other canon builders of the 1960s and 1970s were able to provide through their arguments and generalizations. I am not interested in separating their role as literary historians from their ideological agendas and political goals. Literary history is a construction just as all stories about history are, as David Scott explains in *Conscripts of Modernity*. Like Donnell, Scott insists on considering history writing as the act of telling a story from a particular context and perspective rather than of revealing the truth and making the past speak for itself. Scott turns to the ideas of the "problem-space" and "emplotment" to make the case that certain modes of storytelling can be more useful than others at particular historical junctures.[2] A problem-space, for Scott, is "an ensemble of questions and answers around which a horizon of identifiable stakes (conceptual as well as ideological-political stakes) hangs" (*Conscripts* 4). Problem-spaces are structured around certain questions for investigation, which then demand particular modes of emplotment; for example, "anticolonial stories about past, present, and future have typically been emplotted [as] Romance" (7) because of that genre's suitability for "narratives of overcoming" (8). One of the central insights Scott offers my own project is the historicity of these problem-spaces: "problem-spaces alter historically because problems are not timeless and do not have everlasting shapes. In new historical conditions old questions may lose their salience, their bite, and so lead the range of old answers that once attached to them to appear lifeless, quaint, not so much wrong as irrelevant" (4).[3] Different periods can be identified by the range of possibilities available to writers, and the kinds of political, generic, and formal moves that come to be privileged as seeming particularly useful or urgent to intervene in those circumstances.

In addition to allowing a rethinking of how periodization might be done without resorting to European historical stages or teleology, Donnell and Scott also point to a model for historicist work in which investigators do not try to hide their motives but actively consider their own relationship to the kinds of pasts they construct. As much as I am interested in understanding the past for its own sake, I am aware of my own desires to tell a particular story about that past for the present. It is easy for an academic in the humanities to be nostalgic for a past moment when literature seemed to matter and when literary intellectuals could imagine themselves as translators or even leaders of "the people." As problematic as those assumptions may have been—and part of my project is to highlight contradictions even at moments when a heroic intellectual identity seemed most coherent—it remains tempting. Regardless of how much a contemporary intellectual might want to revive this earlier model, however, as Scott puts it, that moment is "not one that we can inhabit today" (45). *Conscripts of Modernity* makes a strong case that our context demands different political and critical projects than the "progressive ideologies (radical nationalisms, Marxisms, Fanonian liberationists, indigenous socialisms, or what have you)" (1) that Scott groups together as the "anticolonial answers" to a problem-space different from our own (33). My project begins from the same premise Scott outlines in *Conscripts of Modernity*, that "a criticism of the postcolonial present" (9) requires acknowledging that contemporary obstacles to equality and freedom may be similar to but are ultimately distinct from those faced by the generation represented in Scott's narrative by C. L. R. James in 1938, and that the intellectual identities and identifications available today have changed irreversibly.

So in the context of this postcolonial present, what is the purchase of theorizing a comparative history of a Caribbean literary public sphere? With neoliberalism's dogma of privatization as a leading ideology of contemporary imperialism, the desire to speak in the public name or conjure a public into existence seems more crucial than ever. Thinking about the commonalities in the historical experiences faced by the various islands can be useful in formulating solidarities within the region. While the particularities of each island's development may be distinct, the various islands continue to occupy closely related positions within global power structures. The contemporary challenges each island faces in this global context are similar enough that more intellectual exchange within the region will help the project of imagining new futures. Internationalism has been central to the social movements that have brought about progress toward liberty and equality, as my examination of abolitionism and anticolonialism makes clear.

If the comparative form of my investigation is one part of how this project seeks to contribute to regional solidarity, its content—considering how the possibilities available to intellectuals have changed as the result of realignments in the forces of domination during key historical moments—suggests ways that intellectuals today can formulate new roles in the public sphere. As part of that reconsideration, my project analyzes the roles intellectuals have played in oppositional projects of the past, to help think about how contemporary intellectual identities can be similar to and different from these predecessors. The book I coauthored with Elena Machado Sáez, *The Latino/a Canon and the Emergence of Post-Sixties Literature*, looks more closely at some of the critical interventions that contemporary writers have imagined despite the crisis of anticolonialism as an inspirational project; the conclusion of *Caribbean Literature and the Public Sphere* touches on this contemporary moment, with a discussion of Dionne Brand's work as a meditation on how intellectuals can contest new forms of international domination. In this way, postcolonialism is not viewed as signifying the surmounting of colonialism or as its leftover influence; instead, postcolonialism can be understood as a response to the shift in international regimes of hierarchy and domination that both takes account of and reimagines the forms of opposition offered by previous models.

In locating my work at the intersections of the different conversations taking place within the various Caribbean linguistic traditions, in the interstices of the narratives colonial/postcolonial and modern/postmodern, I hope that my project is not "Eurocentric" in the way Hulme criticizes periodization for being. At the same time, I fully acknowledge the modernist impulse for categorization that underlies the narrative I have constructed. I am not sure that I share the view Donnell and Scott sometimes express, that it is entirely possible or desirable to leave behind modernist modes of thought that long to construct grand narratives and explanatory systems. In fact, both Donnell and Scott show in other moments (which I have noted in this preface's endnotes) how difficult it can be to escape from that way of thinking, since even the desire to overcome outdated modes of thought assumes some degree of teleology. At the very least, I have found it productive to tell this story; I can only hope that readers will find it productive to think through as well.

Caribbean Literature and the Public Sphere is positioned in textual dialogue with a number of groups. I have already mentioned the recent wealth of archival work on the nineteenth- and early-twentieth-century Caribbean by researchers like Brickhouse, Cudjoe, Edmondson, Edwards, Ferguson, Lazo, Lomas, O'Callaghan, Paton, Rosenberg, Silva Gruesz, and Smith; the expansion of the archive by these literary historians—to which I hope I have made some contribution—has made it possible to get a fuller picture of the earlier print culture of the region and to start drawing new conclusions about how Caribbean authors navigated publication during those periods. The kind of comparative work between different language groups I am here attempting has deep roots in Caribbean studies, from the collaborations between figures like Aimé Césaire and

Wilfredo Lam or C. L. R. James's work on Haiti from the 1930s to the conversations surrounding Casa de las Américas in the 1960s and 1970s. More recently, the idea of pursuing the correspondences in the region's literary history has animated the work of critics like Michael Dash, Lizabeth Paravisini-Gebert, and Silvio Torres-Saillant, as well as the scholars who have collaborated on James Arnold's multivolume *A History of Literature in the Caribbean*. My work seeks to build on these kinds of explorations.

In addition to these particularly Caribbean conversations, *Caribbean Literature and the Public Sphere* is obviously indebted to the field of postcolonial studies for opening up the canon and enabling the critique of European- and U.S.-centered narratives of history and literature. Works ranging from Edward Said's *Orientalism* to Robert Young's *Postcolonialism* have offered important insights about the relationship of cultural forms to historical modes of power and domination, and more recently Graham Huggan's *The Postcolonial Exotic* and Sarah Brouillette's *Postcolonial Writers and the Global Literary Marketplace* have suggested how sociological approaches to literature like those of Pierre Bourdieu might be translated to the non-European world. Latin Americanist adaptations of the cultural materialism of Bourdieu, Jürgen Habermas, and Raymond Williams by thinkers like Angel Rama, Julio Ramos, and Jean Franco also form an important intertext for this book, as I seek to build on their insights about how the institutions that structure writing and reception are invested with forms of power often not considered in traditional approaches to close reading. My debts to all of these predecessors should be apparent throughout this book; I mention them explicitly at this point to recognize how they have shaped my thinking about history, politics, culture, literature, and the Caribbean.

As important as it has been for me to imagine contributing to these textual dialogues, I have been fortunate to be part of a number of other more embodied conversations about my work. I attended a summer seminar with Manthia Diawara at the School of Criticism and Theory at Cornell University toward the beginning of this project, as well as a National Endowment for the Humanities (NEH) Summer Institute at Johns Hopkins University as I was finishing the manuscript; the readings and discussions from those experiences contributed immensely to the eventual form of this book. I have presented parts of this project at the annual Caribbean Studies Association and West Indian Literature conferences, and both venues have provided invaluable intellectual communities. I have also been invited by a number of universities to present this work, including Ohio University, Kent State University, and the Mona campus of the University of the West Indies. The conversations generated in these conferences and presentations have been crucial to helping me refine my ideas.

Parts of this book have been published previously, and imagining (and sometimes hearing from!) readers further helped me formulate my ideas. Part of chapter 4 was published previously as "Bita Plant as Literary Intellectual: The Anticolonial Public Sphere and *Banana Bottom*" in the *Journal of West Indian Literature* 17, no. 1 (November 2008): 54–67. An earlier version of chapter 6 appeared as "Authority and the Occasion for Speaking in the Caribbean Literary Field: George Lamming and Martin Carter" in *Small Axe* 10, no. 2: 19–39 (Copyright 2006, Small Axe, Inc. Reprinted by permission of the publisher, Duke University Press). Portions of chapter 7 were published as "Readings from Aquí y Allá: Music, Commercialism, and the Latino-Caribbean Transnational Imaginary" in *Constructing Vernacular Culture in the Trans-Caribbean*, edited by Holger Henke and Karl-Heinz Magister, and published by Lexington Books in 2008. Parts of the conclusion appeared as "Post-Grenada, Post-Cuba, Postcolonial: Rethinking Revolutionary Discourse in Dionne Brand's *In Another Place, Not Here*" in a special issue of *Interventions: International Journal of Postcolonial Studies* 12, no. 1 (2010): 64–73 (http://www.informaworld.com/riij). These journals and presses all generously granted me permission to reprint this material here, and I am especially appreciative of the anonymous referees as well as editors David Scott, Victor Chang, Shalini Puri, and Holger Henke, who provided me with helpful commentary on my work.

A number of my colleagues have shown tremendous generosity in reading portions of this book. Leah Rosenberg, Belinda Edmondson, Norval Edwards, and Elena Machado Sáez provided me with excellent feedback as I was revising the manuscript, and Patricia Saunders was a valuable interlocutor and source of advice in many other ways. Cathie Brettschneider has been an ideal editor at the University of Virginia Press, and thanks to her I received extremely helpful revision suggestions from New World Studies Series Editor Michael Dash and two anonymous reviewers. Being able to participate in this kind of community of scholars has undoubtedly made this a stronger book.

The American Literatures Initiative has been very supportive of this project, and Tim Roberts in particular has greatly facilitated the process of turning the manuscript into a book. Andrew Wallace at the Figge

Art Museum helped me find an image for the book's cover. A fellowship from the American Council of Learned Societies (ACLS) gave me time and resources to complete this manuscript; thanks to the ACLS and to Larry Breiner and Faith Smith for supporting my fellowship application. Funding from the Tinker Foundation and Florida Atlantic University's Lifelong Learning Society allowed me to visit archives in Cuba and Jamaica, and I also used travel funds from Florida Atlantic University's Department of English for archival research in Guyana. I want to particularly thank the staffs at the Casa de las Américas in Havana, the National Library of Jamaica, the National Library of Guyana, and the Schomburg Center in New York for facilitating my research. In Cuba, I was able to interview a number of figures connected to the *testimonio* movement, including Miguel Barnet, Nancy Morejón, Angel Luis Fernández Guerra, and Ambrosio Fornet, who were all extremely generous with their time. I also want to thank the fantastic teachers I have had over the years who have inspired in me the intellectual curiosity that I hope this book exhibits. From Amherst College, Leah Hewitt, Andrew Parker, Barry O'Connell, and especially my undergraduate adviser, Rhonda Cobham-Sander; at Stony Brook, Román de la Campa, Robert Harvey, Sandy Petrey, and Helen Cooper; and the wonderful doctoral students and faculty in the Caribbean literature in English program at the University of Puerto Rico, particularly Lowell Fiet, María Cristina Rodriguez, Denise López Mazzeo, Don Walicek, Edgardo Pérez Montijo, Elsa Luciano, Loretta Collins, and Reinhard Sander. And, of course, I must once again wholeheartedly thank Peter and Bruce Dalleo, my first teachers from whom I am still learning.

Introduction

Periodizing the Public Sphere

THE CARIBBEAN POSES MULTIPLE OBSTACLES for literary history. Literary historians cannot seek the traditional unity of the nation in a region comprised of more than a dozen national units; language provides no more stable a ground, with literature from the Caribbean appearing in at least four imperial languages and a number of local languages. Political histories of the region vary from a nation independent since 1804 (Haiti) to a number of islands still not independent (Puerto Rico, Martinique, and Curaçao, among others). If literary history seeks either to make comparisons or to periodize, then, is either possible in the Caribbean case? In the spirit of what Emily Apter calls "postcolonial comparatism," this book suggests that not only is comparative literary history possible, but that thinking comparatively can actually help periodization, calling attention to correspondences among the region's literary histories. Instead of trying to theorize a generic condition across the region, I focus on particular histories to show how changes in political, economic, and social structures have produced different sets of possibilities for writers to imagine their relationship to institutions of governance and publication. I am calling these structures and institutions the Caribbean public sphere. This book looks at three moments in the history of the relationship between writers and the public sphere: first, plantation slavery as an organizing structure of domination and abolitionism as its oppositional discourse; second, the rise of modern colonialism after emancipation and anticolonialism as a discursive project opposed to this new system of order but haunted by gendered contradictions in the image of the writer as political man of action; and finally, decolonization as a moment of transition from colonialism to a new form of international hierarchy and domination, as well as from an apparently assured masculine anticolonial discourse to a postcolonial crisis of the writer's role in the public sphere.

I use the concept of the public sphere as a contextual reality within which writers operate as well as an imagined idea that writers represent in their texts. The two registers of the public sphere—material reality and imagined ideal—interact as a complex dialectic: the institutions and structures of the public sphere shape writers' imaginations even as writers imagine alternative arrangements and new ways of thinking that help create new public spaces and identities. These institutions and structures include actual physical spaces where information is exchanged and social relations are formed, as well as the virtual spaces of print culture and publication where debates are often sparked or extended. These actually existing spaces allow writers to imagine where public debate and community building might be located even as political, social, and economic realities circumscribe the range of possibilities available.

The chapters that follow see writers locating their aspirations for publicness in spaces ranging from the plantation to the pirate ship, the church to the colonial courthouse, the marketplace to the pages of the literary magazine, the carnival parade to the traffic jam. The literary projects I examine show writers trying to envision discursive agents for these Caribbean public spheres: the public is thus in some ways an audience but frequently a more idealized sense of the people (whether the folk, *el pueblo*, or *le peuple*) as something that writing and publication can help produce and bring into existence. Ideas of public and private map in complicated ways onto binaries like reason versus emotion or calculation versus sensitivity: attending to the ways these different categories appear in Caribbean writing over time shows how conceptions of publicness become raced and gendered, and how the process of imagining an embodied public has proven both enabling and restricting.

Theorizing the Caribbean Public Sphere

Jürgen Habermas's theory of the public sphere provides a useful framework for understanding the relationship of writers to this complex matrix of social forces—from political structures and audience to the institutions of publication and dissemination—but translating this framework to the Caribbean context requires that I modify some of his basic assumptions. Habermas's vision of the public sphere is not designed to address the transnational nature of power characterizing a colonial or postcolonial site like the Caribbean. In light of a history where slavery restricted power to a small elite and modern colonialism meant the removal of local power from a population where the proportion of nonwhites made representative government seem terrifying to these elites, the Caribbean public sphere could not possibly develop as the bourgeois public sphere Habermas describes arising in Europe. In the story Habermas tells in *The Structural Transformation of the Public Sphere*, the European literary public sphere emerges as a space of rational debate independent of the institutions of the state, yet claiming the right to critique and intervene in the functions of the state on behalf of the citizenry. Once this public sphere—physically grounded in salons and coffee houses but also articulated in newspapers, pamphlets, and other early literary forms—breaks the church and state's monopoly on power during the seventeenth and eighteenth centuries, public debate becomes theoretically available to all: unlike the feudal model, in which a person's status in society determined how his or her ideas would be received, a public sphere "governed by the laws of the free market" (Habermas 79) means that "the authority of the better argument could assert itself against that of social hierarchy and in the end can carry the day" (36). This newly organized public, where arguments could appeal only to reason rather than rank, thus established itself as a counterpoint to the power of the state: "By the turn of the nineteenth century, the public's involvement in the critical debate of political issues had become organized to such an extent that in the role of a permanent critical commentator it had definitively broken the exclusiveness of Parliament and evolved into the officially designated discussion partner of the delegate" (66). Crucial to Habermas's definition is the way that the western European bourgeois public sphere could be a critic of the parliamentary government, but an officially acknowledged one invested with the power to keep the state in check by its ability to speak in the name of the public. With access to discursive expression severely limited under plantation slavery, and a lack of representative political institutions in the Caribbean during the period of modern colonialism, the idea that local appeals might be heard by those in power could not inspire intellectual projects as it did in Europe.

Attending to the blockages in Caribbean access to the public sphere also serves as a reminder of the reality that even in Europe this bourgeois public sphere did not actually give voice to all of the elements of what was in fact a diverse and conflicted public; the European public sphere was restricted in terms of access to its institutions, by what it would recognize as rational debate, and thus by race, class, and gender. In a special issue of the journal *Public Culture*, the editors, calling themselves the "Black Public Sphere Collective," wonder if Habermas's description of the bourgeois public sphere could be adapted to theorize a black public sphere, which, in their words, has "sought to make Blackness *new* and remove it from the pathological spaces reserved for it in Western culture" (xiii). In other words, the creation of black narratives and cultural forms and their consumption by a black public are part of "a more general process of diasporic world-building" (xiii). In the issue's first essay, Houston Baker critiques Habermas's monolithic construction of the bourgeois public sphere as "overdetermined both ideologically and in terms of gender, overconditioned by the market and by history, and utopian in the extreme" (8). Such a bourgeois public sphere, Baker shows, depended precisely on the exclusion of enslaved people, the poor, and women as nonproperty owners. Building on the work of Nancy Fraser and Bruce Robbins, Baker argues against mourning the decline of this exclusionary bourgeois public sphere, and in favor of conceiving of public space as made up of a "plurality of spheres" (10), among them a "subaltern, black American counterpublic" able to "recapture and recode all existing American arrangements of publicness" (12).[1]

My discussion of the Caribbean emphasizes the existence of these alternative publics. Yet while the abolitionist and anticolonial literary public sphere in the Caribbean may have features in common with the black American counterpublic Baker describes, I also call attention to the differences that come from the distinctiveness of the Caribbean's colonial and postcolonial context. In *Publics and Counterpublics*, Michael Warner defines a counterpublic as a public that "maintains at some level, conscious or not, an awareness of its subordinate status" (56). The Caribbean literary public sphere, in which participants are constantly reminded of their subordinated position in relation to European literature and political debate, would in this way resemble a counterpublic. On the other hand, Warner goes on to add that "a counterpublic in this sense is usually related to a subculture" (56). A counterpublic thus serves a different function than the theoretical "larger public"; whereas the counterpublic is marginal, the "larger public" claims to express "public opinion" (56) and for that reason has been instrumental historically in national projects of imagining a common identity. The Caribbean public sphere that I describe arising during the modern colonial period is a counterpublic marginalized from and thus opposed to (rather than a legitimizing check upon) the true centers of power, but at the same time served the function of Habermas's idealized European bourgeois public sphere in claiming to represent the hopes and aspirations of the majority of the populace.[2] In the Caribbean, anticolonial writers authorized themselves as spokespeople for the nation by imagining themselves speaking for a marginalized counterpublic outside the circuits of power as well as a public representing the nation and aspiring to take control of the state. The main thesis of this book is that the shifting tension between these two demands—of being oppositional to power yet representing the nation—is crucial to periodizing Caribbean literature. I highlight the shifts from a period of slavery in which the majority of Caribbean people were not permitted to be thought of as part of the public, to a modern colonial era in which aspirations to represent a national public and a counterpublic of resistance come together, to a postcoloniality that forces writers to choose between what are now seen as competing projects.

Looking at how writers interact with—and represent their interactions with—the public sphere provides a useful entry into thinking about the various ways that writers have sought to speak to the region's social and political realities in different historical moments. Acknowledging the diversity of approaches taken by Caribbean writers in any era is a challenge for periodization. Rather than trying to reduce these competing discourses to a single logic or spirit of the age characterizing various historical periods, I prefer to look at each of the three moments I examine as distinct fields. From this approach, the periods of plantation slavery, modern colonialism, and postcoloniality can be seen as each structured by a coherent set of rules distinguishing one field from what precedes and what follows. Plantation slavery requires Caribbean writers to make antislavery appeals to a European public because of the discursive monopoly of the planter class within the region; modern colonialism opens up the possibility for a local public sphere through the growth of literacy and print culture as well as the oppositional ideology of literature articulating a counterpublic opposed to foreign power; postcoloniality puts into question this privileging of the literary in light of the discourse of privatized professionalism coupled with new culture industries. The breaks between these moments are not clean, and part of my interest is in the transitions between these organizing systems where the rules that govern how one enters the field, what can be said from that position, and how much prestige that position will achieve are contested and remade. In the Caribbean, the unevenness of the professionalization of literary work and the shifting prestige assigned to the written word intersect with the social power of the field's participants to produce heterogeneous literary fields with a variety of competing discourses.

In emphasizing how writing is part of a literary field, I am adopting a sociological approach resembling that of Pierre Bourdieu.[3] Bourdieu's approach shows how writers operate within a constrained set of possibilities governed by certain historically determined rules, even as they make choices within those rules that can range from accommodation to opposition to more conflicted positions in-between. The variety of choices available is in part because the rules governing the literary field are not necessarily the same ones that govern other social sites. Writers help to define the rules of the literary field, so that close reading of the work of particular writers can show both how they understand the positions available to them and how they work to change the range of possibilities.

Sarah Brouillette frames *Postcolonial Writers in the Global Literary Marketplace* in response to what she calls "Bourdieu's important argument . . . that the rise of a large-scale literary marketplace that made it possible for authors to make a living by writing occurred in tandem with the development of an ideology of artistic purity and separation from economic concerns" (3). In the Caribbean, the ideology of the literary has often been premised on this kind of disavowal of the market. But disinterestness or absolute autonomy has not been the dominant ideology in the region. The idea of the writer's public and political duty recasts critiques or denials of market values as part of an effort to align literature with a counterpublic of resistance. While Bourdieu's framework of looking at literature as a field is useful for analyzing the mediated autonomy of cultural producers, many of his specific observations about how the French literary field operates are not adaptable to the Caribbean.

I have chosen to examine literary writers who represent a wide variety of responses to the shifting place of literature within the public sphere, though obviously this selection cannot approach a comprehensive account of all of the different positions available or taken within a particular field. In some instances, reading texts that managed to achieve privileged positions in the field sheds light on what allowed certain writers to speak to the desires and anxieties of their particular public sphere. In other instances, examining voices that failed to achieve that kind of institutionalization calls attention to moves or choices the field was less likely to valorize. In both cases, I am foregrounding writers who consciously engage with and stage their positioning in the field, in order to think about what their choices demonstrate about the possibilities and limits of their discursive space. Each literary field is structured by specific rules governing which literary acts will gain a hearing in the public sphere and which will not; these rules are created in negotiation between writers themselves as well as between writers and the larger field of power. My literary history is therefore organized around how writers have chosen to interact with that field of power, even if the literariness to which different writers aspire varies widely in—and is often a defining characteristic of—each of these periods.

While *Caribbean Literature and the Public Sphere* focuses on literature, my approach is also a form of cultural studies, an intellectual tradition that in the Caribbean has provided valuable models for placing cultural production in the context of social structures and institutional power without reducing culture to a mechanical expression of that hegemony. Reconstructing the choices available to and made by each of these literary writers is impossible without looking at their relationships to other discourses, from the political to the popular, that have at different historical moments had more or less influence on the field of power. Understanding the rules of the literary field means placing it in dialogue with other fields, although an in-depth examination of the ways these other fields configured the public sphere is beyond the scope of this book: scholars such as Diana Paton, John Garrigus, Moira Ferguson, José Luis González, and others have shown how juridical, political, religious, and popular discourses have contributed to the constitution of a Caribbean public sphere, and I can only hope that my work adds another dimension to understanding that formation.

The relations of power within which various actors negotiate the rules of the literary field are intersected by, but not reducible to, issues of race, class, and gender, and my attention thus extends to the ways in which those identities and the discourses surrounding them impact how writers position themselves. The public sphere is by no means a neutral space, and is heavily coded by assumptions about white European bourgeois maleness as a prerequisite for participating and being heard. *Caribbean Literature and the Public Sphere* therefore explores how writers from a variety of social positions interact with discourses about race, class, and gender, which frequently make complex demands on writing: the supposed incompatibility of blackness and reason, or the anxiety about literature as a private and therefore feminized activity, leads to responses often characterized by contradiction. The writers examined here frequently reinforce but sometimes manage to redefine the inequalities embedded in historical constructions of what it means to occupy a public versus a private identity in a colonial or postcolonial setting.

Periodization thus depends on seeing a coherent field in which writers work within certain rules of the game that make specific relationships with the public sphere possible. Each period can then be defined by a particular field of possibilities available for writers to construct a relationship to a spectral public, partly real and partly imagined. Along with my investment in describing the contours of each of these fields, I am especially interested in looking at the interstices and transitional moments in Caribbean literary history. The persistently peripheral location of the Caribbean in relation to the centers of global power means that one consistent structural element of the Caribbean public sphere is the contradictory push and pull of consolidation and oppositionality. The moments of transition, in which one organizing system gives way to another, are thus especially interesting as renegotiations of power in response to the successes of oppositional challenges. Modern colonialism, in this reading, emerges to close down the libratory energies opened up by emancipation and the end of plantation slavery, just as postcoloniality plays a parallel role in the aftermath of decolonization. My project therefore focuses especially on how Caribbean writers, aligning themselves with these oppositional projects, navigate the transitions and in the process help remake the rules of the public sphere. *Caribbean Literature and the Public Sphere* begins with the mid-nineteenth-century passage from plantation slavery to modern colonialism as a period in which redefinitions in power relations are reflected in the discursive experiments in Caribbean writing; it continues by looking at how anticolonial writing emerges as a way of giving literary intellectuals a privileged public role; and finally, it examines the crisis of that model in the wake of the decolonization period.

Caribbean Literature: Colonial/Postcolonial or Modern/Postmodern?

The story of literature's relationship to the public sphere that I tell in this book—from plantation slavery to modern colonialism to postcoloniality—highlights some of the insights and blind spots in other prominent narratives of Caribbean literary history. The narrative of colonial/postcolonial, for example, may have some explanatory value for the Anglophone islands that attained independence from the British empire during the 1960s and 1970s. But critics who focus on the Spanish- and French-speaking islands tend to figure history by a different narrative entirely, of colonialism/modernity/postmodernity.[4] Edouard Glissant's theorization of the Caribbean's "irruption into modernity" is perhaps the most cited of any line from *Le discours antillais* and has inspired a number of Francophone investigations of Caribbean modernity and postmodernity, such as Michael Dash's *The Other America: Caribbean Literature in a New World Context* or Shireen Lewis's *Race, Culture, and Identity: Francophone West African and Caribbean Literature and Theory from Négritude to Créolité*. From the Hispanic Caribbean, Antonio Benítez-Rojo's *La isla que se repite: El Caribe y la perspectiva posmoderna* has played a parallel role in bringing the framework of postmodernism into Caribbean studies. Silvia Álvarez Cubelo's *Un país del porvenir: El afán de modernidad en Puerto Rico* and Héctor López's *La música caribeña en la literatura de la postmodernidad* both explore Caribbean culture within the narrative of modernity/postmodernity, just as Juan Otero Garabís employs this terminology in discussing the contemporary "modern (or postmodern) cultures" of the region.[5] Larger debates within which these linguistic traditions participate have undoubtedly reinforced the ways that history is narrated. Whereas the English-speaking Caribbean can join discussions of postcolonialism where voices from former British colonies are often the loudest, the Hispanic Caribbean's literary field is more closely aligned with a Latin American studies tradition that during the 1980s and 1990s was dominated by the "postmodernism debate."[6] The contribution of the Caribbean to modernity has reemerged in Francophone Caribbean studies through rereadings of the Haitian Revolution, with Michel-Rolph Trouillot, Sibylle Fischer, and Nick Nesbitt playing leading roles in bringing that island's experience to bear on a narrative of modernity's constitution that usually privileges contemporaneous revolutions in the United States and France.

As diverse as these historical experiences and as difficult as juggling the multiple temporalities of Caribbean history may be, I believe that placing the Hispanophone, Francophone, and Anglophone narratives alongside one another reveals a number of correspondences. In Latin Americanist versions, the colonial period ends during the early decades of the nineteenth century with revolutions and independence; this period is followed by modernity, which passes during the mid-twentieth century into postmodernity. The Hispanic Caribbean, of course, fits poorly if political status becomes a primary emphasis, since in Cuba and the Dominican Republic independence came much later than on the mainland, and in Puerto Rico political independence has not yet been achieved. The Francophone Caribbean yields a similarly diverse and apparently anomalous set of experiences, with Haiti's independence coming before the Latin American mainland and with Martinique and Guadeloupe currently even more closely incorporated into the metropole than Puerto Rico. The Anglophone Caribbean narrative, by contrast, divides history into a colonial period, lasting until the 1960s, and a postcolonial phase, beginning with independence from Britain; this version of history again places emphasis on political status as definitive, and has the added disadvantage of making the preindependence period an undifferentiated past and glossing over the difference between plantation slavery and what followed.

Instead of an emphasis on political status, then, I want to focus on how, throughout the region, broader shifts can be seen in terms of the Caribbean's position in the international world order and how power is therefore manifested in the region. This approach makes visible a first stage in which the experience of plantation slavery dominates the early economic, political, and social organization of the region, even as the models colonial/modern/postmodern or colonial/postcolonial can tend to downplay the importance of slavery as an organizing social and economic system. Identifying plantation slavery as a regional period emphasizes how unevenly different locations experienced epochal change: the distinct forms the emancipation movement took meant that slavery ended at very different times throughout the region, with Haiti dramatically overthrowing this system and establishing its independence in 1804 and the region's imperial powers attempting to come to terms with that event throughout the rest of the century. Britain's abolition of the slave trade in 1807 and then slavery in its colonies in 1834, emancipation in French colonies in 1848, and the final end of the slave system in Cuba in 1886 mark a long transition in the region.[7] The planter monopoly on the region's public sphere meant that any local appeals made by people of African descent would necessarily be discounted or actively censored. But the bipolar nature of power during the plantation period, in which the Caribbean planter class vied with the metropolis, sometimes allowed enslaved people to play these groups against each other. Two forms of opposition to slavery therefore emerged: abolitionism, which used writing to try to mobilize a public but could envision that public only in England; and various popular counterpublics of radical opposition within the region such as music, religion, and physical confrontation. Each of these forms contains elements of a Caribbean public sphere, but the context of plantation slavery did not allow the kinds of alliances between authors and local public that would later be possible.

The end of slavery as an organizing system opened up a range of new opportunities for Caribbean people to participate in the public sphere, but by the late nineteenth century the imperial powers had developed new ways of organizing their relationships with their colonies, which I call the modern colonial system to distinguish it from plantation-based colonialism. Under the plantation system, the region's white upper classes could claim some local autonomy; however, slavery's abolition and the specter of Haiti made it even more important to remove power from the local context lest a future democratic state be controlled by nonwhite people. Unlike in the United States or South America, where in the late eighteenth and early nineteenth centuries the Creole elites led revolutions against colonial control, in many cases the Caribbean planter class actually gave away power for fear of governance becoming more public: the Dominican Republic's decision to return to Spanish rule in 1861 is perhaps the most extreme example, but the annexation movement in Cuba and the willing acceptance of Crown Colony status in Jamaica in 1866 show the same preference among the local ruling classes for stability of unequal social relations over self-rule.

The codification of the modern colonial system during the nineteenth century thus meant the end of whatever limited local sovereignty the colonies had until that point possessed, making possible a very different idea of the public sphere's relationship to the institutions of power. Instead of the plantation public sphere, in which the only local expression permitted was a direct extension of ruling-class power, modern colonialism created a divide between foreign power and regional public articulation. This occurred through the removal of political power from the local context, a reorganization of international relations that took place throughout the region at the onset of modern colonialism.[8] One of the distinctive characteristics of systematized modern colonialism was the removal of virtually all power from the local context to manage and close down the liberationist energies opened up by the end of slavery. This new organization of power ironically (or perhaps better yet, dialectically) allowed anticolonial writers to conceive of their work as occupying the intersection of the demands to speak simultaneously for a public and a counterpublic.

Whether the important dates for the transition to modern colonialism are 1866, the year in which Jamaica's 200-year-old elected House of Assembly was replaced by a Legislative Council appointed by the governor, or 1898, the year in which the United States made explicit its role as a formal colonial power in the region by taking possession of Cuba and Puerto Rico, or even 1915 with the U.S. occupation of Haiti, these new forms of domination arose in the vacuum created by the end of slavery and the rise of modern capitalism based on an ideology of free markets and unfree governance. This system of power dominated the region from the late nineteenth century until modern colonialism began to be dismantled in the mid-twentieth century. The narratives of modern/postmodern and colonial/postcolonial coincide precisely at this point, with all parts of the region experiencing shifts after World War II that reflected the rise of a new international order. The transition to becoming overseas departments of France undergone by Martinique and Guadeloupe in 1946, the approval of a new constitution in Puerto Rico in 1952 designating the island an Estado Libre Asociado of the United States, the Cuban Revolution in 1959, and the end of British rule in Jamaica and Trinidad and Tobago in 1962 are not precisely analogous events. But taken as a whole, these diverse changes demonstrate how, throughout the Caribbean, political status was redefined in the years following World War II as part of a broad reorganization of the region's political, economic, and social structures and relationships that transformed the region's public sphere.

Describing this recent set of changes as postcolonial may seem inaccurate if the focus is only on political status, which helps explain why islands that did not achieve independence during the years following World War II have often preferred the lens of postmodernity for understanding these changes. Referring to this new world order as postcoloniality (rather than postcolonialism or the postcolonial) is meant to convey the sense signified by the term "postmodernity" of a new context that goes beyond political status to include economic, social, and technological changes. If independence is the only measurement, some islands would thus not yet be postcolonial, while Haiti's early independence leads scholars like Martin Munro to call Haiti "postcolonial . . . since 1804" (268). Yet even Munro chooses a date from the post–World War II period as a turning point in Haitian literary history—the title of his book is *Exile and Post-1946 Haitian Literature*—showing that despite Haiti's distinct historical development, that nation's history is characterized by crises and epochal breaks that parallel the rest of the region. Anglophone theories of the postcolonial often dismiss experiences like that of Haiti as anomalous; but in this case the flight into exile that Munro identifies taking place in Haiti after 1946 is part of the larger postcolonial crisis of the writer's public place seen throughout the region. In other words, I am suggesting that a more precise and fuller picture of the region's history sees parallels in even apparent anomalies like Haiti. Juan Flores makes a similar point by suggesting how the "still-colonial" Puerto Rico "stands as a test of the universalist claims of postcolonial theory" (*From Bomba* 36). He brings up Puerto Rico's current status not to emphasize it as unassimilable, but as a reality that redefines how postcoloniality can be understood. Flores describes present-day Puerto

Rico as the "lite colonial" or the "postcolonial colony" (36). On the one hand, these designations insist that the structures of colonialism continue into the present. At the same time, "it is also clear that Puerto Rico is a colony in a different way" (36); domination has "shift[ed] from a primarily political, state- and institution-driven force to a commercial one impelled by markets and oriented toward consumers" (38), making the postcolonial colony subject to "a capitalism that has become Puerto Ricanist" through encouraging the local public sphere to deploy nationalist icons as part of its system of control (37). Once the histories of Haiti and Puerto Rico are acknowledged, postcoloniality can be understood not as the end of foreign domination or even a partial freedom still haunted by the colonial past but as a new form of hegemony born of the decline of the modern colonial system in order to manage the successes of decolonization. There is no law of history that has predetermined how these shifts from one period to another would occur; the interaction of resistance movements with systems of control have dictated the forms of freedom and domination that have emerged.

Rather than reading historical periods such as plantation slavery, modern colonialism, or postcoloniality as organized around a singular logic, then, I want to point to how each is governed by overarching transnational structures of domination that particular islands and writers come to terms with in different ways. The end of plantation slavery or the change in status after World War II did not play out identically throughout the region. But in these two moments, epochal changes were brought about by the need to regulate the forces unleashed by emancipation in the first case and decolonization in the second. The distinct development of each island, as well as the continued persistence of past structures and inequalities, makes it seem almost impossible to draw distinct lines between these different periods; the real topic of periodization is the lines themselves, and the in-between spaces of the passage from slavery to modern colonialism to postcoloniality are what this project explores in the most detail.

I begin *Caribbean Literature and the Public Sphere* with the first of these transitions, the years between the end of slavery during the Haitian Revolution and the belated Cuban emancipation of 1886. In focusing on the end of plantation slavery as a long transition, I follow Chris Bongie's identification in the French Caribbean of what he calls the "curious interregnum" from 1833 to 1848 "in which the old order was slowly dying and a new one had yet to be born" (*Islands* 264). Bongie identifies this interregnum as the apogee of an epochal shift opening up the "'second imperial phase' of European imperialism" (12). He dates the rise of this "absolutely modern colonialism" as initiated "from the late eighteenth century on" (12); Bongie chooses a very early starting point for the forces that I argue coalesce as a new world order with the end of plantation slavery. In calling attention to this interregnum, Bongie's periodization emphasizes the unevenness of this birth; the obvious parallels between this transition and the decolonization process of the twentieth century shed light on the 1950s to the 1970s as a similar moment for redefining power and the public sphere.

My exploration of this twentieth-century interregnum against the backdrop of its nineteenth-century precursor can allow us to see the persistence of colonial structures in our postcolonial world not as stasis but as the reemergence of domination to close down the heady projects of the mid-twentieth century such as the student revolution in Haiti in 1946, the Guyanese People's Progressive Party (PPP) of the 1950s, the 1959 Cuban Revolution, the radical independence movements in Puerto Rico and Martinique, or the attempt at West Indian federation from 1958 to 1962.[9] David Scott invokes all of these experiments—and their passing—in naming the present "after Bandung" (*Conscripts* 1). Looking at this present comparatively shows the similar fate met by all of these attempts to carve out a space of political and economic independence and equality in the world system. Cuba's epic failure in 1970 to produce a large enough sugar harvest to break free of international economic hierarchies, the Central Intelligence Agency–funded opponents of Michael Manley's "We Are Not for Sale" campaign launching a virtual civil war in Jamaica leading to his electoral defeat in 1980, and finally the overturning of Grenada's revolutionary government by U.S. Marines in 1983 appeared to mark the futility of a truly independent Caribbean. As the global order was defeating these projects, what emerged triumphant was a neoliberal ethic of dependence and service: Michel-Rolph Trouillot cites a speech given by François Duvalier on the occasion of Nelson Rockefeller's 1969 visit to Haiti in which Duvalier makes a case that Caribbean people "could be a great reservoir of manual labor for Americans establishing re-export industries" and that "Haiti could be a land of relaxation for the American middle class—it is close, beautiful, and politically stable" (qtd. in Trouillot 200). Globalization thus means privatization perversely performed in the name of a cosmopolitan public dominated by the United States, a privatization whose impact on literary production still resonates. The strong continuity in terms of which countries occupy privileged positions in the new neoliberal world order—primarily the same countries from western Europe and North America that held power in the modern colonial period—often lends credence to those who see postmodernity or postcoloniality as nothing new. While the rise of the International Monetary Fund, the World Bank, and the global culture industry has certainly not led to the dismantling of international hierarchies, the nature of these institutions suggests the management of the global order not by nation-states, as in modern colonialism, but by global organizations; my discussion of globalization and Empire theory in this book's conclusion explores the significance of that distinction.

Caribbean Literature and the Public Sphere tracks how literature has responded to and shaped this history of domination and resistance. The chapters are organized in pairs, with each pair exploring different projects within the same historical moment. The book thus moves forward chronologically, not directly but through fits and starts, sometimes with horizontal or even backward moves from one chapter to the next. The first two chapters tell the story of abolitionist writing's contribution to the end of the slave system, the alternative literary projects that open up in the absence of such an ordering system, and then the rise of modern colonialism to manage the breach created by emancipation. This is a story, then, not of teleology but of successes and failures. The public sphere of abolitionism, as chapter 1 shows, reinforces the location of its public outside of the Caribbean; in appealing to European parliaments and monarchs as agents of change, this form of writing is unable to imagine or craft any concrete relationship with the antislavery energies in the region, which could only express themselves as a counterpublic of resistance. A close reading of Mary Prince's slave narrative and its legalistic form lays out how the successes of abolitionism come not from its absolute alterity to power, but from its operation within the available circuits of politics and publication. Chapter 2 looks at how writers from the 1850s explore alternatives to abolitionism's locating of power in European colonial centers. Trinidadian Michel Maxwell Philip, the Cuban poets published in *El laúd del desterrado*, and Jamaican Mary Seacole create transnational spaces through the tropes of piracy and a deterritorialized market that overflow the boundaries of the European public sphere, even as a direct connection between writer and national public is not yet imaginable.

Chapters 3 and 4 move to the late nineteenth and early twentieth centuries to discuss how anticolonial writers establish the connection between writing and a local public sphere; these chapters also delve most directly into how ideas about literature intersect with discourses of gender. While the monopoly on the local public sphere by the planters during the time of slavery forced abolitionism to locate in Europe the public opinion that needed to be persuaded, modern colonialism created the oppositional relationship between metropole and colony necessary for uniting the nation. Anticolonialism made writing a crucial part of creating a nationalist public sphere by privileging the figure of the literary intellectual, sensitive enough to listen to and thus speak for the people. As successfully as this discourse articulated the linkages necessary for national emergence, these chapters also show how anticolonialism contains the contradictions that lead to its crisis. Chapter 3 focuses on how deploying the idea of the literary intellectual as man of action gave writers like José Martí, Stephen Cobham, and Jacques Roumain a way to bridge the activities of the literary and the political. Chapter 4 then turns to the limits of this project, to examine how Claude McKay's *Banana Bottom* and the locally published little magazines of the 1940s such as *BIM*, *La Poesía Sorprendida*, and *Tropiques* deploy a feminized version of the literary as a space of critique and opposition distinguished from the aspirations to governance embodied by the man of action. Gossip, as a marginalized public sphere where those excluded from the mainstream can pass along information, emerges as one site where the fissures between the rationalizing objectives of the masculine writer and the chaotic energies of the feminized folk appear most difficult to resolve. Furthermore, the rivalry that emerges at the center of anticolonial writing, in which sensitive literary intellectuals must be distinguished from technocratic bureaucrats, foreshadows conflicts within the emerging nationalist middle class. These contradictions in anticolonial writing—between the valorization of manly action by the writers discussed in chapter 3 and the ideology of a feminized version of the literary advanced in the literary journals that are the topic of chapter 4—could no longer be submerged once nationalist movements came to power.

The second half of the book explores the crisis of literary anticolonialism in light of the shift from modern colonialism to postcolonial forms of foreign domination and hegemony. Chapters 5 and 6 look at how Marie Chauvet, George Lamming, and Martin Carter move from writing in a confidently anticolonial voice in their work from the 1950s to uncertainty or despair about their role in the public sphere in the 1960s and 1970s. These chapters lie at the heart of *Caribbean Literature and the Public Sphere*, and detail the transition from anticolonial writing's public voice to its postcolonial silencing. The revolutionary energies of decolonization come to be represented in this period through a return to the eighteenth-century Haitian Revolution, a story that inspired works in the 1930s, 1940s, and 1950s by Alejo Carpentier, Aimé Césaire, Derek Walcott, Edouard Glissant, and C. L. R. James. Chauvet's 1957 *La danse sur le volcan* revives the story of the Haitian Revolution to express the idea that artists and writers can participate in societal transformation through creating a nationalist culture. By Chauvet's novels from the 1960s, however, it becomes clear that the technocratic elite ridiculed or even vilified in anticolonial writing has come to power in the transition to postcoloniality, a development presenting real dangers for the literary intellectual. Lamming and Carter, meanwhile, detail a discursive crisis of authority brought on by the simultaneous demands upon them to be leaders and subalterns. These writers find themselves unable to formulate an alternative project that can satisfy their desire to keep alive the privileged anticolonial position of the writer but also turn over the public sphere to the popular elements of the newly forming nation-state.

In the context of this crisis of anticolonialism, chapters 7 and 8 turn to two innovations in genre from the late 1960s and 1970s that I read as attempts to reestablish the anticolonial authority of the intellectual even while acknowledging the de-privileging of literature in that effort. Chapter 7 discusses how the *testimonio* of Miguel Barnet and the Sistren Theatre Collective attempts to open up access to the public sphere by circumventing the ideology of the literary, even as it hopes to create a new heroic project for the literary intellectual. In chapter 8, cultural studies and the popular culture–inspired novels of Luis Rafael Sánchez and Earl Lovelace appear as another set of attempts to unleash the energies of the nonliterate classes as well as harness those energies for a renewed intellectual project. All of these efforts thus emerge as nostalgic attempts to reconstruct the anticolonial relationship between writer and public while acknowledging its impossibility in a postcolonial problem-space transformed by new social, political, and economic realities. My conclusion moves from this transitional moment, in which conflicted forms such as *testimonio* or the musical novel emerged, to the more clearly postcolonial work of the 1990s and beyond by writers like Dionne Brand. These final chapters therefore detail the sense of crisis over literature's public role, even as ending with Brand allows me to call attention to how contemporary writers seek to create new literary horizons that engage with the postcolonial context while remaining committed to the spirit of abolitionist and anticolonial predecessors. *Caribbean Literature and the Public Sphere* is my own response to these competing demands.

Part One

The Rise of the Caribbean Literary Public Sphere, 1804 to 1886

1   The Abolitionist Public Sphere
and the Republic of the Lettered

WRITING FROM THE PERIOD of plantation slavery displays a
particular relationship to the public sphere. Within the Caribbean, the
planter class monopoly on written discourse meant literature allowed to
circulate locally was almost uniformly aligned with power. Oppositional
forms of writing did emerge and were central to abolitionism, which
sought to bring about emancipation by persuading a public of the evils
of slavery. But in the hierarchical literary field of plantation slavery,
antislavery articulation required European patronage, and the public
targeted by abolitionist writing was European, as appeals to the local
planter class to abolish slavery appeared futile and mobilizing African-
descended people unimaginable. Focusing on the kinds of publics engendered by the written word, then, only emphasizes the lack of a truly
representative local literary public sphere during the period of slavery.
The written word within the region was connected explicitly to the colonial legal system and the newspapers of the planter class; the discourses
best representing the Caribbean majority in the period of slavery were
expressed less in print than in cultural practices such as music, religion,
and popular festivals like carnival.[1] These forms of expression were deliberately excluded from what was defined as public and only allowed to
speak as a counterpublic: defining the written as what counted as legitimate public expression was clearly intended to restrict who could participate.[2] Reading the written record while remaining aware of its limitations allows the productive tracing of a framework for understanding
the discursive structures of Caribbean slave society.

By analyzing what kinds of relationships between writers and public
sphere were available during plantation slavery, I outline the particular
contours of that literary field and show how its structures and institutions—and therefore its rules—differed from what would follow. Mod-

ern colonialism, by contrast, features a new positioning of the writer within the public sphere, which made possible the consolidation of anti-colonial writing reliant on new forms of authority. While the nineteenth century included important contributions to Caribbean literature, Caribbean writers began to think of themselves as part of a local literary tradition during the early twentieth century at the same time as two social factors emerged to enable the particularly anticolonial notion of literature: first, the rise of a local literary public sphere embodied in newspapers and journals open to debating colonial rule; and second, the active connection of those publications to social movements within the region. These factors allowed Caribbean writers to imagine that they spoke for and to an oppositional black counterpublic but also a national public that could be an agent in local governance; their absence in the nineteenth-century Caribbean created a literary field structured around a different idea of the relationship between writer and public.

This chapter examines the abolition movement as an important precursor to anticolonial Caribbean literature, but a precursor distinct in terms of the public sphere it enters. I suggest that the public sphere of slavery and abolition can be best understood as the sort of literary field theorized by Angel Rama in *La ciudad letrada*. Rama describes a restricted form of the Latin American public sphere in which access is only available for a lettered elite, whose discursive monopoly allows societal control. The discursive monopoly of the planter class, maintained through restrictions on literacy and publication along with censorship of the rare oppositional texts that were produced, ensured that the Caribbean situation would be an extreme version of Rama's republic of letters, what I refer to as a republic of the lettered. The institutions of the church and state allowed some oppositional voices to find their way into public discourse, but only via the patronage of the lettered elite. Critiques of power and the status quo were censored and marginalized in the Caribbean public sphere. Abolitionist writing sought to break the discursive monopoly of the planter class, explicitly positioning itself as addressing the public. Yet abolitionism still managed to reproduce the discursive control of the lettered elite and generally limited itself to legalistic appeals that reinforced the idea of Europe as the center of power. Only with emancipation and expanded literacy would the lettered monopoly on discourse be exploded. Abolitionism's project is not the anticolonialism that sought to use print to mobilize a local public. Plantation slavery's field of power led antislavery discourse to what were frequently antinationalist positions, sometimes coming into direct conflict with planter or bourgeois desires for autonomy. This distance from a locally based concept of the nation reinforced a configuration dependent on European patronage in which the Caribbean subject could not assume the place of authorship and authority but required a representative of the European republic of letters to translate her or him for the public. The idea of Caribbean authorship would remain restricted until the ways that Caribbean subjects were able to enter public discourse changed.

Abolitionism and Discursive Monopoly

The debates surrounding slavery illustrate the idea of a public sphere as private people coming together in public via print to argue for the most rational course for the state to pursue. Although Habermas's account fails to discuss the abolition movement as an example of the public sphere at work, Caribbean intellectual and literary historians have recognized the centrality of print and public mobilization to abolitionism. Gordon Lewis calls abolitionist writings part of a "war of words" that "addressed itself, both in England and France, to the rise to power of the bourgeois public opinion of the age" (116).[3] Lewis's emphasis on the European location of this early debate is echoed by Christopher Schmidt-Nowara, who discusses how "the transformation of the public sphere in mid-nineteenth-century Spain, especially in Madrid, created the possibilities for antislavery mobilization" (6).[4] Slave narratives, one of the earliest forms of Caribbean writing attempting to speak for the inhabitants who made up the majority of the region's population, participated in precisely this European literary public sphere, even while the reception of this writing back in the islands was much more restricted. By examining specific incarnations of the abolitionist public sphere, this chapter shows how the actual debates taking place resembled Rama's republic of the lettered more than the idealized liberal-democratic public sphere Habermas describes as existing in Europe during this period or the anticolonial public sphere that would follow. Because of their participation in a patronage system, slave narratives and other forms of abolitionist writing appealed to a variety of conflicting sources of authority, in some cases asking that arguments be evaluated on their own merits but frequently relying on outside legitimation through the invocation of documents and questions of character.

Abolition offered an early model of writing aimed at mobilizing public opinion to bring about social change, but it did not create a Caribbean public sphere. The debate over abolition took place in Europe because of the European literary field's proximity to power and the monopoly on discursive opportunities enjoyed by planters in the slave societies. Selwyn Cudjoe begins his discussion of "the intellectual tradition of Trinidad and Tobago in the nineteenth century" with "The Narrative of Louisa Calderon," which he labels as one of the "first narratives of Trinidad and Tobago's literary tradition" (*Beyond Boundaries* 11).[5] This narrative, which Cudjoe defines as "the extracts from various trial testimonies in which [Calderon] speaks for herself and describes her suffering" (11), was presented in a London courthouse in 1806 as part of the trial of Thomas Picton, the former governor of Trinidad arrested for torturing Calderon. While Cudjoe focuses on the content of Calderon's testimony, I want to emphasize how the context shows characteristics of the abolitionist public sphere. The trial, and Calderon's testimony, clearly found an eager audience and influenced public opinion, as "this case became a cause célèbre in London because it pitted some of the most powerful pro- and antislavery advocates against each other" (14). At the same time, it is important that the proper setting for this debate was considered to be England, not the colony. Although the events leading to the trial took place in Trinidad among actors at the time located in the island, it was unthinkable that a British governor might be tried in the colony because of the power dynamic between colony and mother country as well as the total resistance by the planter class to the idea of allowing a critical public sphere to emerge in the islands.

While in England the abolitionist movement used the press to participate in and influence public debate about slavery and the slave trade, the critiques of slavery made within the region show how much less discursive space was available in the Caribbean. For example, the 1804 writings of the Hart sisters in Antigua discussed by Moira Ferguson in *Colonialism and Gender Relations* take striking antislavery positions but couch themselves as private letters rather than attempts at public mobilization. Whereas Calderon's testimony could spark debate in England, the Hart sisters' narratives found no such audience because the available public forums in the colonies were almost entirely controlled by the planter class. Gordon Lewis's comparative history of early Caribbean thought describes the dominance of this "proslavery ideology," which "reached its zenith in the period between the mid-eighteenth and the latter part of the nineteenth century" (107); he traces this planter perspective through much of the work written within the region during the period of slavery, including that of Edward Long, Bryan Edwards, Moreau de Saint-Méry, Hilliard d'Auberteuil, and Francisco de Arango y Parreño. While in Habermas's account European salons and newspapers engaged in rational debate about the common good, newspapers and other publications in the Caribbean were a mouthpiece for the conservative planters, not a public representing a broad cross section of the national interest. Although later in the nineteenth century these newspapers and printing presses would become instrumental in the creation of an oppositional public sphere that could begin to imagine itself speaking for the broader population—especially as the spread of literacy meant that members of the colored class became printers and newspaper editors (Roberts 153)—the slave system depended on the discursive monopoly of the planter class.

This monopoly on power required the withholding of literacy from the majority of the islands' populations; writing was therefore controlled by a small and powerful minority and reflected their interests. Peter Roberts's history of the writing in the British Caribbean points to the ideology behind these restrictions. Roberts describes how the written word arose for purely "functional" purposes, so that "the primary role of literacy as it developed in the West Indies was to permit easier management and control in church, state and private business" (128) in the form of "record keeping" and "to regulate the movement of slaves" through written passes (114). While an abolitionist public sphere flourished in Europe, then, in the islands those who wrote and engaged in public debate showed no interest in speaking to or for the majority population. When writing began to assume a greater regional importance in the eighteenth century through newspapers, it was precisely in order to defend the plantation system and the inequalities it fostered: "it is only with the increasing challenge to the system of slavery that, as a community, [the planters] were forced to indulge in literacy to defend their position" against the abolitionist movement in England (108). Gordon Lewis concurs that "the majority of pro–West Indian titles" of this period "were improvised answers to the abolitionist writers" (108).

Writing was thus generally conceived to serve a utilitarian purpose and was closely connected to support for the status quo. As Jack Corzani puts it, "those who had literary proclivities remained in the metropole and published works that were generally unrelated to their island origins," since the planter elites were frequently "absentee owners who preferred to live in France" as "the Caribbean island was nothing but the site of their plantation, source of wealth that they self-indulgently squandered in the capital" (467). This is not to say that there was not important or interesting writing to come out of the region during that period: Evelyn O'Callaghan's *Women Writing the West Indies, 1804–1939*, for example, examines a range of female-authored literary endeavors from that period that are often quite critical of social norms. But even in these cases, O'Callaghan acknowledges that when she began exploring this subject, she found that "virtually all the relevant texts were published in England" (15). This fact confirms that nineteenth-century Caribbean writing not strictly aligned with power had no local public sphere to enter. My next chapter shows that to a large extent, the absence of a critical public sphere within the Caribbean during the period of slavery still persisted even when the Cuban poets included in *El laúd del desterrado* or Michel Maxwell Philip's *Emmanuel Appadocca* and Mary Seacole's *Wonderful Adventures* were published in the United States and England during the 1850s.

As much as slave narratives circulated in Europe and contributed to the discursive defeat of slavery, in plantation society slave narratives or other critical forms of discourse were denied entry into any local literary public sphere, forcing the slave population's public expressions into other, nonliterary forms ranging from popular culture to violent rebellion. Local newspapers carried only disavowals of slave narratives or abolitionist materials, rather than anything resembling the rational debate characteristic of a utopian public sphere. Roberts notes the prevalence of censorship in the colonies, where "in the Spanish empire governments exercised direct control over the press" (147), while in islands like Antigua and Barbados, "printers had to side with the government of the day and respect the wishes of the powerful not only to get government business but to avoid being put out of business altogether" (148). Cudjoe describes early newspapers from Trinidad such as the *Port of Spain Gazette*, which "acted on behalf of the planters and generally spat its venom on anyone who spoke of the virtues of emancipation," a perspective connected to the fact that "the editor and proprietor of the *Port of Spain Gazette* was the government printery" (*Beyond Boundaries* 63).

As newspapers and other forms of publication in the Caribbean began to develop, then, they were not necessarily engaged in the critique of power that Habermas sees in the European public spheres of the same period. Angel Rama suggests some of the reasons for this situation. As he narrates in *La ciudad letrada*, literacy had always been aligned with the church and the bureaucratic state in Spain's mercantile New World empire. Rama describes a discursive yet no less real "lettered city," made up of "administrators, educators . . . and other wielders of pen and paper"—a group he calls *letrados*—who "controlled and directed" the physical city from its founding until well into the nineteenth century

(17–18). Under Spanish rule, Latin American writers made up the colonial bureaucracy, authoring laws and maintaining communication with distant monarchs. Writing played a major role in the evangelizing project of the church as well. Rama shows how civilization and Christianity spread by the written word, and control of newly conquered territory depended on codification through writing. Even with the mainland's independence from Spanish rule, the lettered minority continued to author the laws and inscribe the foundational fictions of the recently established New World nations.[6] Despite the new social order brought about by independence, the usefulness of the *letrados* to the institutions of the state remained unquestioned, and the republic of letters in which educated elites maintained a monopoly on discursive power persisted into the second half of the nineteenth century. As long as literature was an integral part of state business and the privileged domain of an almost priestly class, the Latin American *letrados* could rely on their privileged position as guardians of the written word to legitimize their discourse. The republic of the lettered Rama describes thus makes it clear that, despite Habermas's ideal of a public debate where rank could be bracketed, many other factors restricted and influenced who could participate.

I invoke Rama's description of the lettered city because of its emphasis on how restricted and hierarchical this kind of public sphere was, even as the plantation societies of the Caribbean differed in fundamental respects from the settler colonies of Latin America upon which Rama bases much of his argument. If anything, the social gaps produced by slavery made the discursive monopoly of the ruling classes even more total in the Caribbean. Instead of lettered cities where a professional middle class might arise, power in Caribbean society lay in the rural order of the plantation.[7] At the same time, the plantation system meant that the planter class of the islands was tied to Europe more closely than their counterparts in the Latin American mainland were—as Antonio Benítez-Rojo describes, "the economic situation of a Mexican or Peruvian landowner was not related to any kind of monoproductive agriculture meant for export and dependent on the slave trade," and for this reason "the landowners of the great viceroyalties did not feel themselves bound tightly to the mother country, as surely was the case with the slaveholding planters of the Caribbean" ("Power/Sugar/Literature" 57). Whereas independent public spheres arose on the American continent, then, in terms of their relationship with the metropole the Spanish-speaking islands were much more similar to their Caribbean neighbors. Demographics meant that in the Hispanic Caribbean, enslaved people accounted for nearly half of the population—in Cuba, the population of nonwhites in the island, including free blacks and mulattos, made up the majority during much of the nineteenth century—as the culture of the plantation dominated.[8]

The close relationship to the metropole and the culture of the plantation reinforced the connection between writing and power established during the earliest days of conquest. Carlos Alonso describes how "Puerto Rico's long-standing status as a secondary military garrison determined the relatively late arrival of the printing press, in 1806" (147), and Raquel Chang-Rodríguez notes that "the printing press arrived in Hispaniola at the end of the eighteenth century (c. 1782), and was used mainly to publish official documents" (125). When institutions of a public sphere did emerge, it was under the direction of the state: John Garrigus details the deliberate efforts by the colonial state in Saint-Domingue to foster a sense of allegiance to the Crown among Creole planters through the establishment during the 1760s of "the colony's first successful print shop" and other institutions meant to form the equivalent of the public sphere in France (124).

Though not the site of such an overt Enlightenment project during the eighteenth century, Cuba also featured a well-developed publishing industry that was almost entirely connected to the lettered class Rama describes. In 1791, for example, the important newspaper *Papel Periódico de La Habana* began publishing, and a public library was launched in 1793, but both institutions were controlled by a group of "twenty-seven prominent landowners" known as the Sociedad Económica de Amigos del País (Pérez 66). Major histories of the island or the region were written in Cuba by Bishop Pedro Agustín Morell de Santa Cruz in 1760 and councilman José Martín Félix de Arrate in 1830, while in Puerto Rico Fray Iñigo Abbad y Lasierra produced *Historia geográfica, civil y natural de Puerto Rico* in 1782. Representatives of the church and state, these authors took distinctly conservative perspectives: Morell "praises Christopher Columbus' skills and generosity, and speaks of the Indians as barbarians" (Chang-Rodríguez 125); Arrate presents what is a counterpoint to Las Casas's argument for the African slave trade, proposing instead that Indians would make a better labor force; and Abbad "writes like nothing so much as the energetic visiting colonial official" (G. Lewis 265) whose "class and race prejudices" mean his work "cannot in any way be seen as expressions of a wider popular movement" (266). The points of view in this early writing are of a ruling class imagining ways to impose its own conceptions of society onto the virgin land, rather than conceiving of itself in relation to a public; these writers form Rama's lettered city.

The Caribbean during the time of slavery was thus a republic of the lettered in terms of the disciplinary function of writing, even if the creative production did not match the lofty ideal of a republic of letters: as Roberts describes, plantation society used writing for primarily utilitarian purposes, and this form of commercial literacy hardly produced great literature, while Corzani points out that "various ministerial circulars prove that the constant concern of the central government was to avoid the formation in the French islands of a creole intellectual elite" (466). Gordon Lewis supports Rama's observation about Latin America that what little intellectual life existed in the Caribbean was associated with the church, noting that "the settled intellectual class that existed in the island towns, then, was mainly that gathered in the convents of the various orders" (91). Racial hierarchy and slavery's prohibitions on literacy only heightened the association of writing with a privileged minority.

While the planters' monopoly was never total, in the cases where the voices of enslaved people did enter the official record it was almost always through the mediation of writers connected to the church or state. These avenues toward a public sphere allowed some admittedly restricted discursive opportunities for Caribbean peoples. When the state recorded the voices of enslaved people, it was with the goal of managing their opportunities for public expression, though as John Lean and Trevor Burnard show in an article they title "Hearing Slave Voices," even in the state records from the Berbice and Demerara-Essequebo colonies they examine, there is the potential for these voices to disrupt the planter monopoly on discursive power.[9] The opportunities to participate in print culture offered by the church proved even more volatile. The Hart sisters provide one example of how evangelical Christianity could inspire and help articulate antislavery sentiments, and Emilia Viotti da Costa's *Crowns of Glory, Tears of Blood* presents an equally fascinating account of how missionary work in what is today Guyana influenced the formation of oppositional discourses among enslaved people during the 1820s. The legal and religious public spheres within the region where the enslaved began to protest their status would substantially shape the abolitionist writing that gave a literary form to these oppositional energies. But as important as these interstitial spaces of protest proved, the most robust voicing of antislavery discourse located its institutional and imagined authority outside of the region, especially in England, throughout the late eighteenth and early nineteenth centuries.

Abolitionist Discourse in the Francophone and Hispanophone Caribbean

Beginning in the eighteenth century, newspapers provided a public forum for the ruling classes in the Caribbean, but slave owners continued to withhold literacy from the vast majority of the population for fear that enslaved people who became literate might attain a revolutionary consciousness through reading abolitionist materials. Enslaved people appeared not as active subjects of writing, but as its objects: the written word was meant to account for them in ledger books and bills of sale; their presence in newspapers was in advertisements alongside "houses, horses, cows, mules and pigs" (Roberts 143). The result was that as plantation slavery began to come to an end, virtually no popular written tradition existed in any of the islands, and the Caribbean literary field had almost no local autonomy from Europe. Rama dates the challenge to the republic of letters as beginning in the mid-nineteenth century, without directly engaging with how emancipation would have been part of that epochal shift; I hope that my own emphasis on abolitionist discourse calls attention to how the struggle against slavery challenged the *letrados'* monopoly on the written word in a dramatic and permanent way. After presenting an overview of abolitionist activities in the Hispanic and Francophone Caribbean, the last section of this chapter turns to a close reading of a slave narrative, *The History of Mary Prince*, examining the particular workings of the British abolitionist public sphere to show its difference from the European public sphere Habermas describes as well as the anticolonial public sphere that I discuss in subsequent chapters.

Writings by and sympathetic to enslaved people and people of color appeared from the Hispanic and Francophone Caribbean beginning in the late eighteenth and early nineteenth centuries, with some of the more famous figures including French abolitionist Victor Schoelcher and Martinican mulatto Cyrille Bissette as well as the Cuban priest Félix Varela and freed slave Juan Francisco Manzano. While this writing sought to mobilize popular sentiment against slavery, the contours of the public sphere of the plantation period meant that the public being lobbied to enact changes remained European. Lawrence Jennings describes the Société des Amis des Noirs, the earliest French abolitionist society, as "elitist in character" and notes that it "avoided appeals to public opinion" as it "tended to center its activities in the legislative chamber" (*French Anti-Slavery* 2). Alongside the lettered opposition to slavery represented by the Amis des Noirs, the French Caribbean witnessed the best-known radical counterpublic in the region, the Haitian Revolution. The relationship between physical uprisings in the islands and literary advocacy in Europe was complex.[10] C. L. R. James's *The Black Jacobins* seeks to show how actions in Saint-Domingue influenced public debates about slavery and freedom taking place in the French National Assembly during the 1790s. His account has persuaded historians that the emancipation act passed in France in 1794 was less the result of the Société des Amis des Noirs or any other intellectual group, but rather "was forced on the Republic by the slave revolt that began in 1791 in Saint-Domingue" (Jennings, *French Anti-Slavery* 3).

While much of the focus on Haitian agency in ending slavery emphasizes how rebelling blacks used force to make themselves heard by the French public, a number of remarkable documents from that era show how formerly enslaved people and free people of color sought to shape their own future through use of the written word. As early as 1789, a group of free people of color presented their grievances in Paris; their "Address to the National Assembly" was crucial to securing rights for free coloreds, even if the rights of enslaved people were not addressed at this point. Some of the earliest antislavery writings to emerge out of the French Caribbean include letters forwarded by the governor of Martinique to the French government in 1789 signed by "us, Nègres" (Dubois and Garrigus 66) and "the Entire Nation" (67) that threaten "torrents of blood flowing" (66) and declare that "the entire Nation of Black Slaves united together has a single wish, a single desire for independence" (66–67). Rather than private correspondences, these letters make themselves public statements by addressing the government directly and by claiming to speak in the name of the nation. At the same time, these letters locate power to liberate in the French king, and they were tellingly forwarded to Paris, as if they could only effect the change they sought through being sent abroad. The idea among enslaved people seeking freedom that the metropole made a better ally than local powers seems strange when seen through the lens of anticolonial nationalism, but makes sense in the context of the abolitionist public sphere. As even Toussaint Louverture's letters to the French government demonstrate, the idea of a literary public sphere debating the greater good was still imagined to require achieving a voice in Europe.[11]

With plantation slavery creating violent societal rifts that nationalist discourse could not overcome, the rebelling Haitians had to constantly change their attitudes about autonomy from or fealty toward France as the French Revolution's policies toward the colonies shifted. With the rise of Napoleon and the execution of prominent members of the Société des Amis des Noirs, the idea of reasoned appeals as a route to emancipation vanished. Slavery was reinstituted in French-controlled territories in 1802, forcing Haitians to declare independence to protect the freedoms they had won in battle. Unable to reconquer Haiti, Napoleon initiated a strict regime of censorship around the issue of abolition both at home and in the empire. Though Napoleon's reign ended in 1815, the French colonies remained vigilant about suppressing oppositional discourse: abolitionism was frequently blamed for the uprising in Saint-Domingue, and the planters in Martinique and Guadeloupe emerged even more strongly opposed to any questioning of slavery's status quo. The experiences of Cyrille Bissette illustrate the restrictiveness of the French Caribbean public sphere of this period. In 1823, Bissette was arrested in Martinique for his advocacy on behalf of the free people of color and exiled from the islands. Bissette was freed only after an appeal in France and forbidden from returning to Martinique. Instead, he stayed in Paris and along with other free men of color "tried to promote themselves as the equivalents of the white colonial delegates who officially represented in Paris the interests of the colonial legislatures" (Jennings, "Cyrille Bissette" 51). This struggle, over who represented the Caribbean public and had the "right to act on their behalf" in France (30), led Bissette to "petitioning the government, eliciting support from liberal French politicians, and producing dozens of pamphlets and newspaper articles" (30). Silenced in Martinique, only in France could Bissette become a spokesman for the Caribbean public, eventually expanding his agenda to include the emancipation of all enslaved people in French territories. The abolitionist networks that Bissette helped build in France during the 1830s and 1840s—including a journal he launched in Paris in 1834 called the *Revue des Colonies*—appear to have been unthinkable in the plantation colonies themselves in this period.[12]

In the Spanish islands, antislavery advocacy was for the most part forbidden and punished by the colonial authorities. Very little literary opposition to slavery found representation in metropolitan publication, and what did get published, such as the novel *Sab* by white Cuban writer Gertrudis Gómez de Avellaneda y Arteaga, which appeared in Spain in 1841, was banned in Cuba. In the local context, Cuba featured a somewhat more diverse set of viewpoints than the discursive monopoly maintained by the ruling classes in other islands. As Benítez-Rojo points out, as early as 1832 the *Revista Bimestre Cubana*, published in Havana, featured an essay by José Antonio Saco that enlisted what Saco calls the "noble mission of writers" to "save the *patria*" in the movement to end slavery (qtd. in Benítez-Rojo, "Power/Sugar/Literature" 22). This idea of the writer as voice of the nation is crucial to the concept of the literary public sphere and becomes central in Caribbean anticolonialism of the twentieth century. Benítez-Rojo calls attention to Saco's advocacy against slavery as part of a broader fear that an increasing African population would turn Cuba into a black nation, making clear that Saco still saw himself representing the interests of Cuban whites. Although the large white population in Cuba meant a wider diversity of opinions among whites in which planters were not the only ones represented, Saco's vision of the Caribbean public remains limited in its exclusion of nonwhites. Even Saco's limited attempt to construct a national public was perceived as dangerous, however: as part of "the first organized effort by Cuban intellectuals to mount a common front of resistance against the power of the slave traders and the saccharocracy" (23), Saco would face persecution by the colonial government and was eventually forced to leave Cuba in 1834.

This violent policing of public discourse in the Spanish colonies led many Cuban antislavery or anticolonial writers into exile, frequently in the United States as the next chapter on the *filibustero* movement discusses. Those who remained in the island faced significant obstacles to local publication, such as the group organized around one of Saco's collaborators on the *Revista Bimestre Cubana*, Domingo del Monte. Del Monte's salons and publication efforts made the white Venezuelan the dominant figure in the Cuban literary scene of the 1830s and 1840s. Antislavery writing became a major impetus for this group, with del Monte sponsoring publication for free blacks and formerly enslaved people. But the Spanish government largely managed to blunt the impact of these literary movements, censoring and persecuting these authors and preventing their writing from achieving the influence of the British abolitionists. The texts that did get published, like Saco's work or del Monte's own "Estado de la población blanca y de color de la isla de Cuba, en 1839," appealed explicitly to the planter class to humanize slavery in order to prevent future uprisings. In *Literary Bondage*, William Luis describes these texts as part of a dialogue around slavery—with Saco and del Monte at "one end of the spectrum of the bourgeois dialogue" and full-fledged proslavery positions at the other (62). But Luis acknowledges that even Saco and del Monte could not get "outside of the rhetoric of slavers" and "sugar discourse" (32), revealing how positions seeking to speak on behalf of the nonwhite population did not feature in this conversation and remained excluded from the nineteenth-century public sphere.

Taking an antislavery position in Cuba meant stepping outside of the circuits of publication and public dialogue entirely; Luis even defines Cirilo Villaverde's earliest versions of *Cecilia Valdés* as "not antislavery works" because "they passed the censors and were published in Cuba" (4). Del Monte's circle was nonetheless very active in producing antislavery writing, even if it could not be published locally. Anselmo Suárez y Romero wrote the antislavery novel *Francisco* during 1838 and 1839, though it was only published after his death in 1880. Villaverde published short stories in Cuba during the 1830s, including the early versions of *Cecilia Valdés*, but in the 1840s his involvement in nationalist activity led to his arrest and flight to the United States. The height of government repression of this nascent public sphere came in 1844, as thousands of free blacks and mulattos as well as liberal whites were arrested upon accusations of a grand conspiracy to help enslaved people overthrow the colonial government. The result of this probably manufactured "Escalera conspiracy" was a direct attack on the rising power of the free black and mulatto populations as well as on the tenuous antislavery public sphere that del Monte had sought to establish: many blacks and mulattos were executed; a number of del Monte's associates, including del Monte himself, were forced to leave Cuba; and another Afro-Cuban writer attached to his circle, Juan Francisco Manzano, ended up in prison.

Manzano's authorial career typifies the ways that antislavery challenges faced significant censorship within Cuba while access to the abolitionist public sphere in Europe required entry into a patronage system. Formerly enslaved, Manzano managed to publish some poetry in Cuban newspapers during his lifetime thanks to del Monte's help, but after his time in prison, he apparently lost interest in writing. Manzano's narrative of his life of enslavement is described by Ivan Schulman as "the only autobiographical account written by a slave during slavery that has surfaced to date" in Latin America (7), a fact that speaks to the tremendous obstacles enslaved people faced in being heard in the public sphere. Schulman notes that "there is no doubt whatsoever that Manzano wrote his *Autobiography* at Del Monte's insistence" (15), citing a letter from Manzano in which he responds to his patron's request. Luis notes that another of del Monte's associates "corrected the slave's grammar and syntax" (83), presumably shaping the narrative in the process. Getting the autobiography published required still another level of patronage that even del Monte and his circle could not provide, but could only help negotiate: the narrative was not published in Spanish at all during Manzano's lifetime, but only appeared in England when it was printed by the Anti-Slavery Society in 1840. The distance between this literally translated version of Manzano's story and the author's original occasion for speaking embodies the ways in which the lack of a local literary public sphere during the period of slavery challenged the possibility of authorship in a Caribbean context. Benítez-Rojo sums up the contributions of Cuban writers of the 1820s, 1830s, and 1840s by noting that their "texts did not have much of an impact on public opinion within the island, since they were written and published outside Cuba" ("Power/Sugar/Literature" 19). The idea of a Cuban literary public sphere that could debate issues like slavery or independence was conceivable only as something that could exist outside of the region.

Mary Prince and the Abolitionist Public Sphere

Juan Francisco Manzano's ability to publish his work depended on an abolitionist network centered in England; the implications of locating power in this metropolitan site can be seen in the best-known Anglophone Caribbean slave narrative from this period, *The History of Mary Prince*. I want to look at this text to show how it is shaped by not having a Caribbean public sphere it can enter. The critical discussion surrounding *The History of Mary Prince* has centered on the nature of the collaborative process that produced the text: contemporary critics have worked admirably to read past the surface of Prince's text to try to excavate whatever elements of her voice and her agency can be recovered, especially in terms of Prince's evasions and allusions regarding her sexuality and the sexual abuse she has suffered.[13] But even these readings only emphasize how the actual text we have stands in the way of this project.[14] Searching for Prince's authentic voice is an important project for reconstructing the past from a subaltern perspective; I take up these issues of recovering the subaltern voice in the discussion of *testimonio* in chapter 7.[15] My purpose right now is to point to how the concept of the public and Prince's claims on that public are central to the text's publication, even as the challenges that Prince faces in being heard show her context resembling the republic of the lettered Rama describes more than the literary public sphere of anticolonialism. The sources of authority that allow Prince to speak and be heard simultaneously deny her the status of author and control of her own story: only with the end of plantation slavery can the articulation of an oppositional, anticolonial public sphere allow writers to marshal alternative sources of authority and create more recognizably modern authorial projects.

Published in 1831 by Thomas Pringle, secretary of the British Anti-Slavery Society, *The History of Mary Prince* was conceived and deployed as part of the abolitionist fight against slavery. In *Abolition's Public Sphere*, Robert Fanuzzi discusses how the abolition movement in the United States invested its resources heavily in the printing of antislavery materials so as to "ma[k]e the creation of a reading public the principle [*sic*] goal of antislavery agitation, the practical equivalent of abolition itself" (xii). Fanuzzi goes on to explain that this meant that "to 'abolitionize'" (xii) required not just reaching out to or appealing to an already existing public, but actually creating a public through the publication of newspapers, pamphlets, and other materials distributed to those sympathetic to the antislavery cause. While Fanuzzi focuses on the abolition movement in the United States, the printed word and the idea that it could contribute to and shape public opinion were equally central to abolitionism in England. We can see in Prince's narrative how these hopes and aspirations are embedded in the text's construction.

The form of *The History of Mary Prince* points to the ways in which it explicitly orients itself toward a public, conceived as a particular audience but also more generally as an intervention into an abstract debate. A preface by Pringle identifies how the text is meant to act as testimony for what he calls the "tribunal . . . of public opinion" (Prince 56). The immediate context here is a series of court proceedings surrounding Prince and Pringle, beginning with the issue of her freedom but extending into a pair of libel trials involving Pringle as her publisher. When Pringle asserts in his supplement following Prince's narrative that "we might safely leave the case to the judgment of the public" or that "it is incumbent on me, as [Prince's] advocate with the public, to state such additional testimony on her behalf as I can fairly and conscientiously adduce" (108), he is explicitly referencing this context and positioning her narrative as a part of this legal defense. The text as a whole includes witnesses (of which Prince is the most important but certainly not the only one), evidence (including many documents such as letters and newspaper articles), and opening and closing arguments by Pringle.

Yet in addition to serving as a defense of Prince's freedom of movement and speech, the structuring of *The History of Mary Prince* as a legal intervention is meant to serve a second function. Near the end of the supplement, Pringle pivots away from defending Prince and toward his larger goal of putting slavery itself on trial: "after all, Mary's character, important though its exculpation be to her, is not really the point of chief practical interest in this case" (116). Does Mary Prince need to turn out to be virtuous and true, he asks, for slavery to be condemned as wrong? Pringle's appeal to the public is only partially concerned with securing Prince's freedom and clearing her name; he wants his readers to see in this specific story how "the case affords a most instructive illustration of the true spirit of the slave system" (118). Pringle's hope is that the publication of *The History of Mary Prince* and similar slave narratives and antislavery materials would affect the debates taking place in the British Parliament about the future of slavery in the British colonies. Prince's narrative thus uses publication and debate to conjure a critical public sphere able to intervene in legal and political affairs. As in the case of Louisa Calderon, however, that public debate, even when concerned primarily with the Caribbean, can have a hearing only in England. The inability to imagine mobilizing a Caribbean public shapes Prince's narrative. When critics describe how Prince must hide her sexuality or discuss it only in coded ways—Jenny Sharpe, for example, notes the "the truth of her testimony depended on demonstrating that she was a decent Christian woman" (32)—this argument takes for granted that her target audience could only be English. That assumption is embedded in the text's own address: Prince's story makes narrative asides about how she has omitted certain language "too, too bad to speak in England" (Prince 68), and she repeatedly expresses her hope that although "few people in England know what slavery is" (74), once her story reaches this public they will "call loud to the great King of England, till all the poor blacks be given free" (94).

Prince's text seeks a sympathetic hearing in England, knowing that the audience she reaches in the islands will not be open to her calls to end slavery. The exclusion of enslaved people from the Caribbean public sphere meant that simply suggesting that Prince might have a worthwhile opinion on the subject of her own freedom was a repudiation of the slave system; in her introduction to the republication of the narrative, Moira Ferguson notes that proslavery advocates of the time received Prince's story as just such a challenge. The appendix to Ferguson's edition of the *History* includes an article, from the *Bermuda Royal Gazette*, published in 1831 as an alternative narrative liberally quoting Prince in order to refute her, and defending her former masters by including letters from some of the island's planter class that assert her masters' "high character" and "reputation" (152). The official voice of the plantation system, represented in the article in the *Bermuda Royal Gazette*, thus acts as a mirror for Prince's abolitionist narrative. Despite their opposing objectives, both are structured by similar assumptions and demands: both abolitionist discourse in England and defense of slavery from the Caribbean seek to persuade British public opinion through deploying letters and documents to establish the authenticity of the main text. Both the newspaper article and Prince's narrative therefore belong to the system of patronage characteristic of the republic of the lettered in which the text derives its legitimacy from extratextual sources, rather than finding ways to generate textual authority through constructing the kind of relationship between author and public that the anticolonial writers of the twentieth century were able to establish.

As long as the Caribbean relationship to the public sphere remained monopolized by the lettered few, it was only through the patronage of members of that republic of letters like Pringle that Prince's voice could hope to reach the public. Pringle's connections to the world of publication as well as Prince's inability to write her story for herself forced her to rely on this patronage. The narrative is related by Prince but recorded by Susanna Strickland, herself a "recent Methodist convert" (Ferguson, Introduction 11) and aspirant to the lettered city: in the same year that Prince's narrative was published, Strickland also published a collection of poems in London, which Ferguson observes was dedicated to a major figure in the abolitionist movement and feature at least one explicitly antislavery poem (39). Gillian Whitlock notes how Strickland's familiarity with the English literary field made her particularly well positioned to "render [Prince's] life and character 'intelligible' to the British public by drawing on the religious and political discourses of the anti-slavery campaign" (253). In addition to this first level of mediation—that Prince requires a literate Englishwoman to transcribe her spoken discourse— the text is also heavily influenced by Pringle's presence as editor. Pringle admits to having "pruned" Prince's exact words, and his assurance that "no fact of importance has been omitted" further suggests that he and Strickland have decided what is important about Prince's story and what can be left out (Prince 55). Taken together with the fact that Pringle, too, "was a published poet in his own right" (Paquet, "Heartbeat" 144) and that both he and Strickland were members of the same church, we can see the sorts of authorizing mechanisms that allowed Prince to gain entry into this particular public sphere only with the aid and consent of an elite literary and religious lettered class.

The very need for Pringle's preface reveals that a black woman tell-

ing her story in 1831 required authorization from members of the republic of letters. The preface is not the only part of the text that serves to
legitimate Prince: while her narrative occupies a central place after the
preface, Pringle includes numerous footnotes to explain or verify what
she discusses. Prince's story is then followed by a long supplement written by Pringle in which he refers to and quotes from a variety of letters
and other documents that provide a context in which to read Prince's
story. These include letters from her former master, John Wood, which
acknowledge her freedom but also make claims against her morality and
character; Pringle's refutations of Wood's accusations, where he vouches
that he knows Prince well and "she was really a well-disposed and respectable woman" (99); and even a letter from another Antiguan white
who verifies certain facts that Prince relates and supplies material (primarily his observations about the sexual practices of the people of the islands) that Prince herself could not discuss. Finally, Pringle ends the text
with additional appendixes, including the narrative of another enslaved
person. That Pringle saw a need to include all of these materials points
to how little authority Prince's voice had on its own. The effect of all of
these materials is also to turn Prince's story into a tool for Pringle, literally giving the editor the last word: "THAT NO SLAVE CAN EXIST
WITHIN THE SHORES OF GREAT BRITAIN" (125).

I call attention to how Prince's voice requires these various forms of
verification to emphasize how the abolitionist public sphere is not open
to all regardless of rank. Pringle's supplement makes clear that who
you are has as much influence on how you will be received as what you
have to say. The supplement begins with Pringle presenting a letter by
Wood disputing many of Prince's claims; Pringle proceeds to go through
Wood's points to address them and provides documentation to support
Prince's version, but in the process he relies as much on logically refut-
ing Wood's accusations as he does arguing about "character." On the
one hand, Pringle sets out to establish the "unquestionable facts" (117)
by asking his audience to "estimate the validity of the excuses" Wood
makes in his letter (102); to that end, he asks Wood to produce evidence
of some of his claims (103, 108) and wonders about certain contradictions in the slaveholder's narrative, such as why he continued to employ a
slave he found so unreliable and untrustworthy (105). He calls attention
to Wood's "unreasonable" (97) refusal to sell Mary for any price, making the case that the owner "prefers losing entirely the full price of his
slave, for the mere satisfaction of preventing a poor black woman from
returning home to her husband" (118). In light of Wood's anticapital-

ist irrationality, Pringle asks his readers to function as a rational public sphere so that each will "judge for himself as to the preponderance of internal evidence in the conflicting statements" (104), evaluating the arguments "upon their intrinsic claims to probability" (118).

On the other hand, in spite of these appeals to bracketing outside issues and reading the documents internally, the central question that emerges in the supplement is who should be trusted: after Wood calls into question Prince's virtue, Pringle introduces a letter by Antiguan antislavery advocate Joseph Phillips that describes Prince as "respectable and trustworthy" (110) and calls Wood "more severe than the ordinary run of slave owners" (109). This leads one of Wood's proslavery supporters to call Phillips "a man of the most worthless and abandoned character" (112), and at this point the supplement lapses into a series of "testimonies" (113) on each side meant to "vouch for" (117) the various participants. Rama's argument about how the *letrados* assert the primacy of the written word to extend their privilege certainly helps explain Pringle's footnote in which he mentions a woman who wants to testify to Wood's benevolence and then undercuts this endorsement by noting that this woman "has declined, however, to furnish me with any written correction of the misrepresentations she complains of" (117). A public sphere in which a person's social position can be left out of how his or her argument will be received is not what we see in this debate. The medium in which arguments are made matters a great deal, since only written testimony carries weight for Pringle and his imagined readership.

Habermas describes his utopian version of the public sphere as a marketplace of ideas, where each participant can enter and receive a hearing based on the merits of his or her argument rather than status in society. Prince's reliance on patronage obstructs such a direct relationship with the market, but taking her appeal straight to the market appears no more attractive an alternative in Prince's narrative. In *The History of Mary Prince*, the market is not portrayed as a utopian space of free exchange. Prince describes this scene: "We followed my mother to the market-place, where she placed us in a row against a large house, with our backs to the wall and our arms folded across our breasts. . . . At length the vendue master, who was to offer us for sale like sheep and cattle, arrived. . . . I was soon surrounded by strange men, who examined and handled me in the same manner that a butcher would a calf or a lamb he was about to purchase" (62). For a black woman who has been enslaved like Prince, the market is a site that corrupts and degrades all those who enter it. This experience of inequality and exploitation prevents her from feeling entirely comfortable within the market, and becomes a commentary on her distrust of the processes of publication, which also put her private body on display. Instead of seeing the market as potentially authorizing or as a public sphere to aspire to, Prince is forced to seek other routes toward authorship and publication. Her ability to reach the public depends on the patronage characteristic of the republic of letters, to which there appears no better alternative.

Entering the patronage system makes *The History of Mary Prince* a heterogeneous narrative, containing many voices of which Prince's is just one. Sandra Paquet and others have made the case for how Prince's voice can be read through these layers of mediation, and that Prince does have certain sources of authority aside from those granted her by the lettered city: while Prince's ability to conform to recognizably British standards of legal and religious discourse is her primary claim on the public, she also possesses the "authority . . . of the victim and witness" who has experienced firsthand the horrors of slavery (Paquet, *Caribbean Autobiography* 32), as well as her ostensible ability to speak for and even embody her community. These alternative forms of cultural and symbolic capital would be precisely those that the oppositional literary public sphere of anticolonialism would tap into during the twentieth century. They were only tenuously available to Prince, however; the obstacles she faced demonstrate how distant the majority of Caribbean people would have been during the period of slavery from any sort of literary public sphere, and how limited and administered the avenues available to them for having their voices heard would have been. Legal testimonies like Calderon's, protest writing like that of the Hart sisters, and even narratives after slavery's abolition about the apprentice system by someone like James Williams all entered a public sphere structured on the forms of authority that shape the composition and dissemination of Prince's narrative.[16]

As much opposition as these abolitionist circuits faced, and as much as abolitionism as a discourse circumscribed the ability of Manzano and Prince to represent themselves, Sibylle Fischer reminds us that this remained the only viable literary public sphere for the nonwhite writer. Fischer compares Manzano to the other major Afro-Cuban writer of the nineteenth century, Gabriel de la Concepción Valdés, who published locally under the pseudonym Plácido. Even the need for a pseudonym suggests the dangers of publication in an age of censorship, and in fact Plácido was incarcerated at various points of his life because of his poetry and eventually executed by the colonial government in 1844 for his supposed part in the "Escalera conspiracy." Fischer calls attention to the irony that Plácido was never perceived by the abolitionists as a politically committed writer, and stood as an anomaly in his time; only his martyr-dom has allowed him to be absorbed into literary history even though he was never accepted by the literary field during his lifetime. Fischer con-trasts Plácido and Manzano in ways that emphasize the unevenness of the literary public sphere in mid-nineteenth-century Cuba. She notes that whereas Manzano clearly participated in the abolitionist public sphere, Plácido anticipates an uncomfortably modern conception of the writer not then available in Cuba. For this reason, while abolitionism allowed a formerly enslaved person like Manzano to take an antislavery position, Plácido's poetry was much more ambivalent: "Unlike Manzano, Plácido does not decry the suffering of slaves in his writing. . . . For Manzano, writing was a means for securing the support of liberal Creoles and thus eventually achieving his freedom from slavery. The same people who as-sisted Manzano in his attempt to buy himself freedom had nothing but scorn for Plácido's poetry. Ironically, the slave probably was more able to speak his mind than the free mulatto" (Fischer 97). In describing the different levels of discursive freedom available to each, Fischer calls at-tention to the types of authority and institutions each was able to appeal to: "Manzano's writings were passed on through elite abolitionist chan-nels and intended for publication in England, not Cuba. . . . Because [Plácido] was arguably the first Cuban poet to have made a living as a writer, the need to create a space for himself in the marketplace clearly imposed severe restrictions on what [he] could say" (97). In other words, Plácido was attempting to make his way as a modern writer in circum-stances when a modern public sphere did not exist. The next chapters explore how the end of slavery meant a shift from abolitionism as an authorizing structure to the marketplace, thus allowing a more direct re-lationship to the local public but forcing Caribbean writers to reimagine the possibilities for opposition and critique.

All of these examples serve to show how in the English-, French-, or Spanish-controlled islands during the period of slavery, a small group maintained a monopoly on the written word so that entry into the lit-erary public sphere required patronage, approval, and even translation from the literate elites. With power perceived to lie outside the region, the European metropole appeared to be the only plausible location for a literary public sphere where the interests of the nation could be de-bated. Caribbean counterpublics were able to challenge the legitimacy and power of the local ruling class, but during this period that challenge took place almost entirely in nonliterary forms. The next chapter moves from this abolitionist public sphere, firmly located in Europe, to a set of in-between imaginings from the second half of the nineteenth century articulated in the work of Cuban poets in the United States collected in the anthology *El laúd del desterrado*, in Michel Maxwell Philip's novel *Emmanuel Appadocca*, and in Mary Seacole's *Wonderful Adventures of Mrs. Seacole in Many Lands*. These transitional texts imagine a public sphere no longer located in Europe but not quite Caribbean, coded as transnational through deterritorialized images of unfettered mobility and oceanic piracy. The end of slavery allowed these writers to imagine new power relations between Europe and its colonies and new roles for Caribbean writers. At the same time, just as abolition opened up new freedoms, the rise of modern colonialism sought to close down and govern these possibilities. Philip, Seacole, and the Cuban poets, writing in the transition between these two periods of Caribbean history, all locate discursive possibility outside of the established conventions of the republic of the lettered and begin to develop the forms of localized authority that enable a Caribbean literary public sphere.

2 The Public Sphere Unbound

Michel Maxwell Philip, *El laúd del desterrado*, and Mary Seacole

BY THE 1850s, slavery had formally ended in the English- and French-speaking Caribbean—in part because of the successes of the abolition movement in Europe but also because of increased physical resistance by enslaved people within the region—and abolitionism was no longer the avenue into a European public sphere it had once been. Chapter 1 discussed how the abolitionist movement of the early nineteenth century located its public sphere in the European metropolis even as most of the energies of a Caribbean counterpublic remained outside of print. With the end of slavery bringing increases in literacy and access to publication for greater portions of the Caribbean populace, a local literary public sphere able to debate and critique the state began to come into existence during the second half of the nineteenth century. Abolitionism played an important role in ending slavery, but was not a discourse primarily aimed at mobilizing a local population or setting up an alternative to the colonial state.[1] The counterpublic of physical resistance to slavery was no more nationalist: as Sibylle Fischer puts it, "the political unconscious of radical antislavery was not the nation-state" (271). Opposition to slavery opened up transnational liberationist energies that would be closed down in the late nineteenth century as modern colonialism began to organize the world around nation-states and their overseas possessions. Emancipation did not proceed evenly—slavery remained legal in Cuba until 1886—and, as this chapter shows, the unevenness of the passage from mercantile slavery to modern colonialism and the inheritance of abolitionism's public sphere meant that Caribbean writers of the mid-nineteenth century did not quite imagine their public within the framework of the modern nation-state that dominated international relations of this period.[2]

In this chapter, I examine three texts from the 1850s that illustrate the conflicted and in-between positioning of the writers of this transition: the novel *Emmanuel Appadocca* by Trinidadian Michel Maxwell Philip, the anthology *El laúd del desterrado* by a group of Cuban poets in the United States, and the travel narrative *Wonderful Adventures of Mrs. Seacole in Many Lands* all imagine a Caribbean subject and public separate from Europe, yet none locates the site of political possibility for the Caribbean within the islands. The chapter begins by showing how, for male writers like Philip and the Cuban poets, the outlaw identity of the buccaneer becomes the ideal bridge for their deterritorialized oppositional aspirations; the last section then turns to how Seacole seeks authority not as a heroic man of action but via her participation in the market, a maneuver foreshadowing the ambivalent move away from patronage and toward autonomy that enables the anticolonial writing of the twentieth century.

These authorial projects come out of a period of flux in the Caribbean. Even as the end of slavery brought freedom to many of the islands' inhabitants, Europe and the United States tightened their economic and political control over the Caribbean during the latter half of the nineteenth century. These foreign centers exerted renewed control over the region's nascent intellectual scene as well. Many of the major novels from this time period were either published in the metropolis, such as Cuban writer Cirilo Villaverde's *Cecilia Valdés* published in New York in 1882, or remained unpublished, like *Busha's Mistress, or Catherine the Fugitive* by Jamaica writer Cyrus Francis Perkins, which was written in the mid-nineteenth century but only became available when it appeared serially in Jamaican newspapers in 1911. While modern colonialism sought to close down the freedoms opened up by emancipation, in the late 1800s publications critical of the planter class and the state began to appear throughout the region; these newspapers and journals became a major institutional basis of early Caribbean literature as well as anticolonial movements.[3] While the Cuban poets could publish only in the United States, and both Philip and Seacole published their works in London, Europe is no longer imagined as the only potential site of a public or a public sphere in these works. While this public is not quite located in the local Caribbean setting, *Emmanuel Appadocca*, *El laúd del desterrado*, and *Wonderful Adventures of Mrs. Seacole in Many Lands* show how the public sphere becomes unbound after slavery and new possibilities are opened up for its reimagining.

The Man of Action in the Deterritorialized Public Sphere: Maxwell Philip's *Emmanuel Appadocca*

Published in England in 1854, *Emmanuel Appadocca, or Blighted Life: A Tale of the Boucaneers* by Michel Maxwell Philip contains identifiably anticolonial elements in its desire to imagine a nonwhite Caribbean intellectual who is modern, authoritative, and able to enter the public sphere as a full member. Philip, a student of the law at the time of the text's composition who would go on to become an accomplished barrister in Trinidad and eventually mayor of Port of Spain, draws on the tradition of legal discourse as one early Caribbean public sphere. Philip's cousin Jean-Baptiste Philippe had published what Bridget Brereton describes as "probably the first book ever written by a Trinidadian" (*Introduction* 23). Philippe's *A Free Mulatto*, an 1824 protest against the treatment of the free colored class in Trinidad, sought to use writing to open up public dialogue, addressing itself to the British secretary of state. Philippe's writing thus mirrors what the previous chapter discussed as abolitionist appeals in terms of both the invocation of legal authority and the orientation toward Europe. *Emmanuel Appadocca*, on the other hand, uses the image of piracy to locate Philip's imaginative locus of power as a counterpublic outside the colonial courts. But the text does not make the anticolonial move of connecting that challenge to a national public. The deterritorialized nature of Philip's hero thus reflects the transitional status of the Caribbean in a period between the end of plantation slavery and the rise of modern colonialism.[4] The collision between these two systems of power opens up a contradictory space for Caribbean authorship, giving Philip more possibilities than those available in the abolitionist public sphere, but still not enabling the full-fledged national public sphere of anticolonialism.

The publication of *Emmanuel Appadocca* thus positions the audience as once again a "tribunal of public opinion" about slavery and racially based inequality, even as Philip places that trial outside of a national context. In juxtaposing British law with "the laws of the Creator, written on the heart of man at his creation" (Philip 62), the novel appeals to natural goodness more than democratic consensus and, in so doing, calls into question the idea that the English bourgeois public sphere can make decisions for the good of its Caribbean subjects. At the same time, Philip's novel remains heterogeneous in its desires, holding out hope that when presented with the realities of postemancipation racism and inequality, its enlightened readership will see the rightness of Appadocca's cause.

Appadocca, the mixed-race hero of the novel who has been driven to piracy, anticipates the anticolonial intellectual in his ability to speak with an authority that comes from both his widely acknowledged learning and his practical use of language. Leah Rosenberg discusses how he is "a super modern man" (21) because of his command of technology. The novel emphasizes how "the many universities in which he had studied . . . had declared him a man of extraordinary talent" (Philip 89); in addition to this book learning, Appadocca gains knowledge from scientific study of his surroundings. His talent in astronomy demonstrates his ability to see the movements of the heavens and translate that information for the practical navigation of his ship, just as his "contemplation" (116) of society allows him to obtain "an abstracted idea of the manner in which the world turns" (114). His ability to reach such understanding comes from adept senses: even when darkness prevents this enlightened subject from collecting information through sight, he is able "to use his ears for the same earnest purpose as he had done his eyes" (166), or even proceed "under the pilotage of his sense of feeling" (184) by simply putting a moistened finger in the air. His abilities to read from the page or from the natural world extend to his encounters with men: "his studious mind had long been exercised in connecting deductions and his deep knowledge of human actions and their springs" (83). Just as when he reads a letter he is described as "possessing himself of the information it contained" (25), Appadocca's skills as a reader of men or of nature allow him to become the knowing subject able to impose his "will" (26) on either his crew or his environment.

With this knowledge as the basis for Appadocca's authority, his "deep sonorous voice" (58) becomes the physical embodiment of the man of action's power in what I discuss in the next chapter as an anticolonial trope reflecting the literary intellectual's command of language. In fact, the edition of *Emmanuel Appadocca* reissued in 1893 calls attention to precisely these qualities in the author himself, describing Philip's "tall, commanding presence" (9) and "sonorous voice" (7). Even when the first-mate, Lorenzo, betrays "a slight falter in his voice" in discussing the execution of a member of their crew, Appadocca can pronounce the sentence "with the same grave and apparently apathetic coolness which characterised him" (58). While his authority depends on the strength of his voice, Appadocca is as much associated with silence as with speech, even apologizing at the end of a long monologue detailing the experiences that led him into piracy, "but I find I am becoming prolix" (108). Appadocca knows when to speak and when to remain silent, so that when he speaks his orders are immediately enacted. The captain speaks authoritatively because his words are backed up by action—"I make no ungrounded assertions" (211), he reminds his half-brother—and these actions stem "from reason," as he has "long buried impulse" in favor of "act[ing] up to the dictates of the mind" (111). He thus guards his words, so that whereas others use words "to find in conversation the relaxation which the places of amusement of other countries afford," Appadocca is "not inclined to exchange more words with the merchant or any other person in the island, than were absolutely necessary to the accomplishment of the object" (88). This authority, based not on status but on the judicious use of words, allows him to silence his wealthy white father, James Willmington, who "stood dumb before the son" (64) when Appadocca declares himself his father's judge. The book's central struggle between Appadocca and his father is a struggle to control the ability to speak: upon capturing him, Appadocca has his father "bound . . . so tightly behind, that not even a murmur of the prisoner could be heard" (52), and during the trial Appadocca allows that his father as defendant "will be permitted full liberty to express yourself, at the proper time" (62). In exhibiting his ability to restrict or enable his father's occasions for speaking, Appadocca takes away discursive certainty from the planter class his father represents and finds a way to speak with authority.

Yet the place where that authoritative speech can be articulated remains outside existing social structures. While I have emphasized the anticolonial characteristics Appadocca exhibits, Philip's potential hero lacks the true public sphere that would allow him to fulfill his ambitions. After his education in France has left him as able and enlightened as any European gentleman but without a matching fortune, Appadocca realizes that "the only means I possessed was my pen," and so sets out for London because "you must know that literary men are badly paid in France" (99). He finds that he cannot get his work published in England, and to keep from starving he must sell all of his valuables "save my telescope" (100), the instrument that phallically embodies his aspirations as philosopher-king. His experiences lead him to disillusionment with his "fondly cherished hope, that in Europe, the centre of the highest human civilizations, I should have been able one day to bring the stars to mankind, and should have crowned the labours of a life-time, with banishing away some of the ignorance in which the human species was enveloped" (108). He finds that social inequality stands in the way of this Enlightenment project, that the public sphere is not open because "without money, not many can hope to propagate truth" (108). This realization of the material grounds for literature and philosophy leads to his attempt to reconnect with his wealthy father; when the father denies Appadocca because of his race, Appadocca finally sees the social injustice at the heart of Europe, that the wealthy men of London "possess wealth enough to render thousands happy without injuring themselves" (107) but choose instead to follow their individual pursuits. Appadocca can no longer abide by these "false systems" (105) and unnatural laws; he resolves to exact revenge on his father and departs Europe for Haiti and eventually Trinidad.

An unjust social system protects Appadocca's father, since as the father says in his own defense, "men are not punished in society for [my] offences" (65). *Emmanuel Appadocca* is therefore forced to imagine its public sphere outside England, where abolitionists made their appeals, or its Caribbean colonies, where anticolonialists would later mobilize public sentiment. In this transitional moment, where "the laws of the land" (65) protect planters like Willmington, Appadocca locates the potential for justice outside of land and on the pirate ship, an extraterritorial, unbounded space created by the buccaneers' "resentment of injustices" and "distaste for the society of their species" (64). This community is identified as being organized around some of the same affective bonds as the modern nation: the crew's affinity is described as "that mysterious sympathy which instinctively exists between people of the same country, and children of the same soil" (53). But just as they are like a nation, they are equally opposed to and outcast from the modern national system: as one British officer and former classmate of Appadocca tells him, piracy "is an offense which is universally reprobated by all nations" (94), and Appadocca's first-mate understands that his "daily life was a continuous challenge to man, to the powers that ruled the earth" (82). As the men exist outside of the law, yet are disciplined in the extreme to the ship's regulations, the novel articulates both a counterpublic and a public, albeit in deterritorialized form.

The novel's vacillation between the lawlessness of the seas and the discipline and order needed for a nation means that the crew's natural tendencies toward lawlessness are held together not by reasoned debate but by Appadocca's will: his strong rule allows the men to paradoxically be "treated like his children" but also "lead the lives of men" (54). The force of his personality transforms the crew into an undifferentiated mass of industry resembling the "movements of beautifully adjusted machines as they perform their parts" (38); it is his "firmness of mind which enabled him to curb the natures of even pirates, and to establish a discipline on board the Black Schooner that made his men simultaneously act as if they were but the individual members of only one single body moved by but one spirit" (193). Acting as the force that disciplines the men but also allows them to fulfill their potential, Appadocca represents the "black sovereign" figure that Michelle Stephens discusses as the tendency toward an almost totalitarian masculinity in what she calls "black empire" texts of the African diaspora. This "black masculine hero" (Stephens 66) is "strong, focused, intelligent, and educated—both a manly and masculine leader of his people" (61). She names Martin Delany's *Blake* the "ur-text of the genre" (60), but I suggest *Emmanuel Appadocca* as another candidate since it was published five years before *Blake*. Stephens notes the desire in these narratives for the founding of a black nation free from European or U.S. control, and we eventually learn Appadocca's ultimate wish to "lead the men who have followed me so bravely . . . to some remote spot on the fertile vast continent that lies on our right, and build them a city in which they may live happily, quietly, and far removed from the world" (Philip 236). Latin America thus becomes a space where hope for the national solution can be projected, even if it will never be realized within the novel.

In spite of their similar aspirations to become founding fathers, the mulatto Appadocca is fundamentally different from Blake, who "is the pure black revolutionary hero who, racially, is of unmistakably African origin" (Stephens 60–61), and seeks to create a black nation on the grounds of those origins.[5] The crew of *Emmanuel Appadocca* is by no means a potential black state, being strikingly different from a nation made up of "children of the same soil" (Philip 53). Like Melville's *Pequod* in C. L. R. James's reading, the men of Appadocca's *Black Schooner* are an explicitly multinational and multicultural grouping.[6] Onboard can be heard "the jolly songs of all nations, as sung by the different denizens that formed the motley crew of the schooner" (27); the crew speaks English, French, Spanish, as well as various Creoles, and in the early part of the novel this crew welcomes the addition of a black man who speaks a creolized English, a priest and his lily white charge, and a fisherman described as a "mulatto . . . of Spanish extraction" (12). An English officer observes how strange it is that an educated and intelligent man like Appadocca has "freely chosen to herd with the wretched outcasts" (93), but these wretched of the earth become "kindred spirits" precisely because they have "separated themselves, by their deeds, from the world, the world's sympathy, and the world's good and bad" (43). They are a nation, but also a critique of the way that the nation would have been imagined in the nineteenth century as, for example, in Johann Gottfried von Herder's influential formulation of the *volk*.[7]

The closest that this open and multicultural community comes to being reproduced outside of the bounds of the ship occurs in St. Thomas, where Dutch, English, French, U.S., and Latin American ships and sailors are all "drawn together for the purpose of commerce" (87). The absolute rule of trade here means that the port is governed by rules not unlike those of the pirates: when customs officers board Appadocca's ship, they "were easily satisfied, for the easy and encouraging policy, which the Danes have been wise enough to adopt, for the purpose of drawing trade to their little island, did not require many of the forms in the clearance of the ships which might enter its port" (87). Indeed, if, in Appodocca's opinion, all commerce is piracy (113), it is no surprise that the abstract market becomes almost a homeland.[8] At the same time, St. Thomas's danger, revealed when Appadocca is captured there, is that it is too embodied and thus governed by the laws of the land to be an adequate site for this counterpublic of resistance.

Despite their many affinities with an alternative nationalist project, then, the crew's detachment from "soil" also suggests the ways that Philip could not position his project within any existing space, either geographically or chronologically. The novel opens by establishing the setting as in-between. The first words of *Emmanuel Appadocca* are: "Between the north-west coast of Venezuela and the Island of Trinidad there lies an extensive expanse of water, known as the Gulf of Paria" (11). This body of water is where one character declares, "I am at home again; I am on my own gulf" (139). Appadocca himself, when asked which harbor his ship returns to after its adventures, describes how "we sought no other shelter than that which was afforded us by the high and wide seas" (160). Unmoored from land, unable to be either the Caribbean islands or Europe, this setting reflects how Philip had to imagine his public sphere: while England had the institutions that could support his publication and provide readership, Philip could only be marginal there, whereas in Trinidad the institutions of the public sphere were still too limited to allow the kind of Caribbean nationalism or critique of colonialism that *Emmanuel Appadocca* articulates.

As much as this positioning makes *Emmanuel Appadocca* what William Cain in his introduction calls "'Atlantic' literature" (xvii), and in doing so invokes Paul Gilroy's concept of the Black Atlantic, the majority of the novel is not set in the Atlantic, between Europe and the New World. The opening passage goes on to describe its setting in the gulf bordered on one side by Trinidad and the other by "the mainland of South America" (Philip 12), and these are the bodies of land that frame the Gulf of Paria and *Emmanuel Appadocca*. Philip thus places his imagined community between the English colonialism of Trinidad and the freedom of the recently liberated South American continent.[9] Latin America represents, for Appadocca, opposition to British colonialism, as we learn in the story of the protagonist's namesake who fought the English invasion in the name of the Spanish (217).[10] Emmanuel Appadocca's Venezuelan love interest, Feliciana, tries to free him from his vengeful vows, but he cannot get away from the death struggle with his father, and ultimately the oppositional war he is fighting kills both white planter and rebellious son. Caught between conflicting demands, Appadocca exists in a transitional moment, which his location between colony and continent physically manifests. The contours of this contradictory moment appear in the crew's composition, peopled by opponents of the new social order including both black servants like Jack Jimmy as well as members of the "old aristocracy, banished from France" after the revolution, who have become sworn enemies of democracy (110). Appadocca's own ideology expresses a mixture of theological faith in God's laws as well as the intense disdain for feeling or instinct in favor of thought and reason. He is the product of a moment where the old order of slavery is being abolished throughout the region, but new systems of control are only just arising.

Emmanuel Appadocca articulates significant aspects of what would emerge as the literary anticolonialism of Jacques Roumain or Claude McKay: the combination of action and intellect, the idea that sensitivity would enable this enlightened intellectual to listen to and understand his environment and translate that knowledge into an oppositional project. Appadocca prefers absolute opposition to accommodation, labeling as "deceiver[s]" those who "remained in the society of mankind" despite awareness of its injustices (162). But Appadocca's story is ultimately a thwarted romance rather than the foundational fiction of *Gouverneurs de la rosée* or *Banana Bottom*;[11] Appadocca achieves his goal of enacting revenge upon his father, but the novel ends without the union with Feliciana that would offer domesticity and a private self distinct from his avenging persona. Unable to attach his opposition to a national project, Appadocca represents a counterpublic of resistance but still, at the end of the story, has found no public sphere where he can locate himself. The solitary individual, outside of social structures, ultimately proves unproductive for the founding of a new order. Two English officers reflect on a lost time when "we feared God, honored the King, and dealt justly and honorably by all men" but that now "the times, then, are changed . . . and the greatest misfortune is, that such characters as that Willmington, unluckily for humanity, make as many Appadoccas" (205). Philip creates Appadocca as the only kind of hero possible in such infamous times, but Appadocca's ultimate goal—to eventually end his attacks on the British and found a city where his men can be free—cannot yet be conceived of as possible.

The Public Sphere at Sea: *El laúd del desterrado*

The attempt to imagine alternatives to European colonial rule is as central to the poetry anthology *El laúd del desterrado* as to *Emmanuel Appadocca*, and just as Philip figures the pirate as the embodiment of his transnational desires, these Cuban poets writing from New York turn to the *filibustero* as their idealized man of action. Chapter 1 discussed how the careers of José Antonio Saco, Juan Francisco Manzano, and Plácido show the persecution and censorship faced by writers in Cuba who opposed slavery. This chapter explores how the Spanish authorities were no more open to writing that challenged colonial rule. As in the case of the abolitionist public sphere, movements against Spanish rule in Cuba faced enormous obstacles because of the colonial power's discursive monopoly. Colonial restrictions meant that criticism of the government was virtually impossible to publish, driving much of the independence movement underground or into exile. Yet throughout the mid-nineteenth century, a body of writing against Spanish rule emerged in newspapers published in the United States, culminating in the anthology *El laúd del desterrado*. Published in New York in 1858, the volume features work by six of the poets active in U.S. periodicals during this period as well as three poems by José María Heredia, who had died two decades earlier but is included as an inspiration to these political poets.

Involved primarily in the New York and New Orleans exile communities, the writers collected in *El laúd del desterrado* were part of both a literary and political movement. The six active poets included in *El laúd del desterrado*—Miguel Teurbe Tolón, José Agustín Quintero, Pedro Santacilia, Pedro Angel Castellón, Juan Clemente Zenea, and Leopoldo Turla—were all born between 1818 and 1832 and left Cuba for the United States between 1846 and 1853. Kirsten Silva Gruesz calls these writers "Lopecistas" because of their association with Narciso López, the famous *filibustero* who launched military operations from the United States in an attempt to liberate Cuba and died in one such invasion in 1851. For Silva

Gruesz, this allegiance with López allows the anthology to speak "on behalf of the anticolonial cause" (146) seeking to free Cuba from Spain. The anthology certainly features a number of poems articulating a strong desire to end Spanish rule; yet the writers featured in *El laúd del desterrado* present an ambivalent and often contradictory vision for the future of their homeland that, while opposed to Spain, does not always advocate independence or freedom. Their ideology is distinct from the anticolonialism of José Martí that I discuss in chapter 3. Rather than constructing the anticolonial relationship to the public sphere that interpellated the nation as subject of political change, these writers remained outside of the national space and at sea in how they envisioned the public that their writing could persuade to end Spanish rule in Cuba.

The poems included in *El laúd del desterrado* frequently protest against Spanish control. References are made to "Cuba esclava" (Montes-Huidobro 41), as in Tolón's "Resolución," or to Cuba's "chains" (123), as in Leopoldo Turla's "Degradación." Santacilia's "A España" catalogs the deficiencies of the Spanish empire in hopes of convincing its reader of the injustice of Spanish rule. Silva Gruesz points to how the poem transmits its "anticolonial message" (150) through "debunk[ing] national myth-making" (151); the poem begins by recounting the stories of Spain's power and glory that the speaker was told as a boy, before moving on to describing the current reality of that empire's decline. Rodrigo Lazo calls this "ideological unmasking," which serves to establish "a parallel between the poem and a revisionary history" (88). These descriptions of injustice are joined with cries for Cuba to "wake up!" (Montes-Huidobro 66) as in Agustín Quintero's "¡Adelante!" or for "una guerra Cubana," part of the title of one of Tolón's poems. Many of the poems memorialize martyrs of what was still a nascent independence movement—the Grito de Yara that is considered the real beginning of the Cuban wars of independence would not occur for another decade, in 1868. Nonetheless, the poems repeatedly aver commitment to "la lid," or the fight, with Tolón's "La pluma y la espada" ending with the speaker declaring, "I put you down, Pen, to embrace you, Sword."[12]

The anthology thus traces out the relationship between writing and action in similar terms to those of the anticolonial writers of the early twentieth century: poems invoke the ideas that writing can serve to bring awareness to injustice, that it can present alternatives to dominant colonial narratives, but that ultimately writing cannot live up to physical action in the struggle to decolonize. While the writers of *El laúd del desterrado* express those elements of the anticolonial project, the way they

envision their relationship to their public leads them to position themselves as above and estranged from the nation that might enact these
changes. Poems figure change as virtually impossible because of the distance between the poets and their Cuban audience: Clemente Zenea be-
moans how "In vain the people call to me."[13] This typical lament captures the challenges these exiles faced in enacting the changes they de-
sired. Exile, illiteracy, censorship, and other structural limitations of the
nineteenth-century public sphere made their connection to a Cuban public tenuous, as Lazo calls attention to in emphasizing the "real impedi-
ments of how to transport the documents and make them available in a
society where such texts were banned" (17). The question of audience is
encoded even in Santacilia's anti-Spanish protest "A España," which addresses itself explicitly to Spain; this form of address makes it resemble a
liberal appeal to the Spanish government to ease its policies toward the
colonies more than a rallying cry for the Cuban nation.

Despite this rhetorical strategy, which recalls the abolitionist appeals
to the English public seen in chapter 1, the poets of *El laúd del desterrado* did not devote their primary energies to persuading the Spanish
public to change colonial policy. Their location in the United States accounts for much of this difference, and appeals were certainly made to
potential allies in the United States; the existence of U.S.-based newspapers like *La Verdad* and *El Filibustero* attests to the successes the exiles
achieved in convincing North American interests to support their anti-
Spanish agitation. But the publication of *El laúd del desterrado* in Spanish suggests that this volume was not aimed at the U.S. public broadly
conceived. While Spain and the United States were sometimes the targets of lobbying, the group these poems position as responsible for transforming the homeland is most frequently the lettered exile elite. Tolón's
"A Guaimacan," written in the second person, addresses itself to Heredia in invoking the author of "La estrella de Cuba." The poem begins
by naming him as "the valiant voice of a robust song / who there on the
beaches of a sad Cuba" cried out for freedom.[14] The poem ends by answering this cry in calling upon "brave soldiers / to fight or to die be-
neath" the flag of an independent Cuba.[15] By the time the poem arrives
at naming these soldiers, however, an important shift has occurred. The
opening of "A Guaimacan" deploys the trope of grounding itself in the
Cuban landscape popular in many of the poems contained in *El laúd*;
but from there, the poem moves quickly to a setting along the Hudson
and continues by praising Heredia's dedication to Cuban freedom while
in the United States. The "brave soldiers" are the "nobles hijos" and "hi-

jos desterrados" who have been "thrown by the Despot to another land" (49).[16] Like Castellón's "A Cuba en la muerte de Varela," which was also dedicated to an intellectual from the older generation of exiled Cubans, or Tolón's "Canto de un desterrado," "A Guaimacan" explicitly names exile in the United States as the ideal position from which to advocate Cuban independence.

The preface to *El laúd del desterrado*, written in 1858 by editor José Elías Hernández, makes explicit the contradictory implications of such a privileging. The preface emphasizes how all of the writers included are members of "the republic of Cuban letters" and come from "the most illustrious classes in the island";[17] the repeated references in the later poems to the "noble sons" of Cuba reinforces the idea of a class that considers itself entitled to lead. Yet even while Hernández invokes their class background to authorize this lettered elite, he also emphasizes their relationship with the "pueblo cubano" (3): they are "poetas populares" (4), men committed to "nuestra revolución" (3). This simultaneous desire for and fear of the popular demonstrates the conflicted nature of these poets' discourse. Revolutionary commitment is offered as what allows these elite writers to overcome the distance created both by their class and by their location within the United States; what the volume must produce is a way in which physical distance can become a sign of allegiance rather than hierarchy. The preface thus introduces the idea that the anthologized poems will be part of the independence struggle by "reviving a mode of sentiment . . . reminding the people of grand ideas of liberty in the language best suited for preserving that memory."[18] Giving the anthology the duty of keeping alive the words of the "poetas mártires" (3) and inspiring the revolutionary movement, this preface thus attempts to reorient the Cuban republic of letters as an explicitly oppositional counterpublic of resistance.

The exile appears as this idealized oppositional identity in poems like Tolón's "El pobre desterrado" and "Canto de un desterrado" as well as Santacilia's "Salmo CXXXVII de David," which is modeled on the same Psalm that the Melodians would adapt as a Rastafari anthem in the 1970s. The exile positioning becomes linked to revolutionary action through the figure of the *filibustero*, an identity articulated most directly in Clemente Zenea's poem "El filibustero." As Lazo explains, that poem articulates the idea of the *filibustero* as different from other kinds of warriors specifically because of the importance of mobilizing the public sphere in their project: "what differentiates filibustering from a war is that the *filibustero* must appeal to a larger population for support" (59).

The three poems dedicated to Narciso López in *El laúd del desterrado* (by Tolón, Clemente Zenea, and Turla) reiterate the allegiance to action, emphasizing the military aspects of the *filibustero*. These poems declare their commitment to freedom while reinforcing the idea that change would come to Cuba from the outside: Turla's "A Narciso López," for example, praises López for "giving freedom to oppressed people."[19] Taking López as an emblem for the kind of liberation movement these writers envisioned demonstrates the complicated relationship of *filibusteros* with the Cuban public they are seeking to reach and the U.S. institutional framework that shapes their occasion for speaking.

The location of these poets in the United States and their desire to use that site as a staging ground to intervene in Cuba cannot be separated from the growing strength of U.S. manifest destiny ideology. Cuba was central to the process by which the United States began to fashion itself as an international empire and emerge during the nineteenth century as a major power in the Caribbean. Unlike in the British and French islands, where the transition from plantation slavery to modern colonialism simply meant a reorganized relationship with the metropole, the Spanish empire proved too weak to survive this epochal change; in Cuba and Puerto Rico, then, the declining slave system occurred concurrently with the rise of U.S. domination in the region, so that as early as the first half of the nineteenth century, the United States, rather than Spain, was by far these islands' largest trading partner.[20] In the aftermath of the U.S. war with Mexico and the acquisition of vast tracts of Mexican land, the 1850s represented a high point in the movement within the United States to annex Cuba. As Lazo describes, the contributors to newspapers like *La Verdad* saw the annexationist movement in the United States as their most promising ally; their interest in annexation was closely linked to an allegiance to U.S. slaveholders, who frequently supported financially the literary and military activities of these mostly white, upper-class Cubans. The *filibusteros* received patronage from powerful interests in the United States: López's expedition from New Orleans in 1850 was supported by Southern politicians, including Robert E. Lee and Jefferson Davis. Agustín Quintero, who contributes three poems to *El laúd del desterrado*, fought on the side of the Confederacy in the U.S. Civil War, which Silva Gruesz notes may explain "Quintero's fall from the [Cuban] national canon" (152). These alliances called into question the ability of this group to speak for a broad Cuban public in the island and circumscribed the kinds of political projects these *filibusteros* could advocate.

The contradictory ideologies represented by the contributors to *El laúd del desterrado*—who variously advocated annexation and independence, and described Cuba as "enslaved" even while supporting the continuation of plantation slavery—demonstrates how their geographically and temporally in-between context shaped their discourse. The institutions that structured this context offered a field of positions to these writers that did not include the kind of autonomy that someone like Martí was able to carve out a few decades later. Lazo notes that while the longest-standing newspapers of the Cuban exile community such as *La Verdad* were staunchly annexationist, in large part a product of the support they received from the Cuban and U.S. planter and business classes, more radical newspapers did begin to appear in the 1850s, such as *El Mulato*, which openly criticized the plantation system. While the *filibustero* position generally sought to bring change to Cuba from the outside because of fear that widespread social revolution would lead to what had happened in Haiti—an outcome feared even by antislavery white liberals—newspapers like *El Mulato* and *El Independiente* opposed slavery and called for Cubans of all backgrounds to come together to overthrow Spanish rule. Lazo cites an 1853 essay from the English section of *El Independiente*, the newspaper Cirilo Villaverde founded as a reaction against the annexation movement, which argued that "Cuba can yet gain her independence by force of arms, the only resource left to downtrodden people, the only one which, through a process of purification, can adequately prepare them to pass from illimited despotism to absolute freedom" (93). This article, titled "To the Public," articulates a strong revolutionary message critical of the idea that an elite group of exiles, supported by U.S. business interests, could bring "absolute freedom" to Cuba; yet publishing the piece in English and referring to the Cubans able to take this revolutionary step as "them" suggests that even in this case Villaverde cannot quite connect with those he sees as revolutionary agents. Even when publishing in Spanish, the routes to the Cuban public proved frequently obstructed, as journals and newspapers published in the United States and banned in Cuba managed only irregularly to reach this target audience; according to Lazo, the end result was that "texts did not circulate widely enough to prompt a revolution" (17–18), and "by 1855, it became increasingly clear that *filibustero* writers were failing in their efforts to persuade readers in Cuba to rise up against the government" (98). It would be decades before such a project would be fulfilled.

The geographical location outside of the island thus presented the possibility of a critical counterpublic not yet feasible within Cuba, but also made impossible the connection with national space and audience necessary for a successful literary public sphere. This deterritorialized arrangement enabled the positioning that would be so productive to this generation's literary and political action. The public that these writers ended up successfully addressing and mobilizing were other exiles like themselves, captured in terms like *desterrado* or *filibustero* that they used for themselves, their audience, and the agents imagined as able to put an end to Spanish rule. *Desterrado*, generally translated as exile, signifies the idea of being detached from a specific physical space, as Lazo points out: "*desterrado* emphasizes a disconnection from the land, *tierra*" (55). The term *filibustero*, a concept associated with piracy and buccaneering, evokes a different sort of deterritorialization, the community at sea like the "shipwrecked" man Clemente Zenea describes in "El Filibustero." This oceanic public sphere, neither entirely inside nor outside the Caribbean, is the space free of the laws of the land seen in Philip's *Emmanuel Appadocca*. Evocative of the buccaneer's location on the margins of empire and at the edge of legality, the *filibustero* captures the spirit of a transitional moment in which alliance with U.S. commercial interests can be deployed to oppose Spanish mercantilism. The term remained caught up in the onset of the U.S. role in the region as a modern colonial power—one of the most famous filibusterers of the nineteenth century was William Walker, whose invasion of Nicaragua in the name of U.S. manifest destiny uncomfortably reflected on the Cuban *filibustero*'s vision of themselves as liberators (Lazo 6). By deploying the idea of the written word as weapon, in attempting to mobilize a Caribbean public through literature, and in marking out the writer's marginal space as allowing a privileged relationship with a counterpublic of resistance, these mid-nineteenth-century writers foreshadow many of the contours of the literary anticolonialism of the twentieth century.

Navigating the Fall of the Republic of Letters: *Wonderful Adventures of Mrs. Seacole*

While Michel Maxwell Philip in England or the Cuban writers in the United States looked to the pirate or *filibustero* as the man of action who could embody their transnational desires, Mary Seacole's autobiography fashions her as a less romantic or oppositional migratory subject, a "sutler" able to move across boundaries "with a view to gain" (Seacole 5). Unlike Philip with his career as a lawyer or the *filibusteros* and their exile networks in New Orleans and New York, Seacole as a nonwhite female colonial subject found herself seeking to publish her life story in London in 1857 in order to financially support herself. Living via her writing, Seacole thus represents an early model for the modern professional writer. Yet without a Caribbean public to which she could appeal and without resources, Seacole was forced to tailor her narrative to and seek her narrative authority from a British public. This kind of subordinate, marginalized relationship to the public sphere meant that rather than autonomy, Seacole's text shows dependence on other forms of authority. For Seacole, the market occupies a similar role to piracy in the works of Philip or the Cuban poets, becoming a site of discursive authority that enables her to create an interstitial subjectivity. Seacole allies herself to a British empire that transcends narrow national interest and enables her mobility and freedom, even as she locates herself in the margins of that imperial space. Her travels reveal her status between empires as she interacts with both established British control and rising American power. *Wonderful Adventures of Mrs. Seacole in Many Lands* thus appears as a conflicted text that seeks to translate West Indian experience for a British public while it reveals an unfulfilled desire to establish a counterpublic able to critique that dominant power.

Seacole's writing demonstrates an awareness of the positions available to her within this Victorian literary field and the genres it offered. *Wonderful Adventures* resembles *The History of Mary Prince* in terms of the documentation it includes to validate Seacole's voice, but its publication decades after the end of British slavery means that it does not utilize the channels established by abolitionism to enter the public sphere. As William Andrews points out in his introduction to the Oxford University Press edition of Seacole's narrative, this reality is reflected generically in the fact that "Seacole did not write her narrative expressly to advance the cause of antislavery, as so many Afro-American women autobiographers did during her era . . . one does not read her autobiography as part of the slave narrative tradition" (xxvii). At the same time, neither does Seacole's narrative express the artistic aspirations of the later anticolonialists like José Martí or Aimé Césaire who sought to utilize highly stylized language to distinguish their work from professional or bureaucratic forms of writing. This in-between position leads her to cross bourgeois and popular forms in order to insert herself into the tentative discursive space available to her, with the awareness that her inclusion is precarious if not impossible. By choosing to write a narrative that resembles autobiography, memoir, and travelogue, Seacole negotiates genres that in Victorian England were almost exclusively the domain of male, bourgeois subjects.[21] Yet she injects into her narrative the crass language of the market, explicitly identifying her authorial project as a money-making venture. She makes no disguise of the fact that she "wrote her book as an entrepreneurial project to raise money after declaring bankruptcy" (H. Cooper 204). On the contrary, she embraces that cause by ending her narrative describing the circumstances of her bankruptcy and her hope that her readership will have charity toward her. Seacole thus identifies financial independence, rather than physical and spiritual freedom, as the kind of capital the British public can offer the Caribbean subject.

While publication located Seacole's text in England, the narrative itself opens onto a variety of spaces that show how unbounded and mobile her potential public sphere might be: she mentions visiting Cuba, Haiti, and the Bahamas (Seacole 5), and within the course of her narrative travels from Jamaica to Latin America, England, and finally to southeastern Europe to participate in the Crimean War. These travels through a variety of marginal spaces, from the boardinghouse to the war zone, show Seacole to be the prototypical migratory subject, at home wherever she goes. In Seacole's case, the market and her financially motivated travels connect all of these sites. At one stop in Gibraltar, she describes her cosmopolitan delight in being in a city and mixing with the crowds. In this setting, she acknowledges how at home she feels in the marketplace: the tour itself "was rather fatiguing . . . and I was not sorry to return to the market-place, where I stood curiously watching its strange and motley population" (83). Seacole's profession as a merchant requires that she feel at home amid the consumer classes who patronize her. She even runs into a few "kind-hearted fellows" who "had been often in my house at Kingston" as customers (83). She here points to the extraordinary fact that in a strange land, where all else may appear foreign to her, the market remains a familiar, reassuring, and welcoming place. The overtly economic thrust of Seacole's project resonates with her self-conception throughout the narrative, as a shrewd and hardworking businesswoman. She appeals throughout her narrative to her authority as a laborer, contrary to Victorian stereotypes of people of color as lazy and unenterprising, a stereotype that Seacole mentions in her first paragraph. In contrast to the symbolically powerful image of the exile that Martí cultivates, as a disinterested intellectual whose only labor is his art, Seacole fashions herself as a "sutler" (vii), as she is introduced to her readers in the introduction. This term becomes a description of Seacole's literary practice. A precursor to the contemporary Jamaican higgler who travels the same routes as global capital yet operates within the interstices of empire, Seacole the sutler finds her ability to cross borders as well as her opportunities to use those experiences to tell her own story simultaneously enabled and circumscribed by the transnational market that modern colonialism creates.

Seacole constructs an image of herself that suggests she has control of her circumstances, but the documentation that accompanies *Wonderful Adventures* undercuts this self-presentation. Like *The History of Mary Prince*, Seacole's text is edited by an outside hand and supplemented by letters from those who knew Seacole in the Crimea as well as British journalist W. H. Russell's preface, all meant to vouch for the authenticity of her narrative and her credentials as a "plain truth-speaking woman" (vii). As much as Seacole hopes that she can be judged by a modern public for what she has done, who she knows proves just as important to achieving a hearing. Russell paradoxically insists that he "should have thought that no preface would have been required to introduce Mrs. Seacole to the British public" (vii), asserting that her own notoriety gives her an automatic entry into that public, but then goes on to bear "testimony" to her worthiness to receive such a hearing (viii). She cannot take for granted that simply having a tale "unique in literature" will allow her to find a forum to tell it (vii); as her experiences in the Crimea have taught her, "authority" depends on having something that others want (118). As Amy Robinson puts it, "the profit of a particular text is not simply narrative utterance, the story it tells, but also the production of an authoritative voice which produces the conditions for that voice to be listened to, and in this case, to procure donations for Seacole's cause" (542). These forces of supply and demand shape her story, which means that unlike slave narratives, which were assured of a hearing through the abolition movement's patronage, the episodes that Seacole will recount are not primarily about the injustices she has endured but scenes of her own selflessness and heroism. In this case, audience demand is not for recrimination but for stories about the British war in the Crimea. She admits early in her narrative that her participation in that major event is "the one and only claim I have to interest the public ear" (Seacole 26), and relating those events will thus be her main concern. Her narrative is an effort to cash in on the symbolic capital that she has acquired through her service to the British empire: "I trust England will not forget one who nursed her sick, who sought out her wounded to aid and succour them, and who performed the last offices for some of her illustrious dead" (viii).

While the market presents Seacole this chance to establish her own authority, entry into a public sphere that appeals for its authority to English consumers means that her critique of power, when it appears at all, is much more veiled and ambivalent than in either slave narratives or anticolonial writing. As the discussion of Martí in the next chapter shows, one of the main challenges the anticolonialists would face was to construct a critique of power even while relying on the market as a primary source of legitimation. Writing to a British audience that she frequently invokes in asides to her "kind reader" (27), Seacole raises no objection to Jamaica's colonial status; as Sandra Paquet puts it, "*The Wonderful Adventures of Mrs. Seacole in Many Lands* reflects an enthusiastic acceptance of colonialism in the aftermath of slavery" ("Enigma" 651). Critics have intently debated whether Seacole resists or supports British colonialism.[22] Bernard McKenna approaches the question by pointing to how Seacole often makes her critique of racism through reference to the attitudes of people from the United States she encounters in her travels, thus allowing her to oppose white supremacy without disrupting her identification with Englishness. I want to examine Seacole's attitudes toward the United States, but not only to answer McKenna's question of whether her text "supports English hegemony" or "undermines it" (228). I point to how the text's location at the transition from slavery to modern colonialism means that it is also between different imperial models; as a result, the text betrays ambivalence not only toward England but also toward the modern forms of colonialism represented by the U.S. presence in Central America.

The marginal space of New Grenada, where much of the first part of her narrative takes place, is described as a "lawless out-of-the-way spot" (Seacole 13), making it a site of both threat and possibility. The locales she visits in what is today Panama are characterized by squalor and chaos, populated by "the refuse of every nation which meet together upon its soil" (10). Cholera becomes the trope for her visit, though Seacole notes her belief that the sickness was brought from New Orleans and thus reverses typical racist anti-immigrant rhetoric to make North Americans a contagion infecting New Grenada.[23] But while New Grenada thus represents lawlessness and degeneration, it is also a site where social hierarchies break down: "rude, coarse gold diggers, in gay-coloured shirts, and long, serviceable boots, elbowed, in perfect equality, keen Yankee speculators, as close shaven, neat and clean on the Isthmus of Panama as in the streets of New York or New Orleans" (18). This "perfect equality" even extends to a breakdown in the laws governing gender, so that many of the women dress and act as men and "appeared in no hurry to resume the dress or obligations of their sex" (20). Seacole is both energized and fearful of this world in which the "civilization" and "control" ensured in other contexts by British empire no longer operate (19).

Yet Seacole is attuned to the ways in which even amid this break-down, new forms of domination are emerging. She twice disapprovingly mentions U.S. "schemes for annexation" of other parts of the Americas (51), and sees clearly the imperial designs of the racist, vulgar North Americans she encounters. While the United States becomes a way for Seacole to displace her critique of racism and imperial domination, her desires for modernity embodied by the market make even that critique ambivalent. For example, her description of the American railroad project across the Panama isthmus is almost unequivocally celebratory: "It was reserved for the men of our age to accomplish what so many had died in attempting and iron and steam, twin giants, subdued to man's will, have put a girdle over rocks and rivers, so that travellers can glide as smoothly, if not as inexpensively, over the once terrible Isthmus of Darien, as they can from London to Brighton. . . . It is a gigantic enter-prise, and shows what the energy and enterprise of man can accomplish. Everything requisite for its construction, even the timber, had to be pre-pared in, and brought from, America" (10, 12). She marvels at the mo-dernity of this project, subjugating nature and technology to man's ratio-nalizing will. She even applauds the civilizing effect that this moderniza-tion project has had on the region: "Not yet, however, does civilization rule at Panama . . . but seven years ago, when I visited the Isthmus of Panama, things were much worse, and a license existed, compared to which the present lawless state of affairs is enviable" (10). Moderniza-tion, emanating from the United States, boldly spreads progress and civi-lization to a chaotic and corrupt Latin America.

These attitudes seem to be paradoxical: in one breath Seacole rails against U.S. racism and slavery; in the next, she sings the praises of the North Americans' modernizing efforts in Central America, which, she acknowledges, resulted in the deaths of countless African Americans, West Indians, and "Spanish Indians," Seacole's preferred term for the lo-cal population. Though these attitudes may appear to be inconsistent, in fact, her argument against slavery relies on her embracing of the liberal-capitalist project, as does her success at becoming a bourgeois subject able to move freely in the colonial public sphere. While Prince appeals to Christianity and Philip to a more deist idea of natural law, Seacole artic-ulates modern ideals of freedom and the right to sell one's labor on the free market as moral arguments against slavery and discrimination. In each of her critiques of the enslavement and oppression of people of African descent, Seacole implicitly puts forward her own literacy and economic success to contradict stereotypes and racial hierarchies based on the assumption that a black woman like herself could never be an equal citizen to a European man. Whereas Prince needed in her *History* to assert her basic humanity, Seacole believes that her accomplishments have earned her recognition as a bourgeois Englishwoman.

The existence of such a liberal public sphere, where accomplishments can be recognized and authority can be based on grounds other than status, opens up possibilities for Seacole within her story and as an author. But the inadequacies of that public sphere to live up to its ideals produces the heterogeneity of her text. The lettered elite are presented in the story as an inadequate site of authority in this increasingly modern world; rather than rely on patronage, Seacole is repeatedly forced to take matters into her own hands. The most overt example of this comes when she seeks to travel to the Crimea to offer her skills as a nurse to the British war effort. Though throughout her travels she frequently relies on connections to the powerful to help open doors, at least as frequently those connections are not enough. Despite accompanying her inquiries to the War Office or to Florence Nightingale with numerous "testimonials" attesting to her skills as a nurse (77), Seacole is rejected at every turn. Although she momentarily expresses disappointment at this kind of discrimination—that "American prejudices against colour had some root here" in England (77)—she is remarkably pragmatic about the prejudice she faces: "in my country, where people know our use, it would have been different; but here it was natural enough—although I had references, and other voices spoke for me—that they should laugh, good-naturedly enough, at my offer" (78). Seacole decides that if having upstanding British men "speak for" her does not work, then she will simply move to the Crimea on her own to set up a hotel, since she knows there will be a demand for her services; this sort of self-reliance and dependence on a market where patronage fails stands at a significant remove from the republic of letters that required authorization for entry. This episode encodes the same dynamics Seacole faced in publishing her narrative; while she cannot enter this public sphere localized in England entirely on her own terms, she has sources of authority and symbolic capital that she can deploy to tentatively circumvent the "authorities" (80) who are not interested in authorizing her.

The History of Mary Prince, Autobiografía de un esclavo, Emmanuel Appadocca, and *Wonderful Adventures of Mrs. Seacole* each appeared in England during the waning years of the slave system in the Americas, but had limited circulation within the Caribbean; *El laúd del desterrado* was published in the United States and found its ability to travel back to Cuba restricted. Within a few years of publication, all of these texts were out of print; one recent critic could be talking about any of these texts when she describes Seacole's narrative as "all but erased from feminist, Caribbean, and British literary histories" until its rediscovery during the late twentieth century (A. Robinson 537). Yet the final decades of the nineteenth century suggest the emergence of new venues and institutions for Caribbean literature alongside epochal historical developments: on the one hand, the end of slavery in the region in Cuba in 1886, the dissolution of the last local parliament in the British islands in Barbados in 1884, and the formalization of the United States as a colonial power in the region in 1898; at the same time, the reprinting of *Emmanuel Appadocca* in Trinidad in 1893, the publication in Trinidad of J. J. Thomas's *Creole Grammar* in 1869 and *Froudacity* in 1889, the rise of national poet and playwright Massillon Coicou in Haiti, along with the publication in Paris of his *Poésies nationales* in 1882 and Anténor Firmin's *De l'égalité des races humaines* in 1885, and in the 1880s and 1890s the emergence of a model for successful professional writing, José Martí. The codification of the modern colonial system and its division of the world among nation-states and their possessions that took place in the final years of the nineteenth century were thus accompanied by the rise of a local literary public sphere dedicated to critiquing and opposing that power. My next chapter begins with Martí to discuss how this anticolonial Caribbean literature linked itself both to the dominance of foreign power and to the presence of a national literary public sphere unavailable to Prince, Philip, and Seacole.

Part Two

Modern Colonialism and the Anticolonial Public Sphere, 1886 to 1959

3 The Intellectual and the Man of Action

Resolving Literary Anxiety in the Work of
José Martí, Stephen Cobham, and
Jacques Roumain

MODERN COLONIALISM, through its attempts to remove local power from the Caribbean, enabled writers throughout the region to see themselves speaking for a national public as well as part of a counter-public opposed to power. The modern colonial system's attempts to remove power from the region produced a vocal and influential Caribbean intellectual class aligned with the social movements of anticolonialism. The existence of these social movements made it possible for Caribbean writers to imagine mobilizing a local public to give their literary projects the political significance that would allow them to speak with authority. These anticolonial sentiments open up a field of possibilities for writers like José Martí, Stephen Cobham, and Jacques Roumain to craft a heroic role for the literary intellectual, that figure sensitive enough to hear and understand the desires of the people better than either the foreign or local ruling class. While these authors imagine this heroic role for the writer, they struggle to reconcile their anxiety about the efficacy of writing as a passive or feminized activity with their desire to occupy the identity of man of action and spokesman for the nation.

Beginning with José Martí's literary and military participation in the Cuban wars of independence, anticolonial writers constructed a writerly vocation that could combine words with action to make their case for being the ideal representatives to lead the nation. Even though Martí was, like the writers featured in *El laúd del desterrado*, exiled from Cuba by Spanish authorities and forced to publish in newspapers in the United States and Latin America, he managed to connect his authorial project to the nation in a way these earlier writers could not. Rather than relying on patronage from annexationist North American interests, Martí turned to the market as a source of legitimacy, which allowed him to write not only against Spanish rule but also U.S. intervention. Relying on the market for legitimation had significant downsides, but the success of Martí's anticolonialism depended on his ability to work within those limits. Furthermore, Martí was able to position himself as organically connected to the colonial nation, represented by the oppressed and marginalized, by distinguishing himself as a literary intellectual separate from the technocratic or professional elite. The idea of literary intellectuals as sensitive enough to listen to the nation and eloquent in articulating its desires allowed writers to give themselves a place in the anticolonial project. Yet at the same time, being literary threatened to undermine their relevance and exclude them from a public sphere ruled by the practical. This section looks at how Martí and some of the most successful anticolonial writers to follow him managed to imagine the intellectual as spokesperson for both a national public and a counter-public of resistance. Placing Martí alongside the work of a lesser-known writer, Stephen Cobham, shows the ambivalences in that anticolonial ideology. The chapter closes by looking at how Jacques Roumain's canonical *Gouverneurs de la rosée* uses the literary identity to try to resolve some of these ambivalences. This authorial anxiety foreshadows the turn in chapter 4 to an exploration of how coding opposition in terms of the literary enabled a critique from the margins of colonial capitalism even as it eventually isolated the literary intellectual from political and social power.

José Martí and Literary Anticolonialism

In *Desencuentros de la modernidad*, Julio Ramos adopts Angel Rama's concept of the lettered city to show how the crisis of the colonial Latin American literary field is especially visible in the work of José Martí.[1] While the framework used by Ramos remains Latin Americanist, his focus on Martí begins to adapt Rama's approach to a Caribbean context. Ramos sees Martí positioned between two eras, which he describes as the end of the republic of letters and the beginning of modernity. In Ramos's argument, Martí's career thus marks the transition from the patronage system to the market. Although their adherence to the colonial/modern/postmodern narrative means neither Ramos nor Rama discusses the impact of the abolition of slavery and the sudden entrance for the first time of large numbers of black voices into the Caribbean public sphere, we can also see how Martí writes at the moment in which mercantile slavery finally ends in the Americas (in 1886 in Cuba) and modern colonialism begins to arise as a new system of domination (with the United States taking control of Cuba and Puerto Rico in 1898). Just as the writers of the 1950s who are the topic of chapters 5 and 6 draw their authority from their ability to see the conflicts between different worlds, Martí imagines a new role for the writer in the face of the modern colonial system. Martí's anxieties about the writer's feminization or emasculation and his insistence on manly action reflect how this new configuration of the literary field separates the literary intellectual off from the field of power and threatens to make literature a private activity.

My first two chapters discussed how popular expression in the Caribbean was forced into a marginalized position outside of or unrecognized by the official discourse of the colonial state. As literacy spread and writing was no longer controlled by the ruling class, literature became a more popular form of expression. Ramos describes how what he calls modernity opens new possibilities precisely by dividing creative writing off from the government and allowing writers to imagine themselves as privileged interlocutors and opponents of official power. Ramos recounts, for example, how the first novel by Puerto Rican writer Eugenio María de Hostos, *La peregrinación de Bayoán*, published in Madrid in 1863, connects the insertion of the Caribbean writer into the public sphere to the anticolonial project: "The novel in sum follows a young colonial Caribbean writer's itinerary of desire—a desire to inscribe himself by means of writing into the 'public space' [*publicidad*] of the polis in Spain. The writer's ultimate aim (which the character of Bayoán often emphasizes) is to contribute to the independence of his native island, Puerto Rico" (43–44). Although Hostos's eventual espousal of positivism would lead him to later disavow this idealization of the literary intellectual as bearer of the anticolonial project, Martí picks up this project, explicitly making the literary not a mark of irrelevance but a precondition for both understanding the colonial nation and bringing that nation to recognition by the field of power. Unlike Hostos, Martí begins to articulate a "*publicidad*" located not in Spain, nor in the United States, but within the Caribbean itself.

Martí's exilic location outside the Caribbean needs to be taken into account, especially in light of Laura Lomas's argument that the tendency to read Martí "within a national tradition facilitates the efficient commodification of Martí's image" (126). I see Martí's relationship to the nation as central to his project, but Lomas's warning is a good reminder of how Martí's discourse was not a natural outgrowth of his participation in the nationalist struggle but an attempt to overcome the contradictions of his own conflicted transnational context. Like slave narratives and the abolitionist publications, Martí took advantage of his location in the metropolis of New York and his access to metropolitan technologies of publishing and distribution. Yet despite his location, Martí seeks to assign agency to the Cuban masses, unlike the writers in *El laúd del desterrado* who saw upper-class exiles as saviors of the Cuban nation. In examining two of Martí's essays, "El prólogo al *Poema del Niágara*" and "Nuestra América," I want to emphasize first how Martí himself describes the social transformations of the late nineteenth century and the possibilities this epochal passage creates for the writer in the public sphere; second, how he explicitly identifies occupying that public sphere with the nationalist project; and finally, how both in terms of his content and his style he makes the case that the potentially feminized qualities possessed by the literary intellectual—sympathy and sensitivity—can be combined with manly action to make this figure the ideal spokesperson for the nation.

Martí celebrates the democratization of writing implied by the professionalization of the writer, yet works to create a new auratic form of literature based on stylization in order to resist the influence of the culture industry and the rationalized language of progress. Ramos emphasizes how Martí's contradictory project leads him to seek literary autonomy in his poetry even as he embraces the contaminated space created by the market in the *crónicas* he published in newspapers to support himself financially. These contradictions define the writer's position in the modern New World literary field, constrained by the market logic that demands the writer be a waged laborer, yet insistent on writing as "the site of an *alternative* commerce" autonomous from economic considerations (Ramos 84). It is within this contaminated space of critique defined by its literary nature that Martí seeks to carve out a position for intellectual action and public intervention. Martí describes the implications of these social transformations for the literary public sphere in "El prólogo al *Poema del Niágara*," a prologue Martí wrote to a poem by Juan Antonio Pérez Bonalde published in book form in New York in 1882, but appearing in periodicals in other locales, including the *Revista de Cuba* in 1883 and the *Trinidad Review* during the same year under the title "The Lyre and the Harp."[2] Martí chooses Pérez Bonalde as a poet who manages to create a relevant and heroic literature—he praises Pérez Bonalde's ability to "fight with the lyre" ("Poem of Niagara" 308)—without ignoring the ways in which the "infamous times" (309) in which he lives challenge the very possibility of such heroism. Martí shows his admiration for Pérez Bonalde as a poet who manages to withstand the "tearing asunder" (312) of the social order that characterizes modernization and take advantage of his positioning within the newly configured public sphere to critique that system from its margins.

On the one hand, Martí laments the way in which this "tearing asunder" has undermined literature's previously assured public voice. He observes how the writer's prestige is no longer assured by the church and state.[3] The market offers an alternative way of reaching a public, but in entering this sphere writing risks being reduced to its exchange value: modernity is a "gilded" age, "when the only prevailing skill is that of having a well-stocked larder in the house" (308). While Martí insists that Pérez Bonalde's poetry resists the process whereby the material is all that matters—his poetry "is not the work of an artisan turning out articles in mass production" (323)—the epic potential of literature has been undermined, and what we get instead is "intimate, confidential and personal poetry" (310) or "teller[s] of love tales" (308), now that "poets today can neither be lyrical nor epic with any naturalness" (310). Without a guaranteed voice in political matters, the privatization of writing means that the chronicler who tells the story has been split off from the heroic actor who makes history. Martí returns to the language of battle and the poet as "one of those good contenders who fight with the lyre" (308); the new challenge, though, is that despite the heroic poet's readiness for battle, "he appears armed with every kind of weapon in an arena where he sees neither combatants nor rows of seats enlivened by an enormous public, nor does he see a reward" (319). This uncertainty— not about one's commitment to fight, but about what one is fighting for or against—anticipates what we see among writers at the onset of post-coloniality, facing what Martí here identifies as the challenge of North American–dominated modern colonialism, in which Spain's formal empire may be fading into the past but a future of political and economic freedom is not assured.

As much as Martí laments the loss of the assured public voice of the lettered city, he sees in modernity the potential to sweep away the entrenched injustices and inequalities of the past. No longer aligned with the church or the state, writers may feel marginalized, but from this marginal position they can align with a counterpublic and construct their critique. The chaos unleashed by what Martí describes as "an age of tumult and affliction"—the epochal passage coming at the end of the Spanish empire and plantation slavery throughout the Americas— means that "the times for raising obstacles are past; these are the times for demolishing them" (312). The writer's stable place had previously been assured by the hierarchical feudal system: now "men are beginning to walk the entire earth without stumbling; before, they had scarcely started walking when they struck against the wall of a nobleman's mansion or the bastion of a monastery" (312).

In this new world, the sweeping away of established truths and certainties of rank and religion makes possible the democratization of knowledge, what Martí calls in this prologue "a kind of decentralization of the intelligence" (314). He explains that although the heroic poetry of the past may no longer be possible, "genius is becoming less individual and more collective. Man is losing for the benefit of men" (315). He describes the transformation of the spheres of society where "ideas" can travel: formerly, "ideas were to turn into the timbrels of the king's jester, or into the clapper of a church bell," whereas now, "ideas take shape in the plaza where they are taught, going from hand to hand and from foot to foot" (313). This new public sphere—embodied in the literally public space of the plaza, available to everyone regardless of rank—marks a break from a time when critique could only be expressed by the court jester or would be drowned out by church bells. For Martí, this world in which "ideas . . . are born on horseback and ride the lightning with wings" (313) allows the poet as itinerant wanderer, with "eyes burning and feet sore from walking through the still smoking ruins" (316) of the old world, to have a place in the new. By affirming the marginality of this nomadic position, Martí establishes a privileged space for literature to critique colonial modernity, a role that subsequent Caribbean writers embrace.

Although this marginality gives the poet an equivocal or contingent space from which to stage his oppositionality and align himself with a counterpublic, Martí remains "nostalgic for heroic deeds" (315) that require a more centered positioning. In the prologue to *Poema del Niágara*, Martí complains that unless writers can define a new relationship to power and the state, they face emasculation, as "in these days men are like certain young women" (309). Modernity threatens to undermine the possibility of virile heroism and manly greatness in literature unless the writer finds a new basis for his activity: "men would look like weak females [if] they devoted themselves to purifying the honeylike wine of ancient Rome that seasoned the banquets of Horace" (310). In these passages, Martí expresses disdain for a present where the loss of epic wholeness means there is now "no such thing as a permanent work" (311). But he also criticizes those who would try to simply re-create the classical past. Instead of producing the "permanent work"—epic public poetry—modern writers must settle for what threatens to be a womanly form of poetry that confines itself to the private and the personal. Pursuing beauty may come at the expense of the "peaceful strength and laborious development" (312) needed to represent truth. Relegating literature to the private or personal threatens to reproduce the hierarchies of the past where "the only way of expressing human wisdom was by some witty gossip" (313), a form of counterpublic that I discuss in the work of other anticolonial writers such as Jacques Roumain and Claude McKay as explicitly associated with women.

Martí deploys this gendered (and frequently sexist) notion of the artist's relationship to the public and the private to describe the challenges for committed or heroic poetry in abstract terms in this prologue; in the context of his other writing it becomes clear that Martí sees the loss of the potential for literature to be connected to masculine action as especially dangerous in the face of foreign imperialism. As Martí was writing these lines from his exile in New York, he could see U.S. manifest destiny turning its attention to Latin America in general and Martí's Cuba in particular. In addition to his poetry, Martí is best known for his strident essays against U.S. designs on the Caribbean basin. In one newspaper report on the Pan-American Congress held in Washington, D.C., in 1889, Martí urges his readers that "the time has come for Spanish America to declare its second independence" and warns that "only a virile and unanimous response . . . can free all the Spanish American nations at one time from the anxiety and agitation—fatal in a country's hour of development—in which the secular and admittedly predominant policy of a powerful and ambitious neighbor, with the possible connivance of the weak and venal republics, would forever hold them" ("Washington" 340). Just as in Mary Seacole's narrative, Martí longs for the modernity represented by the United States—specifically imagined as independence from European political control and tradition—even while he fears this northern neighbor's imperial designs. This imminent threat explains why Martí deems manly action so necessary, and anticolonial writing will be dominated by these gendered tropes of masculinity; writing is not enough, without a "virile" response, to ensure Caribbean freedom from North American annexation. His return to Cuba to fight for his island's independence exemplifies this conception of the writer as man of action.

Martí imagines the literary intellectual as particularly well suited to fight these battles on behalf of the national public because of his ability to listen to the subaltern classes that colonial power has sought to silence. His most famous essay, "Nuestra América," published in 1891 in Spanish-language newspapers in New York and Mexico, continues the idea of a virile response to North American imperialism, urging the "patria" to "awaken" and construct "weapons of the mind" ("Our America" 288) and emphasizing unity in the face of danger ("the trees must form ranks to block the seven-league giant" [299]). These elements of "Nuestra América" have been much discussed by critics, and Ramos explains that the essay has become such a focal point because it allows "the configuration of a discourse . . . that will later provide the foundation for an emergent Latin Americanism" (251). Ramos describes how this writerly "authority," tied "to the compensatory strategies of a redemptive gaze, is also grounded in a projection of the future, an aesthetic and teleology that postulates the definitive supersession of fragmentation" (254). This romance of redemption is what David Scott identifies as the heart of the anticolonial project: "anticolonial stories about past, present and future . . . have tended to be narratives of overcoming, often narratives of vindication" (*Conscripts* 8). I want to return to this canonical text to show how "Nuestra América" fits into a genealogy of Caribbean anticolonial discourse and lays bear some of its basic discursive formations, by emphasizing how the essay articulates a particular idea of the writer's place within the project of anticolonial nationalism.

In "Nuestra América," Martí makes a case for a nation based on the values of "natural man" as embodied by the "native mestizo" as opposed to "the alien, pure-blooded criollo" ("Our America" 290). Basing new republics on local forms of knowledge is, for Martí, the key to creating the kind of unified and just *patria* that can stave off foreign threats (the "tiger outside") while achieving the consent of the various populations within (the "tiger inside" [294]). It is clear to Martí that these populations cannot rule themselves: "the uneducated masses are lazy and timid about matters of the intellect and want to be well-governed" (291). The only fear is that "if the government injures them they shake it off and govern themselves" (291). At issue, then, is who is best suited to lead in this situation. Martí argues that knowing the nation effectively enough to govern it requires ignoring the fashions of other lands and listening to the nation's "natural man." Martí criticizes "the leaders who try to rule unique nations, of a singular and violent composition, with laws inherited from four centuries of free practice in the United States and nineteen centuries of monarchy in France" (290). Only "natural statesmen" who govern "from the direct study of nature" and thus "know the true elements of the country" can meet these demands (294). The issue is knowing, for "to know the country and govern it in accordance with that knowledge is the only way of freeing it from tyranny" (291). Acquiring this knowledge requires listening to the subaltern populations: the "mute masses of Indians" (289), "the black" and "the campesinos" (293). Creating and assembling knowledge of this sort is clearly an intellectual project, but it is not just any intellectual who is suited for this task. "Nuestra América" attacks the "artificial intelligentsia" (Martí's original phrase is "letrados articifiales" ["Nuestra América" 66]) who provide "false erudition" (Martí, "Our America" 290). He thus distinguishes between the literary intellectual and the professional who "accuses his native republic of irredeemable incompetence because its virgin jungles do not continually provide him with the means of going about the world a famous plutocrat, driving Persian ponies and spilling champagne" (290). This professional who ignores the local in pursuit of economic modernity becomes the foil for the writer who is sensitive to the nuances of Caribbean reality and subaltern expression.

Ramos points to how Martí establishes this distinction through the very language in which he writes, the "highly stylized form of writing" (Ramos 262) that calls attention to its literariness. "Nuestra América" reads not like a political treatise or a sociological study—the kinds of rational knowledge one might expect to form the basis of good governance—but instead like prose poetry. What Ramos calls Martí's "will to style" is the insistence on literature "as the discourse still capable of representing the origin, the autochthonous, and all those marginalized elements left unrepresented and unrepresentable by rationalizing languages in the service of modernization" (262). If the Indian is mute, if the black, though he "sang his heart's music in the night," remains "unknown" (Martí, "Our America" 293), how can the leaders listen to these groups and understand them? Martí answers by noting "dramatists are putting native characters onstage," and "poetry is snipping off its wild, Zorilla-esque mane and hanging up its gaudy waistcoat on the glorious tree" (294). If the elites are unable to recognize the wisdom of the mute Indian and the seemingly unintelligible black, the writer's imagination can help bring that knowledge to light. Placing sensitivity and imagination at the center of the national project, Martí makes his case for why literary intellectuals deserve a privileged place in the public sphere. Yet we can see in Martí, and in the other anticolonial writers, an anxiety that these qualities will be associated with femininity and emasculate their project.

Words and Action in Stephen Cobham's *Rupert Gray*

At the same time that Martí was forging a literary project authorized
to intervene in politics by speaking in the name of both a public and
a counterpublic, the Anglophone Caribbean was beginning to see the
emergence of a literary public sphere. In Jamaica, the Jamaica Local
Literary Association and the *Jamaica Times* provided institutions for
figures like Thomas MacDermot and H. G. de Lisser to begin crafting
a Jamaican national literature in the first decades of the twentieth century: in 1903, MacDermot even launched what he called the All Jamaica
Library to publish locally written works within Jamaica, which, as Leah
Rosenberg explains, "demanded an independence from the metropole to
which many anticolonial nationalists did not even aspire" (34). While
more attention has been devoted to the late 1920s and early 1930s as
the birth of these sorts of institutions in Trinidad and Tobago, literary
historians are beginning to point to the turn of the century as crucial in
that island as well.[4] The activities of the Trinidad Literary Association
and Gray's Inn Literary Association in the 1890s, groups tied to Henry
Sylvester Williams's Pan-African movement and agitation to reform the
Crown Colony government, lead Selwyn Cudjoe to conclude that "during this period, political and literary activities became tightly interre-
lated" (*Beyond Boundaries* 321).[5] Cudjoe also discusses what he calls
"The Big Poetry Row" of 1902, in which a variety of writers used Port
of Spain newspapers to stage a sometimes heated argument over the
value of locally published poetry. That the arguments are framed by attacks on writers for "dumping [their] rubbish on the public of Trinidad"
(354) shows how deploying the interests of the local public had become
a powerful rhetorical strategy in debates not only about politics but also
literature.

    Rupert Gray was published in 1907 by Mirror Printing Works, the
printer of the *Mirror* newspaper, which "began publication in 1898 as a
reformist daily newspaper sympathetic to the political radicals" opposed
to Crown Colony rule (Winer et al., Introduction to *Rupert Gray* xxi).
The novel's author, Stephen Cobham, was a part of the founding of Trinidad and Tobago's Pan-African Association in 1901, and is on record in
the *Mirror* speaking out in favor of more local self-governance. *Rupert
Gray* shows the desire to position the intellectual as integral to the articulation of public demands, alongside a distrust of the literary as creating distance from that public. The previous section discussed how Martí
made literariness an important aspect of authority in the public sphere;

but the image of Martí that has frequently proven more enduring and attractive to subsequent Caribbean intellectuals has been the man of action. Cobham, who has been almost entirely ignored by literary history, may seem an odd match with the other writers discussed in this chapter, Martí and Jacques Roumain, who are two of the most renowned Caribbean writers. The figures who have become the most celebrated anticolonial writers—Martí, Roumain, C. L. R. James, Aimé Césaire, and others—were able to successfully submerge the anxiety that the literary intellectual was not an identity compatible with the man of action. *Rupert Gray*, by contrast, highlights these anxieties.

Rupert Gray shows great interest in sketching out the institutions of the public sphere, exploring their reach as well as their limitations. The world of Cobham's novel is strictly codified in terms of the public and the private, the former associated with the male world of work and the latter associated with the novel's domestic romance. Chapters abruptly shift between Rupert's successes as a black accountant in the bustling mercantile world of Port of Spain and the domestic affairs of his employer's white daughter, Gwendoline, in the family home of Sunflower Manse. After one chapter featuring a long conversation at the family home between Gwen and her friend Florence—of whom the novel says, "what did it matter that she held a physician's diploma . . . women's profession is marriage" (S. Cobham 42)—the next chapter shifts the scene with this opening: "serious developments were meanwhile getting ahead down at the store" (47). Repeated attempts are made to police the boundaries between the serious world of men and the domestic pursuits of women, as when Gwen's father declines to respond to inquiries about his daughter's affairs by declaring it "private business" (79). But the novel requires the crossing of these boundaries through Rupert's visits to Sunflower Manse and his eventual relationship with Gwen. Their relationship blurs distinctions between public and private by interjecting racial politics into questions of love and desire.

The two major plots of *Rupert Gray*—the interracial romance between Rupert and Gwendoline, and his rivalry with another black employee of the same firm, Jacob Clarke—both hinge on public perceptions. In many cases, the opinion that matters is figured as "society": Gwen repeatedly must imagine "what would society say" about her love for Rupert, and can only love him if she is willing to "fl[i]ng away regard for the rules of her order" (27). In other ways, though, both the romance as well as the rivalry are played out not only for the approval of society—Gwen's caste—but for the more nebulous "public opinion"

(82). This public opinion is tied to print, although the novel emphasizes how underdeveloped the literary world remains. Only through Gwendoline's sponsorship can "private theatricals" be performed in her home, and since "the play was written by a native; none of his people therefore cared to read it, and the books lay unsold at the booksellers" (34). With the literary remaining private, newspapers influence public opinion, whether in how the "local press" reporting on her successes in Europe has helped to establish Gwendoline's place in society (9) or how a good review for a local play "appeared in the papers" and led to the author's books selling "with surprising rapidity" (38). The rivalry between Rupert and Clarke, before it moves into the actual legal proceedings of the final third of the novel, takes place in the court of public opinion represented by these newspapers: Clarke attempts to slander Rupert by submitting damaging stories to the *Port of Spain Gazette*, hoping that "the whole stinking affair will fill a column and a half," but is defeated when what in fact appears is an article about Gray's induction into a prestigious English society (76).

Alongside this story of the developing public sphere, *Rupert Gray* tells a story that makes a modern, professional black man its hero and poses his position as a contrast to both the black working class and the literary intellectual. Rupert is an intellectual in his own right, and his story has anticolonial implications: as Rosenberg notes, the novel makes the case for self-government "by envisioning an Afro-Trinidadian as the most prominent politician in a Trinidad with representative government" (27). At the same time, Cobham undercuts Rupert's potential to make alliances with the black working class, embodied in the novel by François Pierre, whose representative class status is made clear when he is described as a "typical working native" (S. Cobham 87). Pierre's inarticulate speech—he stutters and often lapses into French Creole—severely restricts his ability to participate in the public sphere, culminating in the scene where he attempts to help Rupert's case in court but is almost completely unable to make himself understood (111).[6] *Rupert Gray* thus represents the exclusions of the legal public sphere even while presenting literature as better able to speak for Pierre's class. The ability to speak for Pierre enables Rupert to fashion himself as advocate for the oppressed even as Rupert participates in silencing Pierre and enforcing his class status, explicitly scolding him when he tries to offer advice with the rebuke, "Silence, Pierre, and know your place" (16).

As spokesman for those who cannot speak for themselves and heroic man of action, Rupert Gray acts as idealized authorial alter ego within the novel; but *Rupert Gray* also crystallizes the author's ambivalence toward writing as a suspect activity through the figure of Jacob Clarke. More than Pierre, Rupert's true foil is Clarke, who works with him at Mr. Serle's firm and becomes Rupert's rival in the course of the novel. Clarke is thus another member of the black professional class, but embodies qualities that make him the virtual opposite of Rupert. On a most basic level, Clarke is selfish and thinks only of personal advancement whereas Rupert repeatedly imagines his vocation as serving his race: even when Rupert reaches the height of achievement, is recognized as an English gentleman and is invited to stay in England, he asserts his responsibility to his people by explaining that "England is already made. Trinidad needs her sons to make her" (104). Rupert articulates this ideology directly to Clarke, that "we must forward the race . . . we must proffer the sympathetic grip as we confer the knighthood of encouragement, saying: 'Take heart, brother; rise up and prosper'" (48). Clarke's response is to "be revengeful" (47), and he attempts to slander Rupert to Mr. Murchison, one of the firm's white partners. These actions undermine the novel's portrait of the professional class, calling attention to other stories of competitive backstabbing described by one character as "unpatriotic throat-cutting among coloured men" (49). Along with Clarke, there is also the story of the "recent scandal of that coloured professional and his apprentice," a story lacking in details but in which we learn how "one coloured man checkmat[ed] another on the eve of his promotion, merely for the look of a few guineas" (61). Elsewhere, Rupert's "mercantile community" is described as "shallow wits" (84), and it appears that only Rupert himself is able to overcome this environment and become "an exceptional negro" (16).

As much as Clarke represents the foibles of this professional class, his greatest sins in the novel align him with a different group. Clarke shows himself to be too emotional, being "overcome" as "letting his head fall to his knees, he wept for some time" (15); his sensitivity is in contrast to Rupert's logical and reserved demeanor. Clarke also comes across as unnecessarily verbose, giving a long speech expressing his gratitude toward Rupert in an overly obsequious and falsely literary tone: he even makes references to "blindfolded shylock—a miserable exacter of his pound of flesh" as well as Robinson Crusoe (17). His ostentatious speech differs especially from Rupert's pithy response—"Don't mention it, old boy. Don't mind these things. There are negroes and negroes. There are good and bad in every race. This is your chance. Go and win it" (17)—and in their first conflict, Murchison tells Clarke that "Gray's silence has beaten you" (48). The contrast here is between Clarke's overly ornate language and Gray's quiet but confident command of discourse.

Clarke's verbal pretension only foreshadows his greatest crime: he lies through writing. The trope of the dangerous slanders the writer can invent begins in Caribbean writing at least as early as the 1853 anonymous Trinidadian novel *Adolphus*, and continues famously through Daniel Cosway in Jean Rhys's 1966 *Wide Sargasso Sea*.[7] Clarke's first slight against Rupert, applying for a job in New York meant for Rupert, is initially denied by Clarke, leading Murchison to call him "a stranger to truth" (49). Murchison's continued insistence on not just the application, but its written nature—he first asks, "did you not apply in writing" and then "did you not present your application written on four pages of foolscap" (49)—seems odd, but taken with later incidents in the novel further emphasizes Clarke's use of the written word for disseminating his lies. Clarke invents a false version of Rupert's relationship with Gwen that he sends to the Linnaean Society, which results in Rupert being excluded from that group (78). Clarke also takes as a hobby writing slanderous letters to "English papers, warning them against risking the climate of the West Indies" in order to harm local commerce as a way to take revenge on Murchison for not promoting him (88). The novel reproduces one of these letters, filled with negative stereotypes about Trinidad and its people, along with the narrative aside, "Pity some people ever learn to scribble" (88). Clarke's undoing comes from these written lies, as he is eventually arrested, "for that he did . . . forge, sign, counterfeit and publish falsely a paper-writing purporting to be a will" (122), thus making it appear as the novel ends that he will finally be punished for the fictions he has constructed.

The contrast between Rupert and Clarke extends to their preferred modes of expression, for whereas Clarke is associated with writing, Rupert's voice is repeatedly emphasized as his most striking attribute. As in *Emmanuel Appadocca*, the trope of the voice embodying male authority is typical of anticolonial writing. In Alejo Carpentier's *El reino de este mundo*, for example, Macandal is characterized by "his deep, opaque voice [which] made him irresistible to the Negro women" (Carpentier, *Kingdom* 19). When Gwen remembers her first encounter with Rupert Gray and begins to fall in love with him, "the strange music of a black man's voice kept echoing in her ears" (S. Cobham 9); later, her devotion to him becomes complete when she listens to his "rich voice" (34) and "place[s] herself under the subtle fascination of a voice and presence which did havoc to her self-control" (37). For Gwen, Rupert's voice and manly presence are indistinguishable, the complete opposite of Clarke's anonymous and disembodied "scribblings." Just as Rupert's voice wins over Gwen, he becomes a phenomenon in England because of his "conversational powers" (100), and after a speech in which he "project[s] his voice till it curled round the borders of the crowd" (101), he is described as the "lion of the season" who all those "fashionable" want to meet (102).

Clarke and Gray are thus two competing models of what the novel calls "authority" (17). Rupert's authority is benevolent and seems to come to him naturally: he advises Clarke to "handle your authority mildly" (17) and when teaching Gwen she is grateful because Rupert has "not instructed me in knowledge; you have educated me to the acquiring of knowledge" (23). Part of what makes him this ideal teacher is that he is not didactic but acts to uplift his pupil; but equally important seems the mention in the same conversation that he "knows fencing and pugilism . . . that his muscles are so well developed as to have enabled him to lift a heavy load of something or other and toss it on cart" (21). Rupert is thus a "man of action" (104) whose voice is tied to his physical presence. Even as a teacher—a vocation potentially closer to the literary intellectual than the professional, and an occupation that subsequent anticolonialists would invest with a great deal of importance for their project[8]—Rupert only teaches white women, whether it is Gwen or Lady Rothbery, and only shows expertise in practical subjects like "typing" (20) and "science" (54).

This "common ground of science" (54)—where Gray can show himself the equal of English imperialists, as Rosenberg discusses—is not the only field where the protagonist can demonstrate his worth. The novel specifically celebrates "the professions, the service of the Crown, and in commerce" as the sectors of the public sphere in which the white elites "are ready to receive the black man with open arms" (59). *Rupert Gray* thus imagines the public sphere as the market, and follows Rupert's conversation with Clarke about different models of authority with a sudden turn to describing the "love and war of bargaining and barter" of the docks (18). These scenes celebrate that space as the most modern and energetic one available to the hero. The novel opens with a description of the "Port-of-Spain Railway Station" as "the scene of hurrying and hustling" (7), emphasizing this site of exchange as distinctly modern. The scene features characters ranging from "country belles, in the latest style," to "men . . . consult[ing] their watches," to "newsboys . . . hawk[ing] the daily papers," to "a row of hucksters . . . discussing the contents of their trays" (7). Amid these instances of local modernity, Gwen looks out toward the representatives of commerce that connect the island to the outside world: "there out in the distance on the southernmost confines of the shipping, a great ocean liner rode at anchor" (7). The critical introduction that precedes *Rupert Gray* asserts the uniqueness of this vision, arguing that "modernist fascination with the phallic energy associated with machines is rare in Caribbean writing" (Winer et al., Introduction to *Rupert Gray* xlvii); but in Martí's essay on the "Brooklyn Bridge," or Seacole's praise of technological advancement in Panama, or even Roumain's *coumbite* and Appadocca's crew as machine, an ambivalent desire for modernity, embodied by the market as well as technology, appears constitutive of Caribbean writing of the colonial period.

As in the works of Martí or Seacole, presenting the public world of work as an idealized space in which Gray can be recognized for his intellect and accomplishments leads the novel to interrogate the idea of the United States as a new source for this ideology in the Caribbean. Early in the story, an "out-and-out New Yorker" (S. Cobham 29) comes to try to recruit Rupert to serve a place where "we Americans believe in brains" and "a man like you will shine" (29–30). Rupert is tempted by the offer, as "the United States always held a fascination for him" (30). But just as he rejects the British intellectual world in favor of returning to Trinidad to help build its admittedly underdeveloped public sphere, he turns down the offer for reasons the American identifies as "sentiment" (30). Indeed, that offer—which Clarke jealousy competes for even as Gray nonchalantly rejects it—proves to be what drives Clarke to scheme for revenge: "from the day the New Yorker told how Jacob Canaan Clarke tried to get to America, [Clarke] grew very sullen" with "a dark squint in his face" (47). "The American capitalist" (31) thus introduces conflict into "Trinidad's Eden" (51) via the cutthroat competition in which Clarke engages. Lack of solidarity is not limited to Clarke's professional class; the novel's first chapters establish the resentment felt by lower-class people toward Rupert's advancement. The black waiter who grumbles "Nigga too black. . . . Set down close bakra gul, tink heself big guvanah" (10) and the people waiting outside Serle and Murchison's firm commenting "ef me was a merchant nevah keep black book-keepah" (13) demonstrate that Rupert must overcome not only racist power structures but also class divisions within the black community. Fascination with the United States and with market-based modern colonialism as modernizing forces is thus tempered with concern about the inequalities and resentments they breed.

Rupert Gray ends as a successful romance, marrying Rupert to his love and aligning him with the working-class Pierre in a common project to build a "Negro Industrial Institute in the West Indies" that will even include "a day each week . . . for negro literature exclusively" (123). Despite this hasty drawing together of the contradictions the novel has opened up, *Rupert Gray* demonstrates the fissures of anticolonial writing, both in terms of the resentment of the lower classes toward those who might seek to represent them as well as the anxiety of the male writer that literary activity is neither manly nor the most effective way to help his people. For Martí and Roumain, emphasizing the literary as a quality that enables writers to better hear or be sensitive to the needs of the nation, and as something that could distinguish the writer from other middle-class identities, allowed them to cover over these fissures. But the contradictions at the heart of anticolonialism never disappear, and the emphasis in *Rupert Gray* on the voice over the written prefigures the postcolonial developments I discuss in chapters 7 and 8, where the impulse among professional writers to incorporate testimonial voices or music emphasizes the presence of the body and sound rather than the disembodied written word. Literary historians have preferred to read the writers associated with the *Beacon* journal in the 1930s—especially C. L. R. James and Alfred Mendes—as "the beginning of an indigenous literary tradition" in Trinidad and Tobago (Sander 24); the canonization of this moment at the expense of earlier writers like Cobham is directly tied to the process Leah Rosenberg and Patricia Saunders describe by which the *Beacon* writers effectively positioned themselves as spokesmen and leaders of the incipient nation. *Rupert Gray*, written just as the anticolonial movements in the region began to gain strength and provide writers with the connection to the social that could make their work relevant, shows a response to modern colonialism that appears very different from that of Martí, Roumain, or the *Beacon* writers. But keeping Cobham's work in mind when thinking about that dominant form of literary anticolonialism calls attention to the anxieties and contradictions facing the modern colonial writer seeking to enter the public sphere.

Jacques Roumain's *Gouverneurs de la rosée* and the Writing/Action Divide

Rupert Gray expresses the challenge of uniting literature with action along with the temptation to view writing as a cowardly or unmanly activity. The writers most closely associated with Caribbean anticolonialism were those who were able to resolve this divide between writing and action in much the same way that Martí did at the onset of colonial modernity. Jacques Roumain, founder of the Parti Communiste Haïtien and author of one of the major Caribbean novels of the modern colonial period, the 1944 *Gouverneurs de la rosée*, perhaps best embodies the ideal of the literary intellectual fusing writing and political action. The novel is not concerned with the urban middle class like *Rupert Gray* or Roumain's earliest fiction; instead, *Gouverneurs de la rosée* presents a different sort of intellectual. Roumain's novel lays out a vision of the intellectual who is sensitive and yet authoritative, is intimately connected to the peasantry and thus able to listen to and express their aspirations, yet at the same time possesses special knowledge that enables a pedagogical leadership role that can push the peasants forward into resistance against the status quo. While Cobham's inability to entirely submerge the anticolonial project's contradictions may have contributed to his disappearance from nationalist literary histories of the region, Roumain's successful articulation of this project made him a canonical figure in Caribbean literature.

Roumain became the dominant intellectual figure of Haiti's modern colonial period, which has been called a period of "renaissance" for Haitian literature.[9] Plantation slavery ended earlier in Haiti than in any other part of the Americas, with a successful slave revolution bringing about a newly independent nation in 1804. But the transitional period within the Caribbean initiated by the abolition of plantation slavery was especially unstable in Haiti: the island endured a century of political turmoil, including twenty-two different heads of state between 1843 and 1915. The United States looked on the presence of an independent, formerly slave state in the Caribbean as a danger to its regional hegemony; intervention in Haiti was thus contemplated in the U.S. press throughout this period much like the debates about Cuba seen in chapter 2, with Ulysses S. Grant's administration even introducing a proposal to the U.S. Senate in 1870 to annex the entire island of Hispaniola (Bellegarde-Smith 76–77). After a series of military interventions in Haiti meant to assert U.S. dominance, the United States finally took control of the island in 1915 and officially integrated it into the modern colonial system, which divided the region into formal holdings by Britain, France, Holland, and the United States.[10] Haiti's modern colonial period thus includes the U.S. occupation, which lasted from 1915 to 1934 and during which time the local elected government was dissolved and a new constitution favorable to the United States was imposed, as well as the years from 1934 to 1946, during which time the United States no longer occupied Haiti militarily but maintained control over the Haitian government's finances.

The first wave of resistance to the U.S. invasion came in revolts by the Cacos, peasant armies that had opposed the central government before the invasion and became a focal point for resistance during the occupation; these guerrilla revolts were put down by 1920 after the killing of one of the Cacos' major leaders, Charlemagne Péralte. From this point, "during the 1920s Haitian political opposition to the occupation centered around local newspapers, whose editors were promptly and frequently jailed, and also included several attempts to bring complaints about the occupation before international bodies such as the League of Nations" (Schmidt 152). These appeals to an international public were for the most part ineffective, and for much of the 1920s social unrest was sporadic and unfocused. The next major uprising, the student strikes of 1929, set in motion the eventual end of the occupation: what became widespread riots forced the United States to deploy a commission that agreed to begin staging legislative elections and withdrawing troops from Haiti. Roumain was involved in the literary and activist institutions that were at the center of these uprisings.[11] While his cofounding of *La Revue Indigène* in 1927 has come to occupy an important place in literary history as the main journal of the *indigènisme* movement associated with Jean Price-Mars, in the same year Roumain also helped found the more politically active *La Trouée*, whose title means "the breach." The first issue of *La Trouée* opens with the editorial declaration, attributed to Roumain and Richard Salnave, that "our combative name rings out like the call of a drum. . . . It is that of young and ardent souls who are going to pierce the barrier of ignorance and apathy which suffocates us."[12] In addition to publishing poetry and short stories in those two journals, by 1928 Roumain had become editor of *Le Petit Impartial*, which Michael Dash calls "the political organ of this generation" (*Literature and Ideology* 78). Roumain's essays on Mahatma Gandhi in that newspaper suggest how Roumain saw the U.S. occupation as equivalent to British colonialism and parallels the special issue on Indian anticolonialism published by the *Beacon* in Trinidad and Tobago in 1932 that also featured an article on Gandhi.[13] Roumain authored a series of articles in 1928 to "Jeune-Haïti" and "À La Jeunesse," leading up to his founding of the Ligue de la Jeunesse Patriote Haïtienne en Action, an organization that played a key part in the 1929 strikes; by the end of 1928, he was arrested for "misuse of the press" (délit de presse) (Roumain, *Oeuvres complètes* 1212) and spent time over the next few years in prison. Roumain seeks to use his writing to directly exhort Haitians to unite against foreign rule; this activist writing thus marks a departure from what Martin Munro describes as the "depoliticized aestheticism" of the previous generation of Haitian writers such as Frédéric Marcelin and Edmond Laforest associated with the literary magazine *La Ronde* (12).

Gouverneurs de la rosée begins by establishing the past as time of wholeness for the village of Fonds Rouge. Beverly Ormerod calls this "the lost Eden" and points to the novel's Christian allegory (20); such a recalled past also suggests a better time before the U.S. invasion and modern colonialism. While historical markers in the novel are few, we eventually learn that the founding trauma that occurred in the past to divide the villagers against one another was the death of "patriarch" Johannes Longeannis, known as "General Longeannis because he had fought with the Cacos" (Roumain, *Masters* 62). Despite this oblique reference to the colonial experience, in the context of Roumain's activities against the U.S. occupation *Gouverneurs de la rosée* may not seem as readily anticolonial: the novel is not obviously opposed to any immediately identifiable foreign power. While there are some references to a wealthy white American in control of badly needed resources (50)—though even in this example, the situation being described is in Cuba, not Haiti—and there is antagonism between the peasants and the local police, what makes the novel anticolonial is not what it is against, but the particular idea of the relationship between the intellectual and the public that it presents, and the idea that this collaboration can redeem the community.

While the novel may not make explicit historical reference to modern colonialism, *Gouverneurs de la rosée* presents a situation in which most of its characters view power as something removed from their local context. From the opening page, when Délira "called on the Lord" to help her, the narrator remarks: "but so many poor creatures call continually upon the Lord that it makes a big bothersome noise. When the Lord hears it, he yells, 'What the hell's all that?' and stops up his ears. Yes, he does, leaving man to shift for himself" (23). The novel thus allegorizes a situation in which Haitians lack any avenue by which to have their petitions heard by those who control the levers of power. While *Gouverneurs de la rosée* frames that lack of local control in terms of religion rather than geopolitics, Léon-François Hoffmann explains Haiti's history in the same terms, such that "the landing of U.S. Marines and the subsequent occupation of Haiti by white masters seemed another divine intervention in the affairs of Haiti" (367). In *Gouverneurs de la rosée*, one character concludes that "the Good Lord's white" (Roumain, *Masters* 162), suggesting a colonial context behind the fact that appeals for things to get better "with the Good Lord's help" (39) reinforce the peasants' passivity and sense of powerlessness.[14]

The novel's protagonist, Manuel, seeks to encourage his fellow peasants to view the power to make change as something that does not need to appeal to outside sources but can be enacted by mobilizing the community: "Resignation won't get us anywhere. . . . You keep on expecting miracles and providence, with your rosary in your hand, without doing a thing. . . . But providence—take my word for it—is a man's determination not to accept misfortune, to overcome the earth's bad will every day, to bend the whims of the water to your needs" (54). In setting out to bend the situation to his will, Manuel appears as the ideal anticolonial man of action. He is strong enough that while "his bag was heavy . . . he didn't feel its weight" (35). Like Rupert Gray or Emmanuel Appadocca, he is handsome and dynamic, a "real man" (181) who others recognize as a "great Negro" (122) and instinctively address as "Chief" (75). Manuel is immediately able to win over the beautiful Annaïse, who is especially impressed by his "somber voice that hit each sentence hard" (38). While others resign themselves to poverty brought on by drought, Manuel succeeds in finding a spring and overcoming the seemingly insurmountable obstacles preventing that water from being brought to the crops. As Dash points out, Manuel's ability to make his will "etched into the surface of the landscape by the cutting edges of various tools" demonstrates his "mastery" of the world around him (*Other America* 78).

While Manuel thus takes action, the novel also invokes the division between saying and doing seen in *Rupert Gray*. As the other peasants deliberate on whether to overcome their rivalries to help Manuel transport the water, one criticizes "idle talk," asking "what are we going to *do*?" (Roumain, *Masters* 134, emphasis added). In this same exchange, another accuses the men who will not take action of "sitting there like old women telling a rosary about your poverty. . . . We'll take the water! We'll take it by force!" (134). These words, from Gervilen, the villain of the story who eventually kills Manuel, are spoken in favor of *not* cooperating with Manuel and instead taking the water from him; that they so closely resemble Manuel's idea that positive action can be enacted "by force" suggests Gervilen as the ironic flip side to Manuel's heroism that subtly undermines the absolute valorization of action. But the hierarchy of saying and doing is hard to displace: typical of anticolonial writing, but even more dramatically in *Gouverneurs de la rosée* than in *Rupert Gray* or *Emmanuel Appadocca*, talk is gendered as a womanly activity that threatens to emasculate. Characters remark that "women's insults don't lead anywhere, they're just so much wind" (79) or that "the chattering of the women became irritable" (76). Délira calls out to God while her husband, Bienaimé, suffers in silence—even if "maybe he wanted to say something" (24)—and tells his wife to "hush your mouth!" (33). Women gossip: in Annaïse's first appearance in the novel, she stops to "pick up and distribute news" from those she passes on her walk (39). Gossip frequently appears in anticolonial Caribbean writing as a sort of counterpublic where those excluded from the dominant public sphere pass along knowledge. Yard fiction from the 1930s like Alfred Mendes's *Black Fauns* deploys gossip and rumor as a way for its working-class characters—especially black women—to circulate information relevant to them but ignored by dominant forms of communication; C. L. R. James's *Minty Alley* is the story of how its middle-class male protagonist comes to listen to and learn from the gossip from which he is at first excluded. The discussion in chapter 4 of gossip shows how Claude McKay's *Banana Bottom* demonstrates a desire seen in many male writers of this period to rationalize this form of communication through labeling it unreliable, fickle, and womanly.

Whereas the gendering of this division between speaking and action suggests a hierarchy, *Gouverneurs de la rosée* shows that the two activities cannot be easily separated: first, through emphasizing how even though Manuel is a man of action, sometimes those actions involve speaking; and second, through making the women's discursive abilities, and even their gossip, crucial parts of the project to bring redemption to Fonds Rouge. Manuel's first action in the novel is a speech act, as he calls out "Stop!" and the bus driver obeys (34). Throughout the novel, he will be a man of words as much as a man of action. While Manuel's refusal to be passive defines his character, he is not able to end the village's suffering himself, even warning those who see him as savior that the solution is "Not I alone. . . . All the peasants will have a part in it" (89). His role is more than anything else as teacher, who tells first Laurélien, then Annaïse, and finally Délira what must be done to save Fonds Rouge. In a scene with Laurélien, Manuel gives a long monologue on the need for cooperative action and refusing to give up. Though Laurélien initially "almost lost his breath trying to follow Manuel," eventually "a curtain of light began to rise" (75). Manuel's words enlighten Laurélien and transform him into Manuel's first disciple.

The other two characters who pass along Manuel's legacy—a legacy embodied by the "words we won't forget" (178), as Laurélien puts it as Manuel is being buried—are both women. When Manuel describes his hopes for the future to Annaïse, she excitedly tells him, "you've made me dream" (89). From that point, Manuel explains her role in helping to realize that dream: "you'll begin talking to the womenfolk. Women— they're the irritable sex, I don't deny that—but they're also more sensitive and they have more heart. . . . You'll say, 'Cousin So-and-so, have you heard the news?'" (91). Letting Annaïse lay the groundwork for his plan means using the networks of gossip to which she already has access to ready the women for the eventual idea of working together. The plan succeeds, and even circumvents the local policeman, Hilarion, who hopes to seize the peasants' land but notices Manuel "going around talking" and spreading "words of rebellion" (80). When Manuel's plan is set into action, Hilarion "scented a mystery" and goes to Manuel's house only to find him dying (160). Because he cannot imagine that the plot extends beyond the singular man of action, Hilarion is unable to find out what is going on. Once Annaïse has paved the way for convincing the peasants to work together, Manuel explains on his deathbed the entire plan to his mother. With his instruction, Délira goes from waiting for God to bring change to acting herself. She insists that "I've got to talk to those folks" to tell them Manuel's message (180), and when she gets a chance she literally quotes him: "Here's what my Manuel, my boy, told me. 'You've offered sacrifices to the *loas*, you've offered the blood of chickens and young goats to make rain fall. All that has been useless. Because what counts is the sacrifice of a man, the blood of a man'" (181). Using Manuel's speech, described by one character as "a great word, *oui*" (181), Délira persuades the peasants to all work together and enact his plan.

Belinda Edmondson describes the tendency in anticolonial Caribbean writing to establish the masculinity of the man of action through the gendering of the land and the folk as female (60), and Dash points to how Manuel "uses his machete to cut the water free from the earth, a direct parallel of which is his own mark left on the deflowered body of Annaïse" (*Other America* 78). While Manuel certainly represents phallic power, his ability to participate in and use women's networks of communication should not be overlooked: it is precisely through involving Annaïse and Délira in the village's redemption that Manuel avoids establishing a hierarchical relationship between intellectual and public. In *not* dismissing the attributes associated with women, Roumain's novel creates a space for the literary intellectual who can be man of action but is also sensitive enough to the people's desires to lead them effectively. Manuel sometimes appears quite passive and is frequently silent; these are times when he is "thinking" (Roumain, *Masters* 53), "ruminating" (56), or "reason[ing]" (59). Manuel listens to those around him, an activity reflected in his exploration for water, which Laurélien sees as "getting to know the country once again" (58). In contrast to Gervilen, who yells in a "voice stuck deep in his throat, harsh and swollen with rage" (96) or "shak[es] with rage" as "a bit of froth whitened his mouth" (134), when Manuel offers his considered responses it seems that "he's already figured it all out in his head. What he says is reason itself" (123). The novel figures Manuel's process of learning and then speaking for his people as an act of translation: "Manuel had translated into good Creole the exacting language of the thirsty plain, the plaint of growing things, the promises and all the mirages of the water" (131). The formulation of Manuel's work as not only physical but also intellectual proves useful for Roumain to imagine the writer's relationship to the nation. Yet equating the folk with the land—a trope we will see repeated in George Lamming's account of the Haitian Revolution as well as Martin Carter's poetry, both discussed in chapter 6—still risks figuring the (feminized) people as passive and silent, and, like the Indians and blacks Martí mentions in "Nuestra América" or Cobham's representation of Pierre, requiring someone to speak for them.

For the villagers who have grown "tired of that old story" (131), Manuel offers a new narrative where peasants can say "we're *this country*, and it wouldn't be a thing without us, nothing at all," and where local actors can control their own destinies (74). This sort of authorship, where Manuel's words and actions not only speak for but through speaking literally bring into existence the nation, offers Roumain a way of giving the literary a role in the public sphere. Unlike in *Rupert Gray*, the hero of *Gouverneurs de la rosée* is not a modern and professional member of the middle class, but the literary intellectual. *Gouverneurs de la rosée* thus continues an opposition between the technocratic elite and the literary intellectual present in Roumain's earlier writings, from his 1928 article "Le peuple et l'élite" to his first two books, the 1930 story collection *La proie et l'ombre* and the 1931 novel *Les Fantoches*. These early works focus on what Carolyn Fowler calls "the aimlessness of bourgeois existence" (73) among what Dash labels the "parasitic elite" (Introduction to *Masters* 6). The story "Préface à la vie d'un bureaucrate," first published in *Haïti-Journal* in 1930 and then collected as the final story in *La proie et l'ombre*, shows how Roumain's critique of this class distinguishes between the bureaucrat and the "littérateur": the story depicts middle-class capitulation to the status quo as an abandonment of the literary through a protagonist who "once was attracted to politics" and "thought himself a literary man" but ultimately chooses the stability of a "place waiting in the Department of the Interior."[15] Roumain makes the distinction during his 1929 trial; Fowler's biography cites the address Roumain made to the court where he claims to speak in the name not of "a minority of men, dissatisfied because they have no share of the power" but "all Haitians, if one excepts the small percentage of functionaries nourishing themselves at the garbage pails of Cooperation" (276). Roumain emphasizes the difference between the "small percentage of functionaries," who do not speak for everyone, and the minority of literary men like himself who do. Creating in Manuel a character who listens to and understands the folk, but also has special knowledge that allows him to enter into pedagogical relationship with them, allows Roumain to imagine a middle-class identity separate from the professional and aligned with the lower classes. Authority comes from claiming to speak in the name of a national public as well as aligning with an oppositional counterpublic. But the anxiety that opposition to power becomes a private space never disappears. The identity of literary intellectual remains ambivalent as its association with potentially devalued feminine qualities suggests: while in *Gouverneurs de la rosée* the literary can be a manly and authoritative activity, anticolonial writing can only contingently resolve the idea that politics and action remain distinct and privileged activities.

While Rupert Gray and Manuel are fictional characters, the nationalist leaders who came to prominence in the anticolonial movements of the 1940s and 1950s and then to power in the governments of the 1960s and 1970s—Eric Williams, Juan Bosch, Fidel Castro, François Duvalier—are often regarded as these larger-than-life men of action. Norman Manley, as leader of Jamaica's first political party in 1938 and eventual chief minister in 1955, is one of these towering political figures. Rex Nettleford's introduction to Manley's speeches places him within the narrative of anticolonial intellectuals in terms of his ability to unite ideas with action: Nettleford emphasizes how the great man provides "substance rather than mere form" (xii), that he "did not however simply dream dreams; he also worked actively in the shaping [of society]" (xviii) and that "most important of all he transformed these cherished ideas into practice" (xviii). While Manley thus connects theory and practice, all of these examples also imply a hierarchy: speeches are only of value when action is the outcome, so that Nettleford can anxiously assure his readers that his collection of Manley's words "is not concerned with rhetoric—Manley's urbanity and the masculine elegance of a legal style notwithstanding" (xi). Nettleford's language is also a reminder of the gendered associations of action versus rhetoric, and it is worth noting that Manley's political thought is left behind through these speeches, the most public of rhetorical occasions where the body and voice are present for all to see and hear.

In her memoir, Manley's granddaughter Rachel explains how, despite his extraordinary intellect, her grandfather could never understand why he lost elections to the more charismatic Alexander Bustamante. As Rachel Manley puts it: "he had leaned on his wife, asking her for explanations of a simple, but idiosyncratic world which seldom conspired to be logical. It was not losing the election that broke his confidence. . . . It was the fact that he could not comprehend the reasons for his defeat, reasons which his wife easily intuited" (174). Throughout this memoir, Rachel Manley shows how Norman as political man of action can only succeed through his literal marriage to the artistic sensibility of his wife, the artist Edna Manley.[16] This chapter discussed how Martí, Cobham, and Roumain seek to navigate the vexed gendered relationship between art and politics. Cobham's novel in particular calls attention to the tension between these activities, while Martí and Roumain manage to craft an anticolonial project that can give literature a privileged place in the national project. But even these authors are often best remembered as men of action more than literary figures. The story of Caribbean decolonization as a genealogy of heroic masculine heroes can be appealing. Focusing only on the contributions of people like Norman Manley to crafting a Caribbean public sphere, however, can overshadow other stories: for example, while Norman Manley was integral in the development of the weekly newspaper *Public Opinion* in the late 1930s and early 1940s, where debates about Jamaican independence helped persuade the British to allow local elections during the 1940s, his wife, Edna, during the same period was forming the literary circle that would include Roger Mais, M. G. Smith, and George Campbell. Edna Manley and these writers all contributed to *Public Opinion* during the early years of its existence, allowing the publication to appear as an ideal wedding of the political and the literary; but by the early 1940s, as the People's National Party (PNP) began contesting elections, Edna Manley left the editorial board of the weekly newspaper and founded the literary magazine *Focus*. The relationship between these two publications was complicated, as each staked out different turf in the anticolonial public sphere.[17] The interactions and disjunctures between literature and anticolonial politics during this period marked the writing of the modern colonial period, whether in more obviously politically committed writers like Martí, Roumain, and Mais, or the literary practitioners who I discuss in my next chapter. Continuing to trace out these alliances and rivalries helps give a fuller picture of the anticolonial literary public sphere and renders intelligible its crisis during the postcolonial period.

4 The Ideology of the Literary

Claude McKay's *Banana Bottom* and the Little Magazines of the 1940s

THE PREVIOUS CHAPTER DISCUSSED how writers most frequently identified with anticolonialism, such as José Martí and Jacques Roumain, constructed a discursive project that overcame anxiety about writing as a private activity through emphasis on masculine action. Along with Martí and Roumain, other important figures from the modern colonial period such as C. L. R. James, Roger Mais, V. S. Reid, Jacques Stephen Alexis, Frantz Fanon, Pedro Mir, and Jesús Colón deployed this ideal of the writer as man of action as a way to insist on the public purchase of their literary endeavors.[1] These writers became embodiments of anticolonial writing because of their ability to articulate the connection of literature to a counterpublic represented by political movements. But the case of Stephen Cobham shows how his erasure in literary histories of the region may owe not to insufficient political commitment but to *Rupert Gray* too explicitly displaying the anxieties at the heart of the literary intellectual identity.

Alison Donnell makes one of the strongest arguments that the ability of anticolonial writers to align themselves with nationalist political movements led to their privileging by the critics who shaped Caribbean canons during the 1960s and 1970s. Donnell points to how much of the writing of the modern colonial period does not fit into this overtly political model as "perhaps the most obvious and also the most troublesome" aspect of her revisionist literary history:

Many writings from this period simply do not share the same emphasis on establishing a new connection between the Caribbean writer and his or her place, voice, and audience. Indeed, as my attention to Vivian Virtue and J. E. C. McFarlane will demonstrate, certain figures during this period were positively opposed to what was then a revolutionary move, and moreover deemed it their obligation as poets to occupy the aesthetic and spiritual high ground, a position which has never been particularly appealing or persuasive within the critical models after the 1960s. (14–15)

Donnell argues that the idealization of the aesthetic and disavowal of the social that she finds in Virtue and McFarlane is a central if ignored aspect of Caribbean literary history during the modern colonial period. In this chapter, I want to explore this high modernist tendency toward aestheticism—what I call the ideology of the literary—as something not opposed to but in fact an integral part of the Caribbean project of anticolonial literature discussed in the previous chapter. Emphasizing the overlaps in these ostensibly antithetical positions helps us make sense of how both aestheticism and political commitment belong to the same colonial literary field.

I begin the chapter by looking at one of the novels Donnell mentions as among the few from the pre-1950 period to be accepted into the nationalist canon—Claude McKay's *Banana Bottom*—to show how even in that novel the ideology of the literary is what allows the intellectual to speak for both a public and a counterpublic. From there, I discuss how this ideology emerged as important to Caribbean writing of this period, especially in literary magazines that developed in the 1940s. Despite the apparent diversity of these publications—from what are thought of as apolitical, purely literary publications like *BIM* in Barbados, *La Poesía Sorprendida* in the Dominican Republic, the Guyanese *Kyk-over-al*, or the Cuban *Orígenes*, to what are often seen as the more nationalist *Tropiques* in Martinique or the Jamaican *Focus*—all of these publications are united by their ideology of the literary. This ideology, whether articulated by McFarlane in his addresses to the Empire Poetry League, by McKay in *Banana Bottom*, or by Suzanne Césaire and Aimé Césaire in the pages of *Tropiques*, contains a desire to position writing above everyday concerns along with a vision of the literary intellectual as having special political insight to critique instrumentality and materialism. We see this apparently dueling tendency even in McFarlane, whose essay collection *The Challenge of Our Time* contains aesthetic examinations of literature in chapters like "Form" and "The Vehicles of Thought and Their Significance" but also begins with a chapter analyzing the new Jamaican constitution. While Donnell correctly points out that the political solutions McFarlane offered made him a much less attractive model for later nationalist writers, I return at the end of this chapter to show how even his ideas about literature and aesthetics closely resemble what is perceived as the more political writing of McKay or the Césaires, whom I show to be just as interested in occupying "the aesthetic and spiritual high ground" (Donnell 15). Beginning with an examination of *Banana Bottom* makes clear how the idea of the literary as separate from practical, rational, or scientific forms of knowledge—and therefore part of a counterpublic—formed an important part of the anticolonial case for writing's public authority.

Bita Plant as Literary Intellectual

Claude McKay is frequently cited as one of the early-twentieth-century forefathers of Caribbean literature. Donnell shows how in accounts of the region's literary history, beginning with Kenneth Ramchand's foundational *The West Indian Novel and Its Background*, McKay becomes one of the few writers from before 1950 to receive significant critical attention: "in the crucial crossing between Empire and nation that marks the political narrative of [the pre-1950] era, it is clear that some writers . . . are the figures we are encouraged to remember through anthologies and critical studies (Claude McKay, C. L. R. James, George Campbell and Roger Mais)" (50). Donnell points to this canonization as connected to the fact that all of these writers wrote with an explicitly nationalist political project in mind, and it surely helped McKay and James that each was at various times connected to international Marxist spheres. Yet the novel that Ramchand celebrates and has been most credited with securing McKay a place in Caribbean literary history—*Banana Bottom*—is not so far removed from the ideology of the literary that Donnell argues has been marginalized from Caribbean literary histories. Rather than centering his novel around the man of action like Cobham's Rupert Gray, Roumain's Manuel, John Campbell in Reid's *New Day*, or Hilarion in Alexis's *Compère Général Soleil*, McKay chooses a female protagonist who shifts the emphasis away from physical opposition and onto the terrain of the literary. McKay manages to enlist that ideology in the service of a nationalist project just as successfully as Martí in "Nuestra América" or Roumain in *Gouverneurs de la rosée*; attending to how anticolonial authors deploy the literary as a way of staking out space in the public sphere is crucial to understanding the shifting place of writing in the Caribbean.

From his early poetry, to his work as a journal editor, to his novels or autobiographical reflections, Claude McKay was closely connected to the establishment of a literary public sphere. McKay's early career depended on the institutions of the modern colonial period's nascent Caribbean public sphere, with his first poetry published from 1910 to 1912 in the Kingston newspapers the *Daily Gleaner* and the *Jamaica Times*. McKay's poem "The Daily Gleaner," published in that newspaper in December 1911, posits the newspaper as a discursive space open to all—"read by white man, read by nigger"—and explicitly equates its founding in 1834 with freedom for "cullud folks" (*Collected Poems* 5). The poetry McKay publishes in Jamaica from 1910 to 1912, as Winston James discusses, explicitly seeks to speak for those traditionally excluded from this public sphere—poems such as "Quashie to Buccra" voice the point of view of a "we" meant to indicate the black peasantry, while others such as "Passive Resistance" name a "we" that is the urban underclass.[2] *Banana Bottom*, though, steps away from trying to directly speak in those voices—the voices of the folk—a distancing strategy on McKay's part typical of literary anticolonialism. The novel remains invested in the wisdom of that folk's knowledge, but with an awareness that even McKay's early poetry is not the unmediated voice of a group. *Banana Bottom* focuses much more on this process of representation: the novel reflects on the public sphere as a vehicle for the pedagogy and leadership necessary for creating the nation, as well as on the qualities this mediator needs in order to fairly represent the hopes and aspirations of the Jamaican public.

The standard reading of *Banana Bottom* is of the novel's protagonist, Bita Plant, rejecting her early allegiance to European high culture and discovering her Jamaican identity through popular culture. Ramchand summarizes the novel as depicting how Bita "gradually strips away what is irrelevant in her English upbringing" (259). *Banana Bottom* thus demonstrates the successful process of "self-assertion" (272) that leads to "Bita's final liberation and embrace of the folk" (260), an emplotment of West Indian history that Donnell points out dovetails with the nationalist project. The marriage to Jubban is seen as the final achievement of this process: in Wayne Cooper's words, "Instead of marriage to a proper black clergyman, educated to disdain the folk life of the peasants, she chooses to marry her father's drayman, Jubban, whose strength and reliability are emphasized by his total commitment to traditional farming. . . . With the creation of *Banana Bottom*, McKay's picaresque search for psychic unity and stability, begun with *Home to Harlem*, came full circle to rest in the lost paradise of his pastoral childhood" (282). Like Cooper, other critics often read this process within the context of McKay's novelistic trajectory as a whole, as when Tyrone

Tillery argues for *Banana Bottom* as McKay's "last attempt to advance the theme he had unsuccessfully begun in *Home to Harlem* and carried through to *Banjo*: that Western civilization was the Negro's cultural hell and should be rejected in favor of the simple values of the 'folk'" (129).

Recent critics have begun to question this reading: Belinda Edmondson, for example, notices that rather than Bita distancing herself from European high culture, that culture maintains its prestige throughout the novel and even into the final scenes of her reading Blake and Pascal. The novel narrates Bita's rejection of a series of potential suitors on her way to eventually choosing Jubban, clearly ending with her marriage to the folk. But as Bita explores and discards these different possibilities, Edmondson rightly notes that the novel never really rejects the character most directly associated with European high culture, Squire Gensir; Rhonda Cobham even makes the case that far from rejecting Gensir, Bita eventually marries her body to Jubban but her mind to the Englishman ("Jekyll and Claude" 143). Critics often chalk up McKay's inability to fully reject Europe to his middle-class background: Edmondson calls this the "paradox . . . engendered by the position of black West Indian intellectuals . . . who in effect mediated between English discursive and African-derived political systems" (37). In these readings, *Banana Bottom* thus cannot quite fulfill the radical politics to which it aspires. Rupert Lewis and Maureen Lewis make this case most explicitly, calling "McKay's principal failure in the novel" (45) his "simplistic handling of emotional interaction" that "derives from his simplistic depiction of inter-class relationships" (48); "the root of this ambivalence lies firmly in McKay's class background—that he grew up in a British colony, that he came from the peasantry, that his father was a prosperous farmer, and that his family therefore occupied leadership status in the local community" (50). Instead of the earlier reading of *Banana Bottom*, as Bita (and, by extension, the author) successfully casting off privilege and aligning with the folk, these readings argue that McKay's location within the middle class prevents him from accomplishing that objective.

Recognizing that "middle class" to which McKay belonged as itself a conflicted entity might refocus what we assume to be the novel's objective. I read *Banana Bottom* as built around conflicts within the Jamaican middle class rather than between Jamaica and Europe; the novel's anticolonial project may not be primarily the casting off of Europe, but an examination of racial as well as occupational differences within the Jamaican middle class to make the case for the best form of leadership for the local nation.[3] As much as Bita's education in Europe provides a backdrop for the story, that experience is already in the past when the novel begins; the novel invests much more narrative energy in depicting and critiquing class and color hierarchy within Jamaica than in rebuking Britain or its presence in the West Indies. Through Bita's different suitors, the novel explores various models of middle-class allegiance, so that the primary opposition is not really between European literary culture and Jamaican popular culture. What Bita ends up rejecting is becoming part of the professional technocratic brown middle class in order to value an alternative middle-class identity, the literary intellectual. While literary qualities, of sensitivity and verbal acuity, seem emasculating in *Emmanuel Appadocca* or *Rupert Gray* and remain uncomfortably feminine in texts like *Gouverneurs de la rosée*, they become in Bita natural parts of her personality. *Banana Bottom* articulates the anticolonial ideal of the intellectual whose authority is literary in order to show this figure especially attuned to listening to and speaking for all parts of the nation, but also to allow her to align with a counterpublic and stand apart from colonial social structures and capitalist instrumental reason. *Banana Bottom*, through its critique of popular modes of expression like gossip, participates in this advocacy for a bourgeois literary public sphere; but as it establishes the basis for middle-class authority, the novel also shows how conflicts existed over what segment of the middle class is best suited to occupy this role of spokesperson. I want to examine the divide within the middle class between the literary and the technocratic to discuss how anticolonial writers sought to occupy the space of the literary as a way of distinguishing themselves from the utilitarian ideologies of the professional middle class.

Banana Bottom begins by describing both the lack of an ideal literary public sphere and the institutions created by the peasants that serve as a black counterpublic, such as the local church where Bita's return is received. While the novel opens by introducing Bita and briefly sketching out the social relations in the town—setting up in the second paragraph an opposition between "the folk of the tiny country town of Jubilee" and "the Press and official persons" (McKay, *Banana Bottom* 1)—it almost immediately takes a six-page digression to tell the story of Crazy Bow. The detour eventually arrives at Crazy Bow's connection to Bita's story, as it is their sexual encounter that gets her sent to be educated in England. But investing so much narrative space at the beginning in establishing Crazy Bow's back-story makes him the first of what will become a series of men who become mirrors for Bita and show us what paths she might take. While Crazy Bow is described as having "an intellectual bent" (4), his talents lie with the sensual instead of the logical: Cobham points out that both he and Squire Gensir embody for Bita "a culture of sensibility" that is more intuitive than rational ("Jekyll and Claude" 136). The intellectual as artist thus lays the groundwork for a formulation of the literary intellectual who can be distinguished from the more calculating leaders of society.

Crazy Bow's tragedy is an inability to find a place where his artistic expression can be recognized. Described as an especially "precocious child" who early on demonstrates artistic talent and even has the advantage of light skin, Crazy Bow is sent to school with the hope that "the boy would be good for an official job some day" (McKay, *Banana Bottom* 4). But during his education his love of music "knocked everything else out of his head. Composition and mathematics and the ambition to enter the Civil Service" (5). Crazy Bow is in this way alter ego for Bita, who despite her darker skin is nonetheless destined for a "nice bringing-up" (14) and of the class "bound on a preaching or teaching way, the main civilizing professions of the dark peasantry" (15). This career-oriented track is only diverted by Bita's attraction to Crazy Bow. Learning his story shows that what is deemed craziness is in fact his preference to follow his artistic longing rather than a practical career in a locale where such aspirations appear inexplicable; as the novel puts it, "there were no pianos in Banana Bottom" (6), and therefore no possibility that Crazy Bow's art will be appreciated there. When Crazy Bow returns later in the novel, Bita recognizes him as "a true artist" whose performances make his listeners weep, but one who still has no place and "was always wandering" (257). Crazy Bow thus presents for Bita an alternative to entry into the traditional professional class even while his story acts as a warning about the inability of the sensitive intellectual to draw nourishment from his or her people or to locate himself or herself in the local space.

At the same time that Crazy Bow's story demonstrates the lack of opportunities for local intellectuals and artists, his outcome demonstrates an additional danger in the absence of a free and rational public sphere: throughout *Banana Bottom*, gossip is presented as a mode of disseminating knowledge that circumvents official channels but repeatedly results in misunderstanding and tragedy. As in the texts discussed in chapter 3, gossip appears frequently in Caribbean literature of the modern colonial period as a sort of counterpublic where those excluded from the dominant public sphere pass along knowledge. In *Banana Bottom*, when the Craigs and the Days discuss "the controversial articles in the daily newspaper" (96) or Teacher Fearon leads one of the "debating and . . . literary societies" that "nearly all the villages had" (239), they participate in a literary public sphere available to them only because of their privileged status; gossip appears throughout the novel as a more democratic, oral alternative.

While *Banana Bottom* explores gossip as this sort of counterpublic, it is also frequently the catalyst for harmful or even disastrous results. After the sexual encounter between Crazy Bow and Bita that the novel suggests is natural and consensual, Bita's father tries to "hush the matter up" but cannot now that Sister Phibby Patroll, the "village looselip" (10) whose surname suggests the disciplinary side of her activity, has begun to spread news of a rape; as a result, Crazy Bow is given over to the institutions of the official state, tried by an unsympathetic "criminal court" (11), and institutionalized in a madhouse, while Bita is sent abroad and uprooted from her home. Sister Phibby's gossip repeatedly leads to this sort of danger or harm, including Pap Legge's death (147) as well as Tack Tally's suicide after he is mistakenly led to believe that his participation in Obeah killed Pap Legge (151). The novel's final tragedy comes when a hurricane strikes and the island's telegraph system fails. Amid this void of official news, rumors spread about the destruction suffered in Jubilee, prompting the white missionary Malcolm Craig and Bita's father to die trying to get back to the village. As the novel puts it, "thus Malcolm Craig went down to his death carrying Jordan Plant. And all because of exaggerated news" (284).

In addition to the unreliability of gossip, the novel also presents it as sometimes manipulated by malicious actors. In the story of how the peasants of Banana Bottom try to collectivize to get a fair price for their coffee, the experiment is undermined as "some native persons, chiefly those who were employed in minor posts by the whites as shop clerks, foremen on estates or domestics, and who delighted in putting on airs over those who tilled the soil," spread rumors that destroy the peasants' confidence in their collective (20). These false leaders—who are in this incident and elsewhere connected to religious opportunists—mislead and misinform the peasants for their own gain. This trope of gossip as a counterpublic created by the restrictiveness of the official public sphere, which can also be seen in the work of Alfred Mendes, C. L. R. James, Jacques Roumain, and other writers from this period, suggests an anticolonial interest in exploring how groups excluded from official discourse still express themselves; but associating gossip with what McKay's novel depicts as the irrational practices of Obeah and "loose-lipped" women becomes part of the case for how the codification of those networks by male literary intellectuals would benefit the entire nation.

The "minor" functionaries and managers who undermine the plan for collective action are the first of a series of technocrats and professionals who become the novel's foils and villains. As much as *Banana Bottom* demonstrates a desire for the creation of a more formal public sphere where community desires might be openly articulated, the novel shows its suspicion of the class of leaders who already dominate the existing versions of this forum. The depiction of Herald Newton Day allows the novel to explore the clerisy as one segment of this class. One of Bita's suitors, Herald Newton is described by critics as "a racial sycophant" (Cobham, "Jekyll and Claude" 141) and "a Negro who gets a white man's education and learns to despise his own people" (Ramchand 269). As frequently as the novel articulates Herald Newton's relationship with his people in terms of race, though, it also calls attention to his relationship as preacher to the people as audience: after one sermon he tells Bita, "I kept imagining all the time that it was a bigger and better audience" (McKay, *Banana Bottom* 99), and later the narrative notes with some derision that he does not vary his sermons depending on context, but speaks "in the same tone . . . without much thought of the audience" (108–109). While Herald Newton is victim to a colonized racial consciousness, then, he is also caught up in a certain idea about professionalism as well as in the limitations of his chosen vocation; this insensitivity to the specific needs of the Jamaican public suggests the ways in which the sermon or lecture is a less suited model of leadership than a mode of teaching that encourages dialogue with the pedagogical subjects.

Herald Newton's identity as professionalized intellectual is also revealed when Bita notices how "he enjoyed being addressed as reverend" (166). He appears to be pursuing his theological studies primarily to obtain a position, precisely the idea of education Bita denounces in the novel's final scene: "well, she thought, if my education has been wasted it is a happy waste. They were right perhaps who said it was wasted who believed that the real aims of education were diplomas and degrees and to provide things of snobbery and pretension" (314). Carolyn Cooper sees Herald Newton representing the "split" identity created by his "formal education" ("Only a Nigger Gal" 42), a model that Bita must move away from as she "deconstructs the education she receives" (52); Bita's speech from late in the novel, though, shows that she is not rejecting education but the "realm of the practical, which her higher training had always emphasized" (McKay, *Banana Bottom* 191), and aligning herself with something different from "training," the idea that the life of the mind should be pursued purely for its own pleasures.

The clerical tradition represented by Herald Newton Day signifies in the novel both upward mobility for the individual and a potential source of leadership for the community; his eventual discrediting and flight from the story suggest the novel's vision of that tradition's limitations. Bita's cousin Bab, who "did not warm to the notion of a pedagogic or clerical career" (54), pursues what appears to be the only alternative, entry into the civil service. As with Crazy Bow, the civil service is thus presented as "the place where all the intelligent light-coloured young men went" (9) and the most sensible route out of the peasantry.[4] Raised by Bita's father and the son of the same aunt who raised Bita, Bab is yet another of Bita's male alter egos: he is even the first to develop a relationship with Squire Gensir, who is described as Bab's "mentor" and opens his library to Bab just as he will later to Bita (and while critics frequently think of Bita as McKay's fictional alter ego, Bab seems more biographically similar to the author).[5]

Banana Bottom targets this civil service as much as the church as a pursuit at best empty and at worst opportunistic and corrupt. Bab himself becomes disillusioned with this career—especially when learning how little chance for advancement he will have as a black man—and exits the novel after he "emigrated to the United States" (234). Bita learns another brief but important lesson about this profession when she visits the home of the "native gentleman [who] held a handsome post in one of the Civil Service departments" (214). Mrs. Craig brings Bita to his house just as she is getting involved with Hopping Dick—the implication is that the patron wants to match Bita with the younger brother "who had just graduated from a local college and who also expected to enter the Civil Service" (214)—but Bita is appalled when she realizes that while the man "possessed a fine library where he always entertained," he uses the books only for show: "she pulled out one volume after the other and all were uncut," and the civil servant admits, "I don't read much besides the newspapers. . . . But it's nice to furnish a room like this with fine books and bookcases. It is the fashion and gives distinction" (214–215). In owning and displaying these books only for the status that they give him, this character shows the professional class's interest in utility as incompatible with a real appreciation of the literary.

In the context of the vacuity of these other middle-class identities, *Banana Bottom* posits the literary intellectual, sympathetic to the people in a way that the professionals cannot be, as the representative of these people in the public sphere. Sensitivity attunes the literary intellectual to the folk, even as the act of representation requires a distancing from that subaltern status. Bita may marry the folk, but she will not become the folk herself, as evidenced in the scene in which Bita nearly loses herself during a revival meeting but ultimately maintains her identity apart from the other participants. Similarly, in her romantic choices, Bita must learn to be sensitive to her desires and to value feelings that go beyond the rational even as she must not lose her intellectual identity: while she is relieved to not have to marry Herald Newton Day because "her physical self recoiled from" him (110), she realizes that if he had not left she would have gone through with the wedding "even though her spirit and her body were resistant" (180). James Giles, in a chapter called "The Novels: Instinct versus Intellect," makes a case for this binary as the central pivot in McKay's fiction and sees Bita as the "ideal wedding of instinct and intellect" (20); Carolyn Cooper calls this the "body/mind split" ("Only a Nigger Gal" 42) in *Banana Bottom*, and sees marriage to Jubban as resolution of that split in favor of the body. But ending the novel with Bita reading Pascal, where she decides that "the most beautiful of all things" is "the pure flight of the mind into the upper realms of thought" (McKay, *Banana Bottom* 314), makes clear that despite the novel's celebration of spontaneity or sensitivity, it is not rejecting the life of the mind. This final celebration of unfettered creativity—what might be called "thought for thought's sake"—reminds us that even her desire for Jubban, the folk, or the irrational has an intellectual component: just as other writers from the 1930s and 1940s like Aimé Césaire or Alejo Carpentier were drawn to irrationalism via surrealism, McKay turns toward a value system opposed to capitalism's instrumental reason in order to valorize the literary intellectual over the professional or technocratic elite.

Banana Bottom thus does not reject the idea that specialized knowledge is needed for national advancement: the question is which form of middle-class knowledge will be privileged. The tension between an investment in folk knowledge and a desire for a rationalization of that knowledge crystallizes the novel's ambivalence toward folk practices like gossip and Obeah. McKay expresses his own idea of his literary inclination as early as the preface to *Constab Ballads*, his second poetry collection published in 1912. McKay describes how he "had not in me the stuff that goes to the making of a good constable; for I am so constituted that imagination outruns discretion" (qtd. in W. James 55). McKay imagines that his tendency toward creativity makes him unfit for civil service, but it gives him advantages in other potential endeavors: he possesses "a peculiar sensitiveness which made certain forms of discipline irksome, and a fierce hatred of injustice . . . to relieve my feelings, I wrote poems" (qtd. in W. James 55). These qualities—unbounded creativity, a poetic sensitivity, empathy for others—McKay here identifies as what makes him a poet, and would be precisely those qualities that anticolonial intellectuals from Martí to James to Roumain would emphasize as making the literary intellectual particularly suited to speaking for and leading the excluded masses. Through figuring Bita's development in this way, *Banana Bottom* invests its hopes in a literary intellectual class, married to the physical power of the peasantry, as the future for Jamaica. *Banana Bottom* is part of the case made by writers from throughout the region during the modern colonial era for literary intellectuals as leaders of Caribbean anticolonialism as opposed to the technocratic elite of the island. The rest of this chapter examines literary journals of the 1940s as another significant articulation of the importance of the literary in Caribbean anticolonialism.

The Literary Journals: *BIM*, *La Poesía Sorprendida*, and *Tropiques*

Attending to how the literary becomes a way for intellectuals to distinguish themselves from the professional or technocratic elements of the colonial middle class is important for understanding the literary journals that began to proliferate in the Caribbean during the 1940s. These journals draw heavily on this ideology of the literary, an emphasis that has often been read as apolitical. When their politics has been acknowledged, it has been for the nation-building role that they have played in using local settings and language. Literary historians contrast the "predominantly literary" orientation and "quieter nationalism" (Yow 337) of these little magazines with the "sociological consciousness" (Baugh, "History" 238) of more heterogeneous publications such as *Beacon* and *Public Opinion*. But even in this turn toward an apparently more hermetic aestheticism we can see an anticolonial longing to assert the political import of writing. Placing these journals into the broader context of other anticolonial writing can show how they also share a politics that privileges the contribution of the literary through distinguishing it from the practical or the professional. The emphasis on the literary can be seen through looking at journals as varied as the ostensibly apolitical Barbadian *BIM* and Dominican *La Poesía Sorprendida* to publications more frequently read as politically committed such as the Martinican *Tropiques*.

The ideology of the literary was central to the journals that began to flourish in the English-speaking Caribbean during the 1940s, such as *Focus*, *Kyk-over-al*, and *BIM*. Of these Anglophone literary journals, the Barbados-based *BIM* was the longest running and probably the most influential. Founded in 1942 by E. L. Cozier and edited for most of its run by schoolteacher Frank Collymore, *BIM* published continuously for thirty years and launched the careers of Derek Walcott, Kamau Brathwaite, and George Lamming. Ramchand calls the journal "the most West Indian periodical in the islands" (72). John Wickham, meanwhile, states that "no single institution, no other person . . . [has] done as much for the cause of West Indian writing as BIM and Frank Collymore" ("Colly" 16). Lamming emphasizes *BIM* as a public sphere, describing it in an introduction to a 1955 issue as an "avenue by which [Caribbean writers] might reach a literate and sensitive reading public" (qtd. in Baugh, "Frank Collymore" 123). *BIM* was also crucial to extending this notion of the public to go beyond any one island: Reinhard Sander describes *BIM*, along with *Kyk-over-al* (a journal published in Guyana beginning in 1945) and the BBC's *Caribbean Voices* program, as the first West Indian institutions to take a "regional approach" that "helped foster an awareness among the writers in different islands of creative developments taking place in neighboring territories, and encouraged them to see their work as part of a new regional phenomenon" (2).

Despite the central place it has been assigned in the region's literary development, *BIM*'s editorial statements mark it as an unassuming journal that explicitly avoided what Ramchand calls "political affiliations" or "a theory of literature" (72). The journal's editorial policy is expressed in a section titled "What BIM Requires" from the third issue, which appeared in December 1943. The editorial statement outlines stylistic and formal preferences while explicitly asking writers to "give us something with a wide appeal" and to leave political advocacy at the door: "Do not write merely to express yourself or to mend the world or to elevate humanity" (76). *BIM* thus articulates a clear policy of valuing literature for its aesthetics rather than its (political or social) utility, leading a later editor to talk about the "unpretentiousness which has become characteristic of the magazine . . . asserting no doctrine, offering no policy, making no proclamations of intention to fill any vacuum" (Wickham, "Introduction" iv). This space of the literary that *BIM* stakes out apart from the everyday concerns of politics can therefore appear to be in tension with the fact that the journal published many of the writers most closely associated with anticolonialism. In an interview with David Scott, Lamming reflects on the place of literary magazines like these in nationalist movements, noting the irony that Collymore was "completely apolitical" and thus *BIM* during the 1940s "is not connected to a Barbadian nationalism, or a Caribbean nationalism, or any of that. It is going in fact to become that, in spite of him" (Scott, "Sovereignty" 86). Lamming makes it sound like an accident that *BIM* became a vehicle for anticolonial politics and played a part in the decolonization movement. People like Lamming have made the case that the journal was not only not particularly political but not even necessarily nationalist; Edward Baugh describes the philosophy behind *BIM* as the avoidance of a "policy of exclusive West Indianness" ("Frank Collymore" 11). But it is clear in looking through the stories included in *BIM* that at the very least the journal placed significant emphasis on the local as material deserving of literary treatment: one of the journal's editorial statements calling for submissions advises that stories will be accepted "provided they're written in reasonably good English (or Bajun)" and also advises contributors to "regard things from your own viewpoint and experience" rather than writing about "the Alaskan winter" or "Chicago" ("Editor's Comeback" 1). A national project is being constructed here, as early issues of *BIM* contain such features as W. T. Barnes's woodcuts of palm trees or boats, essays like "Rum Ruminations" by the Tippler or "Inkle and Yarico" by E. L. Cozier that connect local events and activities to historical world processes from colonization to tourism, or travelogues of trips to other islands that construct a sense of community within the region.

The ideology of the literary may seem at odds with this nationalist mapping. But the emphasis on the literary becomes part of the critique of colonial society, in which creativity is set up against bureaucracy, beauty against materialism, the literary intellectuals against the technocratic elite of professionals and civil servants. Collymore's stories in *BIM* are a good example of this way of deploying the literary: though critics have emphasized their universal themes of "the dark underside of human beings" and "issues such as alienation and loneliness" (Barratt 167), in fact stories like "The Man Who Loved Attending Funerals" from issue 22 or "RSVP to Mrs. Bush-Hall" from issue 35 are clear critiques of bourgeois society. With Collymore's protagonists drawn from the professional and political classes, revealing the "dark underside" of these characters is part of a broader social critique that underscores the hypocrisy of their claims to rationality or morality.[6] Other contributions to *BIM* such as "In All Their Glory" by A. N. Forde from issue 13 or Edgar Mittelholzer's "The Sub-Committee" from issue 15 continue to present a bank-rupt middle class: Forde's protagonist has grown disillusioned with his job in the post office where he "was drifting further and further away from these people" among whom he had been born (26); Mittelholzer's play shows government functionaries so caught up in protocol that they do not notice a bomb set off in their building. The space of the literary that *BIM* seeks to occupy connects to the war of position taking place in *Banana Bottom* through a critique of the political class of the island and abroad: for example, the first issue contains a puzzle that uses the ages, times in power, and birth-dates of Mussolini, Stalin, Hitler, Roosevelt and Churchill that has the effect of equating all five, and issue 4 features another humorous column of "Simple Political Definitions" mocking the local politicians and elections. While these forms of satire seem too gen-tle to rise to the level of protest, they do register the journal's critical at-titude toward the status quo. This sort of detachment from all politics hardly lends itself to the political commitment typically thought of as anticolonialism, yet articulates the literary as a force opposed to instru-mentality and materialism.

The movements within the Hispanic Caribbean from this period that have been most readily incorporated into comparative Caribbean liter-ary histories have been the *negrismo*, *Afro-antillanismo*, or *indigenismo* of poets like Nicolás Guillén, Manuel del Cabral, and Luis Palés Ma-tos. With their resemblances to the *indigenistes* in Haiti or the interna-tional negritude movement, this turn toward the valuing of black cul-ture marked an important part of the region's struggle for an affirmative identity. Hispanic Caribbean literary journals of the 1940s—critics have focused especially on the Cuban *Orígenes*, while I examine the seldom-analyzed *La Poesía Sorprendida* from the Dominican Republic—have generally been overlooked in this comparative history, as their literary orientation has been read as insufficiently nationalist. Silvio Torres-Sail-lant contrasts the committed poetry of Pedro Mir with what he describes as "the aestheticist, Western-oriented movement known as La Poesía Sorprendida" (226).[7] But the ideology of the literary articulated by these disaffected intellectuals, in which poets rather than politicians and pro-fessionals are presented as heroic opponents of instrumental reason and the materialist status quo, shows how even these supposedly apolitical journals respond to a similar set of demands as the work of more readily recognized anticolonial figures like McKay or Césaire.

La Poesía Sorprendida overlapped in significant ways with its more famous Cuban contemporary, with issue 5 of the Dominican journal featuring poetry by José Lezama Lima, founder of *Orígenes*, and issue 13 including contributions from Cubans like Virgilio Piñero, Eliseo Diego, and Cintio Vitier. This sort of cross-pollination in the Caribbean literary journals of the 1940s demonstrates how much intellectual exchange existed within the region, though only a few writers, like Alejo Carpentier and Aimé Césaire, both of whose work appears in *Orígenes* and *Tropiques*, managed to cross the region's linguistic barriers the way that a visual artist like Wilfredo Lam could. While *Orígenes* was closely associated with the singular figure of Lezama Lima, the editorial board of *La Poesía Sorprendida* at various times featured Dominicans Franklin Mieses Burgos, Mariano Lebrón Saviñón, Freddy Gatón Arce, and Antonio Fernández Spencer, as well as Alberto Baeza Flores, a Chilean, and Eugenio Fernández Granell, a Spaniard fleeing the Franco government. Although the collaborative nature of *La Poesía Sorprendida* may make it more difficult to associate the ideology of the Dominican journal with any one figure, the editorial statements and types of work included from one issue to another still show an adherence to the ideology of the literary.

La Poesía Sorprendida was published in Ciudad Trujillo (Santo Domingo) from 1943 to 1947; the context of the Trujillo dictatorship no doubt shaped the publication, most obviously through the 1944 law preventing non-Dominicans from occupying editorial posts, which forced Baeza Flores and Fernández Granell into secondary positions. Antonio Fernández Spencer, in his 1977 retrospective on the journal, highlights how the journal's critique of the political context was forced into subterranean references, noting that Rafael Leónidas Trujillo is mentioned only once, in an obligatory column praising the centennial of the country's independence. Fernández Spencer calls attention to how this same column salutes great poets "within and outside" the island, thus alluding to "the intellectuals and artists who couldn't live in their homeland" because of the dictatorship.[8] The journal's cosmopolitanism in general might be read as part of this same subtle resistance to the Trujillato's fascist nationalism. The issue celebrating the centennial (February 1944) asks its readers not to stop their celebration at the nation's borders, but to give praise to "all the intellectual workers from both Americas [todos los trabajadores intelectuales de ambos Américas]" (Veloz Maggiolo 46), then goes on to include three Haitian poets. Such inclusiveness was surely a fraught political decision in light of the 1937 massacre of thousands of Haitians sponsored by Trujillo in an effort to purify the Dominican nation.

Many of the journal's editorial statements appear to be veiled attempts to engage with that political context: the centennial issue, for example, asks its readers to "affirm your faith in the creation of a more beautiful, freer and deeper world of tomorrow."[9] Even without the outside enemy offered by European colonialism, then, this Dominican publication connects to a regional anticolonial faith in the literary intellectual's social role. This philosophy becomes articulated through the journal's increasing fascination with surrealism: by issue 6 (March 1944) the final notes mention the connection they have established with "el movimiento surrealista chileno," and issue 7 (April 1944) contains a more detailed reading of some of these Chilean poets. Jorge Carrera Andrade, an Ecuadorean poet living in the United States, contributes the essay "Notas Sobre la Aventura del Surrealismo" in the September 1944 issue, detailing the latest developments in the surrealist movement in Europe. Surrealism becomes for *La Poesía Sorprendida* a way of making art matter, as a challenge to the status quo and a vehicle for imagining alternative worlds. The inaugural issue (October 1943) lays out the journal's orientation in exactly these terms. Baeza Flores describes how poetry's "magic" can "surprise" and even "save" a "crazy world": "poetry is therefore a weapon, less obvious or corporeal but with a force capable of destroying real weapons; because there continues to be an appetite among men for a world of beauty and interior truth."[10] Poetry is figured as a weapon precisely because it does not belong to any particular political point of view; it stands against the ordinary world and allows the poets to occupy a position of alterity and oppositionality.

La Poesía Sorprendida sought to fulfill this mission through creating a local literary public sphere that would expose Dominicans to poets and artists from throughout the Americas and Europe as well as provide a space for local writers. The earliest issues in particular are heavy on works by Breton, Eluard, Blake, Apollinaire, Joyce, Lawrence, and other major figures of the international avant-garde. At the same time, members of the editorial collective built a gradually stronger sense of a Dominican literary scene, beginning by featuring their own poems alongside the international greats and eventually including a diverse range of local writing. Simultaneous with the journal, they created a press that brought out about a dozen short collections by poets connected to the journal. The emphasis on giving the sense of a vibrant local intellectual scene can be seen through the journal's scrupulous accounting of literary events taking place in Santo Domingo, from readings and lectures to new publications. Later issues even begin to include a "Pasado del Presente" section that reproduces an important text from the past by national figures like Pedro Henríquez Ureña (May–August 1946), in order to demonstrate the richness of the Dominican cultural heritage. The later issues also begin to feature more original essays taking on subjects like "How to Read Our Poets" (October–December 1944), showing more investment in the journal as a site not just for poetry to become public but also to debate literary and artistic issues.

La Poesía Sorprendida deploys surrealism as a way to link the valuing of the literary to an oppositional political project. Surrealism serves the same function in Francophone publications like the Martinican journal *Tropiques*, which was edited by Aimé Césaire and Suzanne Césaire along with René Ménil. *Tropiques*, published between 1941 and 1945, was the first journal from the region explicitly aligned with surrealism, receiving direct support from André Breton, who was in exile in Martinique during World War II. The surrealist orientation of *Tropiques* would prove influential for the entire Caribbean, disseminated especially through Aimé Césaire's success: his poetry appeared in translation in the sixth issue of *Orígenes* and is mentioned in an essay in a 1945 issue of *La Poesía Sorprendida* (qtd. in Gatón Arce ix). Césaire also gave a series of lectures in Haiti during 1944, inspiring Jacques Stephen Alexis, René Depestre, and a number of other students to launch the surrealist publication *La Ruche*. Michael Dash notes that Breton himself visited Haiti just before the student uprising there against the pro-U.S. government, and that President Élie Lescot "thought it was Breton who had engineered the revolt that overthrew him early in 1946 and . . . seized the special edition of the student newspaper *La Ruche* which appeared in January 1946 and was dedicated to Andre Breton" (*Literature and Ideology* 158–159).[11]

Just as the Trujillo dictatorship in the Dominican Republic and the Lescot government in Haiti formed the context for the interventions of *La Poesía Sorprendida* and *La Ruche*, *Tropiques* was founded while Martinique was under the Vichy-controlled French government. But the context the journal engages most directly is the longer history of colonial dependence. In an interview with Jacqueline Leiner, Aimé Césaire describes how he conceived of the idea for *Tropiques* upon his return to Martinique in 1941 as a way to fill a "cultural void" in the local public sphere created by the island's "society of cultural consumption."[12] Césaire identifies the local production of culture as antidote to the cultural economy of modern colonialism, a move resembling the emphasis on the local seen in other Caribbean journals of the period. Yet *Tropiques* is hardly the forum for the wide variety of local voices seen either in *BIM* or *La Poesía Sorprendida*; the journal is dominated by the contributions of Ménil and the Césaires, and the little original poetry (as opposed to the reprinting of French poets or the translations of Harlem Renaissance figures) seems almost entirely to be by Aimé Césaire, especially during the journal's first two years. The main contribution of *Tropiques* is instead its theorization of poetics and culture; subtitled a "revue culturelle," all of the issues contain fascinating and frequently polemical discussions between Ménil, the Césaires, and a few other contributors about the goals and possibilities of socially and politically committed art. In this way, *Tropiques* articulates directly the ideology implied in *BIM* and *La Poesía Sorprendida* through its celebration of poetry as the site of alternative knowledge and even revolution. The journal frequently accomplishes this privileging through opposing the literary to the professional.

The first issue of *Tropiques* begins with a poetic essay by Aimé Césaire that sets the coordinates for the journal's idea of poetry and the writer. Narrated in the first person, the essay draws equivalences between the poet, the spokesman, and the warrior:

> A silent and sterile land. I am speaking about ours. . . . I hear screaming steel, drumbeats in the bush, temples praying amidst banyan trees. And I know it is man speaking: now, as always, I am listening. But here is the monstrous atrophy of the voice, the age-old exhaustion, the incredible mutism. . . . No city. No art. No poetry. Not one seed. Not one shoot. Or else the hideous leprosy of imitations. In truth, a sterile and silent land. . . . But it is no longer time to feed off the world. It is a question of saving it. The time has come to gird our loins like valiant men. (A. Césaire, "Presentation" 88)

In this passage, Césaire demonstrates the centrality of the ideology of the literary to the anticolonial project. The poem begins with the notion also seen in Martí's "Nuestra América" of the muted people needing a spokesman to give them voice. The narrator equates the people with the land in the manner Belinda Edmondson describes, and then, like *Gouverneurs de la rosée*, identifies the intellectual as a listener who possesses the sensibility needed to interpret their inarticulate noises. By the end of the passage, the poet has proven why he is the manly warrior who can redeem his people. This celebration of masculine action recalls Martí's or Stephen Cobham's writing, but in demonstrating how the warrior must move through the stages of listening and finding voice, Césaire reinforces the idea of poetry itself as the highest form of commitment.

The next contribution in this first issue of *Tropiques*, an essay by Suzanne Césaire entitled "Leo Frobenius and the Problem of Civilizations," captures the journal's alignment with negritude. The journal frequently celebrates the natural or the irrational as particularly African ways of thought that can be privileged over European rationality. The essays by Suzanne Césaire and Ménil in particular emphasize the "essential" (Ménil, "Lightning Effect" 153), the "essence" (S. Césaire, "Civilization's Discontents" 99), the "true nature" (97) or the "genuinely African ways of thinking and feeling" (S. Césaire, "Leo Frobenius" 83) that can be found in Martinique. Critics like Wole Soyinka and Bill Ashcroft have noted negritude's reinforcing of the binary opposition that associates Europe with scientific reason and modernity, and Africa with a naturalistic primitivism.[13] The essay on Frobenius shows how Suzanne Césaire sees in him a model for thinking about Europe's "craze for science, technology and machines" as resulting in "an imperialist philosophy that has generated the world economy and the encircling of the globe [and] brought humanity to catastrophes as terrible as the wars of 1914 and 1939" (87). James Arnold provides an especially thorough reading of how the thought of Frobenius, Spengler, Nietzsche, Breton, and other European critics of Western rationality influenced the *Tropiques* writers (50–54).[14]

As much as *Tropiques* can be read either as part of negritude's rejection of Europe or as part of a broader attack within Western thought on the legacy of the Enlightenment, the quarrel with science and instrumental reason in *Tropiques* can also be positioned within its Caribbean setting as part of the contest with the professional class we have seen Martí, McKay, and others waging. For both Aimé Césaire and Suzanne Césaire as well as for Ménil, the poet is repeatedly held up as heroically standing against cultural decline and destruction. Ménil in the first issue of *Tropiques* gives the journal "the task . . . to prepare for the Poet's arrival" ("Birth of Our Art" 110) since "the existence of the poet will coincide with our existence for ourselves as approximate people" (111). The journal thus plays prophet to the poet who will redeem the people and make them whole. Suzanne Césaire equates the antitechnological that can bring about "the world re-created" with "Poetry" ("Leo Frobenius" 87); in a subsequent issue, her husband's famous essay "Poetry and Knowledge" declares that "there is someone who saves humanity, someone who restores it to universal harmony, someone who marries a human florescence to universal florescence: this man is the poet" (139). The poet in this essay is the man of action, but is also "pregnant with the world" (140), suggesting that as important as masculine action may be, there is also a need for the poet to draw on and even appropriate the feminine qualities of fertile creativity. Aimé Césaire cites Baudelaire, Mallarmé, Apollinaire, and Breton as possessors of this form of alternative knowledge capable of overcoming "the great silence of scientific knowledge" (134), showing that despite whatever feminine qualities he may possess, the heroic poet is still male. The list of poets also makes clear that, as in *Banana Bottom*, the division is not entirely between Europe and Africa or the Caribbean.

The division, in fact, is articulated repeatedly as between poetic and scientific knowledge. Suzanne Césaire credits surrealism with shedding light on this division: "when Breton created surrealism, the most urgent task was to liberate the mind from the shackles of absurd logic and so-called reason" ("1943" 124). Ménil's "Introduction to the Marvellous," published in the third issue of *Tropiques*, laments the process by which "life withdraws from the living" as a result of the deification of "practical reason" (89). Ménil expresses preference for what he calls marvelous rather than realist writing, describing realism as "an uncertain technique of debased science" (116), an opposition that evokes the much better known essay on *lo real maravilloso* written by Carpentier later in the decade.[15] In the same issue, Ménil argues that "it is consequently in poetry and not in mathematical chattering of Cartesian psychologists that we can read what matters to us" ("Lightning Effect" 154). Much like McKay's Bita or Roumain's Manuel, the literary intellectual thus offers access to a different kind of knowledge that can embody the hopes and aspirations of the nation: "the best lessons about human behaviour must be sought in aesthetics" (Ménil, "Introduction to the Marvellous" 90) because "poems and stories . . . reveal to us a fragment of the world we would like to have lived in" as the aesthetic "responds to our fundamental desires [and] aspirations" (90).

This critique of efficiency, utility, and professionalism in *Tropiques* is rendered metaphoric in some measure, Ménil argues in his preface to the 1978 reissue of the journal, because of the severe colonial censorship the journal faced while the French Vichy government controlled the island ("For a Critical Reading" 69). But that this critique is part of an intraclass struggle with the bureaucracy and professional class can be seen even more overtly in *Légitime Défense*, the magazine of a group of Martinican students in Paris who put out only one issue in 1932 before "French authorities effectively banned the journal by making life difficult for the students, suspending their grants and ensuring that distribution (especially in the Caribbean) was blocked and no further issues were possible" (Richardson 5). Ménil played a part in founding both publications, and both strongly articulate what I have been calling the ideology of the literary. In fact, in an essay published in *Tropiques*, Ménil himself credits the earlier journal as the beginning of a poetic tradition "conceived in 1932 with the publication of *Légitime Défense*" ("Situation of Poetry" 132) and carried forward in *Tropiques*.[16] Ménil in this essay calls the tradition both journals inhabit "Caribbean Romanticism" (132), by which I take him to mean the celebration of poetry as a form of alternative knowledge capable of transforming Caribbean consciousness and society.

The "declaration" that opens *Légitime Défense* makes explicit how this ideology is deployed as a means of what Brent Hayes Edwards calls "class suicide" (191): "emerging from the French mulatto bourgeoisie, one of the most depressing things on earth, we declare (and we shall not retract this declaration) that, faced with all the administrative, governmental, parliamentary, industrial, commercial corpses and so on, we intend—as traitors to this class—to take the path of treason so far as possible" ("Légitime défense" 43). These literary intellectuals thus distinguish themselves from the technocratic or professional elements of the Caribbean middle class, what Jules Marcel Monnerot in an essay from the journal calls "the children of the coloured bourgeoisie" who "go to France—generally successfully—to 'earn' the title of 'Doctor,' 'Teacher' and so on" and thus "adopt the tastes and distastes (as well as the bowler hats) of the French bourgeoisie" ("Note" 45).

While the enemy *Légitime Défense* identifies facing Caribbean self-realization is most easily reduced to the issue of assimilation to foreign values, what is really at stake is a struggle *within* the Caribbean middle class to determine the segment best suited to lead and speak for the Caribbean public. Monnerot thus addresses a later essay to attacking "specialists . . . principally of a professional, familial and military order" ("On Certain Common Characteristics" 59) while positing redemption in "poetry" (63). As McKay does through his construction of Bita, the writers of *Légitime Défense* make it clear that the turn toward poetry is not a distancing from France but from the professional class: Monnerot especially admires how "poetry in France from the eighteenth century to the present has shown a constant effort both to liberate itself from utility as expressed by logic, the subject, expressionism or clarity and, by returning to its own sources, to become less and less limited by language and other conventions" (63). On the other hand, the reality, according to Etienne Léro, is "the exceptionally mediocre character of Caribbean poetry," resulting from poetry writing still being "a job on the side" that "any doctor, lecturer, lawyer, president of the republic" can occupy to "earn a little renown among the mulatto bourgeoisie" (55). What *Légitime Défense* ironically calls for, then, is specialization, for poets to focus on issues of form and aesthetics—an option that, as we saw in Seacole and Martí, only becomes available through market success—since only purity from a corrupt social order can prove their suitability for standing up to and overthrowing that order. The attack on the scientific or the rational is thus part of a broader argument against the practical: in *Tropiques*, Ménil goes so far as to celebrate "absolute poetry" as "poetry *for itself* and not *for us*" ("Birth of Our Art" 110), emphasizing an ideology of the literary as detached from use-value. Yet even in its title, *Légitime Défense* suggests the equation of this radically literary stance with a sort of military maneuver.

Of the contributors to *Tropiques*, Aimé Césaire most thoroughly makes this double move of combining the literary and the political, and it is no coincidence that Césaire collected many of the poems he published in *Tropiques* in a 1946 volume titled *Les Armes Miraculeuses*. Césaire declares poetry's centrality to a successful political project in one impressionistic essay published in *Tropiques*: "the Martiniquan revolution will be made in the name of bread of course; but also in the name of fresh air and poetry (which comes to the same thing)" ("Panorama" 81). Poetry, then, is "the principle of a healthy Caribbean politics: open the windows. More air. More air" (81). Giving poetry this vital role in the reshaping of the Caribbean nation seems to be a great distance from the virtually art-for-art's-sake literary ideology expressed when Ménil talks about "expression without content" ("Birth of Our Art" 110). What is important for understanding this brand of anticolonialism is how, for Ménil, these two ways of thinking are in no way incompatible; in fact, only a few months later in a subsequent issue of *Tropiques* he can imagine salvation in the form of "a man armed with poetic power, standing tall above his people and overturning his country's social life with a single spoken word" ("Lightning Effect" 154). Ménil's "absolute poetry" ("Birth of Our Art" 110), because of its refusal to participate in the instrumental order, becomes a site around which a politics can still be organized. Aimé Césaire's "Poetry and Knowledge" picks up precisely that idealized vision of the poet, who is not "the cold calculator and strategist" but instead can open the way "for humanity's most illustrious dreams" (137). The poet is a dreamer, able to envision an alternative order. In uncoupling the idea of practical but incremental improvement embodied by the professional class and promising a "leap" brought on by "the poet's audacity" (115), the opposition of action and reflection is thus temporarily resolved.

Aimé Césaire's contributions to *Tropiques* articulate two central elements of anticolonial ideology: a critique of Enlightenment rationality as unable to understand Caribbean reality along with a valuing of the literary as better suited to speaking the desires of the Caribbean nation as counterpublic. His support for departmentalization of Martinique in the late 1940s has puzzled many commentators, who see this turn away from independence as contrary to the logic of his earlier writing. Arnold notes that "by 1950 [Césaire] had undoubtedly found that the irrationalist current in his poetry had become a hindrance to him as a Marxist deputy" (178), and goes on to cite Césaire's own description of this split between the role of the poet and the political functionary in a 1971 interview: "the writer is all alone with his mind, with his soul; the politician, not to mention the party hack, unfortunately has to take contingencies into account; he tries to lead but he also has to come to terms with contingencies, and if a *mot d'ordre* is not linked to the reality of things, that *mot d'ordre* is only literature. Consequently, I find that there is no contradiction between what I write and what I do; they are merely two different levels of action" (qtd. in Arnold 180). Transformations in the Caribbean public sphere placed new demands on what Arnold calls "the public man who emerged from the crucible of wartime Martinique" (100); in the same interview, Césaire observes that *Tropiques* "ceased publication . . . precisely because the *cultural struggle* was giving way to the political struggle" (qtd. in Arnold 101).[17] Despite Césaire's insistence on his ability to occupy the position of writer and politician, these quotes demonstrate how by the time of the interview he could not imagine himself occupying those two positions simultaneously: he is only a politician when he acts, whereas when his words are disconnected from the real world he is creating "only literature." Arnold makes a strong case that Césaire was "obliged to deny the inspiration of a significant part of his poetry" (179) in order to think of himself as a politician, a trend associated with the postcolonial crisis of literary authority that the second half of *Caribbean Literature and the Public Sphere* explores. Césaire continued to operate as both professional technician and literary writer, although only through thinking of these as separate activities.

I began this chapter by positioning my own readings of the centrality of the literary to Caribbean anticolonialism in dialogue with Alison Donnell's appeal to critics to engage with work produced by writers more interested in aesthetics than politics. With the ideas about art expressed in *Banana Bottom* or the literary journals of the 1940s in mind, we can see how closely they resemble those of J. E. C. McFarlane, the figure who Donnell positions as the antithesis of the anticolonial tradition because of his politics and ideas about aesthetics. As different as McKay's ideas may have been from those of McFarlane in regards to religion or national independence—and as different in terms of those issues as the positions taken by Collymore, Lezama Lima, and the Césaires might have been—all of these figures celebrate the poet as society's vanguard and display a reverence for the literary as opposed to the practical.[18] The introduction to McFarlane's collection *The Challenge of Our Time* frames his literary explorations in the context of "the recognition of the need for direction" for society (i), a direction that he suggests the literary world can provide if "the means of creative knowledge and informing public opinion were at the same time fostered" (iii). He ends that collection much more forcefully, declaring a decade before Aimé Césaire said virtually the same thing that "the world's poets are also the world's saviours" (213). When Bita reads Blake and finds him "holding the spirit up, up, aloft, proving poetry the purest sustenance of life, scaling by magic and all the colours of passion the misted heights where science cannot rise and religion fails and even love is powerless" (McKay, *Banana Bottom* 268), she sounds similar to McFarlane's observation that "it is thought, and thought alone, that exercises sovereign sway" (28); and while McFarlane's politics may not seem recognizably nationalist, the idea he expresses that "the greatest bane of our present existence is to be found in the over-emphasis which has been laid upon material things" (33) certainly echoes the opposition to capitalist instrumentality seen in the pages of *La Poesía Sorprendida* or *Tropiques*.

While the emphasis on masculine action in the works of Martí, Cobham, and Roumain and also associated with McKay and Césaire may seem far removed from the aesthetic concerns expressed by the editors of *BIM* or *La Poesía Sorprendida*, in fact all of these writers are attempting to assess the conflicted relationship of the literary and the practical in the context of anticolonial politics. As Donnell shows through noting how McFarlane operated in many of the same literary institutions as writers more easily identifiable as anticolonialists, like Roger Mais, the overlapping institutional space occupied by these figures demonstrates how these writers are staking out distinct but clearly related territory within a colonial public sphere in which distinguishing the literary intellectual from the professional class is as urgent a political project as a critique of Europe. As the next chapter shows, identifying this conflict within the Caribbean middle class can enhance the analysis of the triumphs and failures of the anticolonial movement as well as the postcolonial governments that would succeed it.

Part Three

Postcoloniality and the Crisis of the Literary Public Sphere, 1959 to 1983

5 The Expulsion from the Public Sphere

The Novels of Marie Chauvet

DURING THE MODERN COLONIAL PERIOD, writers like José Martí and Claude McKay, as well as journal editors like Frank Collymore, Aimé Césaire, and Suzanne Césaire, made the case for the literary as a crucial quality in governing the nation. But the successes and failures of the region's anticolonial struggles left nationalist intellectuals in a difficult new position during the decolonizing years as they could no longer unify their aspirations to speak for both a public and a counterpublic. This chapter begins the second half of *Caribbean Literature and the Public Sphere*, which examines the effects that the crisis of anticolonialism had on the region's literature. Writers who had conceived of their intellectual labor as oppositional now found themselves at odds with the nationalist movements that became the postcolonial state. While participants in the anticolonial struggle faced persecution from colonial Britain, France, and the United States, as postcoloniality became the region's dominant framework intellectuals faced a variety of pressures from the local governments they had helped bring to power.

Postcolonial or postmodernist critics, influenced by suspicion of nationalism as an exclusionary ideology, have often seen the tragedy of the contemporary Caribbean as the coming to power of the anticolonial intellectuals of the modern colonial period. In *The Other America*, Michael Dash makes this case. According to Dash, Caribbean modernism—defined as "negritude, indigenism, and even Marxism" (*Other America* 62)—harbors in its poetics a desire to close down difference through enforcing an imagined lost purity. Modernism thus becomes a term used to periodize—he looks especially at Aimé Césaire and Jacques Roumain as major practitioners of this kind of poetics—but also to describe an ongoing trend within Caribbean writing, since Dash includes more recent writers like Frantz Fanon, Kamau Brathwaite, and Roberto

Fernández Retamar as adherents to what he characterizes as a dangerous mode of thought. Postmodernism, represented for Dash in decon-
structive play and the carnivalesque (79), refuses to align itself with any
master narrative or ideological position and thus avoids what he calls in
his section on Roumain "The Totalitarian Temptation."

Dash acknowledges that in its origins, "modernity was an emancipatory discourse" (61), but reads Césaire, Brathwaite, and Roumain to argue that their anticolonialism "reinforced the idea of the author as the
fountainhead of truth, of an authoritative self presiding over a totalizing vision and the lure of a nativist politics" (73). Césaire's and subse-
quently Fanon's desire for a violent revolutionary break from the past
paradoxically lends itself to "nostalgia for a prelapsarian, mythic past"
(70); Brathwaite's "History of the Voice" turns into a search for "the
foundational rhythmic utterance" that "is not an inclusive chorus" (72).
The problem, for Dash, is how "Fascist politics are a hidden dimension
to indigenist poetics" (75), and so Roumain becomes the ideological precursor for Duvalier's dictatorship with *Gouverneurs de la rosée* "a Caribbean version of the 'dictator' novel" (78).[1] In making this case, Dash
must argue that writers critical of or even persecuted by these authoritarian regimes actually share a common totalitarian logic. Thus, in discussing Roumain, he suggests that "even those ideologically opposed
to Brouard's fascism were seduced by the retrieval of a terrestrial order,
by the restoration of a luminous center from which would emanate sa-
cred diction, a prelinguistic rhythm, a primal harmony. . . . Roumain's
Masters of the Dew, while normally seen as progressive and quite distinct from the ideology of [Duvalier's] griot movement, paradoxically
reveals an anxiety for establishing a truth beyond words" (76). Dash ultimately makes the case that celebrations of the folk are fascist (75) and
that "what starts off as a dream of liberation from an oppressive Western system of knowledge ends up also asserting a new, closed, hegemonic
system of values . . . the seductive reality of authoritarian poetics is not
far behind these originary fictions" (80).

In identifying negritude, indigenism, and Marxism as precursors to
totalitarianism, Dash argues that literary and political projects based
on racial, national, or class consciousness lead to exclusionary practices
based on distinguishing us from them. While totalitarians like Duvalier
may have claimed intellectual grounding for their regimes in discourses
like *noirisme*, I would argue against ahistorically collapsing all nationalist ideologies or revolutionary movements into the category of fascism.
My discussion of Aimé Césaire and Suzanne Césaire from chapter 4, for

example, showed how the version of negritude articulated in *Tropiques* can be read not only as a reversal of the black/white binary but also as a translation through the prism of race, class, and gender of a number of other binaries, such as reason versus emotion, utility versus the aesthetic, and scientific versus literary thought. Rather than a simple opposition between Europe and the Caribbean, these intellectuals of the modern colonial era connected to various anticolonial currents within European thought such as surrealism to launch a critique of capitalist instrumentality within their own cultures. When anticolonial writers sought to unify the nation, it was not only around the concept of the public as singular but also around an awareness of the nation's existence as a relationally defined counterpublic.

Seeing intellectuals within the Caribbean and their relationship with Europe as heterogeneous and internally conflicted can suggest other ways of looking at the rise of totalitarian tendencies in Caribbean politics. Matthew Smith's *Red and Black in Haiti* details the complicated rivalries between the *noiristes* and Marxists, noting that the technocratic background in law and medicine of *noirisme*'s main theorists like Lorimer Denis and Duvalier gave *Les Griots* a "more scientific than literary" perspective (24). According to Smith, throughout the 1940s and 1950s the *noiristes* excluded and persecuted "the militant left" (136), which included writers like René Depestre and Jacques Stephen Alexis (136). Dash himself, writing about the place of intellectuals within contemporary Haiti, notes how "like Plato, François Duvalier banished intellectuals from his republic" ("Blazing Mirrors" 183). This exile from the public sphere meant that the literary intellectuals discussed in the first half of this book never truly came to power, and were more often victims than perpetrators of the postcolonial violence Dash identifies. Rather than seeing intellectuals as a single unified category, I argue in this chapter that the division of the intellectual field between literary intellectuals and technocratic professionals identified by writers of the modern colonial period, from José Martí to Claude McKay to the literary journals of the 1930s and 1940s, took on a new importance as events such as the Haitian student revolution of 1946, the Cuban Revolution in 1959, and the movement to independence in the British islands during the 1950s and 1960s highlighted the question of governance. The competition between the literary intellectual and the technocratic professional foreshadowed in the previous chapter becomes an overt conflict during the 1950s and 1960s, along the gendered divide of emotion and sensitivity versus scientific reason. This chapter, which looks at the work of Marie Chauvet, and the next chapter on George Lamming and Martin Carter discuss how the literary is forced into retreat in this conflict.

Revolution and the Anticolonial Intellectual in *La danse sur le volcan*

After making his argument for the complicity of the modern intellectual in this purging of the public sphere, Dash turns to the work of Marie Chauvet as taking the properly postmodern "irreverent stand against all totalizing and centering systems" (*Other America* 109). Her depiction of the "wretched pointlessness . . . of literary commitment" (112) in the trilogy *Amour, Colère, Folie* makes Chauvet's work "the full-blown emergence of a postmodernist poetics" (110), as she "holds up to ridicule" and "mock[s]" (112) what Dash calls the modernist tradition of Caribbean thought. Critics like Joan Dayan, Ronnie Scharfman, and Myriam Chancy also focus on Chauvet's critique of Duvalier-style patriarchy and totalitarianism. Dayan joins Dash in contrasting the postmodern distrust of master narratives seen in Chauvet's fiction with the "modernist" or "nationalist" work of her precursors: according to Dayan, Chauvet "go[es] beyond the 'peasant novel' or proletarian visions of Roumain or Alexis" and thus "is scorned by those whose more 'political' agenda demands that they speak for and with the people" (*Haiti* 80). Yet Marie-José N'Zengou-Tayo, in her brief overview of the idea of the committed intellectual in Haitian literary history, argues that "Chauvet expresses her faith in the role of the intellectual and poet as an agent of change" (327), contrasting her work with Lyonel Trouillot's novels, which depict "the end of the leading role usually assigned to the politically committed intellectual in Haitian literature" (332). While both Dayan and Dash, on the one hand, and N'Zengou-Tayo, on the other, see the loss of the writer's place in the public sphere, Chauvet occupies opposed positions in each story, as either the first to give up the writer's public role or the last to keep it alive. I suggest that unlike either Roumain in the 1930s and 1940s or Trouillot in the 1980s and 1990s, Chauvet's career spans a transitional period that falls neither fully within the modern colonial period nor in the emergent postcolonial era. Whereas Roumain can imagine a literary intellectual like Manuel who combines specialized knowledge with the sensitivity to listen to and then speak for his people, and Trouillot has moved away from celebrating the literary intellectual to take his protagonists from minor functionaries like the postal service employee in the 1996 *Rue des pas perdues*, Chauvet's novels navigate a space in-between where the idea of the committed intellectual still seems possible but is becoming severely in doubt.

I begin with an analysis of *La danse sur le volcan* to emphasize how this 1957 novel is invested in the nationalist, modernist project, and invokes the sort of anticolonialism embodied by Roumain and Alexis through telling the story of the Haitian Revolution. Whereas critics looking at the 1968 *Amour, Colère, Folie* have read Chauvet as a postmodern writer primarily interested in discrediting the romance of anticolonialism and the writer's heroic role in social struggles, *La danse sur le volcan* fits more readily into the Haitian literary scene of the 1940s and 1950s. Marie-Agnès Sourieau and Kathleen Balutansky describe how, in this period, "Haitian arts and literature expressed a sense of urgency and hope that the country has not experienced since. René Depestre and Jacques Stephen Alexis, the co-founders of the militant newspaper *La Ruche* (*The Beehive*, 1945), were the major intellectuals of this generation" (35). Depestre and Alexis, as writers as well as leaders of the revolutionary movement that succeeded in overthrowing U.S.-backed President Élie Lescot in 1946, thus stand in for an anticolonial literary generation that "came to an abrupt end under François Duvalier's repressive regime" (35), which took power in 1957. My reading of *La danse sur le volcan* shows how its faith in the literary intellectual makes it part of this anticolonial generation of writing.

La danse sur le volcan looks back to the years leading up to the French Revolution to think about the relationship of the artist to epochal social transformation. Retelling the story of the Haitian Revolution plays an important role in some of the most well known anticolonial Caribbean literature. In C. L. R. James's play *Toussaint L'Ouverture* (later published under the title *The Black Jacobins*), Alejo Carpentier's *El reino de este mundo* and *El siglo de las luces*, Derek Walcott's *Henri Christophe*, Edouard Glissant's *Monsieur Toussaint*, and Aimé Césaire's *La tragédie du roi Christophe*, all appearing between 1936 and 1963, Caribbean writers from this anticolonial generation used the story of one of the region's great revolutionary moments from the eighteenth century to imagine the transformations occurring around them with the end of modern colonialism in the middle of the twentieth. Haiti is not always thought of as part of the same historical narrative as the Anglophone and Hispanic Caribbean, or even as other Francophone islands like Guadeloupe and Martinique. *La danse sur le volcan* connects to this broader anticolonial moment and its ways of thinking about revolution and the public sphere, thus pointing to the broader regional purchase of the anticolonial narrative of heroically overcoming an oppressive past to forge a new future.

Some of the most famous literary renditions of the Haitian Revolution from this period—the plays by Césaire, Glissant, and Walcott, for example—focus on the aftermath of the uprising and the challenges in building a nation-state after a revolution; Chauvet, on the other hand, sets her story in the lead-up to this event, focusing attention on the changes in consciousness that make this revolutionary moment possible, and how these changes affect and are effected by artists as they enter into and interact with the public sphere. *La danse sur le volcan* uses many real historical figures to tell its story, but focuses especially on the coming to consciousness of a young *affranchie* in late-eighteenth-century Saint-Domingue named Minette.[2] Toussaint, Dessalines, and Christophe are completely absent from the story, while major actors like Pétion and Sonthanax appear only as secondary characters. The effect is to foreground the social contradictions of colonial society on the brink of revolution and how competition for the public sphere lays the groundwork for this revolutionary process.

Minette's story involves her development from unaware of the world around her to committed intellectual. When the novel opens, instead of racial consciousness Minette demonstrates only a fear that she will be mistaken for being black: *La danse sur le volcan* consistently foregrounds the discontinuity and possible allegiances between different classes and shades among the island's African-descended population. Minette's mother warns her that the way she dresses might make people think her a runaway slave (Chauvet, *Dance* 8) and urges her to speak what the narrative describes as "affected French as a sign of education and refinement" (13). A new mind-set begins for Minette upon witnessing the horrors of a slave being whipped: after this incident "Minette's view of slavery underwent a sudden and profound change" (45). A little later, seeing slaves being sold makes her imagine that "it would be nothing, nothing at all to plunge a knife into some necks, to poison, to set mansions and plantations to the torch" (115). Her coming to consciousness, then, is largely a growing ability to identify with the suffering of enslaved blacks in the island, and to turn that identification into a common political project.

While these experiences profoundly affect Minette, it is only later that she develops a language for articulating her new worldview, and that process is central to the novel. As she puts it, "'I don't want to be . . .' Minette paused as if searching for a word . . . 'exploited. You taught me the meaning of this word and I have a horror of it now'" (72). Although she has difficulty finding the right word, she manages to; Minette gives credit for her new language to Joseph Ogé, the character who most di-

rectly invokes the anticolonial narrative of revolution. He is the catalyst for Minette's development, introducing her to Enlightenment ideas
about freedom through writers like Rousseau (28) and Abbé Raynal
(73). Joseph thus appears in the novel as the anticolonial intellectual,
the man of action who inspires, educates, and leads his people toward
revolutionary consciousness. The first time Joseph appears, he is fleeing
law enforcement, having been "caught . . . while [he] was teaching some
young slaves to read" (15). Joseph is connected to an underground movement to help and hide runaways, a group with ties to the Maroons, and
toward the end of the novel he is revealed to be the brother of historical figure Vincent Ogé, the French-educated mulatto who led one of the
early, unsuccessful attempts at revolution among Saint-Domingue's free
people of color.[3]

As important as Joseph is to the novel, though, it remains Minette's
story, and in making her story central Chauvet brings in other concerns
in addition to the action-oriented anticolonialism Ogé embodies. *La
danse sur le volcan* specifically figures the anticolonial project as integrally connected to Minette's ability to speak and be acknowledged by
the public sphere. Minette is a performer and aspiring playwright confronting first, the challenges of the color line, and second, the demands
that the market and the public make upon her.[4] The fact that Chauvet
herself began as a playwright and that so many of the anticolonial renditions of the Haitian Revolution appeared as plays points to how drama
enters the public sphere differently from other literary forms. Drama's
appeal to the anticolonial notion of literature seems to come from the
immediacy with which it can speak to and stage social issues in front of
a public.

Public space is virtually inaccessible to those of African descent in
the world of *Danse*. The white society displays an elaborately codified
public sphere, embodied in newspapers, government spectacles, and the
theater. It is precisely these institutions that Minette finds unavailable:
she is excluded from the events of high society, she cannot even afford
entry into events held in the public square (74), and the novel notes that
the most important newspaper, the *Gazette*, "never mentioned Negroes
and mulattoes" (69).[5] The early plot involves Minette's efforts to break
into the white-controlled world of public discourse; when she gives her
first performance, she is described as the "first of her race to leap over
the insurmountable barrier of prejudices" (37), and Joseph acclaims her
as "an honor to her race" (50). The pressure of this role nearly unnerves
Minette, but the novel describes how she is able to perform only by call-

ing to mind two things: first, the presence of "the twenty-one second-ary loges occupied by the persons of color" who she sees as a "powerful chain of solidarity" (57); and second, Joseph's prediction that her "voice is [her] weapon" (50). Her performances are thus framed with an ethical content, a direct connection to her people, and as the equivalent of the revolutionary struggle just beginning to take place: part of what she is learning is how to break away from the ideology expressed by one of the other performers, that "we don't get mixed up in politics. . . . We are artists, nothing but artists" (134).

As she seeks to fulfill Joseph's prophesy and overcome the mind-set that sees art and politics as incompatible, Minette dreams of her performances allowing her to become spokesperson for her people: "Minette considered the performance of such simple, ephemeral plays as a degradation of talent. 'If only these things could serve a real purpose,' she told herself, 'if only one could write the truth and really express the sufferings of the slaves and their desire for freedom in their own language'" (75). But she realizes that she is only allowed to perform as long as her patrons and the surrounding apparatus remain comfortable with her. The local papers initially laud the "liberal ideas of the troupe" as long as "the incident was not injurious to the direct interests" of the "established order" (69); once social unrest begins to sweep the island, though, the newspapers turn on Minette, "criticizing her wardrobe and comparing her—for the purpose of destroying her popularity—with a white actress" (101–102). Within this circumscribed context, and in need of money to support herself, Minette finds herself unable to stage the sort of representations that she would like: she is repeatedly pressured to act as a slave in what are described as "native plays," featuring degrading stereotypes (169). While her sister happily takes on these parts in order to break into the theater, Minette compares acting in these plays to the free people of color who own slaves and make their living off the exploitation of their own people (172).

The novel draws equivalences between Minette's struggles to insert herself into public discourse and the broader social struggles for freedom. The issue of access to the public sphere is not only important to Minette. Slave society is depicted in the novel as a constant competition between enslaved people and masters struggling for discursive dominance. In the early part of the novel, enslaved people appear physically only as they are displayed for sale or publicly punished. After one mild uprising, random blacks are chosen and then "were led to the public square and hanged from lampposts after the mere semblance of a trial" (100). These sorts of tortures are repeatedly called "spectacles" (45, 330), and the novel notes that slaves and free people of color are "explicitly invited to attend" (331). Minette understands that these events have a pedagogical purpose to intimidate, as they are "deliberately staged . . . to remind her, should she ever forget it, of how the back of a slave looked after being lashed with a whip" (45). The public whippings, the display of the body parts of the tortured, and the screams of the victims of this violence are all meant to convey this message about power and control.

The enslaved struggle to speak back, even if their forms of expression are forced underground by the colonial system. The violent policing of public space drives Joseph into hiding, and the other free blacks who Minette finds helping runaways must keep their activity out of the public eye. Early in the novel, enslaved people hardly appear and are almost completely silenced; yet they are able to influence Minette and help change her consciousness through transmitting the necessary messages. The enslaved man who Minette sees being whipped speaks to her without words: "the slave turned his head toward them and stared at Joseph. He hardened his muscles defiantly as though he were making an effort to break the chains, a gesture whose meaning did not escape the colonist. His whip whistled in the air as it lashed across the slave's face. Minette uttered a cry of horror which was lost in the tumult of noise made by the crowd and the clanking of the chains" (44). In this passage, the enslaved person manages to send a clear message of resistance that forms part of Minette's early education. But we also see in the slave-owner's use of violence an attempt to silence this message. In this context, the enslaved population is almost entirely without dialogue in *La danse sur le volcan*, even as their presence is felt in the distant drums (111) and *lambi* (68, 195, 225), sounds that imply threat and rebellion but can only appear to Minette as disembodied noises.

The main obstacle to revolution in *La danse sur le volcan*, then, is articulation. The most basic attempts at resistance or defiance are described as speech acts: "even though they knew their own revolt lacked the strength and organization to be successful, the slaves sought to give it expression" (320) through poisoning and suicide. Yet so much of this oppositional energy is undirected as long as the owners control the public sphere. Joseph and Vincent Ogé attempt to interrupt the dominant narrative and help the slaves articulate an alternative. When he is led to his execution, for example, Vincent takes advantage of the public forum the "spectacle" offers to shout, "Forget nothing that you see here today, my brothers" (333). He creates a counterpublic of "brothers" and gives the event an alternative pedagogical purpose to colonial terror. Vincent's brief speech—delivered with the "deep, resonant timber in his voice and the same slow and careful pronunciation" (333) that recalls Emmanuel Appadocca and Rupert Gray—inspires the revolution as much as his brother's return to Port-au-Prince with the Declaration of the Rights of Man in his pocket (316). While Vincent is executed, Joseph has his tongue removed (326), suggesting how seriously the colonial power takes the struggle over expression. The novel represents Vincent's death and Joseph's muteness as leaving the uprising dangerously without articulation. After the whites betray the agreement they have signed granting the *affranchis* rights, a "crowd of persons of color" gathers outside the theater shouting only "it's unjust" (352) and building toward action. Minette notices Joseph's arrival and that "his inability to speak made his eyes bulge. . . . To think that he had once dreamed of galvanizing crowds to action with his words! The movement had come, the moment for which he had waited all his life. Great rebellious stirrings were in motion and he could not talk to his own people! Instead, hatred was their guide" (352). Minette realizes that Joseph is trying to communicate the overwhelming advantage the police have over this small and unguided uprising, that he wants to "stop the crowd before it went to its certain death" (352). Without Joseph able to take over the spokesperson role, Minette is forced to finally put her voice to the service of her people and connect her status as artist with the broader social movement: she begins to sing "a passage . . . which Joseph had recited eloquently in the past" (352), inspiring the crowd to "beg[i]n singing . . . in chorus" (353). United in this way, the crowd registers their protest against what has happened but avoids "hav[ing] themselves massacred by the National Guard like so many sheep" (352).

Minette's eventual consolidation of the spokesperson role is only part of the romantic fulfillment in the novel. The novel ends with Minette remembering her initial dream that she could redeem and free the enslaved, and realizing that "her dream had taken on the flesh of reality. She had lived long enough to see the cause of the *affranchis* and the Negroes triumph" (369). Yet that romance is undercut somewhat at the end as the narrative point of view shifts from Minette to her love interest, Lapointe, a free person of color who owns slaves but eventually comes around to helping fight for the freedom of all African-descended people in the island. As the narrative gradually shifts away from idealistic Minette and toward the conflicted Lapointe, an ambivalent vision of revolutionary solidarity eventually emerges. Written amid the rise of Duvalier to power, *La danse sur le volcan* is obviously invested in exploring how these sorts of alliances between the free people of color and enslaved people become a crucial part of the buildup to revolution.[6] Lapointe—a real historical actor who became leader of a regiment that joined the British to fight against the revolutionaries (Chartrand 13)—represents within the novel people who would later come to think of themselves as a mulatto class much more overtly self-interested and hostile toward the black population, throughout the story using them as slaves or bargaining chips to obtain their own rights. What I want to emphasize here as well is how Lapointe also represents a counterpoint to Minette's ideas about art and revolution as much as her more sympathetic relationship to blackness. Whereas in Minette's final spokesperson moment she persuades the crowd to avoid bloodshed, Lapointe's every appearance is marked by violent action: his only participation in discursive struggle is also an act of physical provocation, when he "forced his way into the town hall, and seized the lists containing the names of the *affranchis* sentenced to death, and burned them in the street" (Chauvet, *Dance* 354). Seeing Minette crying after her mother and sister are killed in battle, Lapointe offers only this: "Men are like vultures. One must fight, Minette, without tears of prayers. Mercy is no longer fashionable" (362). In shifting to a focus on Lapointe, the novel seems to validate his contention that revolutionary battle is a space for action, for unsentimentality, and for men.

Association with the feminine is enough to discredit those seeking to establish their political credentials. As the *affranchis* debate whether to turn over the enslaved people who had helped their rebellion in return for the granting of rights, Minette and others plead against this idea, suspecting that the whites will kill the slaves and then go back on the agreement: "some of the men protested that this was feminine sentimentality, which had no place in the struggle. The men who agreed with these women were accused of being weaklings" (349). This scene—after which the agreement is broken just as predicted—suggests the complex ways in which Chauvet imagines the intersecting alliances across race, class, and gender lines that the revolution tries and frequently fails to construct.[7] Even as the novel ends with Minette's death and the apparent passing on to Lapointe as model, this ending exhibits extreme ambivalence toward his revolutionary masculinity. Lapointe is a successful military leader of the slaves, but only through "playing on their hatred adroitly, and it was not long before he ruled them like a dictator" (361). He is nearly won over to the utopia Minette had always hoped for, where "people of all colors and classes mingled around him, for the first time without hatred or prejudice" (374); but after her death, he swears himself only to exact horrible revenge on his enemies. The novel ends with Lapointe "learning that a conspiracy had been organized against him, he had the white conspirators arrested and he brutally killed them, without even the semblance of a trial. Two days later, following the example of the proslavery planters and mulattoes, he turned [his plantation] over to the British" (376). Not believing in anything but his own power and self-preservation, Lapointe may be a dynamic man of action, but he lacks the connection to a people or the intellectual sensitivity of Minette and Joseph. The silencing of these literary intellectuals as well as the tyrannical tendencies of Lapointe foreshadow the conflicts within the Haitian middle class that Chauvet explores in *Amour, Colère, Folie.*

The End of Anticolonialism in *Amour, Colère, Folie*

Amour, Colère, Folie depicts a world in which society has been overrun by brutal professionals who see poets as threats and rivals, and the writer has been exiled from the public sphere. Each of the novellas in this trilogy revolves around the impotence and degradation suffered by characters who hope to be writers and heroic actors but are condemned to almost complete failure in their attempts. In all three sections, these aspiring literary intellectuals come into conflict with a militarized secret police supported by complicit doctors, lawyers, and government functionaries. The solidarity between sensitive writers and the folk hoped for by the anticolonial generation has been replaced by a different set of alliances between segments of the middle and lower classes.

The trilogy begins in 1939 and frequently flashes back to earlier periods. Critics have emphasized how despite this earlier setting, the trilogy is meant most directly to reflect on the Duvalier regime: Dayan states that "dates do not matter for the story is the same: blacks and mulattoes fight it out in Port-au-Prince, and the peasants continue to suffer. . . . What begins as the most personal of memoirs ends up a chronicle of Haiti as Duvalier consolidates his totalitarian state" ("Reading Women" 234). While the connection to Duvalier is undeniable, the dates do matter. A major effect of drawing the connection between 1939 and Chauvet's present is to call attention to the postcoloniality of her context: the trilogy emphasizes the ways in which 1939 is the aftermath of the U.S. occupation, which ended in 1934, and that the hopelessness of the present comes out of the crisis of the antioccupation nationalism expressed in many of the flashbacks. The first narrator's memories of her father are of fiery anticolonial declarations: "These great powers call us incompetent: they insinuate themselves into our affairs, demand control of our customhouses and, like jackals, fight over our very hides. I am a patriot, a nationalist, and I will defend what I believe to be the national interest until my dying breath" (Chauvet, *Love* 87–88). Part of this narrator's inability to attach her writing project to a broader social context or political movement comes from a new context in which anticolonial opposition has lost its force. At the same time, the father's patriotism is also xenophobia; just before the U.S. occupation, he applauds the expulsion of Syrians from the country because, as he puts it, "the foreigner has invaded our country" (87). In mourning as well as critiquing the discourse of anticolonial nationalism, *Amour, Colère, Folie* stands at the beginning of the tradition of postcolonial writing that I return to in my conclusion.

The first part of the trilogy, "Amour," is narrated as the diary of its main character, Claire. Claire is a literary intellectual aspiring to make her writing matter: she begins her diary by proclaiming that "my wits were asleep and I have stirred them—with this journal" (4). In connecting the process of writing to an awakening of consciousness similar to what Minette undergoes in *La danse sur le volcan*, Claire echoes the anticolonial ideology of the literary's crucial role in decolonizing the mind. Yet rather than a record of the world around her or her efforts to transform that world, the diary initially revolves around her sexual fantasies and imagined encounters with her brother-in-law. As in all three installments of the trilogy, space in "Amour" is rigidly demarcated between the privacy of the home where Claire spends virtually all of the narrative and the public streets dominated by madmen and prostitutes (38). Diary writing embodies this divide, becoming an intensely private activity conducted while alone in her room and never intended for an audience. As a representative of the formerly landed elite, Clair appears to be interested in writing purely for its own sake and acknowledges that her fear of helping others comes from the same "bourgeois upbringing" that drives her to write (117). She doubts the possibility of "stick[ing] together," realizing that "the idea" that she is "set apart and original, pleases me" (127).

Even more dramatic than the opposition between Minette as spokesperson and the unruly counterpublic in need of guidance seen in *La danse sur le volcan*, Claire's journal retreats into the personal while depicting "terrifying crowds" that she dreams about enacting violence upon her (120). Claire's fear and distrust of the people outside highlight how her literary activity has become detached from any social movement. In this dream, the crowd cheers as Claire is penetrated and beheaded by Calédu, the commandant connected to the U.S. business interests exploiting the town. Calédu is not only associated with the crowd through this dream, he is a representative of the new alliance in which black "upstarts" (30) given uniforms now have power over Claire's class. Calédu is explicitly hostile to the literary intellectuals: the novel describes him "rounding up the poets" (44) and later arresting those who attend literary meetings (124). The sensitive and appropriately surnamed writer Jacques Marti is the first victim of the regime as he protests against Calédu's absolutism, and his brother Joel is forced into virtual silence as a result of this terror. The hostility of this technocrat to the literary is explained in a conversation between Claire's brother-in-law and doctor as a combination of race and class resentment, played out in his violation of women's bodies: "Jacques Marti's murder, the arrest of the poets, the arrest of the grocer, all reveal the excessive zeal of a soldier hoping to attract the attention of his superiors and earn distinction. But the torture inflicted on a certain category of women conceals something else" (118).

In fact, the primary conflict in "Amour" between the writer and the professional class is explicitly gendered: Claire refers to her town as a "dreary graveyard where you see few men besides the doctor, the pharmacist, the priest, the district commandant, the mayor, the prefect" (4). The professional men of the town have no understanding of the literary: Claire visits the prefect's home and remarks that while he maintains an impressive library, "one gets the feeling that they are sitting there for show" (122). Claire, like Bita in *Banana Bottom*, sees government functionaries using books only as a marker of social status and suspects "they have never been opened" (122). Calédu is only the most overtly villainous of these professional men; there are also the "doctors who are exploiting the situation" by selling bills of clean health to Haitian peasants seeking work in the Dominican Republic (131), or even the silent complicity of Dr. Audier in "know[ing] when to keep quiet and to keep the full range of [his] thoughts to [him]self" about the atrocities committed by government agents (44).

The one man who appears to resist both this instrumentality and this silencing is Claire's brother-in-law, the white Frenchman Jean Luze. He is a true man of letters able to bridge both sides of this divide, an accountant who can "talk about music and literature" with the poets who visit (123–124). Whereas the political and the literary have become split off from one another in the other characters, Jean Luze's ability to combine these vocations leads him to repeatedly urge the writers as well as the professionals "to protest, respond to this with a demonstration, face the danger together. . . . Let one person here lead an uprising and the other side will tremble" (42). This sustained faith in the possibility of standing up to Calédu, the government, and U.S. economic interests makes Jean Luze an "idealist" (126). It is no coincidence that this man who represents a throwback to the idea that the intellectual can matter in the political sphere becomes the object of obsession for Claire. But while he may urge action, he also believes that "it's none of my business. It's not up to me to stand up to your district commandant. This is your home, not mine" (42). The presence of this Frenchman in "Amour" only emphasizes that the identity of literary intellectual, so crucial to the anticolonial writer, appears impossible for any Haitian to inhabit in the world of "Amour."

Along with Claire's sexual fantasies focusing on Jean Luze, she becomes equally fascinated with Calédu, as she seeks out stories of the terrible violence that he enacts on other woman of her class. Calédu becomes the man of action that Jean Luze cannot be. With the idea of the literary intellectual as revolutionary opposition an anachronistic impossibility—connected only to women and feminized men—the ability to act appears to be entirely in the hands of the bureaucratic functionary. Writing in this world has become almost entirely separated off from action and the social. In the end, though, Claire does finally take action, leaving the safety of her house to enter public space and stab Calédu in the midst of an uprising (155). This final act of violence that closes "Amour" is hardly treated as heroic, with Claire retreating back into her house "contemplating this blood on my hands, this blood on my robe, this blood on the dagger" (156). The only action possible has become participation in the violence around her.

Claire thus overcomes her paralysis brought on by the gendered division of public action and private contemplation structuring the world of "Amour": Calédu's monopoly of force is broken as new alliances between Claire as writer and the people become possible. But as the trilogy continues, the possibility of effective ethical opposition appears increasingly remote as the divisions such as mind/body, poetry/action, and complicity/resistance—each paralleling the private/public divide—become even more entrenched. In "Colère," the focalizing role played by Claire in the first novella has now been divided among the various members of the family attempting to oppose the seizure of their farm by the ominous uniformed "men in black" (159). Claire ends "Amour" by finally becoming the female equivalent of Jean Luze, a woman of action who no longer writes in isolation but enters the public domain and commits an (albeit ambivalently treated) revolutionary act; in "Colère," action and contemplation become divided between the two main characters, Rose and Paul, each of whom narrates part of the novella. Chauvet reverses the normal gendered associations between these activities: Rose takes action in deciding to give her body to the leader of the men in black in return for a promise that the family's land will be returned, while Paul becomes obsessed with killing this "Gorilla" (261) and saving Rose from his sexual predations, but can only express that desire through unending discourse about his own impotence to act.

By describing in painful detail the sexual violence committed against Rose, the narrative challenges the reader who wants to see Rose's sacrifice on behalf of the family as heroic. On the one hand, Rose feels a certain power in her sexuality: she asks her brother if he knows "what could happen to [him] without my ass-wiggling?" (170). Her actions in some way succeed: Rose is convinced that after the contracted month of sexual exchange is over, her family will retain the land, and she and her brother will be able to use the money from its sale to be educated abroad. Her family benefits in other unforeseen ways as well: her relationship with such a powerful person gives Paul prestige among the other young men who want to join the Blackshirts (254), while her father finds himself "becoming, despite everything, a power broker" as de facto father-in-law to the Gorilla. On the other hand, Rose has only a very limited ability to mitigate her family's suffering and finds her own "submissiveness . . . nauseating" (250). Through forcing the reader to face a first-hand account of Rose's violation—"he rammed himself into me in one rough terrible thrust, and immediately groaned with pleasure" (244)—Chauvet refuses to allow Rose's decisions to remain abstract. Rose takes action and gains some control of her situation, but only within parameters established by the powerful men around her.

Within the family, the mother sympathizes with Rose's decision, while her husband and son can only see Rose as a victim in need of their redemption. Like the men in the family, the mother determines to take action to help her daughter, that "nothing would stop her from doing something, even if it kills her" (225); but as she goes outside and sees "hundreds of thousands of men . . . yelling in unison: 'Hail to the chief of the Blackshirts'" (226), she realizes the futility of her situation. Resigned that she has "failed" in her role as mother to "help [her children] conquer their terror" (228), she also wonders if perhaps she is fulfilling a different motherly role in staying alive: "to attempt again what she had done today, wasn't that, in truth, giving in to the pride of a death justified by them and by her? Should she run straight into suicide, cut short the days she had left?" (228). It is in the context of this fuller understanding of the possibilities available to her that the mother argues with Paul: "what right do I have to judge my daughter when she shows more courage than I do?" (218).

The men of "Colère" cannot come to terms with this world: they insist that they want to act, but can only imagine action as heroic opposition and not the complicit action of Rose or the resigned survival of the mother. Rose recognizes the challenges to masculinity presented by this context: "Grandfather's sterile rebellion, Paul's mute despair, my mother's terror, my father's horrible, humiliating situation, are all reasons to fight. Of all of us, my father suffers the most. Head of the family, the man still responsible for the honor and the future of his children, forced to bow and scrape and kiss the feet of his torturers" (248). Paul, who believes "it's a brother's job to look after his sister" (239), agrees with Rose's assessment, wishing he could join the Blackshirts to have power over "the impotent ones like my father" (238). Despite his aspirations, though, Paul spends most of "Colère" brooding, Hamlet-like, over his inability to play the savior to his sister, blaming his own "self that likes books" for being "soft" (238). His plans to kill the Gorilla are only intellectual fantasies of power; when actually confronted with the reality of killing, Paul finds himself less than a man, wishing "if only I had a gun" that would fulfill his phallic needs (275). The father finally does take action to save Rose, setting up the Gorilla to be killed by one of his henchmen. He uses the family land to compensate this assassin, and the plan works; unfortunately, the ensuing violent chaos leads to the death of the grandfather, grandson, and Rose. In the end, the father's actions result in the loss of the family land and the death of the daughter he sought to save.

In "Amour," Dr. Audier describes the issue of violence toward women as "conceal[ing] something else" (118); he and the other men of "Amour" emphasize the racial and class dynamics of Calédu's torture of upper-class women to show how his violence is a symbolic attack on the group they represent. The violation thus becomes symbol for a struggle between men, as in the anticolonial nationalist idealization of the woman as the land facing symbolic rape from a foreign power. Critics like Dayan, Scharfman, and Chancy argue persuasively that the trilogy as a whole shows the troubling consequence of this formulation: as

Chancy puts it, "Chauvet, unlike her male counterparts, refused to col-
lapse her female character's violations with metaphoric 'rapes' of the nation" (309). The treatment of Rose's body in "Colère," along with the
responses of her father and brother, explicitly invokes the collapsing of
the woman's body and the land so frequently deployed by anticolonialists like Martí and Roumain, with rape acting as the most visceral description of unwanted foreign intervention in the nation demanding the
male writer's redemption of the endangered motherland. Despite the desire of father and brother to inhabit the identity of man of action and
redeem Rose, "Colère" forces the reader to face the possibility that such
redemption may be not only impossible but another form of silencing
and violence as well.

"Colère" thus challenges Paul's idea of himself as intellectual man of
action: in fact, Rose's decidedly unheroic decision to allow her own exploitation turns out to be far more effective than outright opposition to
those in power. As in the trilogy as a whole, the conflict hinges on the
sensitive, literary family—the grandfather who appears in the novella is
marked by his storytelling, while the mother's father was "a poor failed
artist" who drank himself to death (Chauvet, *Love* 178)—up against
the Blackshirts aligned with professionals like the lawyer who brokers
Rose's sexual servitude. In the last section of the trilogy, "Folie," this
conflict becomes most overt, as the novella revolves around four poets
trapped in a room together with the forces of repression and dictatorship
just outside of their door. They can no longer write, and they can no longer intervene in the world around them. "Folie" shows a total inability
of writing and meaningful action to be united and represents the final
alienation and expulsion of writers from the postcolonial public sphere.

The crisis of authority faced by the writers in "Folie" leads Michael
Dash to focus especially on this section of the trilogy to make his case
for Chauvet's postmodernism: for Dash, "Folie" is a condemnation of
"literary commitment" embodied in "the ideal of the paternal creator,"
showing the arrogance as well the "impotence" of these "modernist
myths" (*Other America* 112). This last part of Chauvet's trilogy certainly does present the culmination of the crisis of the author as heroic
man of action. Even more than Claire in "Amour" or Rose and Paul
in "Colère," the poets from "Folie" appear delusional in their longing
to matter and reclaim "all the glory of our forebears" (Chauvet, *Love*
289). Yet Dash's suggestion that Chauvet welcomes the end of the heroic
idea of the writer—that she means to "assault . . . literary modernism in
the Caribbean" (*Other America* 110) through a carnivalesque celebra-

tion of the literary intellectual's downfall—discounts the conflicted perspective *Amour, Colère, Folie* takes toward the end of literary anticolonialism. "Folie" does parody the poet's self-centered desire to lead the people, even as it allows René to be self-reflective about the question of "when did I leave the common people behind" (Chauvet, *Love* 322). In emphasizing historicity in this way—the sense that a time of literature's connection to the public is something lost—"Folie" becomes less a condemnation of literary commitment than a melancholic depiction of its exhaustion. The novella gives the reader no "outside" from which a critique of the ideology as such could be staged; there are no other ideas of the writer or intellectual present in the text, neither the alternative peasant knowledge I discuss in chapter 7 on *testimonio* nor a turn to popular culture as in the novels I examine in chapter 8. The claustrophobia of "Folie," when placed in the context of the cautious hope for a committed artist in *La danse sur le volcan* through the ambivalent possibilities of some kind of mitigated literary identity in "Amour" and "Colère," presents an overwhelming despair that mourns anticolonial modernism more than it seeks to surmount it.

While Dash astutely identifies *Amour, Colère, Folie* narrating the crisis of the anticolonial master narrative of liberation—a crisis that defines Caribbean postcoloniality—he ends up arguing simultaneously that the Caribbean intellectual is totalitarian and impotent, too powerful and totally irrelevant. Recognizing the transitional historical context of Chauvet's text, written amid the decline of anticolonialism, shows how the conception of the writer itself is in flux within each novella. In "Folie," the authorities who order the arrest and eventual execution of the poets have the same dual view Dash articulates, fearing that writers are a threat even while knowing that they are powerless in the new context. The commandant accuses René and his friends of "inciting a mob" (363) and "inciting the crowd" (370), but within the story the poets are never in contact with anyone outside of their home (and their inability to publish their poetry is part of this failure to reach a public [290]); the doctor who oversees the torture of these prisoners recognizes the madness of this accusation, diagnosing that "these men are not in full possession of their faculties. Torturing them will be a complete waste of time" (371). The commandant's paranoia that these poets could incite the people demonstrates the persistence of the anticolonial ideal of writer as leader; but the story demonstrates that for the poets as well as the commandant, this view is delusional in light of the new postcolonial context in which aligning with a counterpublic is dissociated from mobilizing a public.

For Dash, Chauvet's trilogy not only depicts this crisis of the literary but also shows how the literary contains the seeds of the "authoritarian political culture that created the atmosphere of suspicion and terror [toward writers] in the first place" (*Other America* 113). Anticolonialism is nothing to mourn, since, as he puts it, "Chauvet has put her finger on the disturbing reality that suggests that in every intellectual there lurks the monster of all Haitian intellectuals, François Duvalier" (113). Contrary to Dash's identification of modernist writers as accessories to totalitarianism, though, Chauvet's trilogy shows these writers to be opponents and victims of state terror. Instead of seeing intellectuals as an undifferentiated group driven by a singular logic, Chauvet emphasizes different elements of the middle class, including the complicit professionals portrayed throughout the trilogy as cooperating with a fascistic state. Turning to the general transformation of the Caribbean public sphere during the 1950s and 1960s helps place Chauvet's critique of certain brands of Caribbean intellectualism, rather than the intellectual project as a whole, into its context as part of a broader conflict within the intellectual class during the transitional years from modern colonialism to postcoloniality.

Literary Sensitivity and Scientific Governance: The Postcolonial Split

After the publication and then suppression of *Amour, Colère, Folie*, Marie Chauvet left Haiti and went into exile in the United States, as the expulsion of the writer from the Caribbean public sphere took place throughout the region during the transition to postcoloniality. Duvalierism may be the most extreme case of the evacuation of the public sphere to take place in the Caribbean.[8] But other efforts to redefine the forms of power that would follow modern colonialism, whether in Trinidad and Tobago's parliamentary democracy or the revolutionary socialism of Cuba, produced a similar crisis of the public sphere. I am particularly interested in what happened to literature and the group I have been referring to as literary intellectuals in this context. Rather than seeing committed or political writing as necessarily aspiring to totalitarianism, my reading of Chauvet's own relationship to literary anticolonialism suggests that the silencing of writers might more usefully be seen as the outgrowth of the contest for leadership between the different segments of the middle class I have been describing.

The presence of these writers as a counterpublic, claiming to speak for the nation but not necessarily attached to the state, was readily seen as a threat to postcolonial states seeking to define their place in a changing global system. Literary intellectuals could join the nation-building process through ventriloquizing the folk, the testimonial solution discussed in chapter 7, or could produce culture as entertainment channeled through culture industries, as chapter 8 shows. But critique became an activity no longer viable for literature during this period, especially because of pressures from both the state and the market against this kind of writing. In the rest of this chapter, I explore how the changing place of the literary in the Caribbean public sphere can be seen through the differing trajectories of intellectuals like Eric Williams and Ernesto "Che" Guevara, on the one hand, and C. L. R. James, Heberto Padilla, and Walter Rodney, on the other. Williams and Guevara appear in some way as inheritors of the Martían ideal of the philosopher-legislator who demonstrates the privileged positioning of intellectuals in the Caribbean public sphere. But whereas modern colonialism offered opportunities for Martí, Roumain, and others to give creative writing a political function and participate in a nationalist project aligned against the colonial state, Williams and Guevara acknowledge the new terrain of postcoloniality through the ways they distance themselves from that project and identify themselves instead with the forms of professionalism and rationality discussed in chapter 4 as anathema to literary anticolonialism.

The changing relationship between Eric Williams and C. L. R. James shows how the tentative alliance of the professional and the literary becomes uncoupled as these different versions of intellectual leadership are placed into competition. From his activities with the *Beacon* group in the 1930s, to his political organizing in England and the United States in the 1940s and 1950s, James is one of the best examples of the anticolonial intellectual who united his literary and political ambitions. Eric Williams, first prime minister of Trinidad and Tobago, was also a historian whose *Capitalism and Slavery* gives an important anticolonial account of the abolition of slavery, building on James's *Black Jacobins*. During the 1950s, as independence in Trinidad and Tobago became imminent, the two formed an important alliance as Williams invited James to participate in the new People's National Movement (PNM) that was preparing to take power from the departing British. The addresses given by Williams and James in the central square of Port of Spain earned that public space the nickname "the University of Woodford Square" for the national consciousness-raising function of their speeches. The relationship soured in 1960, when James resigned from his editorship at the PNM's main publication, the *Nation*, because of what he perceived as

Williams's capitulation to neocolonialism in allowing the United States to keep a military base in Trinidad and Tobago. James was expelled from the PNM, had the publication of a collection of his lectures suppressed, and left Trinidad and Tobago in 1961. When he returned in 1965, he was placed immediately under house arrest. Released after six weeks and "galvanized into action against the PNM" (Oxaal 182), James tried to establish an alternative Worker's and Farmer's Party to run against Williams, was beaten easily in that year's elections, and left the country in frustration.[9] The intellectual inspiration for Trinidad and Tobago's independence, James found himself unwelcome in the postcolonial nation-state.

While part of the rivalry between James and Williams may have been personal, accounts of their disagreements sometimes point to the different conceptions of history presented in James's *Black Jacobins* and Williams's *Capitalism and Slavery* as part of the incompatibility of their worldviews. Anthony Maingot credits the difference to Williams's "ongoing concern . . . not with voluntaristic revolutionary actions but with the shifts in elite behaviour caused by economic changes. Policy, said Williams, shifts as economic interests change. . . . That was not James's central concern. James was concerned with the masses and their leaders. . . . Distinct from the strict materialist interpretations of Williams, James's conception was more voluntaristic" (149). Williams saw history as a science driven by economics while James focused on the role of mass movements and leaders in bringing about change: thus Williams's view of history is more "mechanistic and deterministic" (158) because his "orthodox Marxist models . . . reflected his academic, non-involved— perhaps even distant—approach to radical historiography" (150). Ivar Oxaal sees the same difference in Williams's argument that "slavery was abolished because it happened to have been in the interest of the most powerful economic faction in the British ruling class" versus James's view that "the ascendancy of the industrial interests were only a necessary *precondition* for the abolition of slavery, the root cause of which was not to be found in the interests of the strong, but in the revolt of the weak" (74–75). Oxaal suggests that how James and Williams understood history led them to their different career paths: "Williams would become a respectable and expert social science technician, an administrator close to the center of West Indian decision-making" as opposed to "the intellectual role James pursued" (76).

I would call this distinction between James and Williams the difference between the literary intellectual and the technocrat. In other writings and speeches, James and Williams even more explicitly articulate opposing self-definitions and ideas about intellectuals. James's *Mariners, Renegades and Castaways*, published in 1953, uses a reading of Herman Melville's *Moby Dick* to meditate on the place of the intellectual in the wake of Hitler, Stalin, and James's own experience being held at Ellis Island as he awaited deportation from the United States during the McCarthy purges. In the reading of *Moby Dick* James presents, "the three American officers represent the most competent technological knowledge, brains and leadership" while "the harpooners and the crew are the ordinary people of the world" (19). While Ahab is thus the totalitarian leader, the villains of the story, according to James, are the complicit bureaucrats and professionals who become the tools that allow the state to manage the nation: "In Russia by 1928, from a revolution, exhausted and desperate, and seeing in the world around it no gleam of hope, arose the same social type as the Nazis—administrators, executives, organizers, labor leaders, intellectuals. Their primary aim is not world revolution. They wish to build factories and power stations larger than all others. . . . Their primary aim is not war. It is not dictatorship. It is the Plan" (14). James goes on to identify "the problem" (14) of our "modern world" (19) as this tendency toward "abstract intellect, abstract science, abstract technology, alive, but blank, serving no human purpose but merely the abstract purpose itself" (15).

Ishmael, as "one of those dreamy young men of education and intellect who cannot live in the world" (40), stands apart from the officers in terms of education and sensibility; he is not the implement of instrumental reason like Starbuck or Tashtego. Instead, Ishmael "is a completely modern young intellectual . . . enclosed in the solitude of his social and intellectual speculation" (40–41). Yet James observes that this potential "literary intellectual"—a term James uses a number of times in the book to describe both Melville's characters and Melville himself—is more obedient to Ahab than any other member of the crew. Ishmael participates in the totalitarian project precisely because it gives him a purpose and offers an antidote to his separation from the natural world and the community of the crew. According to James's reading of Melville's work, the tragedy of his times is both the siding of the technical class with totalitarianism as well as the failure of literary intellectuals to forge a bond with the workers who are the most acute victims of state domination. Later in the book, James lays this out directly through a reading of Melville's novel *Pierre*, and the relationship of the protagonist and the dark and mysterious Isabel. James argues that "Pierre is a literary intellectual. His one chance is to commit himself completely to this immigrant girl. . . . And Pierre cannot do it" (101). *Mariners, Renegades and Castaways* is a lament for the impossibility of this type of solidarity, as well as a clarion call to intellectuals to steer away from the twin temptations of either serving power or withdrawing from everyday life.

While James thus defines intellectualism as opposition to the state and alliance with the nation as counterpublic, Williams interprets the same opposition in a different way. Williams's valuing of technical knowledge moves him away from literary resistance to instrumentality. In a 1958 speech convening the third annual convention of the PNM, Williams emphasizes the importance of "the establishment of the Party Forum, the University of Woodford Square" (Cudjoe, *Eric E. Williams Speaks* 208). In placing the creation of a public sphere alongside the establishment of an elective government and a nationalist political party as the three "miracles" achieved by the PNM, Williams appears to be following the anticolonial script that we see in the next chapter in George Lamming's equating of the West Indian novel with abolition and independence.[10] But the way in which Williams conceives this public sphere sets him at odds with literary intellectuals like James: "Through this forum it has brought political education to the people of the West Indies and introduced a new technique of cold intellectual political analysis based on reasoning and facts as against the empty emotionalism of the past" (208). The opposition to emotion and the emphasis on technique, fact-based analysis, and reason place Williams in stark contrast to the ideals of the sensitive and imaginative literary intellectual. By the time Williams opposes the Black Power revolutions in 1970, he will be criticizing "romantic anarchists of the 'New Left'" who "would carry popularism to insane lengths and be blind to the need for the exercise of leadership" (284); Williams instead emphasizes the vanguardist "role of the party" that shows "the importance of professional training" (314).

The changes in state attitudes and policies toward literary intellectuals like James is reflected throughout the region during this period, most famously in Cuba with the censorship of the film *PM* in 1961 and then with the Padilla affair in 1971.[11] Looking briefly at the intellectual architecture of the Cuban Revolution through the speeches of Che Guevara demonstrates how the conflict between the ideals associated with the literary and those of the technocratic class underlies the changing ideas about the place of literary intellectuals in the public sphere. Guevara addresses the issue of his own background as a medical doctor and member of the professional class in his "Speech to Medical Students and

Health Workers" made just over a year after Fulgencio Batista's expulsion and the triumph of the Cuban Revolution. He sets out to describe what it might mean to be a "revolutionary doctor, that is, a person who puts the technical knowledge of his profession at the service of the revolution and of the people" (113). In this early speech, he uses a story to narrate the need to throw off the technocratic belief that professional knowledge grants power and to stake out allegiance with the literary intellectual ideal of learning from the people:

> None of us, none of the first group that arrived in the *Granma*, who established ourselves in the Sierra Maestra, and who learned to respect the peasant and the worker, living together with him—none of us had a past as a worker or peasant. . . . We, who at the beginning severely punished anyone who touched even an egg of some rich peasant or some landowner, one day took 10,000 head of cattle to the Sierra and told the peasants simply: "Eat." And the peasants, for the first time in many years, and some for the first time in their lives, ate beef. The respect we had for the sacrosanct property of those 10,000 head of cattle was lost in the course of the armed struggle, and we learned perfectly that the life of a single human being is worth millions of times more than all the property of the richest man on earth. (116–117)

The key to leadership is thus knowledge—"a revolutionary must also know the people" (115)—but specifically a knowledge acquired through living among, studying, and listening to the people meant to be governed: Guevara urges the medical students that they can become revolutionaries through "not only visiting these places [where the peasantry lives], but also getting to know the people" (115). Being sensitive enough to listen to the people, a crucial aspect of the literary intellectual's identity as I discussed in chapter 3, is here also Guevara's ideal of good government.

Such continuity, however, does not mean that persecution of the writer was necessarily embedded in literary anticolonialism; Aimé Césaire's explanation cited in chapter 4 of his need to create a political identity distinct from that of the literary intellectual, for example, suggests that the practice of politics sometimes required him to act against, rather than in fulfillment of, the ideas articulated in his art. When Guevara returns to these issues in his 1965 letter published as "El Socialismo y el Hombre en Cuba," he has moved toward the idea that specialized knowledge attained through scientific study of historical processes is what grants the vanguard authority to lead the nation. When the letter discusses the armed struggle against the Batista dictatorship, there are not firsthand stories about learning from the people but instead objective descriptions of "the first heroic period . . . in which combatants competed for the heaviest responsibilities, for the greatest dangers, with no other satisfaction than fulfilling a duty" (Guevara, "Socialism" 213). The vanguard becomes a group of functionaries who "must combine a passionate spirit with a cold intelligence and make painful decisions without flinching" (226). The sympathy and sensitivity to humanity learned from living among the peasantry that Guevara's earlier speech described give way now to the type of emotionless calculation Williams mentions in his speech. The literary intellectual's idea of listening to and learning from the people is less important in Guevara's letter than understanding "the invisible laws of capitalism" (215); the problem of pedagogy now seems to run only one way, where "the initiative generally comes from Fidel," while "the mass carries out with matchless enthusiasm and discipline the tasks set by the government" (214). Guevara opposes this ideal of technocratic knowledge to the inadequacy of literary modes of thought. In calling for the "institutionalization of the revolution" through "a harmonious set of channels, steps, restraints and well-oiled mechanisms which facilitate the advance" of the masses (219), he advocates "the need for technical and ideological education" to bring about more "standardization" of the individual (220). Art is seen as an inferior attempt to address precisely the problematic the revolution is meant to solve, undertaken by "individuals . . . trying to free themselves from alienation through culture" (221). As opposed to these "aesthetic" attempts to address alienation (222), Guevara makes a case for the technocratic vanguard as "the right instrument" for the task (217). The shift from Guevara's 1960 speech to his 1965 letter thus provides a context for how literary intellectuals could come to be seen as competitors with the fulfillment of the revolution. The 1971 Padilla affair, where Cuban poet Heberto Padilla was arrested and imprisoned for supposedly counterrevolutionary activities, becomes the end point of this conflict between different types of intellectuals within the revolution.[12]

A similar story plays out throughout the Caribbean in the 1960s and 1970s. In 1968, historian Walter Rodney, the West Indies' central theorist of the fusion of theory and practice in the figure of the "guerrilla intellectual,"[13] returns to Jamaica from a conference abroad only to be refused reentry to the country and relieved of his post at the University of the West Indies. In Guyana in 1969, poet Martin Carter resigns as a minister in Forbes Burnham's government and becomes the target of violent attacks. In the wake of the Padilla affair, major intellectuals like Antonio Benítez-Rojo and René Depestre, once supporters and partici-

pants in the revolution, leave Cuba amid government pressure and persecution. The persecution of intellectuals grew more severe throughout
the decade, with the politically motivated murders of Rodney in 1980
by Forbes Burnham's government in Guyana, of Puerto Rican novelist
Pedro Juan Soto's son in Cerro Maravilla in 1978, and of poet Mikey
Smith after a political rally in Jamaica in 1983. The decade ends with the
Mariel exodus in 1980 as writers like Reinaldo Arenas leave Cuba, along
with the U.S. invasion of Grenada in 1983, marking an end to the decolonization era and effectively excluding literary intellectuals from the
governing of postcolonial Caribbean nations. The position of the Caribbean writer in the transition from modern colonialism to postcoloniality had not been as precarious since the times of slavery; literature had
officially been exiled from the Caribbean public sphere. In the midst of
this transformation of the public sphere, Caribbean writers were forced
to renegotiate their positioning and reimagine the role for literature and
the writer. The next chapter turns to the work of George Lamming and
Martin Carter as two examples of how committed Caribbean writers
sought to come to terms with the crisis of anticolonialism.

6 Anticolonial Authority and the Postcolonial Occasion for Speaking

George Lamming and Martin Carter

THE DISMANTLING OF THE COLONIAL SYSTEM and the emerging dominance of the postcolonial in the decades following World War II mark a major passage in Caribbean literary history. Chapter 5 described the dangers facing literary intellectuals as their alignment with a counterpublic became identified as incompatible with national consolidation during the 1950s and 1960s. At the same time, many of the writers associated with anticolonial nationalism began to question their own participation in the bourgeois public sphere they had helped to establish. Chapters 7 and 8 look at how *testimonio* and Caribbean cultural studies emerge from this rethinking. This chapter focuses on George Lamming and Martin Carter, two of the most prominent writers of the West Indian literary renaissance of the 1950s, to examine how they positioned themselves and their writing in relation to colonial power and the decolonization struggles. Associating their work with anticolonialism gave their writing a legitimate voice in the Caribbean public sphere, and allowed them to unite the dissociated activities of art and action just as José Martí and Jacques Roumain had. Yet Lamming and Carter press at the limits of the public sphere those writers helped to create, seeing its attachment to the literary as a form of exclusion. Uncertain how to forge a new heroic literary project, these authors reveal how their confidence in the authority of their own literary discourse increasingly wavers, even as they point the way to how a new, postcolonial Caribbean literature might find an occasion for speaking.

The biographies of these two giants of Caribbean anticolonial writing show remarkable parallels. Carter and Lamming were both born in British colonies in 1927, Carter in British Guiana (now Guyana) and Lamming in Barbados. Both began their careers by publishing poetry in local journals in the late 1940s, and then brought out major books in the early 1950s: Carter's poetry collection *The Hill of Fire Glows Red* in 1951, and Lamming's novel *In the Castle of My Skin* in 1953. Both authors published prolifically during the 1950s,[1] and collaborated on the 1966 *New World Quarterly* issue commemorating Guyanese independence.[2] Their literary production slowed considerably during the 1960s and 1970s,[3] though, and in Lamming's case ended completely with the publication of *Natives of My Person* in 1971. Although Carter lived until 1997, and Lamming is still alive, neither author published any major new creative work after Carter's 1980 collection *Poems of Affinity*.

Why did Lamming and Carter stop publishing literary work after such promising beginnings? In Lamming's case, the standard response of Caribbean critics has been that exile eventually took a toll on him, and that extended separation from his homeland drained him of the organic connection to his people that energized his earliest work.[4] For Carter, critics point to precisely the opposite circumstances for his increasing withdrawal from literature: Gemma Robinson notes the standard views, that Carter's lack of access to metropolitan "publishing contracts" (44) and his growing cynicism toward his homeland's "philistinism" (53) made it impossible for him to continue writing.[5] These kinds of readings position Carter and Lamming at opposite ends of the field of possibilities available to Caribbean writers—to stay or to go—with both paths appearing to be equally futile. Yet Caribbean writers from this period, both at home and abroad, did continue to write; looking solely at their location thus inadequately explains the trajectories of Lamming and Carter.[6] Instead of focusing on their geographic locale, I examine the many affinities in the kind of space staked out by Lamming and Carter within a shifting Caribbean public sphere.

I argue that the passage from colonialism to postcoloniality, and its impact on the Caribbean literary field during these years, challenged politically committed writers like Lamming and Carter with a new world to which their literary discourse could not entirely adapt.[7] During the modern colonial period, a particular configuration of literature and politics became privileged, in which literature derived its authority from positioning itself as speaking for both a Caribbean national public and a counterpublic of resistance. The social, political, and economic upheaval at the end of the colonial period—decolonization in the British islands, the Cuban Revolution, changes in status in the French islands and Puerto Rico, the intensifying penetration of North American culture in the form of audio and visual media, the opening up of the Caribbean public sphere to more black and female voices than ever before, urbanization, and massive migrations from the country to the city—worked to undermine the configuration of power and authority that had supported the literary field during the colonial period. As colonialism gave way to postcoloniality, an ideology of the literary that emphasized marginality and opposition found it increasingly difficult to participate in consolidation. Some writers, like the Spiralists in Haiti, withdrew even further into the aesthetic; others, like V. S. Naipaul, chose to position their writing against regional politics.[8] While Lamming and Carter refused to give up on political commitment, their choices resemble Aimé Césaire's decision to discontinue *Tropiques* and seek electoral office. As their rate of publication slowed, Lamming and Carter focused more on giving public lectures, writing speeches for political leaders, and, in Carter's case, even occupying ministerial positions.[9] No longer able to fuse the political and the literary, Lamming and Carter move away from literature to pursue politics by other means.

George Lamming and the Anticolonial Challenge

Much of Lamming's writing can be seen as an attempt to bridge the division between literary activity and political leadership in order to imagine a public role for literature within the Caribbean. Lamming's earliest novel, *In the Castle of My Skin*, is especially marked by this tension. The young narrator, G., writes, but as a purely personal activity: he looks back at one diary entry that describes how "when the year ends and a new year begins I make the same promises, above all to keep a diary. . . . I put the notes away on the shelf and they are never heard of again except someone rescues them from the garbage" (288). Without a public, G. can imagine no reason for writing. Only in the final pages of the novel does his friend Trumper, returned from the United States, begin to hint at the sort of change of consciousness that could give the writer a voice in public. In the passage that gives the novel its title, G. remarks that "when I reach Trinidad where no one knows me I may be able to strike identity with the other person"; in Barbados, that potential for community has been impossible as he has refused to let others know "the you that's hidden somewhere in the castle of your skin" (291). But Trumper insists that his experience of racial consciousness in the United States has taught him that he belongs to a people, and that "a man who knows his people won't ever feel like that" (338). Trumper explicitly connects G.'s lack of consciousness to an inaccurate view of public and private activities: "'I know a man in the states wus like that,' he said. 'He had one funny theory 'bout politics. Said you should leave politics to certain people, 'cause there wus other things to worry 'bout. He had a kind o' theory that the politics only belong to one place and that politicians couldn't do much for the real man. Says the politics has to do with one external relations. . . . They didn't have nothin' to do with people like you an' me and he an' she'" (329). *In the Castle of My Skin* thus ends with a case for seeing politics as internal to every activity, as what gives meaning and authority to even the literary. Lamming's novels of the 1950s develop this idea of the literary as integrally connected to the political. His nonfiction essay collection *The Pleasures of Exile* is in many ways a culmination of this ideology; yet I want to examine it in close detail to show how it is also a transitional text that contains not only one of the region's fullest elaborations of anticolonial ideas about literature but also shows the onset of a crisis of confidence in literary anticolonialism.

The Pleasures of Exile collects ten essays Lamming wrote during the 1950s while he was in residence in England. The chapters vary from the literary criticism of Shakespeare in "A Monster, A Child, A Slave" to the fragmentary travel journal in "The African Presence." For the most part, the book is a description of the old order, the institutions of a colonial literary field, along with prescriptions for how the Caribbean writer can carve out an anticolonial role within that public sphere. The first half of *The Pleasures of Exile* delineates the structures of this field, particularly in the two pivotal essays "The Occasion for Speaking" and "Ways of Seeing," both of which have become canonical essays of Caribbean and postcolonial thought.[10] These essays explain the conditions that lead the West Indian writer to seek consecration in England, especially through institutions such as the BBC, its *Caribbean Voices* program, and the Institute of Contemporary Arts (ICA) in London.[11] While significant commentaries have been written about *The Pleasures of Exile*, nearly all of this criticism focuses exclusively on Lamming's descriptions of the anticolonial Caribbean literary field, in his discussions of the three intersecting figures of Caliban, C. L. R. James, and Toussaint Louverture.[12] Critics have scarcely discussed the ways in which *The Pleasures of Exile* begins to explore another set of questions. The role of the anticolonial writer, according to Lamming, is to rewrite cultural narratives such as *The Tempest*, which have been the basis for political and economic exploitation; but if, as Lamming realizes, Britain is relinquishing its political grip on the region and literature is becoming less and less the primary medium of cultural domination, what does that mean for the Caribbean writer?

Lamming enters a field configured such that even while in their native land, writers "are made to feel a sense of exile by our inadequacy and our irrelevance of function" ("Pleasures" 24). He sees no role for himself in his own society because it cannot legitimate him. While a bourgeois public sphere may exist in the islands, within it the creative writer feels alienation; Lamming explains how in the colonies his occupation immediately distances him from the majority of his countrymen and women, who either have "no connection whatever to literature since they were too poor or too tired to read" or belong to a literate middle class "educated, it seemed, for the specific purpose of sneering at anything which grew or was made on native soil" (40). With little local support or prospects of local readership, the young author looks abroad for potential sites where his writing will be legitimated. His choice to emigrate to England begins, he admits, "with the fact of England's supremacy in taste and judgment" (27). Only with this outside approval can Lamming hope to reach a wide local audience through the colonial schools or be accepted by the colonial elite with a taste for English cultural goods. Lamming talks about the process of becoming a writer and establishing himself in the English literary field in surprisingly straightforward economic terms: he writes that "the West Indian's education was imported in much the same way that flour and butter are imported from Canada," then goes on to call British literature a "commodity" and speaks of "England's export of literature" to the colonies (27). This nakedly economic understanding of cultural production and exchange would have been quite at odds with the dominant Anglo-American literary criticism of the time, the aestheticism of New Criticism and its almost exclusive concern with form and beauty. Perhaps because of his own marginality to the cultural field, Lamming understands the process by which he has become a writer as a struggle to have his talents acknowledged by those with the culturally recognized power of consecration.

In the hopes of reaching a public sphere that *can* authorize his work, Lamming is forced to submit to the rules of the British establishment. Caribbean writing of this time period is encouraged and evaluated in England by reviewers like Kingsley Amis (28) and organizations such as the BBC (44–45). Lamming relates a story about attending a poetry reading at the ICA. He is one of the young poets reading there that night; without a published book as a form of consecrated symbolic capital, it is difficult for the young writer to establish himself, for "a writer without a book is like a cowboy without his horse and pistols" (59). In light of this emasculation, the cowboy deploys other weapons: one young poet reads a poem that "was interpreted by some important poets as an unjust attack upon the greatest and most important of them all: an attack on Mr. T. S. Eliot" (63). This young poet, without the "weapon" of "reputation" (60), forces the literary establishment to acknowledge him, if only to parry his attack, by showing his mastery of their tradition: "he had no horse, but it seemed he owned pistols which were loaded" (63). He cannot be ignored, because he bears precisely the cultural capital valued by the most respected members of the field.

While this unknown poet attacks the field's most venerated tradition, he in fact reinforces its authority by accepting the rules of the game, which dictate the form that his challenge must take. Lamming, as a colonial, possesses the same cultural capital as the English poet; he later notes that no one knows English culture like a colonial, explaining of C. L. R. James, "we can understand why James—once the child of a Victorian classroom—can quote Thackeray for pages" (153). With this cultural capital, Lamming could make the same play for legitimation that he watches the young poet make. In fact, he does just this in rereading *The Tempest*: Lamming is showing his feel for the rules of a game that values a critical study of Shakespeare above all else, and making a sanctioned move within those rules to force the field to account for his voice. But because he does not want to reinforce British authority and acknowledge the legitimacy of a cultural field established as part of England's colonial system of domination, he also has an interest in challenging the rules themselves, from a position outside the game.

To this end, he turns to another source of capital he possesses, his foreignness and alterity to the British literary field. As he puts it, "blasphemy must be seen as one privilege of the excluded Caliban" (9). In recounting his own experience reading a poem at the ICA, he suggests how this is one of the forms of capital the West Indian writer brings or creates for himself or herself in this colonial situation. After reading his poem, he wonders:

> Why and what made those highly contemporary intellectuals clap? . . . I am convinced that it has something to do with a way of seeing. The eyes that rejoiced down on that floor were looking up at a black man who had the audacity to make a poet's journey in public. . . . Each young poet had to sit down after he had read and wait for the examination questions. This is a most painful test. But I was spared it. Someone asked, rather shamefacedly, about the West Indies. I think this reticence might have had to do with doubt about where I had actually come from; and one can't be guilty of this kind of

ignorance in the I.C.A. . . . . The result was an impression of authority. That's why they left me alone. Duty and conscience said that the boy had done his job. (60–63)

The crowd grants Lamming the authority of alterity. His authority to speak of his own experience cannot be challenged because it depends on his place of birth and his skin color, forms of capital none of his audience possesses. Furthermore, his presence at the podium simultaneously reassures and unsettles potential interlocutors; he observes the rules of their game, yet retains the difference and distance marked by his skin color.

Yet despite this "impression of authority" that Lamming's reading earns, not engaging the young poet with questions is another way in which the British literary field contains his challenge (and Peter Hulme discusses how, in a parallel move, the field of Shakespeare studies has tried to ignore Lamming's incursion by simply not responding to it).[13] The Caribbean writer may be allowed to perform, but he still fails to enter into the critical discussion that defines the field. *The Pleasures of Exile* revolves around the question "What is the source of [the West Indian writer's] insecurity in the world of letters?" (23). The story of Lamming's experience at the ICA gives the answer: the source of this insecurity is the dependent basis of the West Indian writers' acceptance in the British literary field. Lamming offers this understanding of his own presence in that field: "Prospero doesn't mind re-marking these frontiers provided Caliban doesn't play the ass with further intrusion; provided, in other words, he doesn't ask for a new map altogether" (202). As unsettling as Lamming's successful mimicry may be to the metropolitan center, as long as he continues to observe and reinforce the authority of the center, the map of social contradictions and power relations remains intact. Put into the position of institutionalized other, Lamming finds his foray into the field emasculated by the "colonial castration of the West Indian sensibility" (49). As a writer without a literary field that values his cultural capital, he is the cowboy without a phallic gun. If there is to be a Caribbean public sphere, autonomous from Great Britain, the writer needs sources of legitimacy other than the institutions of the British literary field. As long as work is judged by British colonial standards and values, as long as this "way of seeing" remains dominant, there can be no Caribbean literary field. The writer's duty, then, is a political one, to "change this way of seeing," of English and West Indians alike, so that the Caribbean may "be released from the prison of colonialism" (36), and writers allowed to enter into a critical dialogue rather than to perform their authenticity.

In the absence of an entirely autonomous set of cultural institutions, Lamming has to imagine sources of authority outside of the British literary field to which Caribbean writers might appeal in order to justify their existence. The central chapters of *The Pleasures of Exile* lay out Lamming's solution to this situation: rather than relying on England for consecration, the proper source of authority for Caribbean writers is the anticolonial movement in the islands. These chapters tackle Shakespeare's *The Tempest* and C. L. R. James's *Black Jacobins* and *Mariners, Renegades and Castaways*. In these chapters, Lamming moves between the figure of Caliban, the figure of Toussaint Louverture, and the figure of the Caribbean writer (in particular James), in order to show the three as interchangeable. The chapter in which Lamming gives his textual analysis of *The Tempest*, "A Monster, A Child, A Slave," begins with a long epigraph from Aimé Césaire's *Cahier d'un retour au pays natal*. Césaire is one of the poets Lamming considers a descendant of Caliban who has created an "authoritative . . . new voice" (49). The challenge of Césaire and other Caribbean writers to Europe refutes "the Lie upon which Prospero's confident authority was built" (117), the myth of racial inferiority and benevolent paternalism that facilitated colonialism. More important, Césaire, the poet who belonged to the Communist Party, agitated against French colonialism, and became a mayor of Fort de France, brings together the literary and political sides of Caliban whose connection Lamming wants to emphasize.

The title of the subsequent chapter, "Caliban Orders History," contains a double meaning, which reveals most explicitly Lamming's conflation of the figure of the writer and the revolutionary. The "Caliban" of this chapter's title is ostensibly Toussaint Louverture. He is the revolutionary hero whose heroic actions managed to dictate to history the course that it would take. At the same time, Lamming's interpretation of Toussaint is filtered through C. L. R. James's *Black Jacobins*. James, the writer, gives Toussaint's story structure, ordering history through narrative. In fact, Lamming posits the Haitian Revolution as a speech act that gave voice to the silenced slaves. He notes that the slaves, as property, "were fed, kennelled, and pushed around as ploughs may be polished, transported, and stacked for safe keeping . . . in the eyes of the owners, they had no language but the labor of their hands" (120). Thus, when the revolution came, "a new word had been spoken . . . the ploughs had spoken" (125).

By equating revolution with the act of speaking the slaves' deepest desires for freedom, Lamming collapses any distinction between the West

Indian writer and those struggling for decolonization.[14] It is no coincidence that Lamming emphasizes Toussaint's ability to read (125) and write (140), and the advantages these skills gave him in organizing and carrying out his revolution. The chapter ends by placing James, Toussaint's most eloquent chronicler, squarely within Toussaint's lineage of Caribbean heroism: "It is wonderful that this epic of Toussaint's glory and his dying should have been rendered by C. L. R. James, one of the most energetic minds of our time, a neighbour of Toussaint's island, a heart and desire entirely within the tradition of Toussaint himself" (150). Lamming thus points to a tradition of struggle and armed resistance from which Caribbean writers may seek an alternative authority from the British literary field. By emphasizing their place as privileged participants in the anticolonial struggles that defined the time period in which *The Pleasures of Exile* was written, Lamming establishes an indisputably authoritative position for the writer in Caribbean society, but one that technological and geopolitical changes were already beginning to undermine.

Although the main thrust of *The Pleasures of Exile* is to offer an alternative source of authority for Caribbean writers trapped in the British literary field, at the same time, Lamming shows an awareness that the established order is shifting and that the new order may challenge the Caribbean writer's admittedly constrained occasion to speak in public. Allusions to the new order occur marginally in the text, especially in the short "interlude" chapters. For example, between the two "major" chapters, "The Occasion for Speaking" and "A Way of Seeing," Lamming inserts the short "Evidence and Example," a five-page chapter in which he describes the funeral of George VI. Elsewhere, appended to the end of "The African Presence," appears a short narrative of Lamming's travels within the United States. These episodes are universally ignored in critical discussion of *The Pleasures of Exile*, probably because of their apparently anomalous and "minor" status within the overall book, appearing as short and cryptic supplementary material. Yet these marginal moments provide the sharpest insight into the emergence of a postcolonial economic, cultural, and intellectual system, and begin to reveal the limits of Lamming's discourse in assimilating this new public sphere.

By continuing to value British taste over the U.S. market, Lamming betrays an attitude toward this new order that is deeply ambivalent. Lamming mentions the United States as a site where a writer might make his or her reputation, only to dismiss this possibility immediately, asserting that "the book had had an important critical press in England; its reputation here was substantial; so it could make no difference what America thought" (26). The United States can provide economic, not cultural, capital: "It was money I was thinking of to the exclusion of the book's critical reputation in America" (26). Lamming still consciously orients his writing toward a literary field based on English taste rather than the autonomy of the American market. When he later travels to New York as a Guggenheim fellow, Lamming is recipient of U.S. rather than British patronage. As a fellow American in the broadest sense, Lamming identifies with the United States ("since the Caribbean was only next door," he writes, "this World was, in a sense, mine" [188]); as a native of one of the United States' neighbors, he has witnessed firsthand the passage of domination in the region from Europe to North America; and as a black man, he admits to a fascination with Harlem and black America. All of these contradictory feelings toward the United States define the unevenly emerging field of Caribbean literature during the second half of the twentieth century, as writers come to terms with their ambivalent relationship to the passing of power from Britain to the United States.

In New York, Lamming for the first time describes meeting a female Caliban, an experience that encodes the ways in which the entire experience of the United States upsets his artistic equilibrium and challenges his discursive certainty. He narrates this encounter very differently from the style he uses to describe his London experiences, as if the woman's presence in the narrative disrupts his most well established devices. In the chapters of *The Pleasures of Exile* that take place in England, Lamming recounts anecdotes about Sam Selvon, Kingsley Amis, T. S. Eliot, Edgar Mittelholzer, and others he identifies by name. By contrast, he never names the Trinidadian novelist he meets in Harlem; she is called only "R." Furthermore, while he rarely wonders whether he, Selvon, and their cohort in England have been changed by their time abroad, he immediately observes of R. that "America had obviously taught her not to care too much if she was wrong" (191). He goes on to make a number of other observations about the effect the United States has had on her, comments that have no equivalent in his discussions of writers in England. It is impossible to separate whether his different approach owes to her gender or her location, both of which make her an anomaly to Lamming. If the reader assumes that these men in England have held tight to their West Indian identity, the experience of the United States appears more challenging to this essence. Furthermore, Lamming's decision to make a woman representative of the experience of West Indians working in the North American literary field has implications about what he sees as the feminization of the role of the writer in this new place.

Despite the emphasis on her difference, Lamming acknowledges that R. is "a Caliban" (191) and a writer like himself. Unlike him, though, she "was a teacher" and "had left Manhattan and gone to live way out in White Plains because a couple had asked her to take care of their dog" (192). She is working on a novel, she moves in the social circles of the "upper crust of Harlem" (190), but she does not enjoy the same privileges to which Lamming is accustomed. She finds that the U.S. literary field does not nourish the writer in the same way that London does. By using a female example to describe the process by which he comes to consciousness of changing attitudes toward writers, Lamming again emphasizes the (im)possibility of writing as a masculine and manly activity: as a writer in the United States, he mentions, "I was not seen as a professional *man* . . . ambitious and bright, perhaps, but poor" (196, emphasis added). West Indian writing in the United States appears to be a more womanly activity than in England; as the emerging center for the Caribbean cultural field, the United States threatens the Caribbean writer with a new form of emasculation via the marketplace.[15]

Like Martí's confrontation with modernity, Lamming identifies postmodern technologies and media as primary threats to the place of the writer in this new public sphere. Martí in the late nineteenth century had found himself forced to rethink the writer's place in the face of the commercialism of the newspaper and the novel; Lamming in the 1950s is confronted with the explosion of more spectral media, such as the radio. A major part of Lamming's anticolonial cultural project involved appropriating and rewriting the British literary canon, in the form of Shakespeare; what role, if any, can this strategy serve if the written word is no longer the primary medium of cultural imperialism? Radio has become the dominant medium of Lamming's age, and a new vehicle of cultural domination: "Prospero may have thrown away his Book; but the art of Radio will rescue his weariness from despair; immortalise his absence; remind us that poetry is a way of listening . . . the art of Radio will rescue his voice from the purgatory of the Ocean which is and may always be a neighbour to eternity" (14–15). Lamming observes that while radio is Prospero's newest weapon, it at the same time heralds a new form of summoning the dead, a potential way of literally giving voice to the illiterate and disenfranchised. For now, radio is the domain of Prospero; but if the radio can rescue Prospero's voice from oblivion, perhaps it can be appropriated by Caliban, in forms like the BBC program *Caribbean*

Voices. While located in London, *Caribbean Voices* broadcast back to the islands the voices of various West Indian writers reading their own poetry and prose, as well as some of the work that was being written by those still in the islands. Lamming remarks on the irony that the radio therefore became simultaneously the vehicle for commerce, administration, and culture in the Caribbean: the *Caribbean Voices* program is broadcast using a medium "where local radio is an incestuous concubinage between commerce and official administration" (65). Lamming thus foresees the ways in which the democratization of the public sphere would coincide with the growth of the culture industry in order to police the new medium.

That radio might be the new vehicle for Caribbean intellectual aspirations concerns Lamming's traditional sentiments, considering the medium's extreme commercialism. Reflecting on radio's privileged form of communicating information, the news, Lamming insists on his preference for literary expression: "News demands a mechanical neutrality of tone whether the voice is giving messages about dying or delight. I was a poet in those days; it is impossible for a poet to evoke sympathy from people who use words as a way of measuring time; and time as the measure of how much money" (51). Literature appears out of step with an audience with different values. The event that sparks these reflections is Lamming's assignment covering the funeral of George VI for the BBC. Attending the ceremony, Lamming observes: "We were witnessing, in the present, the resurrection of a way of behaving" (51). The funeral evokes a residual structure of feeling, a form of mourning steeped in tradition, out of place in the present. The news can hardly muster the proper tone for this somber event; only literary language can describe it with the proper gravity and affect. Both literature and the news convey information, but Lamming suggests that each corresponds to a different mode of structuring experience.

If the funeral setting seems to cast literature as left over from a bygone, dying era, Lamming's crisis when confronted with the ubiquity of British radio only foreshadows the confrontation with postmodernity that becomes most heightened in his visit to New York. Lamming's literary sensibilities are overwhelmed by both the shock of the crowd and the imposing threat of the architecture and technology of the United States. Listening to American radio, he immediately recognizes its difference from the reliable elitism of the British: "The BBC became as remote as the Middle Ages, and no less secure" (189). While British newscasts attempt to strike a tone of decorum, in deference to a set of admittedly out-of-date traditional values associated with nobility and imperial greatness, the newscasts Lamming hears in New York stun him with their haphazard juxtaposition of politics, culture, and advertising. "One had to learn how to take these items of news seriously," Lamming remarks (189). What he cannot decipher is whether this new culture industry is evidence of mass participation or mass deception. As he listens to an advertisement for a film about the assassination of a president, he remembers his own experience passing through customs to enter the country. Thinking back on that event, he wonders how a country confident enough to allow the production of such potentially subversive cultural forms can be so paranoid about harmless immigrants like himself. He concludes that "either [the American government] was too secure to meddle with strangers, or it was much too insecure to take any risks" (190). He is never able to decide whether allowing a film to be made about the assassination of a president shows the revolutionary and subversive potential of the medium, or only proves how secure the system must be to allow such subject matter.

As a flaneur in the city, Lamming begins to wonder whether such a world of instantaneity makes the writer superfluous. The city-space stands as testament to the possibilities of "collective enterprise" (188) and the "triumph of energy over objects" (189); the streets and buildings prove that humankind can order history and landscape. At the same time, the experience of the city also upsets Lamming's poetic sensibility. What can be the role of the writer in such a fast-paced and technologically driven world? When Lamming walks the streets of Manhattan, he can scarcely imagine a role for literature in the shadow of this world. He writes that "literature seemed irrelevant beside the eloquence of those sky-scrapers" (188). The sublimity and shock of New York's urban space preempt Lamming's ability to contemplate the city: "I had not time to think who or what civilisation had built them" (188). In the face of the novelty of his experience in New York, Lamming's usually fluid essayistic style degenerates into "notes which I made as a way of keeping my writing hand at work" (204). This fragmentary form seems to be the only way he can accommodate the new experiences of American postmodernity. This experience points toward an explanation for Lamming's own uncertainty, writing in 1960, as to how he will adapt to the new world: "I am still young by ordinary standards (thirty-two, to be exact), but already I feel that I have had it (as a writer) where the British Caribbean is concerned. I have lost my place, or my place has deserted me" (50). These words foretold the gradual decline in Lamming's literary output, until he stopped publishing fiction completely in 1971.

Listening to the Land in the Poetry of Martin Carter

At almost exactly the same time that Lamming was achieving fame and consecration in London, Martin Carter found himself imprisoned by the British colonial government in Guyana, as a result of his participation in Cheddi Jagan's multiracial People's Progressive Party (PPP). After the April 1953 election that brought the PPP to power, British military forces invaded the country; suspended the constitution, which had granted the colony some autonomy; and overturned Jagan's government. Many of the leaders of the PPP, including Carter, were jailed for demonstrating against the British invasion. Carter spent three months imprisoned at the U.S. Atkinson Air Force Base. During and immediately after this incarceration, Carter authored his best-known collection, *Poems of Resistance*, which explores the Caribbean writer's role in the decolonization movement. Lamming's novels of the 1950s were all published to great acclaim by the London publishing house of Michael Joseph, which around the same time was publishing fiction by authors like Doris Lessing and Joyce Cary. *Poems of Resistance* was the only collection Carter managed to have published in England during this time period. Even this book faced limited distribution; the British colonial government initially banned *Poems of Resistance* in Guyana for fear of its subversiveness, and the book was eventually published in London by Lawrence and Wishart in 1954, whose other titles featured works by Karl Marx and Ho Chi Minh. In this section, I place this collection within the context of Carter's career, and show how his vision of poetry develops from his earliest collections, until, increasingly uncertain of how the poet might speak with authority about a postcolonial Guyana being torn apart by racial conflict between the nation's African- and Indian-descended populations exacerbated by Forbes Burnham's totalitarian regime, Carter stopped publishing poetry in 1980.

Literary critics and political activists alike have read Carter's poetry as an extension of his dramatic actions in the anticolonial movement. Carter's early public career included an unsuccessful run for political office in 1953, a position in the Executive Committee of the PPP, and a role on the editorial board of *Thunder*, the PPP's primary publication. His activism made him an attractive spokesman for international leftist causes as well; Stewart Brown notes that "a few of those early poems . . . have become classics of socialist literature, translated into several Eastern European and Asian languages" (7), and it is probably no coincidence that just after Carter's incarceration in Guyana, a major international socialist press was convinced to sponsor the only poetry collection of Carter's to be published in England until his 1977 *Poems of Succession*, which collects work from all of Carter's previous publications. It has always been tempting to read Carter's poetry as one with his political praxis. Eusi Kwayana, one of the PPP activists jailed with Carter during 1953 and author of the foreword to *Poems of Resistance* under the name Sydney King, admires the "purity of passion" (King 370) of Carter's first collection. Kwayana privileges action as the only ethical response to colonialism: "In a colony there is no room for 'intellectuals.' Everyone must be an activist" (Kwayana 97). Carter's activities as a poet must be made to adhere to this project of struggle: Kwayana thus argues that "*The Hill of Fire Glows Red* did at the level of art what the wage earners were doing in little patches, resuming the struggles of the early quarter of the century" (King 369). Carter's poetry surely promotes this reading of the poet, as the figure who does in his art what the people do in the streets; yet from the beginning, Carter harbors profound doubts about literature's ability to participate in the public sphere. The exploration in Carter's poetry of how the poet becomes translator for inarticulate Caribbean noises leads toward an ultimate uncertainty about that spokesman position.

In his 1951 collection *The Hill of Fire Glows Red*, Carter lays out the most important aspects of his project in two of his earliest published poems, "Looking at Your Hands" and "Listening to the Land." "Looking at Your Hands" insists on action: the poet avers, "I will not still my voice," "I look for fire," and "I do not sleep to dream, but dream to change the world" (Carter, *Poems of Succession* 14). The poet's voice and the cleansing fire of revolution come together as equally necessary for social change. The relationship between writing and action is dialectical; poetry is nourished by action, as action takes its impetus from poetry. His hunger to change the world comes from his knowledge of the injustice of starvation and poverty, a knowledge he acquires: "from books my dear friend / of men dreaming and living / and hungering in a room without light" (14). Carter understands his poetry as an effort to further this knowledge, to press other hands into the collective action necessary for social change. A number of Carter's subsequent poems in *Poems of Resistance* will take up the project of creating the grounds for action.

In "I Clench My Fist," for example, the poet proclaims, "Although you point your gun straight at my heart / I clench my fist above my head; I sing my song of FREEDOM!" (41). The poet, singing his song of freedom, is the anticolonial poet-warrior. As Carter explains in "I Am No Soldier," "I am no soldier with a cold gun on my shoulder"; instead, he is armed with "my poem" (49).

While "Looking at Your Hands" projects itself into the future, suggesting the effect the poem might have on the world, "Listening to the Land" explores the source from which the poet derives his authority to sing for freedom and to dream of changing the world.

> I bent down
> kneeling on my knee
> and pressed my ear to listen to the land.
> . . .
> and all I heard was tongueless whispering
> as if some buried slave wanted to speak again. (15)

The poet, listening to the land, knows that the buried slave has something to tell him, but cannot understand what it is. Carter depicts this process of listening as integral to understanding the past and changing the future.

The trope of the silenced slave and the enunciating poet goes back to the abolitionist public sphere of the nineteenth century and lies at the center of Caribbean anticolonial writing like José Martí's classic nineteenth-century essay "Nuestra América." Julio Ramos describes how, by figuring the writer as the privileged interpreter for the subaltern, the "mute *indio*," and the "scorned Negro," Martí positions the writer as bearer of a different kind of knowledge than that of the "imported book" of the "artificial man of letters"; "hence, literature's claim to priority as an authority in the practice of good government" (Ramos 263). In acting as spokesman for the disenfranchised, Martí assumes that "although the subaltern had to be an *object* of representation and knowledge, s/he could not become a knowing *subject*" (261). The poet, who presumes to publicly speak for the unrepresented, must thus figure them as silent and unable to represent themselves. Carter reconceives the relationship of the poet to the masses in slightly different terms. As in "Our America," the land, tongueless and inarticulate, needs the poet to give it voice. "Listening to the Land" ends by identifying these submerged whispers of the land with the whispers of the past, the deceased ancestors that Lam-

ming's ceremony of the souls conjures to begin *The Pleasures of Exile.*
Yet unlike Martí's mute *indio*, in "Listening to the Land," the past is not
silent; although the land may be incoherent, the past is not. The buried
slave is not waiting to speak, but to speak *again.* The poet cannot quite
hear what the slave has to say, but through listening to the land itself,
the poet should be able to uncover that voice. The subaltern folk and the
land are one, and it is through listening to the land that the poet will find
his people's voice and sing for freedom.

The poet must produce connections to these sources that have been
severed by colonialism. Beginning with "Not Hands Like Mine," *Poems
of Resistance* redefines the project set forth in the earlier "Looking at
Your Hands." As the title suggests, the more recent poem is far less certain of its ability to fulfill the task proscribed by the first one. The earlier poem is an impassioned call to other hands to join the struggle for
freedom. In "Not Hands Like Mine," any such call is much less distinct;
instead, the only sounds to be heard are "a muttering sea" and "hoarse,
groaning tongues," reminders of the "mute" Carib gods, "nameless and
quite forgotten":

> Not hands
> like mine
> these Carib altars knew:
> nameless and quite forgotten are the gods;
> and mute,
> mute and alone,
>
> . . .
>
> Here, right at my feet
> my strangled city lies,
> my father's city and my mother's heart:
> hoarse, groaning tongues. (31)

The gods have almost been forgotten; only within the poem does
any trace of them remain. Rather than foreground the poetic subject, as in "Looking at Your Hands" and "Listening to the Land,"
"Not Hands Like Mine" suggests that the poem, not the poet, can
record the sounds echoing down from the past.[16] Without the poetic
interpreter, though, the sounds of the landscape, of the "strangled
city," are incomprehensible groans and cries the public sphere refuses
to recognize. The difficulty of Carter's project will be the necessary presence of the poet as translator for the folk, a presence whose

individuality threatens to marginalize and silence the people he wants to represent.

A number of other texts from *Poems of Resistance* explore the noises made by the disenfranchised people themselves, apparent to the poet as he listens to the land. "Cartman of Dayclean" makes explicit the connection between the nourishing sounds of the landscape and the Guyanese subaltern subject. The cartman of the poem, the "hidden man," makes "bleeding music" out of the rumbling of the iron wheels of his cart:

> Now to begin the road:
> the bleeding music of appellant man
> starts like a song but fades into a groan.
> . . .
>
> His hopes are whitened starched with grief and pain
> yet questing man is heavy laden cart
> whose iron wheels will rumble in the night
> whose iron wheel will spark against the stone
> or granite burden of the universe. (37)

This rumble carries the same threat signified by the drums, the threat that the iron wheels will spark the cleansing fire of revolution that appears throughout Carter's poetry. At the same time that he identifies this threat, the poet simultaneously naturalizes it, containing the cartman within the poem by making him part of his landscape. Just as the whispering slave, trying to speak again, is part of the land and needs the poet as his channel, the "questing man" becomes the rumbling cart, unable to express himself with anything more than a groan and an incoherent song. If, in Lamming's account of *The Black Jacobins*, revolution is the collective speaking its deepest desire, the cartman of Carter's poem fails to speak.

Carter's most critically acclaimed poems, "University of Hunger" and "I Come from the Nigger Yard," are pivotal parts of his dialectical project of turning the sounds of the Caribbean landscape into poetry, and documenting the process of the people coming to consciousness. Fellow Guyanese poet and *Kyk-over-al* editor A. J. Seymour gives these two poems "pride of place among Martin Carter's poems, because they provide words, like guns, in which he speaks for all colonials everywhere" (103). As in Lamming's imaginary, Seymour considers that books play an equal part to guns in the anticolonial struggle. Carter's words are especially valuable to Seymour because of Carter's ability to speak for those involved in the struggle.

The poem "University of Hunger" begins with the image of "the pilgrimage of man the long march" made by "they who had no voice in the emptiness" (Carter, *Poems of Succession* 34).[17] This march is the process by which those with "no voice" make themselves heard. The poet records the "sea sound of the eyeless flitting bat," "the cruel wind blowing," "the shell blow and the iron clang" (34–35) of the plantation. These sounds create a claustrophobic world, dark and hopeless. But toward the end of the poem, "The beating drum returns and dies away. / . . . The cocks of dawn stand up and crow like bugles" (35). In the final verse of the poem, when the shell blows, it marks the people's coming to consciousness. Driven by the sounds of the distant drum and the crowing cock, the poem ends with the people marching out of oblivion and into the poem. Yet who are the subjects of this process, who I have just too easily referred to as "the people"?[18] The first lines of the poem suggest an absent subject. When the subject of "University of Hunger" appears, it is named as "they." The poem has no first-person narration, and the poem records no direct or indirect speech whatsoever. Despite the incorporation of nonstandard language in the poem, the same formula appears as in previous poems, where the people appear as the mute landscape: "They come treading in the hoofmarks of the mule" (34), "They come like sea birds" (35). Carter depicts the people who are marching into consciousness as silent and downtrodden; their stirring can only be represented by the poet, not enacted within the poem by the marching men themselves.

Carter's "I Come from the Nigger Yard" attempts to resolve this paradox of representation. The poem is narrated by a persona who is presumably one of the brethren of the silenced and oppressed marchers. The narrator locates himself as a peripheral man, confined to the shadows. The first three stanzas describe how he has leapt, crept, searched, and walked into a world that refuses to acknowledge him. These stanzas paint the dark visual landscape of the narrator's world, the "dark hut in the shadow," the "aching floor on which I crept," the "nigger yard of yesterday" (38). The fourth stanza acts as a pivot between the discouraging past of the first three and the fiery promise of the final three. The first half of the poem emphasizes the isolated suffering of the narrator in a barren land, as he has trudged toward what he still hopes will be "the wide streets of to-morrow" (38). In the fourth stanza, we hear the distant echoes of a community: "And there was always sad music somewhere in the land / like a bugle and a drum between the houses / voices of women singing far away" (39). The music, like the poem, may not be bright and cheerful, but the flood of sounds from the bugle, the drum, and the singing women have guided the narrator forward. It is through this community and these sounds that he was "born again stubborn and fierce / screaming in a slum," finding his voice "screaming with hunger, angry with life and men" (39).

In this world, where speech was restricted to "judges full of scorn / priests and parsons fooling gods with words," the man from the "nigger yard" was only "a dog tangled in rags" (39); like the dog, he had a voice, but could not use it to form words to describe his condition. The last lines project the poem as the product of a yet unseen future, when the angry screams will have been turned into articulate poetic language. The conditions for this transformation are a time "when the whole world turns upside down" (38):

> It was pain lasting from hours to months to years
> weaving a pattern telling a tale leaving a mark
> on the face and the brow.
> Until there came the iron days cast in a foundry
> Where men make hammers things that cannot break
> and anvils heavy hard and cold like ice. (39)

This revolutionary resolve, hard and heavy and unbreakable, makes it possible for this man from the "nigger yard" to speak his pain. Carter imagines a world in which the privilege that allows him to write poetry will be extended to the rest of society.

These poems show the poet trying to accommodate and transcribe the sounds of a subjugated population seeking to be heard in the public sphere. Another series of poems from *Poems of Resistance* move from this emphasis on aurality to focus on the written word. These poems—"Letter 1," "Letter 2," "Letter 3," and "On the Fourth Night of the Hunger Strike"—are narrated from prison; it is as if the space that confines the poet's body demands the circumscribed epistolary form. Like the more orally infused poems, the prison letters are filled with the voiceless noises of Carter's surroundings. In the poems from outside the prison, the noises of the landscape and the people give the poet life and hope; within the prison, the noises threaten him and his poetic project. As he listens to the crash of the rifle, "the stamp of feet" and the "tramp of a soldier" (47), he realizes that these sounds make it impossible for him to listen to the land and the people. The skyscraper and the radio made Lamming wonder if literature had become irrelevant; Carter finds himself trying to write while confronted by the authoritarian side of that technology, the prison. He understands his imprisonment is not just about disciplining his body but also his ears: "This is all they want me to hear" (47), he realizes; the system of power wants him to hear only the martial sounds of order rather than the chaotic stirrings of the people.

During his imprisonment, the moment when the poet most clearly shows his involvement in the cause, the isolated poetic subject is also most starkly separated from his people:

> This is what they do with me
> Put me in prison, hide me away
> cut off the world, cut out the sun
> darken the land, blacken the flower
> stifle my breath and hope that I die! (44)

Unlike many of his other poems, a strong first person apparently identifiable as the poet himself narrates each of these prison letters, and stands at a remove from the collective masses outside the prison walls. His thoughts are especially personal: he considers himself and his individual plight, and wonders about his son and his wife. He derives strength and hope as much from the visit from his wife and the letter from a comrade as from the thought of the struggle. In prison, the poet most readily sees that even at the moment of his deepest commitment, his poetic project will always separate him from his people.

Carter's *Poems of Shape and Motion*, written just after *Poems of Resistance*, shows the poet attempting to regain the "purity of passion" that had allowed him to fuse his earlier poetry with collective action. "I was wondering if I could shape this passion / just as I wanted in solid fire," the poem begins; "I was wondering if I could make myself / nothing but fire, pure and incorruptible," it continues (55). This collection marks a transition for Carter, away from the fiery optimism of the early poetry. Completely uncertain of himself, he can only wonder if his project, of shaping his passion into the poetry that can spark a revolution, can be fulfilled. The poet cannot allow himself to be consumed by his subject; as long as his authority depends on his ability to translate for the silenced subaltern, he will not be one with them. True purity, true oneness, betrays the poet's privilege as truth-speaker, as Carter shows in the first poem of 1961's *Conversations*, "Groaning in the Wilderness":

> Speaking with one on a pavement in the city
> I watched the greedy mouth, the cunning eye
> I reeled and nearly fell in frantic terror

seeing a human turn into a dog.
Recovering, I studied this illusion
and made a stupid effort to be strong:
I nodded and agreed and listened close.
But when I tried to utter words—I barked! (62)

In the earlier poems, this process of listening and trying to imitate the "voices hardly human" (62) of the folk provided the poet with his songs of freedom. In "Groaning in the Wilderness," he so accurately ventriloquizes these voices that he reproduces an animalistic yelp of suffering. Without some degree of reflection and poetic distance from experience, the poet cannot produce a comprehensible discourse.

In this poetry of the early 1960s, collected in *Conversations* and *Jail Me Quickly*, Carter shows his discourse breaking down as he loses faith in his earlier poetic mission. The sounds of the landscape and the people that appeared in the earlier poetry fade out; even the poem "Voices" is completely silent. One poem's title asks "What Can a Man Do More?" (72). The answer is that there is nothing more that he can do. In the poem "They Say I Am," he acknowledges the many demands made on him: "They say I am a poet write for them" (61). By this point in his career, he no longer believes that he can be the people's poet, he who "can articulate for them their innermost longings" (Carew 107). He replies "A poet cannot write for those who ask / hardly himself even, except he lies." The poem continues:

Poems are written either for the dying
or the unborn, no matter what we say.
That does not mean his audience lies remote
inside a womb or some cold bed of agony.
It only means that we who want true poems
must all be born again, and die to do so. (Carter, *Poems of Succession* 61)

Carter identifies what needs to happen for the people to have a voice in making poetry: they must have a voice in all other aspects of their lives, and for that to happen, they must be born again into a new world. This is the world that many, including Carter, hoped decolonization would inaugurate. While the young Carter may have believed it his duty to listen to the folk and give them voice in his poetry, at this stage his poetry indicates that it is up to the people to speak for themselves. He can no longer convince himself of his role as a spokesman for his people, and the heroic poet of resistance of the 1950s gradually fades from the Caribbean literary scene. In place of this conception of the writer, the testimonial impulse, which is the topic of my next chapter, emerged as a way of listening to the voices of the "folk." This desire to supplement literature with other voices began to gain literary authority in Cuba and Jamaica in the late 1960s and 1970s in the work of Miguel Barnet, the *Savacou* anthology of 1971, dub poetry, and the Sistren Theatre Collective, and moved into the privileged space once occupied by Lamming and Carter.

Both Lamming and Carter express hope in the promise of independence, the end of colonialism, and the beginning of a better world. The years that follow Lamming's final novel in 1971 would be characterized around the Caribbean by the betrayal of that promise, whether in the increasing totalitarianism of Forbes Burnham in Guyana, the political war in Jamaica between supporters of Michael Manley and Edward Seaga, the alienation of intellectuals in Fidel Castro's Cuba and Eric Williams's Trinidad and Tobago, or the failure of the Grenada Revolution. The 1970s ended with disillusionment and disenfranchisement for intellectuals throughout the region. As Caribbean postcoloniality unfolds, Carter's poetry moves away from the forceful declarations of his earliest work to an ultimate loss of faith in the ability of literature to intervene in the public sphere. Like Carter's poetry, Lamming's essays in *The Pleasures of Exile* stand precisely at the hinge between two worlds, simultaneously averring the writer's commitment to the struggle against colonialism while also expressing anxiety about what the coming of North American dominance will mean in the postcolonial era. Lamming and Carter, two of the figures who defined the Caribbean literary field and the role of the Caribbean writer during the 1950s, found that the upheavals of decolonization brought about changes that shattered their conception of literature and politics. At the same time, both Lamming and Carter hint at some of the new possibilities opened up by postcoloniality; their own reluctance to invest literature with all of their utopian impulses comes in some degree from the realization that women and the folk no longer need the professional male writer to represent them. Confronted by this new world, Lamming and Carter, the great anticolonial writers, were unable to adapt their literary discourse, and were forced to find new methods—speech writing, political organizing, government service—for expressing their political aspirations.

7   The Testimonial Impulse

Miguel Barnet and the
Sistren Theatre Collective

BY THE LATE 1960S AND EARLY 1970S, a new configuration
of the Caribbean public sphere was beginning to be consolidated, and the
literary field found itself being redefined. Chapters 7 and 8 explore two
responses by Caribbean writers—the testimonial impulse and the turn to
popular culture—that show how new relationships between writer and
public structure this postcolonial space. Alison Donnell begins her discussion of "critical moments in anglophone literary history" with what
Laurence Breiner has referred to as the "Savacou debate," the heated exchange that began in reviews of the anthology of new writing presented
in the journal *Savacou* in 1971 and continued in essays throughout the
1970s by some of the major critics of Anglophone Caribbean literature.[1]
Social and political changes taking place by the 1970s make possible in
Donnell's account "the emergence of a shared agenda in terms of content, style and form [that] enabled a community of critics to articulate
collectively the shape of decolonised narratives, and thereby to set the
principles for a regional literary history in motion" (31). Contemporary
Caribbean literary history—what I am calling its postcolonial phase—
is, for Donnell, initiated in the 1971 *Savacou* issue and the Association
for Commonwealth Literature and Language Studies (ACLALS) conference in Jamaica with which its publication coincided. The *Savacou*
issue became a site of contestation as reviewers criticized or lauded the
anthology's attempts to redefine the relationship between intellectual
and public. The main innovations of the anthology were the inclusion of
apparently unlettered voices, which is the topic of this chapter, and the
overt inspiration from music, which I examine in chapter 8. These efforts to redefine intellectual work come as responses to the shifting place
of literature in the postcolonial public sphere, though, as these chapters
show, each project retains elements of anticolonial desires.

While the anticolonial writers I examined in previous chapters imagined themselves speaking for and articulating the ideals of a group they figured as the folk or *pueblo*, the *Savacou* anthology features a different logic based on an immediacy of voice: that the role of the lettered poet (the anthology was edited by academics and professional writers Kamau Brathwaite, Kenneth Ramchand, and Andrew Salkey) is to provide a space for the unlettered to enter the public sphere himself or herself and speak in his or her own voice. Giving Bongo Jerry a place of prominence in the anthology is part of the same impulse that led Mervyn Morris to edit and publish Louise Bennett's performances in 1966 along with an essay "On Reading Louise Bennett, Seriously" in 1967. The most vehement attacks on the new anthology, from reviewers like Eric Roach, who explicitly positions himself as representing a previous generation, argue for literature requiring a kind of distillation process: "for the poet . . . language, mined from the ore of tribal speech, is purified in his head, becomes molten in his heart and is poured out into the form of the poem to harden for all time" (Roach 6). By contrast, Brathwaite's introduction to the volume ends by celebrating how this collection "has brought the writer out of the tower, out of his castle, out of his ego" ("Foreward" 9). The new writing lacks the anticolonial aura—the reference to Lamming's castle here is overt—but, for Brathwaite, this democratization of literature is precisely its value in a postcolonial setting: "until recently, the writer was hero, was one of the elite; his distance overseas added to the glamour of this ideograph. The reader was his pupil; told what to think; must follow if he could. . . . All that has changed" (9). The substance of the *Savacou* debate shows the testimonial impulse at work as the Caribbean made its transition from modern colonialism to postcoloniality.

The same questions raised in the *Savacou* debate—of uncovering a cultural history apart from what Europe might recognize, of literature's ability to represent the different language registers typical of a colonial setting, of the possibility or even desirability of the subaltern speaking—are crucial questions for postcolonial studies. Subaltern studies is frequently associated with South Asia, with Robert Young even arguing that the centrality of *testimonio* in Latin American studies comes from the influence of the subaltern studies movement in India of the 1980s on Latin Americanists like John Beverley (352). I suggest that while the terms may be different in the Caribbean discussions of the 1960s and 1970s—Miguel Barnet and Kamau Brathwaite do not use the word "subaltern," for example—the testimonial impulse inspiring Caribbean literature of the decolonization era is at the center of subaltern studies as well. In fact, with Beverley's earliest writings on *testimonio* as a representation of the subaltern voice, "Anatomía del testimonio," appearing in print in 1987, the year before the publication of Spivak's "Can the Subaltern Speak?," and with both texts written while Beverley and Spivak were colleagues at the University of Pittsburgh, postcolonial studies needs to acknowledge its Caribbean influences by seeing *testimonio* as a precursor, rather than an inheritor, of subaltern studies.[2]

Testimonio in Latin American studies has generally been theorized as a rejection of traditional European conceptions of high literature, displacing the bourgeois novel with a new, working-class way of organizing existence; Beverley expresses this position when he writes that *testimonio* "represents the entry into literature of persons who would normally, in those societies where literature is a form of class privilege, be excluded from direct literary representation, who have to be 'represented' by professional writers" ("Margin" 29).[3] This chapter looks at the two most influential testimonialists from the Caribbean, Miguel Barnet and Honor Ford-Smith, though other well-known testimonial texts to emerge from the Caribbean include Dany Bébel-Gisler's *Léonora: L'histoire enfouie de la Guadeloupe*, and the testimonial imprint can be seen on texts of this period from the folk theater of Derek Walcott to the decision to use nonprofessional actors and documentary-like techniques in the Jamaican film *The Harder They Come*.[4]

In addition to seeing themselves writing against an exclusionary literary public sphere, Barnet and Ford-Smith both identify a newer threat to Caribbean cultural production in the 1960s and 1970s, a strand of their work less emphasized by critics: the infiltration of the Caribbean public sphere by a North American culture industry determined to commodify every corner of postmodern life. Barnet and Ford-Smith formulate *testimonio* as a way of recuperating, or even manufacturing, a pure, indigenous Caribbean culture free from the dictates of international capitalism. In this context, Barnet's project becomes a retreat into a mythical indigenous past still kept alive in rural Afro-Cuban culture; Ford-Smith's, by contrast, emphasizes urban working-class women as the repository of an alternative native cultural sensibility. In this chapter, I examine both how Barnet and Ford-Smith frame their testimonial project—that is, how prefaces and other paratextual materials describe the testimonial process in which a subaltern subject relates his or her story to an intellectual transcriber—as well as how these endeavors are carried out—that is, the subjects chosen as native informants, the episodes included in the narrative, and the stylistic choices made by the transcribers. Examining *testimonio* in theory and practice shows the genre identifying the crisis of Caribbean anticolonialism even as it attempts to keep alive a public voice for postcolonial literature by aligning with a subaltern counterpublic.

From Poet to Transcriber: Miguel Barnet and the Crisis of Literature in Revolutionary Cuba

By insisting on its claims to collective action and to culture's political contribution, *testimonio* might be read as a last gasp of Caribbean modernist anticolonial literature; yet despite the compelling efforts that the genre's practitioners have made to position themselves in this way, I do not want to lose sight of how *testimonio* is nonetheless shaped by the postcolonial public sphere that frames its production and dissemination. Barnet's first two forays into *testimonio*, the 1966 *Biografía de un cimarrón* and the 1969 *Canción de Rachel*, navigate what the two texts overtly gender as the masculine world of anticolonialism and a feminized postcoloniality. The prostitute Rachel stands in for a commercialized public sphere while Esteban Montejo evokes the era of anticolonial struggle and becomes, for Barnet, the emblematic heroic modern subject.

Barnet began his career not as a testimonialist but as a poet in the early years of the Cuban Revolution. Yet the obstacles Barnet faced in finding publication and prestige as a poet appear to have led him to seek out a new literary form. William Luis alludes to the potential "political motivation" ("Politics of Memory" 483) of the move into *testimonio* as a way for a poet from a privileged background to declare his or her allegiance to the revolutionary government through identification with a member of the subaltern masses. Luis also elliptically notes that Barnet "was associated with the second generation group of poets known as El Puente," a group that "fell out of grace [as] many group members were considered antisocials and homosexuals and were sent to rehabilitation camps" (485). Vera Kutzinski fills in some blanks, criticizing Luis for "skirt[ing] the issue of Barnet's homosexuality" (294) even though Luis does obliquely speculate that Barnet's sexuality may have led to his marginalization in revolutionary Cuba: "During this period, Barnet had gone unpublished in Cuba. Perhaps Barnet seized upon the story of Montejo as an opportunity to resume a public literary life" ("Politics of Memory" 485).

Whatever the truth of Barnet's relationship to the Cuban authorities during the 1960s, his early poetry received a mixed reception from the revolutionary establishment. Barnet's first poetry collection, *La piedra fina y el pavorreal*, was published in 1963 by Ediciones Unión, the imprint of the revolution-sanctioned writers' union, and received encouraging reviews and a cover blurb written by Roberto Fernández Retamar. His second collection, *Isla de Guijes*, was published in 1964 by El Puente, the group mentioned by Luis, and had a very limited distribution.[5] In addition to these collections, Barnet consistently published his poetry in journals outside of Cuba, particularly in France and Mexico. After the publication of *Biografía* in 1966, though, Barnet's poetry began to appear in the prestigious literary journal published by the revolution's official cultural institution, Casa de las Américas. This organization named Barnet's next collection, *La sagrada familia*, as a finalist for its literary prize in poetry in 1967. By 1971, Casa de las Américas had created a new category for prizes in *testimonio*, showing how quickly the revolutionary government encouraged the genre's consecration. *Biografía*, with its close alignment of the writer with the heroic anticolonial subject, assured Barnet's acceptance into the literary establishment, and he quickly became one of Cuba's cultural heroes, occupying important administrative posts, including director of the Union of Cuban Writers and Artists, and later the founder and director of the Fundación Fernando Ortíz.

Barnet's shift away from poetry and toward *testimonio* depended on his own specific circumstances, but throughout the Cuban artistic field during this period we can see a reconfiguration of literature's place. The development of *testimonio* is among the most marked developments, but not nearly as dramatic as the rapid ascent of the film industry in the island. In his comprehensive book on the subject, Michael Chanan labels Cuban cinema "a major site of public discourse that at the same time enjoyed a de facto autonomy because of a privileged relationship to the source of power and authority" (17).[6] He describes how writers and artists concerned about censorship or lack of support in other endeavors gravitated to the Instituto Cubano de Arte e Industria Cinematográficos (ICAIC) as a space of freedom and exploration; in one notable example, "when the journal *Pensamiento Crítico* was shut down, one of its editors, the writer Jesús Díaz, was invited to join ICAIC (where in due course he would make a number of notable films . . . and also become secretary of the party branch)" (7).

Film emerges, then, as a way to revive the aura of anticolonial writing but also create a more direct immediacy between artist and audience: not only can the medium circumvent the requirement for literacy, it can offer the presence of the body and voice in a way the written word cannot. Barnet's *testimonio* develops out of the same set of demands in the transitional period of the 1960s, when the model of anticolonial writing is in crisis. In addition to its anticolonial desires, *testimonio* responds to the new contours of postcoloniality as well. Most obviously, the genre's postcolonial elements can be identified in its reaction to the North American cultural imperialism that became an acute concern throughout the region after World War II. As Barnet discusses in his essays from *La fuente viva*, *testimonio* develops out of a desire for a Caribbean essence at just the time when urbanization and modernization projects are tying the region more closely to the international culture industry. In particular, Barnet sees Caribbean writing as potentially reinvigorating the practice of literature, which he argues has become stale and irrelevant in more technologically advanced countries.

At the same time, Barnet's conception of *testimonio* depends on the breakdown of the anticolonial literary field. As chapter 3 discussed, Martí's modernist project developed as a solution to a literary field characterized by the "emergence of a subject profoundly divided, split by the incisive opposition between the priority of action and the supplementarity and suspect passivity of representation" (Ramos 269). Martí's modernism, then, in attaching writing to anticolonial collective struggles, contingently managed to bridge this divide. Barnet, in trying to carry the mantle of Martí's heroic literary project, faces a new Caribbean where Cuban independence, increasing literacy, and new technologies have changed the terrain. *Testimonio*'s bifurcated authorship comes in relation to these shifts, offering a new solution to the split between representation and action, which Martí's commitment to anticolonial struggle can no longer solve. As much as *testimonio* seeks to imbue literature with social coherence by fusing the author with his heroic subject, this effort simultaneously underscores the distinctness and difference of author and subject, leaving literature an uneasy supplement to collective action.

The introduction to *Biografía de un cimarrón* is especially telling in this regard, as one of the few places in the text where the writer speaks in his own voice. That voice is conflicted about its relationship to the informant and to the text (and context) as a whole. The postcolonial author has none of the assured authority of the anticolonial intellectual. While Esteban speaks in the first-person singular throughout his portion of the text, Barnet speaks only in the first-person plural ("nuestro interés," "olvidamos a la anciana"). It is as though Barnet's narrative persona in some way incorporates and accounts for Esteban but always needs him, whereas Esteban's voice can stand on its own. The relationship between the two voices remains ambivalent throughout *Biografía*.

These contradictory anticolonial and postcolonial impulses are everywhere apparent in Barnet's theorizations of *testimonio*. Barnet offers his reflections on the genre in a number of essays, two of which in particular sketch out what he reluctantly calls a methodology: "La novela testimonio: Socio-literatura" and "Testimonio y comunicación: Una vía hacia la identidad," published respectively in 1970 and 1980 and reproduced as the first two chapters of *La fuente viva*. In these two essays, Barnet tries to explain what makes *testimonio* an appropriate genre for revolutionary Cuba. He begins by positing a crisis in literature, in particular the novel, throughout the world: "What we call the novel, with all of its rules, has failed, is not effective for us, doesn't serve us."[7] The literature of the industrialized North has failed to represent the "verdadero hombre" (*La fuente viva* 14), getting away from nature and the essence of everyday life. In *The Pleasures of Exile*, Lamming notices a similar cultural gap in the West between writers and the natural world, embodied by the people who work on the land. As Lamming puts it, "more people read in England . . . but the badge has changed; and we have the situation where the literate are divided into classes: intellectuals and the rest" (*Pleasures* 44). Barnet makes the same observation when discussing why in his mind Cuban writers in particular and third world writers in general are best suited for the task of revitalizing literature. In Europe, by contrast, "for many years there have not been any social movements of importance, no political explosions, and the literature has reflected this inoculated state of affairs."[8] Barnet expresses a sentiment typical of the Caribbean anticolonial writers who came before him, that literature derives its energy from its relationship with collective social movements. The task of the revolutionary writer, then, is to find an organic literary form that can represent the public while giving voice to a counterpublic. An adherence to sterile forms of the European novel in the third world, as part of a slavish devotion to all things European that Barnet describes as the "culto criollo" (*La fuente viva* 19), appears in "La novela testimonio" as a major threat to the Caribbean establishing its own "literatura de fundación" (18).

While Barnet's nationalist opposition to colonial mimicry of European high culture seems typically anticolonial, the postmodern massification of culture presents a new threat to the development of an authentic and revolutionary literature in the Caribbean. In "Testimonio y comunicación," Barnet identifies "una guerra psicológica" (46) being waged against ordinary people throughout the world by mass media and consumerism rather than by high culture. In this attack on "the values of the people's own culture," foreign culture industries force-feed the Cuban people "dreams that are not their own."[9] This commercialization of culture debilitates the majority of the people, deluding them by substituting mass culture for popular culture, and promoting individualism over collectivity. Art in these societies has become complicit with advertising: Barnet uses the example of Andy Warhol's pop art as a foil to contrast with the "arte auténtica"[10] to which *testimonio* aspires. With this commercialization of the public sphere in mind, Barnet calls for a literary withdrawal into truly and authentically Cuban culture, a move that he likens to the general national campaign to "consume our national products."[11]

Testimonio, then, unlike the products of the global culture industry or European high modernist literature, should be a popular form but one produced by the people rather than imposed on them. In this way, *testimonio* moves beyond Caribbean anticolonial modernism, to draw its poetry from the people rather than speaking for the silenced masses. At the same time that Barnet proposes a popular literature, though, he refuses to surrender the didactic function of the writer to show the people the way forward toward revolutionary consciousness. Thus while the testimonial writer should "return the spoken word to the people,"[12] it is the writer whose "sense of history" (Barnet, "Documentary Novel" 23) allows him to identify and distill the "legitimate" hopes and dreams of the people. The tension between these two functions, that of channel through whom the voiceless can speak and that of teacher who can "contribute to an understanding of reality" (23), comes from competing postcolonial and anticolonial demands on the writer.

Esteban, as a virtual contemporary of Martí (both were born in the 1850s), allows Barnet, from the vantage point of the 1960s, to position himself, and the revolution of which he is a part, as heir to an anticolonial lineage traced back to both Martí and the *cimarrón*. Much like Martí, Esteban expresses an ambivalent fascination with modernity, situating himself within the modernizing project yet very much at its margins. The narrative begins by establishing Esteban's relationship to the natural and spiritual world as the source of his authority: "The long and the short of it is that I know everything depends on Nature. Nature is everything" (Barnet, *Biography* 17), he declares with certainty. The narrative thus begins in the pastoral world of the mountains to which the *cimarrón* retreats when he flees slavery and from which the Cuban Revolution will originate. Throughout the narrative, those with knowledge of and links to this natural world will be invested with authority. For example, Esteban distrusts "today's medicine" (51), insisting that "nature is full of remedies" (99) that modern doctors fail to use. In suggesting that their commercial interests lead them to recommend expensive medicines with less curative abilities than common herbs, Esteban casts aspersion on both their efficacy and their trustworthiness. He contrasts himself as one who respects nature and is not driven by profit, setting himself and his narrative against modernity and its duplicitous contradictions.

Choosing Esteban as his informant allows Barnet to emphasize the modern colonial period as a time of idealized masculinity. In his preface, he describes the fortuitous process by which he found Esteban:

> In the middle of 1963, a page appeared in the Cuban press dedicated to various elderly people, men and women, who had surpassed 100 years of age. . . . Two of those interviewed called our attention. The first was a 100-year-old woman; the other, a 104-year-old man. The woman had been a slave, as well as a *santera* and spiritist. The man, although he did not refer directly to religious topics, showed in his words an inclination towards superstitions and popular beliefs. His life was interesting. He talked about aspects of slavery and the War of Independence. But what most impressed us was his declaration that he had been a fugitive slave, a *cimarrón*, in the mountains of the Las Villas province.[13]

What becomes of this woman? The next sentence provides an unsatisfying answer: "We forgot about the old woman and a few days later, went to the Retirement Home where Esteban Montejo was living."[14] As Vera Kutzinski asks, if Barnet's project was African religious vestiges in Cuba, why would he choose Esteban, who had no direct religious expertise, over the old *santera*? The decision appears to come from Esteban's ability to embody the ideals of masculine anticolonial resistance. Participating in wars against slavery and Spanish rule, Esteban's life has been one of manly action. Even recreation allows Esteban to display his virility. As Kutzinski notes, in celebration of independence Esteban claims to have "had more than fifty women in a week" (Barnet, *Biography* 190). Even without women, the men are quite capable of showing off their masculinity: for example, Esteban describes playing games such as one in which "four or five hard salt crackers were placed on the wooden counter or any board, and the men had to hit the crackers hard with their dicks to see who could break the crackers" (29).[15] With his masculinity securely established, Esteban can observe the presence of homosexuality among the enslaved without regarding it as a threat to his own identity, saying "it never mattered to me, sincerely. I believe that everyone marches to his own drummer" (41).

As much as Esteban idealizes the male camaraderie of the countryside, he disapproves of Havana, overrun by Americans and cheap women, a decadent city where "pimps had free reign" (192–193). Barnet's second *testimonio*, *Canción de Rachel*, is set precisely in the city-space of republican Cuba, which Barnet continues to depict through this sexualized imagery. Cuba before the revolution is contaminated and penetrated by foreigners who drive Rachel to a shallow and hedonistic lifestyle. Rather than the *cimarrón*, the emblematic character for Cuba under U.S. domination is the nightclub dancer, a virtual prostitute for foreign tourists and the local aristocracy. Rachel herself, brought by her mother's friend Rolen to the theater, sees that "the show was like a cheap circus where two or three young girls danced showing off for the young men in the first row" (Barnet, *Rachel's Song* 14). When she tries to look up at the ceiling in shame, Rolen "would take my head and lower it, obliging me to watch them" (14). This same Rolen arranges for a teen-age Rachel, "thirteen or fourteen, but with a woman's body" (14), to join the company herself to "pay for the electricity, or the rent" (15).

While these early scenes identify Rachel as a victim of the commodification of Cuban culture and identity, she quickly becomes herself a victimizer of Cuban masculinity; a series of aristocratic and bourgeois men fall under her spell and find themselves emasculated. Rachel's relationship to one of her employers typifies this shift from victim to victimizer. Rachel sleeps with him because he has power and position, but she feels as though her sexuality gives her the upper hand: "it cost him dearly. . . . Poor Don Anselmo! There are many sad, hopeless, life-sized puppets like him out there. Women are fundamentally bad. We abuse men. I confess" (48, 52). Rachel's relationship with her longtime lover, Adolfo, continues to fit this formula. While his refinement and money make him appear to be Rachel's superior, he worships her and even accompanies her to a party "dressed as a Dutch girl, and I as a noble Andalusian" (41). In contrast to the slaves in *Biografía*, who despite their homosexual practices never appear to be anything but the epitome of masculinity, the upper-class men of *Canción* take female lovers yet are unmasked as androgynous and impotent dandies.

The structure of *Canción de Rachel*, whereby men interject their fragmentary impressions of Rachel into her monologue, is meant to perform this marginalization of the men. Yet even though the intention may be to push the masculine voices to the text's margins to reflect how republican Cuba is characterized by a feminized public sphere, another effect is to make Rachel's testimony appear to be insufficient on its own. Through Barnet's own framing of Rachel's discourse, men's voices are given a higher truth value than Rachel's: in *Canción*'s prefatory note, Barnet explains the text's structure, whereby "characters . . . appear in the book, and . . . complement the central monologue"; not incidentally, these counternarrators are "by and large men" (5).[16] These men explicitly ground their attacks on Rachel in their authority as men: "But as for me, as a man, as a citizen and as a revolutionary, I think . . . [s]he was the animal that took advantage of this Republic. . . . Rachel is the best example of prostitution, the vice and the lie wrapped in a red ribbon that reigned in this country" (58–59).

Even Esteban appears in *Canción* to criticize Rachel's characterization of the race riots of 1912 as a "stupid uproar [that] calmed down when the Americans arrived" (55–56). This is only the most obvious example of what Ángel Luis Fernández Guerra explains as the strategy of counterposing Rachel's more outrageous beliefs with the interjections of more reliable voices to force the reader to produce a space behind her consciousness to inhabit themselves.[17] This process turns her testimony into a depthless surface not unlike the superficiality of postmodern pop culture. She even admits that "I can talk a bit but with no details. Whatever I might tell about is on the surface" (93). Montejo's testimony acts as a control in *Canción*; its intervention in *Canción* as counternarrative suggests *Biografía*, by contrast, as a self-aware narrative possessing its own depth and truth value and not supplying its reader with an outside or alternative position from which to take an ironic distance from the text.

Esteban lives at one with nature, is a fountain ("la fuente viva") of folk knowledge, and combines his skill as a storyteller with the manly action of anticolonial struggle. Rachel, by contrast, is the postcolonial artist not connected to the revolution, co-opted by global capitalism and forced to prostitute herself to the market. She lives in a society of "spectacle" (95), and she herself "was no true actress [but] a farce" (92). She describes her greatest talent as "faking": "Faking is very simple. You can't imagine how simple it is. Much less recognize it. Just imagine the results and you'll see that without some of these tricks, the greatest entertainer would go under" (47). These passages emphasize that Rachel is not a genuine artist, and indeed, the narrative as a whole associates her with the artificial and unnatural. While *Biografía* creates an epic world of organic wholeness for Esteban to inhabit, Rachel's difference is especially apparent in her distanced relationship to hard work and nature. In contrast to Esteban's detailed descriptions of the pleasure he took in backbreaking factory work, Rachel revels in how she "used all [her] little tricks to work less than anyone" (47), living off "prostitution" (59) rather than honest work. Her only relationship to the natural world that Esteban reveres is highly mediated and laughably artificial: for example, she believes strongly in astrology, that "the world is ruled by the stars" and that "the harmony of the earth is due to them" (110), yet admits that she knows more about Paris than about the countryside of her own Cuba.[18]

The depictions of Esteban and Rachel thus allow Barnet to periodize Cuban history in a way that posits the Cuban Revolution as a way out of capitalist postcoloniality. Although Barnet sets each of these *testimonios* in the somewhat distant past, *Biografía de un cimarrón* at the turn of the twentieth century and *Canción de Rachel* during the first few decades of the century, he deliberately draws connections between past and present. While its action spans the earliest years of the Cuban Republic, *Canción* is clearly meant to evoke the Batista period of the 1950s, whereas the battles against slavery and Spanish occupation depicted in *Biografía* cast the spirit of the Cuban Revolution as a return to the heroic days of the Cuban wars of independence. Barnet's prefatory notes to each text spell out this intention. *Canción* begins by identifying Rachel with the republican era: "Rachel's confessions, her troubled life during the scintillating years of the Cuban *belle époque* . . . have made possible a book which reflects the frustrated atmosphere of republican life. Rachel was . . . a true gauge of the country's social and political activities" (*Rachel's Song* 5). The preface to *Biografía*, meanwhile, puts forward a genealogy that establishes Esteban's contemporaneity: "his tradition as a revolutionary, first as a run-away slave, then in the war of independence, later as a member of the Socialist Party, comes to life today in his identification with the Cuban Revolution."[19]

Through her contrast with Esteban, Rachel becomes a perfect representative of all of the social, economic, and cultural forces of postcoloniality that threaten the possibility of an authentic, indigenous Caribbean culture. In the figure of Rachel, Barnet identifies the threat to Cuban independence as the United States and a locally complicit feminized bourgeoisie, who together during the modern colonial period managed to turn Cuba away from the heroic masculine tradition Esteban represents. Nightclubs, cabarets, and other accoutrements of the tourist industry have eroded Rachel's Cuban identity and forced her to prostitute herself by performing for an international culture industry. Barnet's periodization also suggests the challenges facing the postcolonial author: Esteban's authority depends on his relationship with anticolonial struggle, whereas Rachel's superficiality and falseness are produced by Cuba's first experience of postcoloniality. She becomes the dangerous threat of the postcolonial artist corrupted and feminized by the market. For postcoloniality to make a break from the republican period, Barnet suggests that Cuba must return to the path of the *cimarrón*; for the postcolonial writer to maintain his relevance and heroic masculinity, he must embrace *testimonio* as a way of avoiding commodification and aligning with the uncontaminated folk.

The End of Anticolonial Politics and the Beginnings of the Sistren Theatre Collective

Jamaican texts from this moment of transition display elements of two different emerging models of postcolonial Caribbean culture. On the one hand, some islands, such as Cuba, were turning away from international markets and seeking to develop an inward-looking form of independence, accompanied by the desire among cultural workers to uncover an indigenous culture outside of foreign domination accompanying this move: *testimonio*'s creation by Miguel Barnet and its consecration by the Casa de las Américas occurs in this context. For other islands, most dramatically Puerto Rico as well as Trinidad and Tobago, postcoloniality meant full incorporation into North American capitalism, with fiction by Luis Rafael Sánchez, Ana Lydia Vega, or Earl Lovelace borrowing from the contaminated language of the market to create new artistic forms. Jamaica in the 1970s found itself negotiating between Cuba's total withdrawal and Puerto Rico's full incorporation. From 1955 to 1972, following the Puerto Rican model, "official government policy [in Jamaica] encouraged and welcomed foreign capital" (Beckford and Witter 66). But in 1972, with the victory of the People's National Party (PNP), led by Michael Manley, official policy changed. Manley, under the slogan "We Are Not for Sale," pursued a policy of rapprochement with Cuba and resistance against U.S. imperialism. As a result of these competing demands, the island was torn apart in what amounted to a virtual civil war between rival political parties. The Caribbean cultural scene of the 1960s and 1970s responds to these various demands, dedicating itself, on the one hand, to the testimonial project of recuperating the voices of the subaltern folk, as in the *Savacou* issue or Barnet's *testimonios*, and, on the other hand, to understanding the contours of postcolonial exploitation through depicting exploitation not in terms of traditional colonialism but via new forms such as the tourist industry and the culture industry, as the next chapter examines.

Michael Manley described democratic socialism as the effort to achieve postcolonial freedom, to "create an economy that would be more independent of foreign control and more responsive to the needs of the majority of the people at home" (39). As Robert Carr notes in an essay about Manley's legacy, the project was explicitly framed as the taking back of the public sphere from foreign capital and its local representatives: "The process Manley describes [as democratic socialism] is primarily a process of decolonization, of moving to change the 'public' represented by state government from the (local and international) financial elite to the bulk of the population" (233). Carr argues that while Manley's government may have only been in power for eight years, the impact of democratic socialism in Jamaica is reflected in the expansion and redefinition of the public sphere: "The electoral figures bear witness to the historic involvement of the masses in the political process: [in the 1980 election] out of one million registered to vote, a record 86.9 percent voted" (233).

The Jamaican literary scene of the 1970s reflects the impact of Manley's project, both in its form and content. Just like the *Savacou* anthology, Jamaican drama of this period became invested in making the subaltern heard. Earlier attempts to create an indigenous theater in the 1930s by figures like Una Marson and Frank Hill presented a clearly middle-class perspective, though one often fascinated by or longing for working-class and peasant culture. At the same time, performances that spoke in the voices of the lower classes, such as Louise Bennett's, were for many years dismissed as comedy rather than serious drama. The turn toward folk theater by those identified as serious artists emerged during the transition from modern colonialism to postcoloniality as Derek Walcott joined the Little Carib Theatre Workshop in 1959 (renamed the Trinidad Theatre Workshop in 1962). In Jamaica, Trevor Rhone and the Sistren Theatre Collective became important parts of this postcolonial attempt to deploy drama as a way to give voice to the people, a parallel to the investment in cinema in Cuba.

Sistren was originally a group of working-class women organized by Manley's government as part of a full employment initiative. All accounts of Sistren begin with the importance of that social program for the group's development: "There would never have been a Sistren if there hadn't been an Impact Programme . . . consciously or unconsciously, the PNP had made a space within which women could begin to organize around their own concerns" (Ford-Smith, "Sistren Women's Theatre" 122). The group's first performance came in 1977 when Honor Ford-Smith, a young graduate of the Jamaica School of Drama, "was invited to direct a play for the Workers' Week concert. Thirteen women from the special employment programme came to our first meeting" (Sistren Theatre Collective, *Lionheart Gal* 10). These plays were explicitly testimonial: their first performed piece, *Downpression Get a Blow*, grew out of the discussions and improvisations of this first meeting, and Ford-Smith emphasizes that the group initially worked "without written material" ("Sistren Women's Theatre" 123) but instead based their performances on the group's own experiences. "I did a lot of listening to stories," Ford-Smith remembers, emphasizing the dialogic process of creating their plays (124). The group stayed together and became a full-time collective, continuing to formulate and perform plays and workshops based on issues like teen pregnancy, Jamaican history, domestic abuse, and political violence. Their work—from testimonial-based performances to a later collective autobiography—framed itself as the cultural equivalent of democratic socialism, the withdrawal from the networks of international capitalism as part of the effort to create a local, Jamaican public sphere. The rest of this chapter looks at how Ford-Smith theorizes a collective, popular theater centered around working-class women, and then moves to a discussion of how those theoretical issues play out in the group's testimonial collection, *Lionheart Gal*.

Sistren's testimonial project is explicitly positioned between a desire to keep alive anticolonialism and a sense of the ideology's exhaustion. The essay "Notes Toward a New Aesthetic," in particular, outlines the group's conflicted artistic and political goals. The essay acts as a description of Sistren's methodology and is written by Honor Ford-Smith, the group's director, or as she calls herself in this essay, its "facilitator." This antihierarchical gesture of refusing to call herself director is typical of Ford-Smith's terminology; she prefers to think of her players as "cultural workers," and thus "in a continuum with other workers in society" ("Notes" 29). She distinguishes Sistren's "cultural work" from any idea of "the arts" as "somehow transcendent and unrelated to ordinary life, [as] cordoned off from economic and political processes" (27). By contrast, Sistren emphasizes the organic wholeness of the political and cultural spheres. Ford-Smith deems this kind of work of reconnection urgently necessary because of a "segment[ing]" of "knowledge" (28) that relegates women's issues to the domestic sphere and intellectuals' concerns to a hermetic conception of art. By subverting this segmentation, "cultural work is part and parcel of a process of empowerment both at an individual and at a social level" (28). In this strand of the essay, then, Ford-Smith valorizes the importance of cultural work in the political struggle, lauding "the anti-colonial movement" and "the women's movement" as "two important historical movements which enabled the idea of cultural worker in the post-colonial world to be significantly developed . . . by naming a space within the specifics of everyday life that could be conceptualized as a basis for resistance" (27).

While at this point Ford-Smith invests culture with a political mission, in other moments she reserves for political action a privileged importance that culture cannot replace. In the same paragraph, she flatly states that cultural work "is not in itself a political action," and that cultural work may want to "carry responsibility for articulating and enacting political positions," but "it cannot do this" (28). Even this statement (cultural work "cannot do this") is highly ambiguous, failing to distinguish whether the "this" that cultural work cannot do is *articulating* or *enacting* the political. In fact, this essay goes on to show itself to be an effective articulation of political positions, and that Sistren has on many occasions enacted palpable (and successful) political change. Ford-Smith describes the most committed intervention that cultural work can hope to make as "using theatrical form as a rehearsal for change" (29).[20] She gives this example of how Sistren's performances can be such a rehearsal: "in work done some years ago in the sugar belt in Jamaica, we used forum theater models to train women to confront local government officials, to marshal the arguments and group cohesiveness needed for the process" (29). While this intervention succeeded, and the women got their demands, she reiterates that "it was the actual meeting with the councilor that won an improvement in the community water supply" (29). As much as Ford-Smith posits Sistren's practice as overcoming the modern separation of labor that devalues culture, she repeats the same gesture by reifying "actual" political intervention ("action") as a limited activity that art can only approach but never actually undertake. Despite this reification of "action" as the only valid means of political intervention, Ford-Smith lays out the ways in which Sistren *does* intervene politically, in particular in its reorganization of relations of production, which makes every member of the group a part of the creative process.

Consumer society is repeatedly identified as the enemy: cultural work's success is defined as "subverting the constraints of working within the market" (27), and collective theater's accomplishment is identified as its ability to "undermine the subordination of the creative process to market forces" (29).[21] In an interview, one of the original members, Pauline Crawford, explicitly opposes Sistren to "commercial playwrights" (Di Cenzo and Bennett 91) who fail to act as "role models" in their work; the very fact of market popularity seems here incompatible with "the message [Sistren] wants to put across" (91).[22] The challenge, in trying to put a "product before the public" (Ford-Smith, "Notes" 32), is to navigate between this type of (postcolonial) commercial co-optation that targets not a public but a consumer, as well as the elitist (anticolonial) literary ideology that assumes "the cultural worker is . . . more innately individualistic or sensitive or creative than the rest of us" (29) and thus thinks of himself or herself as above the (issues of) audience. The goal of Sistren is not only "making visible through theater hidden knowledge and submerged cultural codes" (30) but also "to break with rigid and hierarchical definitions of labor as they have come down to us in the Western theater tradition" (29), in order to find a creative process able not only to incorporate popular form and content but also to involve subaltern subjects themselves in the creation of art.

The role of the "facilitator" (similar to what Barnet calls the *gestor*) in this form of cultural production, and by extension in any testimonial project, thus becomes particularly crucial and particularly vexed. In workshops as well as public performances, the facilitator bears the tasks of recognizing and evaluating what constitutes "hidden knowledge"; helping the group develop techniques that turn this knowledge into methods of empowerment; and deciding which of the improvisations should be put on in public performance and what needs to stay "invisible for very real reasons of survival" (31). In the recording of these performances or testimonies in print, Ford-Smith, like Barnet, shapes the final product not only through the kinds of questions she asks but also as the editor who finally textualizes the informants' oral stories. The relationship of informants to director/writer/editor is complicated even further by each participant's relationship to language and literacy. Ford-Smith never tries to gloss over her privilege as "an apparently white Jamaican" whose family and educational background separate her in many ways from the "thirteen black Jamaican working class women" who make up the rest of the group (31). Yet neither does she entirely explain away how her relationship to the group "re-echoes traditional re-

lations of patronage between the light-skinned upper class which traditionally has dominated the country and the black working class" (31).

The texts produced by this alliance bear the force of these power relations in their language. The written versions of Sistren's plays appear in
the voices of the collective: when Ford-Smith transcribes the group's play
Bellywoman Bangarang for *Contemporary Drama of the Caribbean*, or
when *QPH* appears in *Postcolonial Plays: An Anthology* with the credit
"original text developed by members of the Collective and scripted by
Hertencer Lindsay with assistance from Honor Ford-Smith" (Gilbert
xiii), these plays end up speaking almost exclusively in what Ford-Smith
calls "Patwah," the creolized Jamaican English that is a marker of race
and class. Ford-Smith's writings about Sistren, meanwhile, speak in the
theoretical voice of an academic Standard English. This disjuncture is
nowhere more apparent than in *Lionheart Gal*. The text contains fif-
teen stories told by the members of the collective, twelve transcribed
by Ford-Smith and three written by the "middle-strata members of the
group" for whom "the oral interviews did not work well" (Sistren Theatre Collective, *Lionheart Gal* 16).[23] Ford-Smith includes her own story
in the volume, "Grandma's Estate," written in an English that could be
described as Jamaican Standard, but is virtually indistinguishable from
British English.[24] This disjuncture becomes a productive space for *Lionheart Gal*, but hints at the continuities between Sistren and the elitist elements of the anticolonial writers' desire to speak for the folk.[25]

Ford-Smith's introduction to *Lionheart Gal* begins by describing
two models of Afro-Caribbean womanhood—Nanny (Ni) the Maroon
leader, and the nanny who served in the plantation house during slavery. Similar to the *cimarrón* and Rachel, one embodies ultimate oppositionality and public resistance, the other private acquiescence and incorporation into a dehumanizing system. But Ford-Smith argues that this
overly simplified opposition insufficiently represents the realities of the
nanny and Ni, and the confusion between their names is only the most
obvious sign of how the opposition between them is deconstructed. Even
though Ni led runaway slaves in revolt against plantation owners, "she
did this until 1741 when she was granted a land patent in the Parish of
Portland . . . the granting of the land patent to Ni had a contradictory
effect. It created within the slave colony a homeland (apartheid-style) for
the free blacks, but in a sense, since the war had ended, it contained the
revolutionary potential of the Maroons within the island as a whole"
(2). The contradiction of the Maroons is that although they fought for
and managed to win their own freedom from the British, they stopped

short of confronting the slave system as a whole or freeing hundreds of thousands of other Afro-Jamaicans in bondage. Anticolonialism, while bringing about certain victories, is judged here as ultimately only partially successful.

As much as this introduction seeks to complicate the image of the warrior Ni, Ford-Smith also hopes that *Lionheart Gal* will help recuperate the figure of the passive and submissive nanny. As she puts it, "the work in this collection indicates that the two images of women may not, in fact, be as opposite as we have been taught to believe" (2). One of the goals of *Lionheart Gal*, then, will be to show the quotidian resistance of the nanny, the "ways in which ordinary women have determined their own struggles for themselves and the ways in which they have assessed their own victories and defeats" (2–3). The stories thus will continue, in the anticolonial tradition, to serve a didactic purpose and participate in the struggle: "these discoveries may suggest ways of re-inventing the terms of struggle and the strategy itself" (3). But the reevaluating of the nanny clearly is meant to go beyond anticolonial models of oppositionality. Ford-Smith suggests that the Ni/nanny opposition can itself be understood as a sort of periodization in which the terms of oppression and exploitation have changed, and thus demand new kinds of responses that are not as ready to privilege public rebellions over private ones. She explicitly identifies Ni as "the Maroon leader of the eighteenth century" (1), as if to emphasize her distance from the present day. She includes the idea of historical change in the emergence of the nanny figure: "thereafter, the second image of the Caribbean woman began to come into being as the centuries progressed" (2). While Ford-Smith identifies these two figures as "opposite ends of the spectrum of colonial past and present" (2), that statement might be amended to associate Ni with the anticolonial and the nanny with the postcolonial. The nanny's strategies are particularly important to understand in light of the postcolonial realization that there is no ultimate site of refusal, that "those who win struggles rarely do so by confronting the oppressor on his own terms" (3), especially in a spectral postmodernity where "the authors of these processes, the elite, are as invisible as ghosts" (4).

The introduction positions the stories from *Lionheart Gal* as theorizing a new form of committed postcolonial Caribbean literature in the wake of modern colonialism's end. A number of themes emerge from the stories, but three recur most frequently and appear to be most important: first, the migration from the country to the city, narrated by nearly all of the women; second, violence across all levels of Jamaican society, from domestic abuse to politically motivated massacres; and third, the coming to consciousness of the women about everything from their own bodies and sexualities, to the political and economic workings of the international system. In the rest of this chapter, I use examples from a number of the stories to discuss how the treatment of each of these themes marks *Lionheart Gal* as a postcolonial Caribbean text.

In addition to engaging in a dialogue with the Manley government of the 1970s, *Lionheart Gal* emphasizes another sociohistorical marker, the urbanization and industrialization of Jamaica immediately following independence. Nearly all of the stories narrate the move from country to city, and how that move is associated with the decline of a rural subsistence economy in favor of integration into an international capitalist system. In "'Exodus' A Run," the narrator 'locates her story in "dem days Labour [the Jamaica Labour Party (JLP)] did inna power" (49). The JLP, following the Puerto Rican model, encouraged foreign investment and the consolidation of small landholdings. In "'Exodus' A Run," the emphasis on the interests of larger estates comes at the expense of the rural peasants: "More a dem farmer start come out to group meeting as election time did near. Dem say dem couldn't get no fertilizer. Is only di big farmer get fertilizer, when is all a dem did vote Labour" (49). This story goes on to recount the coming to consciousness of the countryside folk, and their election of a PNP delegate to support their interests. At the same time, it illustrates the decline in the viability of small farming, and the move to urban centers by many of these displaced and dispossessed peasants.

Similarly, "Country Madda Legacy" begins with the narrator's announcement that she has decided not to stay in the country: "From me very young me decide seh me nah go do no farm wuk. . . . Is a hard life in country" (81). By observing her father "do some breed a back breaking wuk" (81), and her "stepmadda" who "used to wuk fi one a di bigger farmer" (83), she concludes that both the type of labor and the relationships of production demanded by the countryside are not the life she wants to live. Another story reminds us that these were the days before "di seventies [when] di government pass di minimum wage" (97), and that unionization was discouraged and unionized workers frequently intimidated (98). While moving to the city hardly solves any of these women's problems, their stories give a picture of a postcolony reorienting itself economically and socially during the years following independence.

In addition to this overtly sociological content, the stories of *Lionheart Gal* depict a society filled with masculine violence directed at all the wrong targets. In "Veteran by Veteran" and "Foxy and di Macca Palace War," the narrators watch poor men from various ghettos around Kingston, armed by Manley's PNP and the Central Intelligence Agency–backed JLP, killing one another in a senseless war. Foxy sees this and realizes that the political leader has distributed these weapons to the poor "because him wanted was to control di people living in di Underworld" (263). While the women show repeatedly their ability to organize themselves against exploitative landlords and abusive family members, as long as the men are fighting one another, they are never challenging society's real centers of power. The narrator of "Veteran by Veteran" finally sees that "is like di politicians no waan working class people fi live good for when dem have dem political differences is always inna di working class area dem fight it out" (190).

Robert Carr calls attention to this political violence as a form of lashing out by those abandoned by a political system whose public sphere has not become open to all: "The men are here engaged in a struggle to the death, and it is their machismo combined with their disaffection from the social pact, as much as what they stand to gain from the support of their political bosses, that drives them" (259). In addition to machismo, Carr alludes to another component of the men's violent reaction as their "disaffection from the social pact." *Lionheart Gal* further identifies domestic abuse, like the political violence of the warring ghetto-dwellers, as the product of a postcolonial crisis of masculinity. Ford-Smith argues in her introduction that both of these forms of violence work against the potential alliances of working-class people that could challenge the unflinchingly corrupt ruling classes. She refers to this "effect of the ideology of male dominance" as being to blame because of the way it "reinforces the interests of men across class lines and divides the interests of men and women of the working class by justifying male privilege and giving black men a stake in the system of domination" (Sistren Theatre Collective, *Lionheart Gal* 5). As systemic underemployment forecloses the opportunity for men to construct an identity as a provider for their families, violence against one another and abuse of women thus become the only perceived avenues for these men to show their manliness. The men become emasculated, as in the case of the father in "The Emancipation of a Household Slave," who "was too meek and mild . . . me stepmadda dominate him" (114).

What Ford-Smith identifies as the "ideology of male dominance" undermines the possibility of solidarity based on class. The narrator of "A Working Woman," for example, laments the ways that people mistreat one another and especially women: "to deal wid di public is a terrible ting. Dem treat all workers bad, but dem more tek advantage when yuh is a woman" (101). This public is oppressive rather than libratory as male resentment over female empowerment contributes to the atmosphere of violence. The narrator of "A Working Woman" draws her conclusions about the public's inherent cruelty when a "working class man" attacks her after she sells him an improperly marked container of ice cream. He justifies this overreaction by saying that when he brings home the wrong type of ice cream, his woman gets upset at him. The man thus positions himself as victim of these two women, the one for whom he must buy ice cream and the other from whom he must buy it. He portrays himself as powerless at the hands of these women, and forced to deploy the only power available to him, violence.

The last story, "Ava's Diary," features another man frustrated by the perceived power of women over men in postcolonial Jamaica. This story narrates how the writer's "baby-faada" becomes increasingly abusive as she becomes more and more successful in her endeavors with Sistren. From the beginning of their relationship, "Bertie love to lick me" (285). She blames an atmosphere of socially accepted violence against women: "Fi-him friend do it too and him follow fashion. Is a style wid dem. Some a dem love talk bout how dem a 'control dat dawta'" (285). Initially, she is embarrassed and ashamed to seek any help, but when she joins Sistren, she finds a community of women who can relate to her situation. Yet rather than alleviating her problems, things begin from that point to get worse: "I think Bertie must be jealous about my work in Sistren" (293), she writes in her diary. After she begins to go on tour to Barbados and is preparing to leave for Canada, he nearly beats her to death. He calls her friends in Sistren "lesbians" (301), leading her to conclude that his eruptions reveal an insecurity about her belonging to a strong female community: "Why do men always feel threatened anytime we woman begin to exchange thought and experience?" (293).

The relationships described in "Ava's Diary" reveal the overall mission of Sistren, the purpose with which Ford-Smith and her players imbue postcolonial art. The testimonies that Sistren presents in plays or in *Lionheart Gal* are meant both to build a community of women willing to publicly speak about their common experiences and to serve a practical pedagogical function of creating an informed and aware nation. The dysfunctional "public" described in "A Working Woman," where, as Ford-Smith mentions in her introduction, "the effect of the ideology of male dominance is to mystify the relationship between the accumulation of wealth for the few and the impoverishment for the many" (5), requires Sistren to take on the pedagogical mission of anticolonialism to shed light on these forms of ideological blindness. But whereas the anticolonialists presented this message from above, it is important to Sistren that their dramatic pieces be created out of real stories of the subaltern experience and performed in the counterpublic voices of Jamaican Patwah.

As much as the plays, *Lionheart Gal* illustrates Sistren's desire to organize the public sphere for a new pedagogical project; the trajectory of nearly all of the stories is from ignorance to consciousness. To stage this narrative of coming to consciousness, "Veteran by Veteran" begins with the narrator confessing her ignorance about politics—"dem time deh me never have no thought bout politics. Me never understand notten bout it" (180)—before later getting into a passionate argument defending the PNP. "The Emancipation of a Household Slave" starts by illustrating the narrator's naïveté as she imagines what coming to the city will be like, and she soon comes to be exploited because of her innocence; but again, the second half of the story shows that she has learned not to be taken advantage of, as she battles her stepmother for control of her paycheck. The inability to understand their situation puts these women at a particular disadvantage with regard to issues like domestic abuse, birth control, and domestic labor. A number of the women become pregnant because of their self-described "ignorance" about sexuality; the statement in "Me Own Two Hand," that no one "never tell me notten pertaining to pregnancy" (167) is repeated almost exactly in "Rock Stone a River Bottom No Know Sun Hot" and "Criss Miss." Sistren is meant to form a direct answer to this kind of naïveté. As the narrator of "Foxy and di Macca Palace War" notes, Sistren's first play, *Downpression Get a Blow*, developed from the women talking to one another, becoming aware of their common experiences, and wanting to discuss their issues in a public forum that could help other women: "Plenty women used to talk bout di children dat we have and di baby-faada problem. At first, me was shy to talk bout myself. . . . Me never discuss it wid nobody. When me come meet Didi and hear she talk bout her baby faada and how she hate him after she get pregnant, me say, 'Well if yuh can say your own me can say mine, for we actually deh pon di same ting'" (273). Sistren's plays thus become a Brechtian tool of what Ford-Smith describes as "conscientization," or the "move from the personal to the structural analysis" ("Sistren Women's Theatre" 125). This is an especially important tool for the working-class women who are meant to be the audience of Sistren's performances and workshops because, as the narrator of "Country Madda

Legacy" explains, these poor women lack consciousness because "dem no get fi look beyond what happen to dem to what cause it, cause dem so busy wid hard wuk" (Sistren Theatre Collective, *Lionheart Gal* 81).

In this way, we can see how Sistren's testimonial project, like Barnet's, continues in its pedagogical aspirations to retain the anticolonialist notion of the intellectual as bearer of a special knowledge, or as best suited to distill the positive aspects of an idealized public imagined as the folk. Seeking to create an art opposed to imperial power and the market seems to demand a complicated desire for but distancing from this counterpublic. These anticolonial elements can be seen most clearly in the theoretical discourse surrounding their practice, and in the vexed relationships to language within the group. At the same time, Sistren, more successfully than Barnet, points the way to a postcolonial art engaged in the quotidian process of nation building, especially in their attention to community and their practical concern with women's everyday lives. In these moments, when the group truly achieves a dialogic rather than a didactic conversation with the popular, Sistren shows what a committed postcolonial Caribbean culture might resemble. Instead of imagining politics only in anticolonial terms, as a contest for the state, Sistren points to the sort of everyday politics that can inspire postcolonial critique, as when Ford-Smith advocates "challenging the boundaries between the domestic and the public spheres" to redefine "sexuality and everyday life [as] an arena for discussion and political praxis" ("Notes" 28). My next chapter turns to how this redefinition of art's relationship to the popular is part of this postcolonial rethinking of politics.

8 Cultural Studies and the Commodified Public

Luis Rafael Sánchez's La guaracha del Macho Camacho and Earl Lovelace's The Dragon Can't Dance

TESTIMONIO ATTEMPTS TO KEEP ALIVE the anticolonial ideal of the intellectual as representing the public while remaining engaged in counterpublic critique in the face of the postcolonial crisis of that model. A prominent strain of postcolonial Caribbean literary criticism mirrors this tactic by turning toward popular cultural, especially music, as a more authentic way of giving voice to the nation than the high culture of the modern colonial period. The first part of this chapter discusses that trend in the work of scholars such as Gordon Rohlehr, Juan Flores, Carolyn Cooper, Lisa Sánchez González, and Juan Otero Garabís, literary critics who have increasingly incorporated analysis of popular music into their work as a way of decentering high culture. Yet the idea that aligning with music might allow literary intellectuals to make their work more popular—described by Jean Franco as "the ideal of community persist[ing] among the intelligentsia in the form of nostalgia . . . evoked by music" (211)—is inextricable from the rise of postcoloniality in the region as an increasingly commodified, massified form of domination, as Sylvia Wynter explains in her two-part essay "We Must Learn to Sit Down Together and Talk About a Little Culture." Caribbean criticism and creative writing of this period thus make the turn to popular music to reinvigorate the literary while maintaining a deep suspicion of the culture industry's influence on the dissemination of culture. I follow discussion of the rise of Caribbean cultural studies with an examination of two novels from the 1970s—Luis Rafael Sánchez's *La guaracha del Macho Camacho* and Earl Lovelace's *The Dragon Can't Dance*—to show the competing desire for popularity but disdain for commercialism exhibited by critics and novelists alike as they occupy the contradictory space between anticolonialism and postcoloniality.

Caribbean Literary Studies and the Cultural Turn

The 1970s marks a particularly important moment of shift and flux in the Caribbean, from the possibilities promised by the liberation struggles against modern colonialism to the realities of a U.S.-dominated postcoloniality. Looking at the 1970s also makes visible how this political and social transition has coincided with a cultural one: just as literature was finding its role in the public sphere in question, the decade witnessed the golden age of socially engaged salsa and the rise of reggae in both local Jamaican politics and the imagining of an international black diaspora.[1] In a colonial public sphere that privileged high culture, anticolonial writers like José Martí, Aimé Césaire, Claude McKay, and George Lamming sought to inhabit the written word as a cultural weapon in the battles for decolonization. Postcoloniality brought uncertainty about that system of values; the result is an increased movement into cultural studies for Caribbean writers and critics, as popular culture becomes the site for intellectuals to channel the utopian aspirations once invested in literature.

The notion that aligning themselves with popular music would allow literary intellectuals to democratize their practice and regain their public role becomes the inspiration for a number of postcolonial literary works that draw on popular music, from dub poetry to novels like Daniel Maximin's *L'isolé soleil*, Colin Channer's *Waiting in Vain* and *Satisfy My Soul*, Pedro Antonio Valdéz's *Bachata del ángel caído*, Mayra Santos-Febres's *Sirena Selena vestida de pena*, and Angie Cruz's *Let It Rain Coffee*.[2] This trend in literary production is paralleled in the academic rise of Caribbean cultural studies. The field of cultural studies follows the attempts made in *testimonio* to turn to popular culture as the last authentic repository of Caribbean identity in the face of cultural imperialism, at precisely the moment in which international culture industries have become dominant in the production and circulation of visual and aural forms. Within the context of these competing demands, cultural studies becomes a strategy for addressing the postcolonial crisis of literary authority. Edgardo Rodríguez Juliá's *El entierro de Cortijo*, describing the famed Puerto Rican musician's 1982 funeral, functions to mourn the end of a cultural epoch while brilliantly depicting this crisis: after a group of girls at the funeral call Rubén Blades, the *salsero* who most directly connects to the intellectual tradition of anticolonialism,[3] "un pendejo" (136), the narrator wonders, "is any authority at all possible?" (73). The final lines of Rodríguez Juliá's *crónica* ask: "we are living in the age of ghostly intentions and unburied gestures, tradition burst into a thousand clashing pieces, so that how are we to reconcile so much madness with so much tenderness?" (73). Just as the writings by Martí discussed in chapter 3 manifested the lettered intellectual's simultaneous desire for and fear of popular culture during the transitional years from mercantile slavery to modern colonialism, texts from the passage to postcoloniality demonstrate a similar attempt to draw inspiration from the cultures of the urban folk even while maintaining suspicion of the market's influence on these mass cultures.

The movement in Caribbean literary studies from strict attention to literary texts to a criticism centered around music and popular culture begins to be seen in the 1970s in the work of influential literary critics such as Gordon Rohlehr. Rohlehr emerged as a major authority on West Indian literature during the *Savacou* debate of the early 1970s, in a series of essays about the nature of West Indian poetry and the relationship of literature to orality and the subaltern folk.[4] Rohlehr defends the testimonial impulse behind the *Savacou* anthology but suggests that despite a number of poems in which writers like Mervyn Morris and Victor Questel explore the challenges of translating music into poetry, the volume does not go far enough in giving space to actual untranslated popular music.[5] In "West Indian Poetry: Some Problems of Assessment," one of his most expansive responses to criticism of the anthology, Rohlehr supplies close readings not only of Bongo Jerry's poetry but also of "Bongo Nyah," a "popular song, which was danced in Trinidad and Guyana merely because of its exciting beats," in order to show the sophisticated social critique articulated by that song (135). Rohlehr argues that "music generally predicts the course of things in Jamaica" much better than "any of the poetry . . . emanating from the Mona Campus" (139). This observation about music as an important point of entry into West Indian social reality runs throughout Rohlehr's writings. While Rohlehr published extensively on West Indian writers such as Lamming, Brathwaite, Roger Mais, and Derek Walcott, he also repeatedly returns to analysis of popular music; *Calypso and Society in Pre-Independence Trinidad*, for example, adopts the techniques of textual analysis to show how music is "one of the surest guides toward an understanding of our milieu and our moment" (vi). Rohlehr's dual interest, in literature as well as music, makes him an important pioneer in the trend toward cultural studies that emerges full-blown during the 1990s among Caribbean literary critics.

Rohlehr's growing investment in cultural studies and music as a supplement to literary studies is a trend visible throughout the region. Elena

Machado Sáez and I discuss in the first chapter of *The Latino/a Canon and the Emergence of Post-Sixties Literature* how in Latino-Caribbean literary studies, Flores, Sánchez González, and Otero Garabís explain their parallel trajectories toward music as a better expression of the subaltern nation, less implicated in elite upper-class institutional formations (which Rohlehr invokes as "the Mona campus"). The suspicion of literature, as "institutionalized" and "canon-forming" (Flores, *From Bomba* 184), "affianced to brutal institutional partners" (Sánchez González 188), and distanced from the "pueblo" (Otero Garabís 155–156), leads to a movement toward music in the work of other major Caribbean literary critics during this time period. The opening pages of Carolyn Cooper's 1993 *Noises in the Blood*, for example, contrasts her latest work on Jamaican popular culture with her early career studying the poetry of Derek Walcott: "These essays on Jamaican popular culture have their genesis in my 1977 doctoral dissertation 'A Different Rage: An Analysis of the Works of Derek Walcott, 1948–1976.' They can be seen as a mirror image of the much earlier work; a transgressive reversal of ideological positions" (13). In this introduction, Cooper suggests that her earlier work, dealing with "Establishment Walcott" (14), was too literary, too concerned with "a western literary form" (3). She marks her turn to popular culture as explicitly "transgressive" and oppositional to the high cultural values literature represents, positing music as a marginal form, "a body of knowledge that is often devalued both at home and abroad" (xi).

Flores, Sánchez González, Otero Garabís, and Cooper suggest the reasons that the Caribbean literary field during the last decades of the twentieth century begins to de-privilege literature, in particular by inverting its relationship with popular cultural forms such as music. These critics focus primarily on the postcolonial impulse toward suspicion of literature as part of the desire for indigenous cultural forms: for each critic, literature is aligned with the high culture of the Caribbean's ruling classes and foreign imperial powers, whether England or the United States. The novel, with its "assimilationist proclivities" (Flores, *From Bomba* 183), has abandoned its stake in the political and can no longer represent a Caribbean form of knowledge to use against the metropole. To serve this function, music must be imagined as both popular (within the local setting) and marginal (in the global context). Positioning music as voice of both the public and an oppositional counterpublic re-creates the anticolonial ideas of the literary and becomes a useful fiction for academics seeking to "turn history upside-down" (Cooper, *Noises* 174) and give political significance to their literary endeavors. Cultural studies becomes a way to create a public role for an increasingly privatized literary field.

As productive as this trajectory in Caribbean literary studies has been, Sylvia Wynter's "We Must Learn to Sit Down Together and Talk About a Little Culture" raises a number of issues that challenge the assumptions of this cultural turn.[6] Wynter, writing in 1968 and 1969, identifies a new situation in the Caribbean that undermines any effort to reanimate the anticolonial concept of the folk: "the concept of 'people,' better expressed by the Spanish 'pueblo,' is vanishing fast" ("We Must Learn, Part I" 25). Wynter discusses this new situation as a "suburban" (26) existence where "it was easier to fight 'manifest unfreedom' in 1938 . . . than to grapple with 'seeming freedom' as we now must do" (30), a description perfectly capturing the transition from anticolonial opposition to the crisis of postcoloniality. She describes this crisis as "another facet of exile" where even writers at home have become distanced from a direct relationship with their people (25). This exile from the public sphere, what she calls "the exclusion of the West Indian writer from West Indian life" (26), occurs precisely as the citizenry of the postcolonial nation begins to be shaped into a public: "the writer who returns from exile at the metropolitan centre to 'write for his people' . . . must come face to face with the fact that his 'people' has become the 'public'" (25).

Thinking about the people as a public has certain benefits, which Wynter identifies as a challenge to the "writer who consciously sets out to write for an elite" (25). "Art for Art's sake" (24) is no longer possible as this hierarchy of high and low culture is collapsed. But uncritical celebrations of this leveling are equally inadequate, as "the writer, who, wanting to write 'for the people' falls into the trap of writing for the consumer" (25). In other words, the fiction of an uncontaminated and authentic folk becomes increasingly unsustainable at the same time that postcolonial reorganization is integrating the Caribbean into the postmodern world system: "the public in the Caribbean, equally like the public in the great metropolitan centres, are being conditioned through television, radio, and advertising, to want what the great corporations of production in the culture industry, as in all others, have conditioned them to want" (25). Wynter distinguishes between the anticolonial ideal of the people as collective actors and the postcolonial reality of a public as a collection of private individuals, linking this discontinuity explicitly to the massification of culture and communication in Caribbean society. She is interested, then, in slipping the yoke of the European literary tradition but also in the political implications of replacing that tradition with a model of culture based on consuming the popular products of global and local culture industries. Wynter provides a lens for seeing how Caribbean cultural studies, in de-privileging literature as unpopular and at the same time turning to some of the most commodified forms such as popular music, can tend to reinforce the crisis of the literary and the valuing of consumable products.

Wynter emphasizes the contaminated nature of postcolonial culture: she reads the market as a mechanism of censorship no less dangerous than the "Soviet . . . 'trial' of writers" (25), with "market commissars" determining what will be allowed to become public and circulate (26). Jean Franco, writing in the 1990s, echoes Wynter's concerns with "the literary intelligentsia's diminishing importance and displacement from public discourse" in Latin America (197), and the associated "angst" as "the utopian vision of the future . . . has now vanished" (196). Franco observes that "the utopian vision was sustained in large part by a literary intelligentsia whose medium was print culture" (196), arguing that the rise of television and the mass market's role in disseminating literature have undermined the potential for a politically oppositional culture. The challenge Franco identifies is maintaining this distrust of the market and popularity without falling into an elitism that prefers the "nomadic margins" (205) to actual engagement with the contaminated desires of the Latin American and Caribbean majority populations. Wynter similarly seeks to avoid the elitist stance against popularity as well as the populist turn toward music and "mass culture" ("We Must Learn, Part I" 25), seeing both as equally unable to allow the intellectual to occupy a space of critique and "constant revolutionary assault against" the "inauthenticity of the so-called real" (24).

In distancing herself from both of these stances, however, Wynter finds herself in a virtually untenable position. She eventually decides that although "books have a function in West Indian society[,] West Indian writers have none" (25). Intellectuals located in the university—the institution that becomes the target of Wynter's critique most explicitly in Part II of the essay, and the location of Rohlehr, Cooper, and Otero Garabís (who have all spent most of their careers in universities in the Caribbean) as well as Flores and Sánchez González (both employed in the U.S. academy)—in profiting from "the separation of mental from physical work" (We Must Learn, Part I 29) have become a "technocrat elite" divided off from the "consumer mass" (30). Wynter is thus arguing against the anticolonial idealization of the folk as still applicable to her postcolonial context even while she repeats the gesture made by Martí, Aimé Césaire, and McKay to oppose their own marginalized literary sensibility to an intellectual entrenchment in the institutions of the professional class. The irony here is that through deriving authority from institutional location, postcolonial intellectuals no longer have to venture into the contaminating space of the market as the anticolonialists did—as we saw in the first half of the book, Martí, McKay, Roumain, James, and others supported themselves at various parts of their careers through publishing in the newspaper, and that medium's market demands shaped their discourses. Wynter overlooks this uneven and impure heritage of anticolonialism, preferring to emphasize the "revolutionary intention" of the previously "coherent culture" (28) in order to try to establish an uncontaminated past to return to. But refusing to see a productive side to the market leaves Wynter without any way of imagining a positive relationship for the Caribbean writer or intellectual to postcolonial culture other than imagining a romantic return to a previously more revolutionary moment.

Wynter's essay calls attention to how imbuing the field of literature and literary criticism with models and methods learned from popular culture walks a fine line with acquiescing to the dictates of the culture industry, which has little time for as unmarketable a product as literary work, even as she tacitly acknowledges this as one of the few strategies available for giving postcolonial Caribbean criticism a voice in the public sphere. Wynter thus expresses an overwhelming pessimism about the possibility of a positive or oppositional popular culture in the postcolonial Caribbean, in contrast to the optimism of Cooper or Sánchez González about music's ability to articulate subaltern desires. While these critics take sides for or against the massification of Caribbean culture, creative writers like Sánchez and Lovelace keep alive the utopian ideal of literature as a space structured by these competing demands but also able to embody contradictory points of view. Postcolonial Caribbean writers have had to engage with both the challenges and opportunities offered by entry into the global marketplace, but cannot shy away from the realities of the market as a distinguishing feature of postcoloniality. The postcolonial literary field is marked by an ambivalent mourning of the anticolonial concept of literature able to participate in political action, as intellectuals and artists are torn between reinstituting and destabilizing anticolonialism's authority by investing the printed word with the sounds of popular music. The rest of this chapter looks at how Luis Rafael Sánchez's *La guaracha del Macho Camacho* and Earl Lovelace's *The Dragon Can't Dance* imagine the field of possibilities made available to the writer by the spread of popular music and its associated discourses.

La guaracha del Macho Camacho: Navigating Dead Ends in Commodified Culture

La guaracha del Macho Camacho and *The Dragon Can't Dance* explore the redefinition of the public, the private, and the political amid the reconfiguration of urban space in San Juan and Port of Spain during the early years of postcoloniality. These novels take as their content the crises of literature and masculinity, attempting to resolve these crises primarily on the level of form. *La guaracha del Macho Camacho* and *The Dragon Can't Dance* draw on, incorporate, and modify the popular, massified forms of the people in the making of art. Both novels prominently feature a critique of the relationship of Caribbean popular cultures to the culture industries accompanying Operation Bootstrap in Puerto Rico and Eric Williams's efforts to imitate that process in Trinidad and Tobago during the 1960s and 1970s. Both novels explore how urbanization, the language of mass communication, and commercialism threaten the possibility of art as much as progressive politics in the Caribbean of the 1970s. Lovelace and Sánchez show how postcolonial Caribbean literature seeks to simultaneously live up to and break from the past by navigating between the contaminated world of commercial culture and elitist conceptions of high literature.

La guaracha del Macho Camacho appeared in 1976 as a landmark event for Caribbean literature written in Spanish. Efraín Barradas speculates: "I don't think that in the history of Puerto Rican literature there had been another novel as commented upon by its contemporaries in the initial moment of its publication as *La guaracha*."[7] Politically, the mid-1970s in Puerto Rico was marked by the first popularly elected pro-statehood government; public intellectuals like Luis Rafael Sánchez were struggling to define their place in this society, while at the same time, salsa was experiencing its *edad de oro* with socially engaged performers like Eddie Palmieri, Hector Lavoe, Willie Colón, and Rubén Blades. For writers and critics envious of the public voices of these *salseros*, *La guaracha del Macho Camacho* suggested the possibility that literature could enter that public sphere. Arcadio Díaz Quiñones writes of the effect the novel had on Puerto Rican intellectuals in his introduction to the edition republished in 2000: "*La guaracha* had immediate repercussions. . . . It allowed a considerable number of Puerto Ricans to inter-vene, from literature or criticism, in cultural debates."[8]

Questions about the public, culture's role in forming that public, and the nature of the public formed by popular culture are at the heart of the novel. *La guaracha del Macho Camacho* begins by interpellating its audience as a public with a direct, second-person address: the first line reads, "If you turn around now, a cautious turn, a cautious look, you'll see her sitting and waiting" (Sánchez, *Macho Camacho's Beat* 5). The reader as audience thus becomes implicated in the story, but only as an omniscient voyeur, passively consuming the scene presented. The impli-cations of this positioning are made even more explicit in the short di-gressions between each chapter, which interrupt the main narrative to promote Macho Camacho and his *guaracha*: in the first of these, an un-named DJ addresses readers with the anonymous yet intimate "ladies and gentlemen, friends," going on to describe Macho Camacho's can-onization by "the distinguished public" as "the one who says so" (15). Readers of the novel are thus placed in a similar position to the charac-ters within who find their communities through listening to the radio or watching television, a sort of "phantom public" (to use Bruce Robbins's term) connected virtually by their status as consumers.[9] In this context, the products of popular culture—Macho Camacho's song, *El Show de Irís Chacón*, and the novel itself—connect communities and create op-portunities for people to imagine themselves as a public, even if the con-tours of this public are severely restricted.

The novel's plot and setting reinforce this sense of stasis and restric-tion. The duration of the novel lasts only a few minutes and contains almost no action: the narrative shifts between a traffic jam where we find Senator Vicente Reinosa and his son, Benny, stuck in separate cars; a mistress awaiting the senator, alternately called La China Hereje and La Madre; and the senator's wife, Graciela. The enormous traffic jam, the *tapón* that is part and parcel of Puerto Rican industrialized moder-nity, frustrates the drivers at the same time that it freezes everyone in their place. It stops the action and ensures that virtually nothing hap-pens throughout the novel; even the suggestion of change or mobility in this world appears unthinkable. The novel treats the predatory relation-ship between the senator and La China Hereje as symbolic of Puerto Rico's relationship to the United States; Reinosa, explicitly aligned with the United States as part of the island's pro-statehood party, acts as lo-cal bourgeois politician whose wealth and position of power allow him to take advantage of La China Hereje, the lower-class woman who needs his money. As in anticolonial writing such as Martí's "Nuestra América" or Roumain's *Gouverneurs de la rosée*, imperialism can be read on the body of the native female.

For the critics who *La guaracha del Macho Camacho* has allowed to, as Díaz Quiñones puts it, "intervene in cultural debates" (15), the status of popular culture within the novel has been the source of fundamental disagreements. In fact, the turn toward cultural studies has often been enacted directly through Sánchez's novel. Lisa Sánchez González and Juan Otero Garabís, for example, both use readings of the novel to make their move away from literature and toward music as the articulation of a transnational public. Sánchez González's last chapter, on what she calls "Boricua cultural studies," begins with a discussion of *La guaracha del Macho Camacho*: "Macho Camacho's *guaracha* gives voice, in an unmistakably Puerto Rican accent, to a collectivizing realization . . . the shared experience of hearing it . . . provides its characters—and its readers—a dynamic moment for . . . re/turning to what has been perhaps the only genuinely inclusive national articulation in Puerto Rico's history: popular music" (165). The novel's stylistic resemblance to popular speech and music allows it to be "anti-canonical" (165) as it breaks down hierarchies between the spoken and written word (166). Yet while Sánchez González sees the novel opening up new spaces for academic study of Latino/a popular culture, Otero Garabís understands it as an effort to close down and control the threats of the U.S. culture industry on Puerto Rican identity.[10] Otero Garabís reads Luis Rafael Sánchez's resistance to the contaminated world of popular music as a privileging of experimental literature as an autonomous space, independent of market concerns: "the novel aspires to create with the reader an intellectual community that, although contaminated with the play of mass culture, maintains the necessary distance to write."[11] Citing an interview in which the author of *La guaracha del Macho Camacho* posits "Puerto Rican literature as a wall against the unbearable vulgarity of assimilation,"[12] Otero Garabís argues that the novel allows Sánchez to critique the growth of commercialism and offer the lettered city as a bastion against foreign penetration and the dilution of a literarily constructed, Spanish-speaking *puertorriqueñidad*.

These readings appear to be at odds: popular culture functions in the novel either to subvert or reinforce the positioning of the literary. But both sides agree that the major concern in *La guaracha del Macho Camacho* is whether literary language is possible in the postmodern Caribbean. In either case, language is hopelessly corrupted by radio, music, television, and film; the only difference is whether we should celebrate or lament the impossibility of a literary public sphere. Understanding the positioning of such a public sphere in the world of *La guaracha del Macho Camacho* depends on the novel's particularly gendered division of space: for virtually the entire novel, the women remain privately sequestered in a variety of inside locations while the men are almost always in the public space of the streets. In the opening scene, as the reader watches La China Hereje passively "sitting and waiting" (Sánchez, *Macho Camacho's Beat* 5) while the senator "climbs into his car of cars and nice as you please he goes off in his car of cars" (7), this dichotomy of inside/outside is scarcely broken. From this point forward, the streets will be almost exclusively the domain of the senator and his son, while La China Hereje, Doña Chon, and Graciela will stay within their homes, apartments, and, in Graciela's case, her therapist's office.

Yet to conceive of the inside as private and outside as public gives only a most superficial understanding of space in *La guaracha del Macho Camacho*. These are not the same streets where anticolonial resistance fighters like Pedro Albizu Campos battled colonialism. The outside, male space of *La guaracha del Macho Camacho* is one of extreme inaction and total atomization: the senator and his son spend the entire novel in their respective cars, stuck in the traffic jam that has turned the public space of the street into the postcolonial superhighway. Each of them is by himself and unable to interact or communicate with any of the other drivers despite their common experience of stasis. The radio waves are the only thing circulating through this static, supposedly public world, in the form of Macho Camacho's *guaracha*. Senator Reinosa and Benny are thus passive recipients of the culture industry, unable to produce any meaning of their own through the collective process of exchange or communication. While a traditionally bourgeois division of space would conceive of the public, male sphere as one of production, where men enter the world to prove their worth, in *La guaracha* the men are passive consumers rather than active creators.

The women, meanwhile, may remain inside, but these apartments and houses are the site of production, of exchange, and of communication totally lacking in the male world. The apartment in which the novel opens is an extreme example of the domestic space as site of commercial exchange: it will be the place where La China Hereje puts her private body on sale to the senator. Along with this apartment, La China Hereje's house is an important setting and scene of most of the novel's dialogue, as she and her neighbor, Doña Chon, discuss everything from work, to popular culture, to their families. These women create the novel's version of the salon where Puerto Rico's politics, economics, and culture can be debated. Although these conversations, too, are dominated by the sounds and images of the culture industry, the women's creativity, as I discuss below, manages to mitigate somewhat the culture industry's colonizing force.

This breakdown of masculine public space challenges the ability of language to convey meaning within the novel's world. The disintegration of the literary public sphere is coupled with a degeneration of language among both the island's masses and elite. The senator, whose high social and educational level should make his speech the most "fine and refined" (64), in fact speaks a political double-talk that saps his words of any precision. His son can barely express himself at all: "What I mean is that I want to give myself the tremendous ecstasy of being the first teenager in the country to burn gasoline in a Ferrari. Or what I mean is that a Ferrari is some kind of wild airship that, that, that, I know what I want to say but I don't know how to get it all together, that, that, that . . . " (57).[13] The corruption of language, which appears to begin among society's elite, infects the upwardly mobile, such as the therapist's secretary, who tries to imitate the refined speech of her superiors: "The receptionist adduces: the excessivity of cold is causified in her by the neatisity of our conditioner of airs" (84). The upper classes speak this decorative language almost entirely emptied of meaning, while language among the novel's lower-class characters appears to be irreparably compromised by the culture industry. The narrator condescendingly describes the receptionist's advertising slogan telephone greeting "Hola Hola Pepsicola" (Sánchez, *La guaracha* 136) as "colonized ingenuity" (Sánchez, *Macho Camacho's Beat* 34). The conversations between La Madre and Doña Chon are often laughably nonsensical. When Doña Chon advises La Madre that "life is a bundle of dirty clothes," La Madre responds, "Doña Chon, you're the kind of person who could do a good job at writing guarachas" (147). The degeneration of language among the lower classes reaches its apogee in La Madre's son, El Nene, mute from birth and unable to express himself at all.

Yet the existence of the novel itself, and its public success, proves that literary language and a literary public sphere are not impossible. Instead of an elitist withdrawal from the corrupted popular language of the masses into some theoretically purer literary language, *La guaracha del Macho Camacho* manages to make do with the contaminated language and put it to literary purposes. *La guaracha* is a bricolage of the hollow phrases of popular and elite speech, strung together by commas and semicolons until they add up to make sense. The novel creates a literary discourse saturated by the language of the nightly news ("People have got to know whether or not their President is a crook. Well, I'm not a crook" [131]),[14] the advertising industry ("In Manatí she took two Cortals and with an artificial relaxation announced, singing and trilling like an announcer for Colgate: *Cortal, when taken, stops the achin'*" [83]), and political sloganeering ("Senator Vicente Reinosa—Vince is a prince and easy to convince" [17]).

The finished product, *La guaracha del Macho Camacho* itself, is not the elevated bourgeois form of literature that the senator's Hispanophile wife, the novel's protector of traditional values, holds in high esteem. *La guaracha* violates in both form and content each of Graciela's precepts that literature should be "objective, democratic, well put together . . . forget slums, forget Puerto Rican independence, forget characters who sweat: everything that's written should be refined and elevated" (86). Neither, though, is *La guaracha* precisely like the romance novel that Graciela condescendingly observes the receptionist reading (29). The receptionist listens to Macho Camacho's *guaracha* as she reads her romance novel, consuming both cultural products simultaneously; the romance novel belongs to the same mass culture as the *guaracha*, a world that Graciela considers "low class vulgarity" (35) and a world from which Sánchez's novel stands apart. Instead of valorizing the *guaracha* and the popular culture from which it springs as an antidote to the inauthentic culture of the comprador class, *La guaracha* refuses to align itself completely with the testimonial impulse to search for cultural authenticity in the figure of the subaltern.

In the Cuban and Jamaican testimonial works discussed in chapter 7, the voices of women and blacks in particular were sought out to represent the silenced subaltern, just as reggae and salsa musicians of the time period, from Bob Marley to Willie Colón, were aligning themselves with this counterpublic in language and in performance. In the novel, the DJ repeatedly identifies Macho Camacho as this resistant performer. The DJ emphasizes Macho Camacho's allegiance with the ghetto, in particular through his blackness: "What Macho Camacho has put into his *guaracha* is his soul, that heart of his that's also the great heart of a man who's gone hungry. Yes, ladies and gentlemen, friends, gone hungry the way a man does who's sweaty and poor and bears the mark of the color of sufferance. Because he's no mulatto, black is what he is, pitch black" (99). The DJ's discourse locates in

Macho Camacho's cultural product, the *guaracha* that his much-celebrated suffering has produced, a form of resistance in opposition to or outside of the empty shell presented by the culture industry. The novel critiques this overly utopian reading of popular music, suggesting that in fact the packaging of Macho Camacho is only another layer of the control and commodification of culture. Contrary to the DJ's characterization of Macho Camacho as spokesman of the subaltern, within the scope of the novel the *guaracha* appears to be as hollow and as much a part of the disciplinary system as the upper-class's elitist conception of culture. The system that creates and disseminates the *guaracha* aspires to totalitarian control; the song is described as establishing "absolute rule" (27) and "a regime of absolutism" (45). The DJ calls Macho Camacho himself "the priest or pastor or preacher of the thing" (129), suggesting his song's complicity in the religious deification of commodities, the thingification of Puerto Rican society.[15] In Macho Camacho's *guaracha*, life is a thing ("la vida es una cosa fenomenal"), a depthless phenomenon without context or consequence. The *guaracha* paints a picture of life as nothing but hip music, dancing, and sex, a notable distance from the violence, poverty, and frustration that the characters actually experience as life.

In one of the rare moments in which someone inside the novel sees through this surface and speaks with some lucidity, the *guaracha* enters to silence the protest. La China Hereje observes the scene on a bus: "The country doesn't work," proclaims another passenger, repeating it over and over "facing a red traffic light that was black because the traffic signal wasn't working" (11). He arrives at that conclusion through sustained thought about the situation, going from superficial phenomena to superstructural causes: "Because the light has gone, because the light goes every afternoon, because the afternoon doesn't work, because the air conditioning doesn't work, because the country doesn't work." His protest is greeted with two reactions:

> The passengers signed up in two opposing parties: one a minority of timid people in agreement and the other a vociferous majority who proceeded to intone with a verve reserved for national anthems Macho Camacho's irrepressible guaracha *Life Is a Phenomenal Thing*, the deeper tones provided by the driver . . . the bus afire with the shrieks and roars of the majority party, the bus afire with the torches of happiness held high by the passengers of the vociferous majority party: happy because with the neat swipe of a guaracha they had crushed the attempt at dissidence. (11–12)

As this passage illustrates, "Life Is a Phenomenal Thing" serves the quasi-religious function of a national anthem in Sánchez's novel. The song's inane lyrics and irresistible beat induce La China Hereje and her neighbors to ignore the social *tapón* that has them trapped, and instead dance their troubles away.

These seductive powers allow the *guaracha* to crush dissidence, or at least confine it to a manageable minority. The song seduces those in the upper classes, such as Dr. Severo Severino, who confesses his fascination with the song, or the senator, who finds himself whistling the tune alone in his car. The allure for them is the subaltern blackness and sexuality the song expresses. To the lower classes, the *guaracha* offers a vision of success that could be theirs, like *El Show de Iris Chacón*, which La China Hereje watches with religious devotion. Macho Camacho, packaged to the lower classes as a poor, black urban dweller just like them, gives the illusory hope that even the most disenfranchised can achieve fame and fortune through the entertainment industry. When La China Hereje watches Iris Chacón, she imagines herself in her place: "The Mother wanted to dance like Iris Chacón and gain continental fame with her anarchic buttockry. The Mother wanted to be transformed into another Iris Chacón and lose herself and find herself" (41). La China Hereje, Senator Reinosa's kept woman, takes hope in the show because "Iris Chacón isn't kept by anything except the danceable impulse of her body" (164).

An Adornian reading of *La guaracha del Macho Camacho* might see the complete domination of this disciplinary system; the novel suggests that control is never absolute. The *guaracha* may be mass produced as a means of pacifying the population, but the ends to which people put the song are beyond the control of this culture industry. Though the song may have totalitarian aspirations, the lyrics never appear within the novel in their entirety, coming together as a whole only as an appendix. Within the novel itself, certain lyrics appear in fragmentary form, giving the impression that the song exists only as it is deployed by particular characters or the narrator. Within the context of this specific deployment, the characters use the *guaracha* to produce their own meanings: the song can inspire the man on the bus to protest as readily as it encourages others to ignore this flawed life. In the same way, Sánchez appropriates and deploys popular culture for his own uses in creating *La guaracha del Macho Camacho*.

While protests may appear to come from a minority, that minority is never silenced in the novel. The *tapón* that has immobilized and ossified Puerto Rican society makes resistance appear futile, but the multitude nonetheless insists on resisting. Although it achieves no obvious purpose, countless drivers loudly protest their frustration by blowing their horns: "Foreseen and collective and conscious recognition of the uselessness of protest but: a chorus of horns proceeds, altogether, *todos a una* . . . the enwheeled multitude brakes, guarachas, advances, brakes, guarachas, advances, brakes, guarachas, advances" (51). The *tapón* opens up the possibilities for lucidity for some of the characters, such as the man on the bus who realizes that the country does not work. As the *tapón* persists, the drivers begin to leave their cars and to take in the reality of their circumstances: "All chaufferdom, the whole passagerial flock, had risen up onto the car roofs in order to find out what the fuck is going on up ahead: a swirl of asking asked by those who have no access to the privileged positions from where one can appreciate what the fuck is going on up ahead" (122). The drivers' goal is for greater insight, to be able to see the transnational spaces interpolating their Caribbean reality and the corporate expansion of the United States. *La guaracha del Macho Camacho*, like *The Dragon Can't Dance*, imagines these connections as overarching, floating through the air in television commercials and radio broadcasts—a system of control the people below cannot see without a more privileged vantage point. Although the *guaracha* enters again in this scene to deflate the tension, the threat has been established that the multitude will be incited to more than permanent partying.[16] This unfulfilled threat appears to be the most that Sánchez imagines postcolonial literature is able to offer.

The Dragon Can't Dance and the Commodification of Resistance

Despite the challenges to a popular literary project that Wynter and Sánchez identify, Lovelace offers *The Dragon Can't Dance* as a new aesthetic produced within the context of a postcoloniality in which cultural production and social action appear to have become disconnected. Sandra Paquet, in an essay that helpfully periodizes Lovelace's nonfiction alongside the 1970 Black Power uprising in Trinidad and Tobago as well as the Grenada Revolution that I return to in my conclusion, notes that in the period between these events, Lovelace's essays seek to question Black Power rhetoric and the anticolonial idea of the writer's relationship with the folk. As Paquet puts it, that "claim to a folk sensibility is prefaced in binary terms that couple V. S. Naipaul and George Lamming, despite their vastly different styles and politics, and dismisses them both and their generation of writers as bourgeois and

unredeemably colonial" ("Vulnerable Observer"). This desire to recon-
figure the writer's positioning, echoing Brathwaite's critique of *In the
Castle of My Skin* in the *Savacou* foreword, is part of the context out
of which Lovelace writes *The Dragon Can't Dance*. Paquet highlights
the political and social transformations the novel responds to; I want to
also point to how the novel explicitly relates the writer's changing role to
cultural and technological innovations. While the novel's ambivalent relationship with music is most obvious, Lovelace's narrator also criticizes
television for presenting a world "too smooth, too easy," lacking "the
guts of the struggle" of everyday life (*Dragon* 222). Against these new
media, *The Dragon Can't Dance* posits literature as a form suited for
thinking together what it calls the "contradictions" between "resistance
and surviving," "rebellion and decency" (178). The crisis presented in
The Dragon Can't Dance is of the inability of its characters to come
to terms with the contradictory impulses of anticolonial resistance and
postcolonial nation building in order to create cultural forms that can
participate in public because they are not disconnected from the struggles of everyday life.

The Dragon Can't Dance takes place in a fictional Port of Spain
neighborhood during the years between the mid-1950s and early 1970s.
The novel offers a variety of public spaces that express overlapping communities: the country fields of slavery and indenture, the urban streets
of carnival and anticolonial organization, the calypso tents and athletic
stadiums of entertainment and national identity, and Woodford Square,
the center of Port of Spain where Eric Williams's speeches consolidated
his popular power in the 1950s. The novel narrates the transformation
of these spaces, as well as the changes in the communities and cultures
expressed in them. While the novel features a patchwork of characters
who live together in the slum known as Calvary Hill, the action revolves
primarily around four men—Fisheye, Aldrick, Philo, and Pariag, each
associated with a carnival figure (the Bad John, the Dragon, the Calypsonian, and the Spectator, respectively). As Linden Lewis notes, this cast
of male characters allows the novel to "present several versions of ma-
saculinity" (166); I am emphasizing how the story therefore explores the
different tactics each deploys to come to terms with the rising dominance
of the postcolonial system and its challenge to both collective action and
masculinity. By structuring the novel around carnival, Lovelace emphasizes the performativity of each man's identity. All of the men experience various levels of unemployment and underemployment through the
course of the novel, which limits their ability to create a public, working

persona. Instead of being able to express themselves in the public world of the workplace, they are relegated to the in-between space of the Yard, the outside space connecting a collection of houses set apart from the rest of the city and thus neither entirely public nor entirely private.

The historical narrative of *The Dragon Can't Dance* moves through three stages, showing the progressive uprooting and isolation of its characters with modernization and postmodernization. The narrative begins from the simple peasantry of the rural village, an idealized collective, "virile" space (Lovelace, *Dragon* 92).[17] From this rural collectivity, where in the language of *The Dragon Can't Dance* each man dreams of "the possibility that he could, in company with men, make something happen" (80), the novel moves to the urban centers of the modern colonial era, where the public space of the street becomes the site where displaced peasants come together to fight against colonialism; finally, the novel ends in Lovelace's present of the late 1970s, the postcolonial city of the Yard and the suburb, where the streets have been turned over to cars and advertisements, and the possibility of creating a public self through labor or anticolonial struggle has been virtually eliminated. The novel describes the movement of the characters from the country to the city to the suburban world, and the parallel passage from what it calls the "religion of rebellion" inherited from slavery, to the posturing of the carnival, to eventual "accommodation" with materialist culture (207). Within the context of this passage, the novel explores how a self can be fashioned, how the artist redefines his (and, for the novel, the artist is male) function, and the potential of literature to speak in the public sphere.

As much as the novel focuses on the four men, the young girl Sylvia acts as a pivot around which their stories revolve. With virtually all of the men unemployed and unable to contribute anything productive to their postcolonial society, Sylvia has something that the market desires, her private self, her body; available to her is the opportunity to turn herself into a commodity and marry the licentious rent collector, Mr. Guy. When Guy forces himself upon Sylvia during her adolescence, her mother stands by and allows this harassment since she cannot afford to pay her rent. Sylvia's exploitation is especially painful because she represents "that hope that had lived in the Yard . . . that beauty of which she was custodian out of her innocence and daring and speed, the belief that there was ahead a better life" (165). Like the island on the eve of independence, filled with hope that the end of empire will restore the men's masculinity by freeing the island from its predatory relationship with England, Sylvia's exchange with Mr. Guy of her body for loans and money stands in for Trinidad and Tobago's status after independence as a developing country forced to have its economy and resources controlled by the World Bank and the International Monetary Fund via corrupt local businesspeople and politicians. Postcoloniality is a feminized status, then, and as Sylvia sells out the island's virginal possibility the novel coarsely labels hers "the apprenticeship of being the whore" (39). By the end of the novel, however, the idea of Sylvia's betrayal becomes more complicated, suggesting that reading her behavior through an anticolonial lens may no longer make visible the full picture: "And it struck [Aldrick]: maybe she had not given up hope for life, for living. Maybe she had not so much chosen Guy as refused the impotence of dragons. . . . Sylvia had not surrendered; she was simply turning, turning from the dragon to herself" (217). Aldrick here acknowledges that amid a set of bad choices, Sylvia may be choosing the more difficult yet more honest option; as Aldrick puts it, "maybe it was easier to rebel . . . maybe it was purer; but, it wasn't the truth" (173). Philo, too, comes to suspect that "[Guy's] love for Sylvia . . . was something that the girl could exploit to her advantage" (230). Their apparently predatory relationship offers a possible model, however unattractive it may appear, for Trinidad and Tobago and the Caribbean more generally in the postcolonial world system.

While the female body thus becomes the site for Lovelace to explore how to carve out a space in a commodified global system, Fisheye remains throughout the novel the spokesperson of the alternative, high priest of the "religion" of "resistance," the "purity" inherited by the people on Calvary Hill from "their ancestors all through slavery, carried on in their unceasing escape—as Maroons, as Runaways, as Bush Negroes, as Rebels" (24–25). This mythical past is what the artists of decolonization drew on, whether in Aimé Césaire's *marron*, Miguel Barnet's *cimarrón*, or Lamming's Caliban. In *The Dragon Can't Dance*, Fisheye brings this spirit with him from the countryside as he moves to Port of Spain "just after the war" (62). He encounters in the post–World War II city a new world: he feels a sense of isolation, separated as he is from the organic relationships of the countryside, and initially creates a masculine public persona for himself through productive labor. But as even that avenue is closed to him, he develops a sense of uselessness, the feeling that his strength and skill are wasted in the city, that the work he finds does not allow him to show off the kind of man he is. Only when joining a carnival band, which battles against other bands, does he feel his masculinity affirmed: "in this war, in this army, Fisheye at last found the place where he could be a man, where his strength and quickness had meaning and he could feel pride in belonging and purpose to his living" (68).

The story of Fisheye's experience in the steelband parallels the triumph of the decolonization struggle after World War II and the rise of the People's National Movement (PNM) and its policy of encouraging commercialization and industrialization. The heroic battles Fisheye fights during the 1950s give way to an era of peace coinciding with the election of the PNM in 1956. Fisheye regards this peace not as triumphant achievement, but as cowardly surrender. As the bands begin to orient themselves toward sponsorship, their oppositionality is undermined: "Sponsors did not like violence in the bands. Indeed, one of the conditions of sponsorship was no misbehaving in the band" (83). At the same time, the bands go from being made up of men like Fisheye, committed to their communities and fighting against the status quo, to being artists concerned only with form: "The steelband tent became a concert hall. Where fellars had talked about battles, they talked now about music. . . . Battles on Carnival days between rival warriors became contests of skill between competing orchestras, warriors became critics of music" (75–76). The sanitizing effect of commercial sponsorship on the bands leaves no place for Fisheye's idea of culture as committed to political action. When independence fails to bring social transformation, Fisheye becomes an unpleasant and guilty reminder to his neighbors of the unfinished decolonization struggle, leader of "the small guerrilla band that was not so much guerrilla as the last remains of a defeated army, that refused to surrender, indeed, to acknowledge defeat, that would keep on fighting even after hope for victory had ended, out of not knowing what else to do" (178–179). He continues to practice the religion of resistance inherited from the days of slavery even as his neighbors become, in his eyes, bought off by marginal material gains.

One of the central ironies of *The Dragon Can't Dance* is the fact that Fisheye fashions this revolutionary masculine identity from images associated with Hollywood film: "Every night almost, he went to Royal or Empire, whichever was showing a western double; and after the show, walking home up the Hill, the picture fresh in his mind, walking kinda slow, he would feel for a few moments his strength, his youth, his promise fill him, and he would walk, the fastest gun alive, his long hands stiff at his sides, his fingers ready to go for the guns he imagined holstered low on his hips" (64). Looking to the cowboy to construct his revolutionary persona, Fisheye recalls Lamming comparing himself as "a writer without a book" to "a cowboy without his horse and pistols" (*Pleasures* 59) as well as Jimmy Cliff's character in the Jamaican film *The Harder They Come*.[18] Lovelace's characters highlight the postcolonial reality in which social reproduction becomes increasingly appropriated by foreign culture industries, such that even positions of rebellion are manufactured within the system. Indeed, as Aldrick will later realize, part of the failure of Fisheye's rebellion is his inability to articulate his performance of resistance in any language other than that given to him by the culture industry. When Fisheye does finally undertake a revolutionary act, leading the commandeering of a police jeep, he vindicates his neighbors by showing the hollow ineffectiveness of his performed resistance. Through its depiction of Fisheye's rebellion as parallel to carnival (occurring on a Monday and Tuesday and described in a chapter called "The Dragon Dance"), *The Dragon Can't Dance* reworks the postindependence Black Power uprisings that occurred throughout the Caribbean during the late 1960s and 1970s and figures them as local performances that, in trying to uphold the banner of the anticolonial struggle, never touch the new system of power.[19]

While Fisheye continues to battle against an enemy he cannot identity, Pariag, who moves from the country to the city just after Fisheye, suffers at the margins of an economic system he is trying to enter. Living in an otherwise Afro-Trinidadian neighborhood, Pariag embodies Indo-Trinidadian exclusion from the nationalist public sphere, feeling the alienation and atomization of the city even more acutely than Fisheye. Initially, his only relationships are with people with whom he has economic exchange: his employer and the customers he services on his route. When Fisheye shakes him down for money, Pariag feels almost happy to have this interaction, which makes him a part of a community (103). As when he later establishes himself as the neighborhood's shopkeeper, Pariag from the beginning is forced to integrate himself into the Yard through accommodation with postcolonial Trinidad and Tobago's economic system of relationships.

After years of living this marginal existence on the Hill, Pariag finally achieves a secure place in the community, first by buying a bicycle for himself, and later by opening his own business at the end of the novel. Pariag chooses what is apparently the only alternative to Fisheye's unending stance of oppositionality, and in the process *The Dragon Can't Dance* aligns its only Indo-Trinidadian identity character with the feminized accommodation represented by Sylvia. In purchasing the bicycle, Pariag is the first resident of the Yard to violate the unspoken "code . . . of non-possession" (119), a gratuitous transgression because the acquisition of material comforts suggests accommodation with the status quo. In the world of *The Dragon Can't Dance*, the major contradiction West Indian independence makes its characters face is the choice between whether they want to continue fighting against imperialism or to take whatever victories they have won and try to enjoy them. Pariag's bike (and eventually the car acquired by Philo) represents the pole of accommodation, the transforming of the street also seen in *La guaracha del Macho Camacho* from the collective space of the anticolonial struggle into an atomized space where private property–owning individuals interact without actually interacting.

Fisheye and Pariag choose sides with or against the institutions of power; Aldrick initially wants to keep faith in the religion of resistance, but grows more and more agnostic as the novel moves forward in time. When Aldrick is first introduced, he is working on his carnival costume with what is described as almost religious fervor: the narrator emphasizes the "spirit of priesthood" (49) with which he approaches his carnival character, the dragon. For Aldrick, the dragon represents the lost meaning of carnival, the struggle for freedom and emancipation from slavery, which were carnival's original roots.[20] Carnival is an opportunity to take over the streets and demonstrate to the state the power of the people; it is this "memory burning in his blood" of slavery and emancipation that "invested him with an ancestral authority to uphold before the people of this Hill" (134). Aldrick's lament is that the costumes have gone from threatening devils and dragons to "fancy devils, with lamé and silk and satin" (209), an aestheticization of carnival's history of struggle and oppositionality.

As the novel's title suggests, Aldrick eventually finds that he can no longer continue dancing the dragon dance. Even while participating in Fisheye's uprising, Aldrick maintains a sense of skepticism that distances him from the other, more strict adherents to the religion of resistance. While in prison afterward, Aldrick begins to seriously contemplate the meaning of the dragon dance. He realizes that he and his friends, the last followers of the religion of resistance, are as embedded into the system that they are combating as Pariag or any of the other people whom they consider to have sold out. "Is like we ain't have no self," Aldrick explains in the language of Hegel's (and Fanon's) master-slave dialectic; "I mean, we have a self but the self we have is for somebody else" (202). He tries to make Fisheye and the others see that their resistance is an act, a subordinated role that they play because they can find no other way to accommodate themselves to postcoloniality. Aldrick forces himself to accept and engage with rather than oppose and fight against a Trinidadian public sphere based on the exchange of commodities, but also on the interaction of differences necessary in a multiracial society.

While Aldrick becomes an organic intellectual, the calypsonian Philo must come to terms with the passage from colonialism to postcolonialism as a cultural producer. *The Dragon Can't Dance* ends with Philo's perspective, moving with him from the communal urban space of Calvary Hill to the dull conformity of the Diego Martin suburb. Like Macho Camacho, Philo represents the entertainer who makes it, who validates the system by proving to his people that they, too, can become rich and famous through unhesitating belief in the culture industry and its commodification of their racial and ethnic identity. Although he moves away from Calvary Hill, Philo's repeated insistence that "I is we," that his success and articulateness have not separated him from the people he wants to represent, resembles the anxiety of the Caribbean author: "I want people who know me when they look at me to say, There is Philo! There is me! . . . You have to let the fellars know the kinda man I is, Aldrick. I is we" (170–171). In ending the novel with Philo, Lovelace points to the complicity of postcolonial Caribbean art with power, but also the potential of Caribbean art to represent and critique the postcolonial system.

Like Sylvia and unlike Fisheye and Aldrick, Philo finds that he has something that he can sell, something that the market values: his private self and raced body. Philo accommodates himself to this system by exploiting his skills as a calypsonian, and by creating a song about his sexual exploits. Though he has made his career singing songs of protest, Philo finally gets his major break when he decides to abandon that tradition, telling Aldrick, "Man, year in year out, I singing about how people hungry, how officials ain't doing their duty, and what I get man? What I get?" (127). The "Axe Man" calypso that makes him famous breaks from social commentary to, as he puts it, "sing what the people want to hear" (126), a song of self-ridicule recounting fantastic sexual performance. The religion of protest is replaced with a religion of diversion, a religion of entertainment "sanctif[ied] . . . in song year after year by the island's leading calypsonians" (33). Sponsored by visiting tourists and local carnival organizers, this new tradition serves both as an export commodity for foreign markets and to distract the local population from their everyday lives.

Yet even within this apparently benign tradition of entertainment, Philo finds a place for social commentary: as the novel ends, he is writing a new calypso satirizing the cookie-cutter suburban society in which he now lives. Lovelace does not allow the reader to naively believe that Philo's insight into the reality of his situation gives him a privileged vantage point to oppose the system: "Philo sat back, a smile coming on to his face, thinking: 'Jesus Lord! I figure them out! I find them out!' believing that this knowledge on its own, this 'finding them out', set him apart from his neighbors and above them" (228). The narrator acknowledges that Philo may only be deluding himself; nonetheless, Lovelace allows his characters to settle for these partial and temporary moments of insight. Just as Fisheye never manages to truly find an intellectual articulation for the energy of his oppositional struggle, Philo never attaches his artistic insights to any social project.

In ending with Philo, and with him hearing that Sylvia has run away from Guy possibly to be with Aldrick, *The Dragon Can't Dance* shows the postcolonial artist's parallels with the prostituted female character. Aldrick rather than Guy winning Sylvia might be read as a bolt of unexpected hope into an otherwise hopeless situation, a conclusion typical of the traditional nineteenth-century romance: Aldrick and Sylvia's union might seem to tie up loose ends and signal the novel's withdrawal from the public world of history and politics into the private world of the family. But this reading views the novel's resolution only from Aldrick's perspective; even Philo and Aldrick have by now dismissed the simplistic notion of personal relationships as a feminine space outside of history. In fact, it is Sylvia's decision to run off; as the novel ends, she has revealed herself to be an active subject rather than a passive symbol of promise or corruption. Her decision redefines what constitutes politics and culture within the world of the novel. By this point, the reader has been invited to see the limits of Fisheye's conception of the public as a masculine space of battle and Philo's expression of the calypso as market commodity. In the idealized bourgeois familial realm of the nineteenth-century romance, the private remains reserved for social reproduction while the pursuits of politics and career take place outside in the public world. The Yard, as a place in-between the public and the private, bears little resemblance to this model. Just as the culture industries have taken over much of the role of social reproduction, private life has become commodified as the market penetrates increasingly into every realm of the everyday. When Sylvia turns away from Guy to pursue Aldrick, the novel has imbued this personal decision with an ambivalent political weight: although she refuses the choice between what Stuart Hall calls "that endless either/or, either total victory or total incorporation" (24), she is exercising choice, choosing what she will do with her body and her desires.

Unlike the anticolonial fighter or the postcolonial artist, Sylvia's choice over how to exercise the rights won in the anticolonial struggle suggests new, personal bases for social movements and battles to be waged. The political, the novel suggests, resides not only in public struggles for control of the state; it also exists in struggles for economic, cultural, and sexual self-determination.

What we see in both of these novels is an attempt to create a new heroic and masculine public role for the writer in a context where even that identity has been commodified. Whether in the novels of Sánchez and Lovelace, the hybrid texts of Barnet and the Sistren Theatre Collective, or the academic activities of Rohlehr, Flores, Cooper, Sánchez González, and Otero Garabís, all of these efforts emerge as negotiations with the new social, political, and economic realities of the region that nostalgically seek to reconstruct the anticolonial relationship between writer and public while acknowledging its impossibility in the postcolonial problem-space. The temptation to retreat from the literary as an elite form into a politically enabling invocation of the popular unites all of these intellectual projects, and has proven invigorating for contemporary Caribbean studies. But as Wynter, Franco, and the novels of Sánchez and Lovelace suggest, this intellectual move is conditioned by the new forms of domination and new configurations of the public sphere that characterize postcoloniality. While insisting on the continued purchase of the anticolonial horizon of liberation continues to animate politically committed work, my conclusion looks to the writings of Dionne Brand to think about how such projects might redefine their relationship with that narrative.

Conclusion

The Postcolonial Public Sphere

CARIBBEAN LITERATURE AND THE PUBLIC SPHERE has explored three periods in Caribbean literary history. Chapters 1 and 2 looked at the decline of plantation slavery and rise of modern colonialism from 1804 to 1886; the key dates in this long regional passage go from Haitian independence and the British abolition of the transatlantic slave trade through the imposition of the Crown Colony system up to the end of slavery in Cuba. Chapters 3 and 4 examined how anticolonial writing developed as a response to the codification of modern colonialism, especially in the face of U.S. imperial involvement in the region that became a dominant force with the seizure of Cuba and Puerto Rico in 1898 as well as the occupation of Haiti that began in 1915. Chapters 5 through 8 focused on the transition away from this modern colonialism in the years between 1959 and 1983. Those dates deliberately evoke the triumph of the Cuban Revolution and the downfall of the Grenada Revolution as bookends to the decolonization period; ending my discussion of the transition from modern colonialism to postcoloniality in 1983 calls attention to the period we presently occupy as initiated by the U.S. invasion of Grenada. In this conclusion, I want to tentatively point to some of the implications of thinking about the postcolonial period as a post-Grenada public sphere, and look at the positions this kind of postcoloniality makes available to contemporary Caribbean writers.

From the restrictive republic of the lettered and excluded counter-public of the plantation, to the consolidation of an anticolonial literary public sphere, to the crisis of postcoloniality: the story told in this book is not a teleology, but neither does it return us to where we began. *Caribbean Literature and the Public Sphere* has argued for understanding different periods as defined by distinct relationships between intellectuals and their public that respond to changing configurations of transnational power. The post-Grenada present can thus be understood as a new global order that necessitates new intellectual responses. The contemporary commodification of public space has meant not only the deprivileging of revolutionary discourse, but of literature itself. While the 1960s and 1970s witnessed the varied responses to the crisis of the anticolonial public sphere discussed in chapters 7 and 8, the years since the invasion of Grenada appear as the full-blown emergence of postcoloniality. The deterritorialization advocated by former nationalist writers like Edouard Glissant and Antonio Benítez-Rojo becomes emblematic of this post-Grenada period. Glissant's move from aligning himself with the Martinican independence movement to becoming an apostle of globalization in the 1990 *Poétique de la relation* parallels Benítez-Rojo's shift from director of Cuba's Casa de las Américas in the 1970s to deconstructionist of master narratives in the 1989 *La isla que se repite*.[1] The enormous influence of these two theorists during the 1990s demonstrates the resonance of this postmodern turn, to what Román de la Campa suggests is "an unbridled celebration of new intellectual horizons that should provide the basis for our own critique" ("Resistance" 92) and might "provide a way out of this fashionable cul-de-sac" (115) of the loss of faith in modernist conceptions of politics.

In this conclusion, I look at two alternative models for understanding this contemporary moment—through the lens of either globalization or Empire studies—before turning to the work of Dionne Brand as a particularly postcolonial rendering of the post-Grenada context. In the process, I suggest a way of periodizing Caribbean literature that does not discard the idea of the postcolonial but defines that periodization in relation to the concept of the public sphere and the crisis created by the successes and failures of anticolonial movements. Brand's writings locate themselves as politically engaged postcolonial texts through their relationship to the anticolonial project, simultaneously paying homage to and critiquing the limitations of a model by now acknowledged (though perhaps not accepted) as having passed. This rethinking of the writer's relationship to the political produces a literature of mourning that locates itself in the aftermath of the literary public sphere's decline even as it seeks to keep alive the legacy of this apparently exhausted model.[2] I end with a discussion of Brand's *In Another Place, Not Here* as an engagement with the anticolonial faith in the intellectual addressed in the first half of *Caribbean Literature and the Public Sphere* and the testimonial desire to go beyond the intellectual from the second half, even as the novel points to the new directions that Caribbean literature has taken at the turn of the twenty-first century.

Postcolonialism, Globalization Theory, and Empire Studies

Using postcoloniality as a periodizing concept remains controversial in the Caribbean: when a number of islands in the region are not even nominally independent, implying that colonialism has ended can seem to undercut ongoing political struggles.[3] I therefore use the term to signify not the end of empire but the rise of a new international regime. Graham Huggan suggests how the imperfect terminology of postcolonial studies might be recoded in this sense: "postcolonialism's regime of value relates to an ensemble of loosely connected oppositional practices, underpinned both by a highly eclectic methodology of 'cultural embattlement' and by an aesthetic of largely textualised, partly localised resistance. . . . Postcoloniality, on the other hand, is largely a function of *postmodernity*: its own regime of value pertains to a system of symbolic, as well as material, exchange in which even the language of resistance may be manipulated and consumed" (6). Postcolonialism, according to Huggan, is an intellectual practice meant to combat the effects of modern colonialism; postcoloniality is a form of domination that arises amid modern colonialism's declining power, and in fact responds to and seeks to co-opt the anticolonial forces—among them postcolonialism—unleashed during the decolonization era.

Huggan's assumption of a cause-effect relationship between postmodernity and postcoloniality (where one is a "function" of the other) is undoubtedly problematic: my discussion of how the Caribbean public sphere is part of a transnational negotiation of power relations has sought to disrupt precisely this view, of power originating in the metropole and only occurring secondarily elsewhere. Calling attention to these two "posts" as parallel ways of understanding how global relations entered a new phase in the second half of the twentieth century allows us to make sense of the points of convergence in the historical narratives of Anglophone colonialism/postcoloniality and Latin American colonialism/modernity/postmodernity, which have framed this project. In the Anglophone narrative, the postcolonial is a contemporary moment in which "the continuing operation of imperialism in its broadest meaning explains why the term 'postcolonial' is generally used rather than 'post-imperial' . . . history has not yet reached the 'post-imperial' era" (Young 27). This emphasis on the unfinished project of postcolonialism dovetails with Hispanophone definitions of a postmodernity characterized by "a sociopolitical reality . . . being felt in Latin America through the neoliberal political regimes that came about in the eighties" (de la Campa, *Latin Americanism* 4), where "the Center . . . aims at appropriating the periphery's alterity and its anti-hegemonic protagonism" (Richard 218), and "the public sphere is taken over by the electronic media . . . turn[ing] it into a *mise-en-abyme* and politics into an icon, image, or simulacrum" (Sarlo 251). Postcoloniality and postmodernity each name trends that emerge in the post–World War II Caribbean and that form the context for the writers discussed in the second half of this book: the rise of nationalist parties to power in the name of the people; these regimes' ambitious industrialization projects, leading to high levels of debt and monetarist interventions by the International Monetary Fund; an increased reliance on the tourist industry, coupled with dependence on North American culture industries. All of these developments have meant a new mediatized public sphere where writers can no longer rely on the authorizing discourses of anticolonialism.

Amid this sense of the inadequacy of established models in providing tools for understanding and intervening in these realities, two other major frameworks have emerged to compete with the postcolonial as a way of understanding the novelty of the contemporary period: globalization and Empire. Many critics have written about how the most popular versions of globalization discourse can tend to present an overly celebratory vision of contemporary exceptionalism: Thomas Friedman's idea that "the world is flat," for example, clearly belies ongoing global hierarchies.[4] Ali Behdad, while critical of postcolonial studies, sees globalization as an even less useful paradigm: "the quick academic shift from postcolonialism to globalization . . . has ironically short-circuited the possibility of understanding the ways in which the geographical and cultural displacement of people and things by European colonialism informed the so-called cartography of globalization today" (70–71). While postcolonial studies has been rightly criticized by people like Arif Dirlik for focusing on the inequalities of European colonialism at the expense of a sustained engagement with contemporary forms of domination and exploitation, globalization as a framework can tend to discount the ways that the locations of the haves and have-nots are remarkably similar today to what they were at the height of modern colonialism.

The growing field of what I call "Empire studies" seems to promise to correct the blind spots of globalization theory. If one of the disadvantages of postcolonial studies is the term's suggestion that the stage of international inequality has been surpassed, Empire studies insists on the fact that power and domination still structure the global order.

The foundational text of this field, Michael Hardt and Antonio Negri's *Empire*, emphasizes the novelty of the present just as globalization theory does: "our basic hypothesis is that sovereignty has taken a new form composed of a series of national and supranational organisms united under a single logic of rule. This new global form of sovereignty is what we call Empire" (xii). They read this new form not as a sign of liberation: "the decline in sovereignty of nation-states, however, does not mean that sovereignty as such has declined" (xi). Instead, Empire has arisen to govern the energies released by decolonization: "the end of modern colonialisms, of course, has not really opened an age of unqualified freedom but rather yielded to new forms of rule that operate on a global scale" (134). One major critique of *Empire* has been its downplaying of U.S. domination in this new global order, a critique that became especially vocal as the U.S. wars in Afghanistan and Iraq, launched just after the book's publication, suggested a resurgence of colonialism. Hardt and Negri respond in *Multitude* by explaining how "at least since the early 1990s, U.S. foreign policy and military engagement have straddled imperialist and imperial logics" (60). The failure of the United States to reimpose a territorial empire on the British or French model may actually support the authors' contention that modern colonialism is no longer the dominant form of international organization, even as these military actions unmask the fiction of globalization as nonhierarchical.

The other major criticism of Hardt and Negri has been for constructing a vision of Empire that is too totalizing: as Vilashini Cooppan puts it, "because Empire can be everything, there is no need to oppose it, or, more modestly, to critique it" (97). This criticism resembles one of the most incisive critiques of another founding text, Edward Said's *Orientalism*, for creating a Foucauldian system in which resistance had no place. I would argue that postcolonial studies, as an academic field invested in non-European contestations of the colonial archive, is in fact born from this critique of the focus on the powerful in *Orientalism* and the colonial discourse analysis it inspired.[5] The totalizing vision of Empire produces the same problem; Empire studies is much less attentive than postcolonial studies to the ways in which the rest of the world has challenged and forced the reshaping of imperial sovereignty. Consider Hardt and Negri's own description of their project:

> The genealogy we follow in our analysis of the passage from imperialism to Empire will be first European and then Euro-American, not because we believe these regions are the exclusive or privileged source of new ideas and

historical innovation, but simply because this was the dominant geographical path along which the concepts and practices that animate today's Empire developed—in step, as we will argue, with the development of the capitalist mode of production. Whereas the genealogy of Empire is in this sense Eurocentric, however, its present powers are not limited to any one region. Logics of rule that in some sense originated in Europe and the United States now invest practices of domination throughout the globe. (*Empire* xvi)

One of the catalysts of postcolonial studies has been to contest this idea that capitalism and modern sovereignty "originated in Europe and the United States," rather than in the interactions of those regions with the rest of the world. Although *Multitude* clearly attempts to correct the tendency of *Empire* to focus exclusively on the powerful—the Cuban Revolution, the African National Congress, and the Zapatistas are discussed, though fairly briefly, and Frantz Fanon even figures in a footnote—Hardt and Negri are still more comfortable describing the present world as "postmodernity" (*Multitude* xvii, 4, 78, 192, 194, 199) rather than as "postcoloniality," a word the authors never use.

Empire studies thus exists as a continuation of the frameworks of globalization or postmodernism more than postcolonialism, in the sense of Walter Mignolo's reading of "postmodernity [as] the discourse of countermodernity emerging from the metropolitan centers and *settler colonies*, while postcoloniality is the discourse of countermodernity emerging from *deep-settler colonials* where colonial power endured with particular brutality" ("(Post)Occidentalism" 92). The value of postcolonial studies, Mignolo continues, comes from its accounting of "subaltern rationality" to attend to new transformations of power and domination from the counterpublic perspective of those who have been its victims: "subaltern rationality, or whatever you want to call it, nourishes and is nourished by a theoretical practice that was prompted by the movements of decolonization after World War II" (91). It is this connection to the projects of decolonization that Empire studies lacks. I find postcolonialism's relationship with anticolonialism, while sometimes troubled, nonetheless makes it a far more useful framework for thinking about the contemporary Caribbean. Postcolonialism's dual vision, of acknowledging the novelty of the present even while trying to learn from and live up to past social movements, becomes a central marker of contemporary Caribbean literature like Dionne Brand's attempts to think through the post-Grenada context.

Is the Post in Postcolonial the Post in Post-Grenada?
Dionne Brand's *In Another Place, Not Here*

Dionne Brand's writing returns over and over again to Grenada, to the events that the author witnessed and participated in during the time she spent working with the People's Revolutionary Government in 1983. Brand first attempts to represent her experiences in Grenada in the 1984 poetry collection *Chronicles of the Hostile Sun*. Written just after the U.S. invasion, these poems are wrought with hopelessness, declaring "the dream is dead / in these antilles" (Brand, *Chronicles* 40), that "you can only fight it with the silence of your / dead body" (43), that "the illiterate and oppressed / . . . have no words for death, / therefore no real need for life" (49). *Chronicles of the Hostile Sun* emphasizes death and despair, apparently closing off the optimistic horizon opened up by revolutionary anticolonialism as the book ends with the poet completely severed from any connection to the people or role in their struggles: "In this hotel / something woke me / there was no noise / no voice / no radio / none of my companions / things would happen now, without me" (75).

These poems emphasize temporal immediacy; while Brand's later essays and fiction often recount the same events, the later texts do not confine themselves to the timeframe of the revolution and invasion but look back on these events from some distance. In taking this position, these works allow a perspective not seen in *Chronicles of the Hostile Sun*, reflecting on what Grenada means for those living in its aftermath. The essay "Nothing of Egypt," from the 1994 collection *Bread Out of Stone*, literally opens with the words "After Grenada" (131), as the author wanders Ottawa remembering the U.S. invasion. Living with the wounds opened up by that experience not only forms the background of this essay but also one of the major organizing themes of the collection as a whole. Just as "Nothing of Egypt" yokes together the North American and Caribbean context as "vibrant and hopeful days, the seventies" (136), other essays such as "Bathurst" and "Brownman, Tiger . . . " reflect on the break between contemporary Caribbean-Canadian cultures and the civil rights–era "Movement" (70) in which Brand participated. Showing the chronological parallels between these different geographical sites emphasizes the cohesiveness of a decolonization era throughout the Americas, as well as its virtual disappearance in the present. Brand contrasts the memory of the decolonization period in the Caribbean and a present-day reality that is much different.

In other words, these essays are postcolonial in their attempts to come to terms with an era of decolonization which can increasingly appear like a distant and irrelevant past. The younger version of herself that Brand remembers in her essays believed that all things were possible, that "I could do anything" (72); the narrator in *Chronicles of the Hostile Sun*, on the other hand, is willing to judge the dream dead. Brand's later writing stakes out a space between those poles. In "Bathurst," Brand marks the younger version of herself as "then" (72), and acknowledges that, by contrast, "the full press of Black liberation organising has ground down to a laborious crawl" as "we're now battered by multicultural bureaucracy, co-opted by mainstream party politics, morassed in everyday racism" (77). The essay "Brownman, Tiger . . . " describes a new generation that "came along [when] Fanon was dead, Rodney had already been killed" (102). Yet Brand refuses to occupy the despondent ground of her poems written in the immediate aftermath of Grenada: a decade later she is "hopeful," she insists that "something's happening" (77). Her vision of the past remembers both the pride and sense of purpose the movement provided, as well as the sexism and patriarchal structures it replicated and still supported. Whether in the image of the activist's funeral, complete with eulogies (134), or the idea of Grenada as something to be "mourned" (140), the period of decolonization has become a time to reflect on rather than inhabit.

The specific past Brand evokes lays down a recognizable set of markers to periodize the difference between "then" and "now": a generation—"my generation" (102)—raised on Fanon and Walter Rodney versus a generation where "what was left was the commercially altered remains of the sixties Black revolution" (102). Her timeline alludes to how the decolonization process gave writers a public role through connections with anticolonial movements, even as postmodern commodification of resistance threatens to neutralize this oppositionality. Whereas the modern colonial period of the first half of the twentieth century saw the development of an anticolonial form of literature in which Caribbean writers such as José Martí, Jacques Roumain, or Martin Carter could confidently assume the position of spokesperson for the nation, postcolonial writing facing the omnipresence of the market in a post-Grenada Caribbean can only long for a time when the writer could have such a political role. Brand's writing is postcolonial in how it mourns this anticolonial mode even as it tries to imagine a new politically engaged writing project.

Brand's *In Another Place, Not Here* presents the decolonization period's hopes of revolution as something gone but not dead, as belonging to a different time but not totally irrelevant to the present one. This postcolonial perspective allows Brand to both pay homage to as well as critique and rethink the spaces available to the writer and the forms of discourse associated with Caribbean anticolonialism. Verlia's story, as that of the diasporic intellectual who must return to reroot herself in the island through working the soil and proving her solidarity with the peasantry, clearly evokes literary anticolonialism, whether Claude McKay's *Banana Bottom*, C. L. R. James's *Minty Alley*, or Jacques Roumain's *Gouverneurs de la rosée*. Yet *In Another Place, Not Here* focuses on the limitations of Verlia's ideas about the relationship of politics to the public and the private, and explores Elizete's alternative relationship to Verlia's political projects.

As anticolonial intellectual, Verlia is credited with helping "wake [Elizete] up" to her male lover's abuses and generally give her a consciousness about her situation (Brand, *In Another Place* 6). At the same time, though, the novel shows the intellectual's lacks and learning process. In particular, the novel depicts in Verlia's journeys a desire for inhabiting the public sphere and a flight from the private. Verlia leaves Toronto and her relationship with Abena because "she needed a mission outside of herself," feeling that there is "nothing more hopeless than two people down to themselves for company" (97). She later reflects that she left because "I couldn't just live in a personal thing . . . Not enough" (102), with ellipses in the original text marking Verlia's inability to name exactly *what* is not enough. The issue for Verlia is not only having a life that matters, that is acknowledged by a public sphere where she is triply excluded as a queer black woman. Even more, Verlia longs for a form of solidarity that can only be expressed through the "immolating of oneself" (207), as in the passage from Fanon she remembers: "The colonialist bourgeoisie has hammered into the native's mind the idea of a society of individuals where each person shut himself up in his own subjectivity, and whose only wealth is individual thought" (159). Yet within Verlia's narrative, this deconstruction of individuality is also a suppression of her own desires, a denial of a private self connected to feeling and emotion that has the practical effect of sending her back to the closet. When she reassures Abena that despite the breakdowns she has been having, "it's just my body. My head's straight" (191), Verlia articulates a view of the personal, embodied self as an obstacle to doing a job that requires her to stay "straight."

Imagining the ideal anticolonial subject as purely public leads Verlia to seek to eliminate the realm of feelings: in decorating her room, for ex-

ample, "she wants it bare, everything bare. No photographs, no sentiment, no memory" (156). Instead, she assembles newspaper clippings to
create a public past to take the place of her personal background: "bits
of newspapers are her history, words her family" (164). But working
amid the revolution, she finds the return of the repressed as she continues to think about Abena and her family: in her diary, she records thinking of them and then how "I feel so small . . . it weakens me to think of
them" (213). Remembering Abena produces the same effect: "I called
Abena and became sad. I don't why. She sounded sad. My imagination
or my period" (208). Emotion, here dismissed as feminine, biological,
and a potentially imagined and unreal fiction, presents a clear threat to
the purely rational anticolonial persona Verlia seeks to create.

Yet even in keeping a diary, this most personal form of writing, Verlia shows the function the private can play for her. Indeed, the novel deconstructs the opposition of intellect as public and emotion as private
by framing political action and solidarity through the passage from Che
Guevara that Verlia returns to: "She wants to live in Che's line. She's
memorized it, memorized it, 'At the risk of seeming ridiculous, let me say
that the true revolutionary is guided by great feelings of love.' There is
a way that she lands in the middle of that line, falls as if in love herself"
(165). The form of love Verlia tries to live up to is a sort of abstracted,
rationalized love of the people in general; Guevara's next sentences (not
reproduced in the novel) ask that "revolutionaries idealize this love of
the people" but not "descend, with small doses of daily affection, to the
level where ordinary people put their love into practice" (Guevara, "Socialism" 226). Much of the narrative of *In Another Place, Not Here* is
about how the boundaries between these two forms of love break down,
suggesting a postcolonial politics must account for the intersections of
public and private identities and alliances. Verlia's love of Elizete is for
her as a person as well as for the oppressed peasantry of which she is
a representative. It is this embodied love that allows Verlia to begin to
"come close to the people" (Brand, *In Another Place* 203) and establish
the grounds for her solidarity with them.

Verlia's mode of enacting that rerooting, through a sexual relationship with a peasant, rehearses a common trope of anticolonial writing
that Brand criticizes in the essay "This Body for Itself." In that essay, she
argues that the anticolonial novel in which the intellectual fascination
with and desire for the peasantry is so often played out through a sexual
relationship uses the black woman's body as object for the intellectual
male's redemption. Brand says of Roumain's *Gouverneurs de la rosée*:

"Here it is the woman as country, virginal, unspoiled land, as territory for anti-colonial struggle. These are not writers with bad intentions, but their approach to the Black female body is as redeemer of the violated" (*Bread* 35). Elizete represents for Verlia the terrain of her rerooting just as Annaïse becomes the land for Manuel in *Gouverneurs de la rosée*. Yet *In Another Place, Not Here* offers what is absent from anticolonial texts like *Minty Alley* and *Gouverneurs de la rosée*: the perspective of Maisie or Annaïse. The narrators of those novels take the point of view of their intellectual protagonists, Haynes and Manuel, respectively, while *In Another Place, Not Here* reverses that gaze in opening with Elizete's voice. Elizete is allowed to express her resistance to any political project that depends on her objectification, not only complaining about the empty content of Verlia's words like "co-operative" and "Revolution" (Brand, *In Another Place* 13) but even resisting Verlia's desire to know and understand her: "I tell she I not no school book with she, I not no report card, I not no exam" (77). Literary intellectuals of anticolonialism expressed their faith in acting as translators for the folk; Elizete refuses to be a text.

In presenting Elizete's voice, *In Another Place, Not Here* invokes the strategies of *testimonio* discussed in chapter 7; but just as the novel's postcolonial perspective expresses nostalgia for but also a critique of Verlia's anticolonial identity, it similarly calls attention to both the potential and limits of *testimonio*. *Testimonio* simultaneously expresses a postcolonial impulse in seeking to erase the presence of the professional writer, creating the pretense of the folk-subject speaking without mediation, even while prefaces and author's notes remind the reader of the heroic anticolonial work the professional writer has done in seeking out and setting down this story. The ideal is, as Jean Franco puts it, that in *testimonio*, "the intellectual virtually disappears from the text in order to let 'the subaltern speak'" (54); the reality is that the intellectual whose position in the public sphere has been challenged can reassert some authority through *testimonio*. Within the *testimonio* discussed in chapter 7, the presence of the professional writer disappears—nowhere in his first-person narration does Esteban Montejo mention Miguel Barnet, the author who set down Montejo's story in *Biografía de un cimarrón*—even while paratextual elements such as Barnet's introduction conjure back into existence that presence and reinforce its authority.

Brand does not allow the presence of the intellectual to hide or remain unexamined in *In Another Place, Not Here*; Elizete and Verlia exist in relation to one another, neither one being privileged over the other. Brand's novel thus becomes about the relationship of intellectual and folk as a narrative of desire, but one where the desire of the folk-subject is actually explored as well. From the first chapter, the novel makes Elizete a desiring subject. While Verlia is defined as the dreamer imagining a better world, the novel also explores Elizete's more quotidian dreams of mobility and escape: "I dream of running, though, to Aruba or Maracaibo" (11). Just as Verlia's desires for Elizete become embedded in her abstracted desires for union with the folk, we get to see Elizete's desires for Verlia as reflective of her own larger dreams and aspirations: "she looked like the young in me, the not beaten down and bruised, the not pounded between my legs, the not lost my mother, the not raped, the not blooded, the not tired" (15–16). Elizete sees her own potential in Verlia, and their relationship becomes a way of realizing herself. In putting the two narratives together, *In Another Place, Not Here* makes them exist in relation to one another, neither romanticizing the woman of the folk as representing the absolute alterity that drives revolutionary opposition nor presenting the intellectual as heroic but isolated vanguardist leaping ahead of the people. The existence of these two characters on a continuum is nowhere more apparent than in Elizete's journey to Toronto, where she shows that the folk-subject can become as mobile and cosmopolitan as the intellectual. In her travel, Elizete takes the position of enlightenment seeker searching to "know" the city where she arrives even if "somehow this place resisted knowing" (69).

Both characters express a clear desire to overcome the boundaries separating them, and readers of *In Another Place, Not Here* have noticed a number of ways in which the novel dissolves the boundaries between Elizete and Verlia. Mark McCutcheon looks at how the liquid imagery is used to show the fluidity of identity, while Ellen Quigley discusses the use of pronouns to deterritorialize each character's subjectivity. But neither character is able to fully understand the other, let alone to become other herself. Ultimately, "there was a distance between them that was inescapable and what they did not talk about. At times [Elizete] saw someone she did not know in Verlia. . . . How could she know Verlia" (54). What finally stands between Verlia and Elizete is the same thing that Verlia tries to sublimate in her section of the narrative: the body that each occupies and can never be occupied by the other, even if sexual union comes closest to realizing that desire. For Elizete, too, the body is an unwelcome reminder of her history: "Heavy as hell. Her body. She doesn't want a sense of it while she's living on the street. She doesn't think of the scars on her legs, she doesn't hide them, she doesn't think of Verlia touching them" (54). Just as the biological realities of personal needs and desires keep Verlia from successfully leaping into an unmoored future, not shaped by a past of suffering, the body weighs down Elizete and marks the possibilities available for her. The novel suggests the body as the personal, private aspects of identity that the anticolonial narrative of public redemption most desires to overcome, but cannot totally leap out of.

To the Last Post

In Another Place, Not Here thus reveals itself to be a postcolonial text through its desire to both inhabit and critique the narrative of revolutionary decolonization. While the stories of Verlia and Elizete invoke these anticolonial predecessors, there is a third character in the novel who explicitly takes a post-Sixties stance: Abena. The lover who initiated Verlia into the movement but who has been left behind, Abena represents the other possibility for the intellectual who did not choose Verlia's self-immolating path. Abena does not join Verlia because "she'd been paralysed" (238), and while Verlia's story is marked by movement and taking action, the novel's penultimate chapter explores Abena falling into stasis. Verlia judges Abena harshly, not so different from the "sellouts" who argue for "going slow" (177). Abena will not commit to revolutionary action because, Verlia suspects, "maybe Abena was hiding something, maybe there was some reason that wasn't really about the struggle at all but personal" (186).

Despite Verlia's continued insistence on enforcing the boundaries of the personal and the public in thinking of Abena this way, however, the novel has already shown that even Verlia's involvement in the movement fulfills for her both personal and political needs. What we ultimately see in Abena is a reoriented intellectual project, not organized around heroic contests for power but the everyday struggles of ordinary people. Abena, tempted by hopelessness, scoffs to herself "as if anybody would dream" in the aftermath of what she has seen (229). But she has not completely given up. Abena is part of the "something happening" that Brand describes in essays like "Bathurst," as "people figure out how to do the day-to-day so that life's not so hard" (*Bread* 77): "[Verlia] didn't know how Abena kept it up, just content to break the rules, a passport here for someone running, a car to Buffalo, a health card, a pay cheque under the table. Small things, Abena said, small things are the only things you can do sometimes" (Brand, *In Another Place* 193). As the novel ends, Abena is only just turning to think about herself, about how "she like to fix others" (239) but has not been able to figure out her own troubled relationship with "emotions" (239). In ending with Abena in dialogue with Elizete as the two try to come to terms with Verlia the intellectual-as-savior as well as their own identities as women and political actors, *In Another Place, Not Here* posits the central questions for revitalizing the place of the intellectual in the postcolonial public sphere: of what kind of relationship Abena and Elizete can forge, and of what kind of new political projects that alliance can work toward in the face of apparent defeat. In supplementing its desire for solidarity and representation with respect for the other's ultimate difference—embodied most explicitly by differences in gender, sexuality, race, and class—*In Another Place, Not Here* explores how postcolonial projects can carry on the legacy of anticolonialism even while following Glissant's call for a politics based on "the right to opacity for everyone" (*Poetics* 194).

Telling a story about the past to reflect on the present, *In Another Place, Not Here* fits squarely into the tradition of Caribbean historical fiction. Anticolonial writers such as C. L. R. James, Alejo Carpentier, and Aimé Césaire looked to the Haitian Revolution to try to imagine how its successes and failures could speak to their historical moment; by the late 1940s and early 1950s, George Lamming, V. S. Reid, and Jacques Stephen Alexis were already resurrecting the social unrest of the 1930s as inspiration for crafting their own engaged literary projects. Brand is part of a new generation of writers from the 1990s and beyond that Elena Machado Sáez and I discuss in *The Latino/a Canon and the Emergence of Post-Sixties Literature*—writers such as Elizabeth Nunez in *Beyond the Limbo Silence*, Margaret Cezair-Thompson in *The True History of Paradise*, Julia Alvarez in *In the Name of Salomé*, and Ana Menéndez in *Loving Che*—who look back to the era of decolonization to set up a thwarted romance and mourn the loss of the forms of hope that moment presented.

Postcolonial Caribbean literature can therefore be defined as distinct from what came before in terms of its inability to inhabit the revolutionary narrative in the same way as its anticolonial predecessors. Yet works like *In Another Place, Not Here* point the way to a rethinking not only of the intellectual's public role but also assumptions about race, class, gender, and what sorts of identity can be public. This emerging postcolonial writing—Caribbean works of art in an age of privatization—shows how previous forms of opposition and resistance represented by the decolonization struggles of the midcentury may no longer be adequate as models for contemporary movements but can provide inspiration for future projects. My hope is that attending to the complexities of abolitionist and anticolonial models in *Caribbean Literature and the Public Sphere* will contribute to the rethinking of Caribbean literature's new horizons for the twenty-first century.

Notes

When translations into English are available, I have referred to the page numbers of the English version. When translations are not available, I have given my own translation in the body of the text and provided the original text along with page number in the endnotes.

Preface

1. When I refer to the Caribbean region, I include the islands between Florida and South America as well as the parts of the mainland with historical and cultural connections to the islands. Because of my own language limitations, I leave to other scholars an examination of how the literary histories of the Netherlands Antilles compare to what I have found in the English-, French-, and Spanish-speaking parts of the region.

2. Donnell contends that she is not interested in Scott's project of "determining at any conjecture what conceptual moves among the many available options will have the most purchase, the best yield" (Scott, *Refashioning* 7, qtd. in Donnell 5), though I am not sure it is so easy to get away from positioning one's own priorities as a privileged conceptual move. In Donnell's case, showing how the questions posed by the nationalist generation have made much pre-1950 Caribbean writing "unknown" and "unknowable" (11) emphasizes the urgency of formulating a different set of questions: "opening up an archive of uneven and unpredictable writings will yield a sense of an unstable past that may be less directly useful to a teleology of literary nationalism, but more honest to the cultural transitions and transactions from which Caribbean literature took its first soundings and made its first voicings" (50). In assigning her project such ambitious goals—to present a "more honest" view of literary history—Donnell makes a strong case for the purchase of her conceptual move, regardless of how she frames her "more modest objective" (5) and the misgivings she expresses regarding Scott's mode of advocating certain critical moves instead of others.

3. Scott's formulation of the relationship between problem-spaces—as one in which "old answers" can be dismissed as "lifeless" and "irrelevant" (*Con-*

scripts 4)—seems strangely romantic, especially in light of Scott's observation that one of tragedy's lessons is to question the view "that the past can be cleanly separated from the present" (12). In my conclusion, I describe my understanding of postcoloniality as constructing this kind of tragic mourning relationship with anticolonialism, acknowledging its passing but nostalgically refusing to give up its spirit. My "Emplotting Postcoloniality" goes into more detail on the ironies of Scott's own embeddedness in the modernist desire for the new in his calls for understanding the present as something completely different from the past.

Introduction

1. Baker refers to Robbins's introduction to *The Phantom Public Sphere* and Fraser's essay "Rethinking the Public Sphere: A Contribution to the Critique of Actually Existing Democracy."

2. Habermas writes that "wherever the public established itself institutionally as a stable group of discussants, it did not equate itself with *the* public but at most claimed to act as its mouthpiece, in its name, perhaps even as its educator—the new form of bourgeois representation" (37). Speaking in the name of the public as a mode of national consolidation is one side of what we can see in Caribbean anticolonialism, although it is always tempered by the simultaneous awareness by members of this public sphere of their existence as a counterpublic.

3. For more on Bourdieu's understanding of the workings of the literary field, see *The Field of Cultural Production*.

4. There are certainly major exceptions to this generalization about the Anglophone tendency toward a colonial/postcolonial framework versus the Francophone and Hispanophone preference for colonialism/modernity/postmodernity: my conclusion returns to some of the Anglophone objections to the idea of postcoloniality, and my introduction discusses Flores and Bongie as two critics who productively bring together the discussions of modernity/postmodernity and colonialism/postcolonialism. It is worth noting that Flores and Bongie each positions himself as something of an outsider to the fields of Latin American and Francophone studies. A number of critics associated with the Casa de las Américas in Cuba, such as Fernández Retamar in "Calibán," also consider postcoloniality alongside postmodernity in ways that resonate with my own project; Cuba, too, might be understood to offer a critical positioning at a skew to dominant tendencies within the field.

5. "Una época en que se comienza a reconocer las culturas modernas (o posmodernas) como mezcla entre las tradicionalmente separadas alta cultura y cultura popular" (Otero Garabís 14).

6. The debate over postmodernism's relationship to Latin American studies is summed up in Beverley, Oviedo, and Aronna. Beginning in the 2000s, Latin Americanists like de la Campa in *Latin Americanism* and Mignolo in *Local Histories/Global Designs* showed the field's increasing investment in the "postcolonial debate." See Moraña, Dussel, and Jáuregui.

7. Blackburn presents an excellent comparative overview of the movement toward emancipation throughout the region.

8. In 1833, the French attempted to address the transition from plantation slavery to modern colonialism with a "so-called colonial constitution" (Jennings, *French Anti-Slavery* 36) in which "most real powers remained with the metropolitan government and its colonial representative, the governor, who proposed the budget, had total initiative in legislative matters, and retained the right to decree by ordonnances" (35–36). The solution for the English-speaking islands was a change of status, which meant tighter control by the metropole and the end of local autonomy: beginning with Trinidad in 1810, with the Morant Bay rebellion in Jamaica in 1865 giving the process a renewed sense of urgency, and ending with Barbados in 1884, the islands of the British West Indies became Crown Colonies, an administrative arrangement Bridget Brereton describes as "formally autocratic" because of its refusal of local representation (*Race Relations* 25). In Cuba and Puerto Rico, meanwhile, the transition away from slavery began even before its abolition, as "mechanisms to effect a smoother transition to free labor were adopted in anticipation of the loss of slave labor—in other words, concurrent with, rather than after, abolition" (Scarano 50). The mid-nineteenth century saw enormous class struggles in the Spanish-controlled islands: in Puerto Rico, laws that forced squatters and peasants to become hacienda workers attempted to regulate these new relations (a conflict depicted in Manuel Zeno Gandía's 1894 novel *La charca*), while in Cuba the same forces exploded in the wars of independence that began in the 1860s. In Haiti, Cuba, the Dominican Republic, and Puerto Rico, where revolution and the decline of the Spanish empire threatened to release these islands from an international system dominated by Europe, the United States stepped in to impose modern colonial controls toward the end of the nineteenth century.

9. Harvey looks at the structures of the contemporary international order such as the International Monetary Fund and World Bank that were designed at the Bretton Woods Conference in 1944 to manage the declining power of modern colonialism as an organizing system; the Bretton Woods Agreement that came out of that meeting would be redefined in the early 1970s, leading Harvey to identify 1973 as the onset of postmodernity in the Western world. It is not surprising that the institutions created in 1944 could not fully address the decolonized world if we consider the 1950s and 1960s as a period of reorganization of global relations in which new directions were not inevitable and were defined in response to the social movements of the time. Harvey makes the case for considering the economic organization of the post-1973 period as distinct from what came before in the second section of *The Condition of Postmodernity*, titled "The Political-Economic Transformation of Late Twentieth-Century Capitalism." While Harvey's account focuses too exclusively on the United States and to some extent Europe, Amin analyzes these processes from the perspective of the rest of the world. Klein also shows how redefinitions in global capitalism

took place outside of the United States or Europe, following Harvey in identifying 1973 as the onset of this new era but showing the role of the Pinochet coup in Chile in the developing doctrine of free market fundamentalism.

1. The Abolitionist Public Sphere and the Republic of the Lettered

1. The field of Caribbean cultural studies has made invaluable contributions to foregrounding popular culture as a site of Caribbean world-making. Price-Mars's *Ainsi parla l'oncle*, Brathwaite's *Contradictory Omens*, and González's "El país de cuatro pisos" remain foundational works in examining how those excluded from official discourse found other modes of expression, and scholars like Cooper, Flores, Rohlehr, Sánchez González, and others continue to expand on these important interventions.

2. The idea that these forms of expression were pushed out of the public sphere echoes Glissant's formulation of a "forced poetics" in *Le discours antillais*.

3. Gordon Lewis's discussion of what he calls the "antislavery ideology" is only one example of an important body of work on the abolition movement. For the particular focus on the role of writing in opposing slavery, see Hurwitz, who helpfully analyzes the ideological parameters of abolitionist writing.

4. Schmidt-Nowara gives a fascinating account of the transnational nature of abolitionism, arguing that "the origins of the Abolitionist Society" that rose to importance in Madrid in the 1860s "lay not so much in Spain, nor in the Caribbean's major slave society, Cuba, but in Puerto Rico" (38). While he makes a convincing case for this argument, he nonetheless comes to the conclusion that while Puerto Rican (and to some extent Cuban) activists were able to mobilize other intellectuals in opposing slavery, their venues for doing so lay almost exclusively in the European metropole.

5. Tobago did not become part of an administrative unit with Trinidad until 1889, so I refer to the colony before that date simply as Trinidad.

6. Anderson and Sommer emphasize the centrality of the written word to the new nationalisms of Latin America in the nineteenth century.

7. Of the "urbanization of Spanish America," Rama writes: "rather than stemming from agrarian growth that gradually created an urban market and trade center, rural development here followed the creation of the city" (11). The novelty of this situation, brought about by the vastness of the Spanish empire and the rapidity with which it was conquered and settled, stands in contrast to the Caribbean islands. See the chapter "De la plantación a la Plantación" in Benítez-Rojo's *La isla que se repite* for a historical account of the process of settlement in the Caribbean region.

8. For more on the demographics of the various islands, see Knight.

9. Lean and Burnard point out that "alone of the British possessions in the Caribbean, [Berbice, Demerara, and Essequebo] had an official known as a Fiscal who was responsible for ensuring that the *Rule on the Treatment of Servants*

and Slaves that the Dutch had instituted in 1772 as a way of curbing slave unrest was adhered to by planters. Under the terms of the British acquisition from the Dutch in 1803, they were obliged to retain the bureaucratic structure of the colonies, and thus the Fiscal remained. The significant feature of his office was that slaves had the right to appeal to him for redress for violations against the slave code" (131). Landers discusses how the Spanish legal code in Latin America provided similar, highly circumscribed opportunities for enslaved people to register grievances or appeals in her essay "African American Women and Their Pursuit of Rights through Eighteenth-Century Spanish Texts." Garrigus argues for the notarial records in Saint-Domingue as a sort of proto-public sphere for free people of color (95). All of these examples show the interstices in which nonwhites could find entry into a legal public sphere set up to exclude them.

10. The introduction to Matthews's *Caribbean Slave Revolts and the British Abolitionist Movement* provides a good overview of how various historians have sought to understand the relationship of the actions of slaves and the printed advocacy of the abolitionist movement.

11. A number of Toussaint Louverture's letters to the French Directory and to Napoleon are reproduced online at http://thelouvertureproject.org. "A Refutation of Some Assertions in a Speech Pronounced in the Corps Législatif by Viénot Vaublanc," a letter Louverture sent to the French legislature in 1797, is reproduced as Document 31 in Dubois and Garrigus.

12. The *Revue des Colonies* explicitly saw itself as influencing public discourse. Brickhouse cites the first issue, which presents "its own self-identified goal of bringing the 'greatest publicity' and thus a 'clarified public opinion' to the subject of 'the suffering and oppressed classes' of the colonial world" (89). But this abolitionist public sphere is clearly metropolitan: Jennings notes of the *Revue des Colonies* that "in the colonies the authorities did everything possible to impede its circulation" ("Cyrille Bissette" 54). See the chapter in Bongie's *Islands and Exiles* titled "1835, or 'Le troisième siecle'" for a discussion of Bissette's writing in the *Revue des Colonies*.

13. Probably the first and perhaps still the best example of this recuperative effort (aside from Ferguson's recovering and editing of the text itself) comes in Paquet's "The Heartbeat of a West Indian Slave." Paquet's essay begins with the premise that despite the circumstances of its publication, Prince's "narrative retains a qualitative uniqueness that is distinctly West Indian, distinctly a black woman's, and distinctly a slave's" ("Heartbeat" 131). Paquet appears to significantly modify this argument in her later book *Caribbean Autobiography*; although that book features a chapter with the same name as the earlier essay, the chapter reworks her reading of Prince's narrative. The book chapter begins with a discussion of the "productive alliances" Prince was required to form (Paquet, *Caribbean Autobiography* 30), noting that it is her relationships with members of the British establishment that "make her voice as historian of West Indian slavery possible and credible to a British audience" (31). Paquet's ambiva-

lence over these questions is understandable, and remains one of the best places to begin thinking about how to read this text.

14. Rauwerda presents what may be the fullest critique of the idea that Prince's voice is recoverable in *The History of Mary Prince*. Drawing on Spivak's "Can the Subaltern Speak?" Rauwerda argues that not only does the "wealth of material that surrounds and shapes" Prince's story demonstrate "how manipulated and externally constructed the narrative really is" (399), but that even within the story, although "it initially seems that Prince names herself" (400), in fact it is Pringle who has named her, as the footnote on page 84 of Ferguson's edition reveals.

15. Prince's narrative forms an intriguing precursor for the *testimonio* of the postcolonial period; Cesareo discusses *The History of Mary Prince* as a form of testimonial discourse and in particular the "politics of erasure that structure . . . subaltern writing" (114).

16. Paton's introduction to *A Narrative of Events, since the First of August, 1834, by James Williams, an Apprenticed Labourer in Jamaica* explicitly discusses how, though "Williams's *Narrative* is not technically a slave narrative" (xvii), Paton nonetheless sees "the most immediate and most important British/Caribbean predecessor to Williams's narrative" as "*The History of Mary Prince*" (xxxii). Paton points in particular to how Williams's text depends on the same system of authentication as Prince's narrative. Though Paton notes the peculiarity that Williams's narrative was "authenticated by black knowledge and truthfulness" via the advertisement preceding the narrative written by a black minister, I would add that the legitimating power of the church follows on Rama's idea of the lettered city; Williams's situation further resembles Prince's in terms of how his narrative circulated in England as part of antiapprenticeship discourse, even while "the Jamaican pro-planter press launched a vigorous attack" on Williams and his editor (xxxviii).

2. The Public Sphere Unbound

1. Eudell presents a different point of view, suggesting the ways that antislavery discourse contained many of the ideas that would later organize postemancipation societies in the New World.

2. During the years following slavery's abolition, Haiti also saw the rise of local publication, though its distinct place in the nation-state system meant that writers attempting to connect to a public or establish an independent public sphere had to forge a relationship with the newly founded state. The connection to the state often meant opportunities for writers, but did not lend itself to independence or critique. Fischer credits Henri Christophe for his "conscious effort to create a national culture" (259) through enlisting writers in his regime, but Dash and Gordon Lewis see a more coercive relationship between these early writers and the state. Dash is particularly critical of Baron de Vastey, who he acknowledges as "the most important ideological figure in early Haitian history"

247 Notes to Chapter 2

(*Literature and Ideology* 4) but blames for the "degeneration of Haitian writing into court poetry and propaganda for the various presidents of Haiti" (5). Lewis sees an early nationalism in the pamphleteers like de Vastey and the historians of the 1840s and 1850s, but admits that they represented not a broad public but "all the class and cultural bias of their authors," who "certainly did not envisage a Haiti in which the unlettered masses would be master" (259). Rather than a public sphere able to critique the status quo in the name of the people, Dash and Lewis describe a form of writing aligned very closely with the state, not so different from Hénock Trouillot's dismissal of writing from this period as the work of an "une petite élite rapaces, anti-progressiste, anti-peuple" (98). A local literary public sphere would flourish in Haiti during the anticolonial opposition to the U.S. occupation that I discuss in chapter 3.

3. Local libraries and schools began to be founded in the region during the second half of the nineteenth century, and a handful of works of poetry or fiction published locally have been uncovered from this time period: Cudjoe notes that the Trinidad Public Library was founded in 1851 and discusses the "rise of a vigorous press, 'a liberal press'" (*Beyond Boundaries* 194) in that island during the 1870s; at the same time, the introduction to the reissued edition of *Adolphus, A Tale*, describes how that anonymously penned novel was published serially in 1853 in the *Trinidadian*, an "anti-white, anti-government" newspaper recognized as a mouthpiece for the free colored class (Winer et al., Introduction to *Adolphus* xxiv).

4. Cudjoe's description of Philip's historical context emphasizes the conflicting forces at work in this period; Cudjoe oscillates between describing Trinidad in the 1850s as "the first flowering of a distinctive national voice" and noting that "nothing said here should blind us to the fact that, of a population of 70,000 people in 1853, two-thirds of the population could not speak English, seven-eighths were illiterate, and nine-tenths 'go barefoot' as the *Trinidadian* reported on December 24, 1853" (*Beyond Boundaries* 120).

5. Perhaps even more than *Blake, Emmanuel Appadocca* expresses the ambivalence that Stephens identifies in black empire texts: "desire on the part of marginalized modern black subjects to tell global stories of the race in the context of empire and conquest" even while "represent[ing] the survival of alternative ways of imagining political community and multiracial democracy" (59). Stephens discusses how even in *Blake*, the "new trope for a revolutionary black masculinity" of the "Negro seaman, a mobile New Negro detached from territory" (67) to some extent mitigates the territorial nationalism that the Black Emperor figure seems to embody.

6. C. L. R. James describes the crew in *Moby Dick* as "a pack of ragamuffins picked up at random from all parts of the earth," adding that "nearly all on Ahab's ship were islanders, and in fact, nearly all the nations of the globe had each its representative" (*Mariners* 18). James also calls attention to Melville's designation of these men as "isolatoes," making them very similar to the outcasts who people Appadocca's *Black Schooner*.

7. During the second half of the eighteenth century, Johann Gottfried von Herder formulated ideas about the nation that would become influential throughout Europe and its possessions during this period. Musgrave explains: "According to Herder, a *Volk* was a community bound together by blood-ties and characterized by a particular language, culture, religion and set of customs. Like the family of which it was simply a wider extension, the *Volk* was supposedly a 'natural unit.' Every *Volk* had the right to develop its own political institutions uninfluenced and unimpeded by others, and thus to express in the political realm its own unique national character. Each *Volk* must therefore possess its own separate state. The 'most natural state,' in Herder's opinion, was a 'community with its own national character.' Multinational states were 'artificial contrivances, patched-up fragile contradictions . . . devoid of inner life'" (5).

8. See Cudjoe's afterword to *Emmanuel Appadocca* for a discussion of how "Philip intends a broader indictment of Western civilization and colonialism which he notes is nothing more than a 'licensed system of robbing and thieving' around which 'the civilized world turns'" (263).

9. I discuss how V. S. Naipaul sets *A Way in the World* in the Gulf of Paria as a way of negotiating between the literary traditions of the Anglophone Caribbean and Latin America in my essay "Ways of Looking: The Global Vision of V. S. Naipaul."

10. In *Adolphus*, a text that ran serially in Trinidad at almost the same time that *Emmanuel Appadocca* appeared in England, "Venezuela, the country to which Adolphus and his companion flee, is presented as the paradigmatic example of a free country, the kind of society the coloured Trinidadian should aspire to achieve, the kind of democracy they would like to construct in their homeland" (Cudjoe, *Beyond Boundaries* 121). *The Slave Son*, published in 1854 and reissued in a companion edition with *Adolphus* in 2003, also ends by going from Trinidad to Venezuela as a move toward freedom.

11. Sommer discusses the role of romance in Latin American fictions of nation building.

12. "Te dejo, Pluma, por ceñirte Espada" (Montes-Huidobro 48).

13. "En vano me llama un pueblo" (Montes-Huidobro 95).

14. "La voz valiente del robusto canto / Que allá en las playas de la triste Cuba / Alzaste porque suba / Grito de Libertad y no de llanto" (Montes-Huidobro 49).

15. "Y ansiosos volarán, bravos soldados, / ¡A vencer o morir bajo su estrella!" (Montes-Huidobro 49).

16. "El letargo pasó. De nobles hijos / Lanzados por el Déspota a otro suelo" (Montes-Huidobro 49).

17. "En esta colección no presentamos ningún nombre que no sea ventajosamente conocido en la república de las letras cubanas . . . la revolución ha surgido del seno de las clases más ilustradas de la isla" (Montes-Huidobro 3–4).

18. "Revivir de algún modo un sentimiento . . . recordar al pueblo grandes ideas de libertad en el lenguaje más propio para que se conserven en la memoria" (Montes-Huidobro 3).

19. "Quien así como tú se sacrifica / Por darle libertad a gente opresa" (Montes-Huidobro 113).

20. According to Pérez, while Cuba traded almost exclusively with Spain in the eighteenth century, by 1850 trade with the United States represented 39 percent of foreign trade while trade with Spain was only 19 percent, and that "by 1877, the United States accounted for 82 percent of Cuba's total exports, followed by Spain (6 percent) and England (4 percent)" (84).

21. See Pratt for a general discussion of travel writing and the bourgeois subject, and Hawthorne's "Self-Writing, Literary Traditions and Post-Emancipation Identity" for a more specific discussion of genre in *Wonderful Adventures*.

22. Seacole frequently makes judgments about the people she encounters based on national stereotypes, suggesting her logic is based more in a reductive version of biology than the rationalism she sometimes espouses. McKenna, Hawthorne, and Baggett seek to show how Seacole does construct a critique of racism, inequality, and exploitation, albeit a mitigated or hidden one displaced onto other subjects, such as how her darker-skinned friend was treated while visiting England.

23. Of New Grenada, Seacole writes: "Before the passengers for Panama had been many days gone, it was found that they had left one of their number behind them, and that one—the cholera. . . . The poor Cruces folk did not hesitate to say that this new and terrible plague had been a fellow-traveller with the Americans from New Orleans or some other of its favored haunts" (24). Her description of cholera in Jamaica makes the same association: "In the year 1850, the cholera swept over the island of Jamaica with terrible force. Our idea—perhaps an unfounded one—was, that a steamer from New Orleans was the means of introducing it into the island" (9).

3. The Intellectual and the Man of Action

1. See especially Ramos's third chapter, "Fragmentation of the Republic of Letters." Rama describes a similar process in his chapter "The Modernized City," though Rama emphasizes the continuity between the *letrados* and literary writers much more than Ramos does.

2. Cudjoe mentions the appearance of Pérez Bonalde's poem in Trinidad, and points out that the editors discuss Martí's prologue in their own analysis of the poem (*Beyond Boundaries* 274).

3. Of the role of the church, longtime patron of the arts, Martí writes: "there is no painter who succeeds in coloring, with the novelty and transparency of bygone days, the luminous aureolas of virgins, nor is there a preacher or religious singer who puts any fervor or words of conviction into his phrases and imprecations" ("Poem of Niagara" 311). In this statement, Martí manages to

distinguish modern art as not necessarily religious, while also expressing what seems to be nostalgia for a strangely sexualized version of that past.

4. Sander and Levy provide crucial background to the vibrant Trinidadian literary public sphere of the 1920s and 1930s. Rosenberg and Cudjoe have begun to call attention to the literary institutions of even earlier periods.

5. The introduction to *Rupert Gray* by Winer et. al. provides an excellent discussion of the political climate of the 1890s. See especially xx–xxxi.

6. Pierre's failures to represent himself in the courtroom evoke the situation that Faith Smith identifies as a crucial context for the publication of J. J. Thomas's *Creole Grammar* in 1869: according to Smith, "Thomas's prefatory remarks in the *Creole Grammar* make clear his concerns that members of Trinidad's working class were being rendered voiceless by legal and religious institutions" (97).

7. The 1853 anonymously authored novel *Adolphus* also features a plot that involves the manipulation of writing leading to tragedy, a fact in that novel directly tied to the lack in Trinidad of a functioning public sphere: "alas, at that time the suffering class, possessing no public organ, could neither send forth nor yet receive any thing like correct information" (7); from there, it notes that "schools, except of a certain stamp, were altogether discountenanced by the authorities, or at least not encouraged" (9), such that its main female character can only enlighten herself through the private library of Padre Gonzalvez (11). Daniel Cosway's role in *Wide Sargasso Sea* is discussed by Gregg (110–111).

8. Rosenberg notes that "middle-class teachers led the nationalist movements of the early twentieth century. [Thomas] MacDermot, who edited the All Jamaica Library and developed Jamaica's first yard fiction, had first been a teacher. Teachers dominated the readership of the *Jamaica Times* and were the backbone of both its political and literary nationalism. In Trinidad and Tobago, Stephen Cobham had been a teacher before authoring *Rupert Gray* and C. L. R. James was a teacher when he wrote 'Triumph' and *Minty Alley*" (209). See also Cudjoe's *Beyond Boundaries* (366).

9. Garret refers to a Haitian renaissance in discussing poetry from the 1920s, 1930s, and 1940s; she takes Roumain's cofounding of *La Revue Indigène* in 1927 as a pivotal moment in her narrative. She lists the "internal causes" of the renaissance as "the social unrest and economic and political instability of the country in the early years of the present century, the intervention of the Government of the United States in the affairs of Haiti, the ethnological studies of Dr. Price Mars, and the dissatisfaction of the young poets with the past generation" (53).

10. Plummer provides a helpful account of the rise of U.S. influence in Haiti and the context leading up to the U.S. invasion. The details of the occupation itself are treated by Renda and Schmidt.

11. Shannon discusses the role of Haitian intellectuals during the U.S. occupation.

12. "*La Trouée*! Notre nom combatif éclate comme un appel de tambour. . . . C'est celui d'âmes juvéniles et ardents qui vont percer la ligne d'ignorance et d'apathie qui nous étouffe" (Roumain, *Oeuvres complètes* 433).

13. In March 1932, an article titled "Mahatma Gandhi" by Rev. C. F. Andrews appeared in a special issue of the *Beacon* on India; later that year, an "India Section" was launched in the newspaper, and another article with the same title by Beatrice Greig appeared in the August 1932 issue.

14. Alongside the passivity encouraged by this apparently Christian belief system, Vodou offers a more complicated ideology in the novel, where men can actually become gods (Roumain, *Masters* 69), even if only for the duration of a ceremony. See Dayan (*Haiti* 83–84) and Mahabir (79–86) for more on the ambivalent position of Vodou in *Gouverneurs de la rosée*.

15. "La politique t'attira un temps; tu ne fus jamais qu'un demagogue puéril; tu te croyais littérateur (tu le crois encore), tu écrivis des manifestes, des poèmes et un livre que personne ne lit. . . . Allons, ressaisis-toi: tu es ce qu'on appelle un type qui a tout ce qu'il faut pour réussir: famille honorable, pas de loyer, et une place offerte au Département de l'Intérieur" (Roumain, *Oeuvres complètes* 131–132).

16. Rachel Manley repeatedly associates the public world of politics with the rational Norman, while the artistic world is the realm of the intuitive Edna. Brown's biography of Edna reinforces this gendered opposition between Norman's rationalism and his wife's emotional sensitivity, even extending it to Edna's parents: "in the struggle within [Edna] of two worlds, the one Christian, rational, the other Animist, instinctual, the fact of [her father's] presence had been a powerful argument for the former: through him she might yet have entered the caviling world of her family. His death severed that argument; it cast her adrift, for the time being at least, on her own inner ocean of imagination" (34). The subtitle of Brown's book, *Edna Manley: The Private Years, 1900–1938*, renders this gendered opposition in terms of the early married life of the Manleys as private and opposed to the public years that follow Norman's entry into electoral politics.

17. I look at the relationship between *Public Opinion* and *Focus* in more detail in the essay "The Public Sphere and Jamaican Anticolonial Politics: *Public Opinion*, *Focus*, and the Place of the Literary."

4. The Ideology of the Literary

1. Anxiety about the relationship of writing and action leads to shifts in how authorial identity is defined by all of these writers. James employs the phrase "man of action" to describe heroes like Toussaint Louverture (*Black Jacobins* 206) and Leon Trotsky (*C. L. R. James* 109), though in his 1953 reading of *Moby Dick* the relationship between the "literary intellectual" Ishmael and the "man of action" Ahab becomes more complicated (*Mariners* 42). In *The Writer in Transition*, Hawthorne reads Mais's work as a negotiation of the writer's

public role. Munro evokes the idea of Alexis as man of action in calling him "the epitome of the Haitian patriot, a descendant of Dessalines" (38), but also looks at how Alexis becomes a model for post-1946 deterritorialized writing. A number of productive readings of the masculinism of Fanon's discourse can be found in Read's edited collection. Torres-Saillant provides an excellent examination of Mir's writing as "anti-Trujillo" and "aggressive to the status quo" (231) while also noting Mir's use of the anticolonial trope of "association of the exploitation of the female laborers and the exploitation of the native land" (230). Dalleo and Machado Sáez look at how Colón "captures the relationship of the artist and intellectual to this anticolonial ideology" (21) even as his writing reveals anxiety about that role.

2. Winston James describes how in "Quashie to Buccra" as well as "Hard Times," "the troubles of the peasants are . . . given voice" (60–61), and how McKay in "Passive Resistance" "makes himself a member of the collective 'we' in whose voice the poem is enunciated" (88).

3. Lewis and Lewis pay significant attention to *Banana Bottom*'s depiction of the Jamaican middle class. While other readers make note of the novel's critique of what Lewis and Lewis call *assimilés*, their essay anticipates my own argument in seeing how the critique of the middle class is not total, and is connected to a broader "dichotomy between the rational empiricism and technological slant of the Caucasian world, as against the spontaneity, vitality, and visceral quality of black culture" (47). For Lewis and Lewis, though, this critique is a sign of McKay's romantic naïveté, that he "never outgrew Jekyll's influence" (47) and that he "read very little of Marx and apparently none of Lenin" (48). His "ambivalence" (50) thus places him into the "pre-nationalist phase of our historical and cultural development" (51). While I agree with Lewis and Lewis's emphasis on this ambivalence, the way the novel embraces and explores these contradictions seems to *enable* McKay's anticolonial political project rather than to make it a failure.

4. C. L. R. James, speaking of why he chose to leave Trinidad and Tobago to pursue his career as a writer, describes how if he had stayed, the only possibility open to him as a talented black man would have been "to be a civil servant and hand papers, take them from the men downstairs and hand them to the man upstairs" (qtd. in Sander 29). James thus echoes McKay's critique of the complete lack of creativity available in this profession making it a less desirable option than an unfettered literary life.

5. Aside from biographical similarities—the friendship with a well-read Englishman and voracious reading in his library, the move to the city and attempts to work for the colonial state, followed by disillusion and emigration to the United States—McKay attributes at least one of his own stories to Bita's cousin: Bab hears Squire Gensir complain about interacting with English people who are not of his class and then asks the squire "how then he was able to tolerate the manners of the peasantry" (*Banana Bottom* 82); in his autobiography,

McKay recounts Walter Jekyll's railing about "middle-class upstart[s]" and asking his mentor, "But Mr. Jekyll, how can you tolerate me? I am merely the son of a peasant" (qtd. in R. Cobham, "Jekyll and Claude" 127).

6. My essay "Shadows, Funerals and the Terrified Consciousness in Frank Collymore's Short Fiction" expands this argument to show how Collymore's short fiction from *BIM* participates in many of the debates about the folk and decolonization present in more recognizably nationalist writing.

7. *Orígenes*, edited by José Lezama Lima and José Rodríguez Feo and published between 1944 and 1956, has frequently been discussed in terms of its almost hermetic stylization as a retreat from politics. Hassan notes, "it is somewhat difficult to perceive any explicit politics in *Orígenes*" (11); the journal was known especially for publishing experimental poetry, in line with Lezama Lima's own preferences for what Bejel calls "Mallarmean symbolism" (223). Pellón uses some of the same adjectives to describe Lezama Lima's "densely metaphorical, hermetic, and epiphanic style of writing" (215).

8. "*La Poesía Sorprendida* saluda, en tan señalada fecha, a los dominicanos—de dentro y de fuera—que laboran en la sensibilidad y la inteligencia, la grandeza dominicana; . . . los intelectuales y artistas dominicanos que no podían vivir en su patria" (Fernández Spencer xxxi).

9. "Afirma su fe en la creación del mundo más bello más libre y más hondo de mañana" (Veloz Maggiolo 46).

10. "No sabemos si la poesía nos sorprende con su deslumbrante destino, si nosotros la sorprendemos a ella en su silenciosa y verdadera hermosura. No sabemos si ella sorprende este mundo nuestro y es su hermosura quien mantiene esa fidelidad secreta en la escondida, interior y grande esperanza. No sabemos si el mundo loco corre a ella, porque precisa ahora correr como antes, como siempre o como mañana; o si ella corre a él porque necesita salvarlo. La poesía siempre mágica, callada, total en su soledad y su resplandor inucitado de vida, ¿Por qué no ha de ser sorprendida? ¿Por qué—como las grandes bellezas mágicas—no ha de sorprenderse, de vez en cuando, de sí misma y de contener su mundo—el mundo? Necesitamos de ella en un planeta sordo, para que ella sea la estrella de la sorpresa y lo inesperado de su luz. La poesía, es entonces un arma, menos evidente, gráfica o corporea, pero con una fuerza capaz de desbaratar esas mismas armas reales; porque sigue siendo la apetencia del hombre de un mundo de belleza y de verdad interior" (Baeza Flores 1).

11. Depestre describes the influence of Césaire and Breton on the overthrow of Lescot in "André Breton in Port-au-Prince." Matthew Smith also discusses the surrealist orientation of *La Ruche* (*Red and Black in Haiti* 75–76).

12. "J'ai toujours été frappé par le fait que les Antilles souffrent d'un manqué. Il y a aux Antilles un vide culturel. Non que nous nous désintéressons de la culture, mais les Antilles sont trop exclusivement une société de consummation culturelle" (Leiner v).

13. See Soyinka's *Myth, Literature and the African World*, quoted in Ash-

croft's essay "Globalism, Postcolonialism and African Studies," for a discussion of negritude's relationship with European binary thought. Fanon also contributes significantly to this critique (102-106).

14. McKay was also influenced by this intellectual tradition: both Rhonda Cobham and Winston James note that his mentor, Walter Jekyll, was "an ardent disciple of Schopenhauer," and thus "deplored the enervation of modern Western civilization" (R. Cobham, "Jekyll and Claude" 125).

15. Although more has been made of Cuban painter Wilfredo Lam's connection to Aimé Césaire, Carpentier contributed an essay to the January 1945 issue of *Tropiques*, raising the question of how much Carpentier's own ideas about the marvelous real were influenced by Ménil.

16. Edwards argues that critics have "overemphasized the importance of *Légitime Défense*" (191) and in particular that "the debt of Césaire's *Tropiques* . . . to *Légitime Défense* . . . has long been in question" (194). He points especially to Aimé Césaire's own distancing from *Légitime Défense* and argues that the importance of surrealism to both journals has been exaggerated.

17. Dash's "Aimé Césaire: The Bearable Lightness of Becoming" further explores how "the politics of Césaire's heroic, modernist stance have always been ambiguous" (738).

18. The rethinking of McFarlane's work that Donnell urges at least tacitly endorses a questioning of the idea that what she calls his "loyalty" (48) to the British empire was necessarily conservative. McFarlane makes a case for the empire as a sort of hybrid, multicultural fellowship, which he opposes to the fascistic tendency toward national purity that he sees as the other possibility in the world of the 1930s; he calls this bringing "a new meaning to Empire" and labels the idea of "reconciling with the Empire the clashing interests and outlooks of divers races . . . at once a grave danger to humanity and an unparalleled opportunity for human progress, co-operation, and understanding" (15). In trying to imagine a form of sovereignty that allows for diversity even while remaining suspicious of the nation-state system, McFarlane seems not so far from some of his better-known contemporaries, the "black empire" thinkers like Marcus Garvey, Cyril Briggs, Claude McKay, and C. L. R. James, who Stephens describes as "attempt[ing] to construct an oppositional form of black nationalism and political representation in an international imperial world that did not yet recognize black colonial subjects as national peoples" (3).

5. The Expulsion from the Public Sphere

1. Dash adopts the idea of the "dictator novel" from González Echevarría. González Echevarría equates authorship with authoritarianism to make a case that the dreams for utopia by Latin American intellectuals set the stage for totalitarian regimes in that region. The process he celebrates, by which "the great figure of the author has been replaced by the uncertain figure of the writer" (70),

resembles the shift from anticolonialism to postcolonialism that takes place in the Caribbean during the 1960s and 1970s.

2. Fouchard, writing during the same period as Chauvet, gives a historian's version of Minette's theater career.

3. Fick provides a good account of Vincent Ogé's rebellion (82–84). She emphasizes how Ogé "shunned slave participation in the revolt" even as other leaders among the free people of color argued for enlisting the support of slaves in their uprising.

4. Chapter 9 of Fischer's *Modernity Disavowed*, titled "Literature and the Theater of Revolution," gives a helpful overview of the theater scene in Saint-Domingue during the end of the eighteenth century. The article by Camier and Dubois, "Voltaire et Zaïre, ou le théâtre des Lumières dans l'aire atlantique française," also provides important background on the interrelation of the theater, the market, and the Saint-Domingue public sphere.

5. Garrigus discusses the struggle over the public sphere between whites and free people of color in eighteenth-century Saint-Domingue in chapters 4 and 5 of *Before Haiti*.

6. Nicholls remains one of the definitive chroniclers of the political conflicts and rivalries between blacks and mulattos in Haiti as well as the place of race-based ideology in Duvalier's rise to power.

7. This incident from *La danse sur le volcan* depicts the infamous treatment of the group of armed slaves known as the Suisse who were betrayed by the free people of color they had fought alongside. In his history of the Haitian Revolution, Dubois calls this episode "a tragic betrayal that would not be forgotten, and a taste of the internal conflicts among different groups of African descent in the colony that were to come" (121).

8. Michel-Rolph Trouillot argues for understanding the Duvalier years as an intensification of Haiti's historical tension between the state and civil society. Trouillot distinguishes between the state, as political apparatus, and the nation, as the people governed, with civil society as the mediating force between them. Trouillot therefore makes a case for a strong civil society—which he defines as made up of "formal institutions" like "schools, clergy, press, trade unions" (17) as well as less formal institutions like the family—as a defense against totalitarianism. As "the bodies and sodalities usually termed 'internal and private'" (19) that exert ideological influence and can act as a check on the state, Trouillot's civil society resembles Habermas's "private people, come together to form a public" (25). My preference for the term "public sphere" rather than "civil society" comes from the former's emphasis on not only institutions but also discursive struggle as part of the process by which state and nation interact.

9. A brief overview of this falling out between James and the PNM can be found in Grimshaw. For more details, see Oxaal.

10. Much like the anticolonial writers, Williams emphasizes the importance of the public sphere as a site of struggle in decolonization, evidenced by his

emphasis on speaking in Woodford Square as a crucial part of building popular support for Trinidadian independence. In a 1955 speech, he explains his decision to "let down my bucket where I am, now, right here with you in the British West Indies" (Cudjoe, *Eric E. Williams Speaks* 165)—in other words, to return to his birthplace and build a social movement to work toward the end of British rule—by telling a story about the lack of "intellectual freedom" (112) and freedom of expression in the islands. He details the hostile responses he receives to publishing books of history critical of the role of sugar and slavery in West Indian society, and how these responses jeopardize his position with the Caribbean Commission. One of his superiors asks him if he is aware of the controversy his histories have caused, leading Williams to call attention to the ways in which the planter class's desire for control of the public sphere conditions these responses: "I had seen a hostile review in *The Antigua Star* and another in the *West India Committee Circular*, both papers of the planters" (116). This 1955 speech explains the importance of creating an alternative space of expression for the process of contesting colonial discursive power.

11. In 1961, Sabá Cabrera Infante and Orlando Jiménez Leal codirected *PM*, a short film that showed images of Havana nightlife. Cuba's Film Institute refused to show the film, deeming it self-indulgent and bourgeois. In the arguments that followed, the island's leading cultural publication, *Lunes de Revolución*, edited by Guillermo Cabrera Infante, was closed down, and Castro issued his famous "Palabras a los intelectuales." For a fuller discussion, see Luis's "Exhuming *Lunes de Revolución*."

12. After Padilla was forced to make an obviously staged public confession, what became known as the Padilla affair marked a break for many leading intellectuals in Latin America and Europe who had been sympathetic to the Cuban Revolution, including Jean-Paul Sartre, Simone de Beauvoir, Julio Cortázar, and Carlos Fuentes. Padilla writes about his experience in *Self-Portrait of the Other*. Miller discusses the incident in the broader context of Cuban politics.

13. See Part II of Hill, *Walter Rodney Speaks: The Making of an African Intellectual*, for Rodney's formulation of the "guerrilla intellectual."

6. Anticolonial Authority and the Postcolonial Occasion for Speaking

1. Between 1951 and 1954, Carter published four books of poems, culminating in his most highly regarded collection, *Poems of Resistance*. Lamming published four novels as well as *The Pleasures of Exile* between 1953 and 1960.

2. The *New World Quarterly* issue commemorating Guyanese independence shows how decolonization allowed a variety of different projects to exist side by side; in this issue, poetry and creative work by Lamming, Carter, Harris, Guillén, Carew, and Mittelholzer appears alongside contributions from Burnham, Jagan, Rodney, Fanon, and James. Only a few years later, such an inclusive gesture would be unimaginable in the deeply divided postcolonial Caribbean.

See Lamming, *On the Canvas of the World*, for the contents of the 1966 issues of *New World Quarterly* commemorating both Guyanese and Barbadian independence.

3. After his "Poems of Shape and Motion" appeared in *Kyk-over-al* in 1955, Carter took a hiatus from creative writing until 1961; during the 1960s, he published two major new collections, *Conversations* in 1961 and *Jail Me Quickly* in 1963, and in the 1970s he published *Poems of Succession* in 1977, a compilation of his earlier poetry as well as some new poems. Lamming, meanwhile, published no new novels from 1960 to 1971, at which point he published his final two works, *Water with Berries* and *Natives of My Person*.

4. Brathwaite typifies this view, that "no novelist, no writer—no artist—can maintain a meaningful flow of work without reference to his society and its tradition" ("Sir Galahad" 37). Brathwaite's essays helped make this the established, commonsense view of the effect of exile on the writer. Brathwaite cites a number of writers, including Lamming, to support his position. Brathwaite quotes Selvon as another source: "'I badly needed this school,' *The Trinidad Guardian* reports Samuel Selvon as saying on his return recently to Trinidad and Tobago. 'I do not think that I could have written another book set in the West Indies without coming back to live among my people again'" (33). Of course, while Selvon did return to Trinidad and Tobago during the 1960s, the return was short-lived; he relocated to London, where he lived until 1978, before moving to Canada, where he lived until his death in 1994. During the last two decades of his life in exile, after Lamming had stopped publishing fiction altogether, Selvon continued to publish four new novels, a collection of essays, and a number of plays.

5. Gemma Robinson begins by posing the same question I ask here: why did Carter move, in Rohlehr's words, "from rhetoric to reticence"? Her readings of Carter's poetry of the 1960s, collected in *Conversations* and *Jail Me Quickly*, make a major contribution to answering this question.

6. Extended exile seems to have had no negative effect on many of Lamming's and Carter's generation, who continued to publish extensively after they had stopped: Selvon, Naipaul, Clarke, and Harris all have written prolifically into the 1990s and beyond during their residences in London and Canada; and exile proved equally productive for slightly older writers like Mittelholzer and Rhys, as well as younger writers like Phillips, Riley, and Kincaid.

7. Lamming describes this disillusionment in an interview with Scott: "There is a period when (I see it now as almost an innocence in a way) I believed—and I think this was shared by certain people of my generation—that the writers, the artists, were actually creating something new" ("Sovereignty" 161). He concedes that "at some stage I had come to feel that if I had anything of relevance and value to say that could be immediately effective in however minimal a way, it would be more effectively done by that statement, by that lecture-form, than by the novel-form" (198).

8. Glover explores the complicated relationship to politics and aesthetics that Spiralists Frankétienne, Jean-Claude Fignolé, and René Philoctète constructed in the context of the Duvalier dictatorship.

9. In the interview with Scott, Lamming details how he became more involved in political activities from the 1960s forward, particularly the Grenada Revolution, organizing conferences and writing speeches for Maurice Bishop. Much of this work appears in Lamming's two collections *Conversations* and *Coming, Coming Home.* Carter, who like Lamming became a prolific public lecturer during the 1960s and 1970s, acted as Guyana's minister of information from 1967 to 1970 before resigning in protest of Forbes Burnham's increasingly oppressive methods. See the published version of the lecture "A Free Community of Valid Persons," in which Carter outlines his grievances against Burnham's government.

10. For example, "The Occasion for Speaking" is chosen to begin the anthology *The Post-Colonial Studies Reader.*

11. The BBC's *Caribbean Voices* program and Heinemann's Caribbean Writers series are just two of the British institutions that supported and consecrated the same writers aligning themselves with anticolonial movements during the 1950s. Recent scholarship is reconstructing this important aspect of Caribbean literary history. For an overview of the origins of Heinemann's interest in African and Caribbean writing, see Huggan. For more on the crucial importance of the *Caribbean Voices* program for preindependence Caribbean writing, see R. Cobham, "The Caribbean Voices Programme and the Development of West Indian Short Story Fiction," as well as Griffith and Nanton.

12. For example, see the introductions to Nair and Simoes da Silva, the chapter "Autobiographical Frameworks and Linked Discourses: George Lamming's *The Pleasures of Exile* and C. L. R. James's *Beyond a Boundary*" in Paquet's *Caribbean Autobiography,* or Nixon. All of these critics center their discussion of *The Pleasures of Exile* around Lamming's rereading of *The Tempest.*

13. Hulme's "Reading from Elsewhere" describes the initial reaction to Lamming's essay on *The Tempest* as "in effect saying 'very interesting, but not actually speaking to the *real* Shakespearean text'" (233). The irony is that because Lamming offers not merely an appropriation of the story of *The Tempest,* Hulme argues, but rather a true reading with techniques acknowledged as legitimate by the field of criticism, "Lamming's understanding of *The Tempest* has outlasted that of Leo Marx, published in the same year" (234).

14. Nair describes Lamming's literary project in terms of its relationship to social movements: "Since, in Lamming's view, the Caribbean novel has had a major role to play in giving voice to the peasant struggles that overset the predicted trajectory of dominant, that is, Western history (except in a Marxist formulation) and that were primarily responsible for challenging colonial dominance, it is not surprising that he gives precedence to the novelist over the historian" (3).

15. Edmondson divides her study of Caribbean narrative into two sections, first discussing male authors in exile, then female writers classified as migrants. Lamming's observations about R. evoke this gendered division of labor in *The Pleasures of Exile*.

16. Of this technique, Jeffrey Robinson writes: "In the course of *Poems of Succession*, one ceases to be addressed by a recognisable personality or persona (revolutionary or, as in 'The Fourth Night of the Hunger Strike' or 'I am no Soldier,' ideal sufferer) [but] by the poem itself; in other words, most of the poems after 1955 are statements that generate their own authority instead of deriving it from an implied speaker" (5). This concept, of a poetry whose authority does not derive from an implied speaker, is one of the primary sites of contestation in the *Savacou* debates of the 1970s, the ensuing dub poetry movement, and the work of the Sistren Theatre Collective, all of which is discussed in chapter 7.

17. Lalla suggests that while "University of Hunger" may not be a direct transcription of West Indian–spoken Creole, its nongrammatical uses of language function as a way "to remind readers of the code they represent" (107). Through foregrounding his language's reliance on and defiance of the codes of Standard and non-Standard English, Carter can "counter traditional poetic discourse by intercepting Standard structures in a number of ways" (106), signaling to the reader a meaning beyond the received Standard. Through the use of this decentered language, the poem pursues the project of exploring the "formation" of "the collective mind of a people" (106) alongside the poet's close attention to the sounds of the land.

18. Seymour argues that the subjects of this poem are "rural, disheartened men who have little, who are hungry, who are marching to the capital city in their multitudes to demand in confrontation some redress. . . . All they have is their hunger and deprivation, but they are men" (105). While the marchers are not named, Seymour's insistence that "they are men" is confirmed in the last line of "University of Hunger": "O long is the march of men and long is the life / and wide is the span" (Carter, *Poems of Succession* 35).

7. The Testimonial Impulse

1. Participants in this debate included Brathwaite, Ramchand, Rohlehr, and Wynter. Breiner presents an overview of the *Savacou* debate, what was seen to be at stake, and the various positions taken.

2. Spivak's essay "Three Women's Texts" discusses Fernández Retamar's Caliban as a "nostalgia for lost origins" that risks "effacing the 'native'"; against this tendency, Spivak insists on Caliban as a "name in a play" that exists only as "an inaccessible blankness circumscribed by an interpretable text" (245). This point in "Three Women's Texts" contains a footnote to the then forthcoming "Can the Subaltern Speak?" as an elaboration of this argument: Cuba thus becomes Spivak's jumping off point for the discussion of subalternity.

3. In the United States in the 1980s and 1990s, progressive academics like

Beverley, Sommer, Harlow, Yúdice, and Sklodowska seized on testimonial discourse as a model for building the cross-class social movements between intellectuals and oppressed subalterns that could elude the hierarchies of the bourgeois public sphere and better represent the social experiments taking place in Nicaragua and El Salvador. Representative selections of this debate can be found in Gugelberger. In light of the postcolonial crisis of literature's ability to intervene publicly, it is worth noting how successfully Latin American *testimonio* was able to speak in the public sphere. See Beverley's *Against Literature* and Gugelberger's introduction to *The Real Thing* for more on *testimonio* and the "Canon Wars" of the late 1980s, and how these debates spilled from the academy into wider media discourses.

4. Collins discusses her interview with *The Harder They Come* director Perry Henzell, and his emphasis on how "actors improvised some of the dialogue in order to capture with authenticity Jamaican urban speech, rendering obsolete the original scripted dialogue." She also refers to how "Henzell has made known over the years his artistic commitment to bringing the camera close to 'real people' and authentic locations" (47), evidence of what I would describe as the film's testimonial impulse.

5. The cover of Barnet's first collection, *La piedra fina y el pavorreal*, features this blurb by Fernández Retamar: "De los poetas surgidos con posterioridad a la Revolución, con la cual se halla desde luego estrechamente identificado, Barnet es uno de los primeros en encontrar *voz propia*." Despite this promising debut, only 1,000 copies of his second collection were printed, and it went virtually unreviewed.

6. Tomás Gutiérrez Alea both personifies the new Cuban artist and uses his films to depict the shift from the anticolonial writer to the postcolonial filmmaker. Gutiérrez Alea establishes the continuity between his own project and anticolonial writing in frequently explicit ways: for example, one of his earliest films, the 1964 *Cumbite*, is an adaptation of Roumain's *Gouverneurs de la rosée*, and his disdain for bureaucracy in other films from the 1960s like *Las doce sillas* and *La muerte de un burócrata* invokes the ideology of the literary I discussed in chapter 4. By Gutiérrez Alea's most famous work in 1968, *Memorias del subdesarrollo*, the literary intellectual has become an untenable identity: Sergio's inability to create comes as he is completely disconnected from the revolution happening around him and wrapped up in nostalgia for the modernist writer-as-man-of-action embodied by Hemingway. The film even parodies the anticolonial trope of connecting with the feminized lower classes through sex. But while the novella by Edmundo Desnoes upon which the film is based is permeated by hopelessness about the place of the writer, the film features cameos by Rene Depestre, Gutiérrez Alea, and even Desnoes himself, thus suggesting that relevant intellectuals *are* possible. The connection of Gutiérrez Alea and Desnoes to the film industry seems to function similarly to Depestre's blackness. What has been discredited is the kind of intellectuals who in Cuba, whether in

the form of Martí or the early Desnoes or Barnet, were white, bourgeois, and associated with high literary forms. The filmmaker, in particular, emerges in Gutiérrez Alea's work as the intellectual able to inhabit the anticolonial persona no longer embodied by the writer, so that Gutiérrez Alea can state in an interview that the film "achieved its goal" of "communicat[ing] with the Cuban public" (Burton 188). By the time he makes *Hasta cierto punto* in 1983, in which the main character is a documentary filmmaker who has an affair with a dockworker, the director has become the postcolonial equivalent of the literary intellectual of the anticolonial period.

7. "Lo que llamamos novela, con todas las de la ley, falla, no nos resulta eficaz, no nos sirve" (Barnet, *La fuente viva* 12). Much of this essay appears in translation as "The Documentary Novel," but significant portions from the opening section are omitted, including this citation.

8. "En Europa occidental no hubo durante muchos años un movimiento social de importancia, no hubo explosiones políticas y la literatura tuvo que reflejar ese estado de cosas inocuo" (Barnet, *La fuente viva* 15–16).

9. "Se manipulan conciencias en una acometida feroz contra los valores propios de una cultura. . . . Los pueblos de nuestra América han sufrido el inmisericorde bombardeo de píldoras doradas para sueños que no son los suyos" (Barnet, *La fuente viva* 44–45).

10. "Los sistemas de comunicación capitalista podrán invertir todos sus recursos en exaltar el disfrute de una sopa de tomate, mediante el anuncio de una bella, bellísima lata Campbell. Nosotros queremos que el modelo único de nuestra cultura sea el alma del pueblo" (Barnet, *La fuente viva* 59–60).

11. "La campaña de consumir productos nacionales" (Barnet, *La fuente viva* 48).

12. "Devolver el habla al pueblo y otorgarle el derecho de ser gestor de sus propios mensajes, ésa es la verdadera vía" (Barnet, *La fuente viva* 49).

13. This preface is not included in the English translation. The translation I supply here is of this passage from the original: "A mediados de 1963 apareció en la prensa cubana una página dedicada a varios ancianos, mujeres y hombres, que sobrepasaban los 100 años. . . . Dos de los entrevistados nos llamaron la atención. Uno era una mujer de 100 años; el otro, un hombre de 104. La mujer había sido esclava. Era además santera y espiritista. El hombre, aunque no se refería directamente a tópicos religiosos, reflejaba en sus palabras una inclinación a las supersticiones y a las creencias populares. Su vida era interesante. Contaba aspectos de la esclavitud y la Guerra de Independencia. Pero lo que más no impresionó fue su declaración de haber sido esclavo fugitivo, cimarrón, en los montes de la provincia de Las Villas" (Barnet, *Biografía* 7).

14. "Olvidamos a la anciana y a los pocos días nos dirigimos al Hogar del Veterano, donde estaba albergado Esteban Montejo" (Barnet, *Biografía* 7).

15. "La operación para ese juego era de poner en un mostrador de Madera o en un tablón cualquiera, cuatro o cinco galletas duras de sal y con el miembro

masculino golpear fuerte sobre las galletas para ver quién las partía. . . . Otro juego de relajo era el de la botija. Cogían una botija grande con un agujero y metían el miembro por él. El que llegara al fondo era el ganador" (Barnet, *Biografía* 28). This passage, and other particularly sexually expressive ones, are omitted from a recently released new edition of *Biografía*, reprinted in 1998 by the Spanish publisher Ediciones Siruela as *Cimarrón: Historia de un esclavo*. The new edition comes with a new introduction written by Barnet, raising the question of whether these omissions are his or the result of an editorial decision made by someone else.

16. Barnet finishes by summarizing his process: "*Rachel's Song* speaks of her, of her life, as she told it to me and as I then told it to her." Since the English edition of *Rachel's Song* loses some of this sense, I have provided my own translation. The original is: "Otros personajes que aparecen en este libro, complementando el monólogo central, son generalmente hombres de teatro. . . . *Canción de Rachel* habla de ella, de su vida, tal y como ella me la contó y tal como yo luego se la conté a ella" (Barnet, *Canción* 5). This formulation captures the complexity of the divided speaking subject of *testimonio*.

17. "Allí [el Alhambra] se condensó el gusto de una época, sus veleidades. El corazón de la futura cultural 'pop.' . . . Rachel es una presa difícil dentro de las ambigüedades de la superestructura. Propicia una pista zigzagueante. El fondo de su información está *detrás* del escamoteo diametral con que ella discurre su monólogo. En *Biografía de un cimarrón* no existe ese *detrás*" (Fernández Guerra 534).

18. Rachel's relationship to the stars resembles the obsession with astrology of the character Mouche from Carpentier's canonical Cuban novel *Los pasos perdidos*. In the same year that *Los pasos perdidos* was published, Adorno wrote about what newspaper astrology columns could reveal about the alienated U.S. cultural unconscious. See Adorno, *Adorno: The Stars Down to Earth and Other Essays on the Irrational in Culture*.

19. "Su tradición de revolucionario, cimarrón primero, luego libertador, miembro del Partido Socialista Popular más tarde, se vivifica en nuestros días en su identificación con la Revolución cubana" (Barnet, *Biografía* 12).

20. Puri's chapter "Beyond Resistance: Rehearsing Opposition in Derek Walcott's *Pantomime*" discusses theater as "specially endowed with political possibilities" (107). Puri's critique of the postmodern academy's cult of transgression and her own preference for seeing literary "resistance and transgression . . . as potential preludes to political opposition rather than as superior alternatives to it" (107) is very much in keeping with what Ford-Smith here describes as her idea of the relationship of culture and politics, although I question the distinction between those two activities even in Ford-Smith's own theorizations.

21. Ford-Smith repeatedly emphasizes the radically democratic ways in which Sistren has leveled the process of cultural *production*, but in the essay never comes to terms with cultural *consumption*. She mentions toward the be-

ginning of "Notes Toward a New Aesthetic" that "cultural work done in one context very often loses resonance in another" and that "the lyrics of reggae and the philosophy of rastafari is very often meaningless to those who consume the musical products" (28). Yet she leaves behind this insight, and this essay hardly explores what a progressive theory of cultural consumption might look like. Sistren's own experience, performing primarily in Jamaican settings for small audiences of their choosing, suggests that producing for and consuming the local is especially valued. See the introduction to the Sistren Theatre Collective's "Bellywoman Bangarang" for a brief narrative of how Sistren developed their "policy toward a stronger focus on particular target audiences, community education in collaboration with community groups" (81) in response to their experiences with hostile male audiences.

22. Many "commercial playwrights" since the 1970s have also used Patwah in their plays. Crawford particularly highlights the group's commitment to presenting a positive "message" and being "role models" (Di Cenzo and Bennett 91) as what set them apart from "the humour and soft porn and violence" (90) of commercial theater.

23. While Ford-Smith makes no overtures in her own story to bringing together Patwah and Standard English, "Ava's Diary," one of the two stories written by another member of the group, does. As a diary, this story emphasizes its textuality, yet plays on the opposition of oral and scribal by shifting between linguistic registers. The first two paragraphs mark this shift with the subject pronoun, moving from Standard English "I" to Jamaican Patois "me." The story begins: "The day I graduated from primary school everybody in the yard wanted to see how I looked—my mother, my father, Tangy, Chico, Blues, Goddy, Granny, Mammy and all the others on the road" (Sistren Theatre Collective, *Lionheart Gal* 283). In the second paragraph, the subject pronoun and orthography change to the stylized textualization of orality characteristic of the other stories: "When me finish dress and come outside me see Bertie, di one dem call Plain Man, a ride up and down pon him bicycle pon di road. Him waan fi look pon me" (283). The rest of the story shifts back and forth between these two styles, alluding to the movement along the linguistic continuum typical of Jamaican speech.

24. Carolyn Cooper, who is otherwise sympathetic to *Lionheart Gal*'s project, criticizes Ford-Smith's decision to allow her story to appear more literary than the others. She writes: "Den nou, 'Grandma's Estate' an 'Red Ibo.' Mii neva laik hou di tuu a dem jos primz op demself iina suo-so Inglish. An dem no ina no taakin bizniz, mi dier" (*Noises* 92).

25. One of the group's other members betrays this potentially paternalistic attitude in an interview in which she describes how "[w]hen we first started, we wanted a forum to put across women's issues because women were still seen as secondary. They were the most oppressed" (Di Cenzo and Bennett 84). Casting oppressed women as "they" instead of "we" indicates the imperfect forms of solidarity the testimonial project built.

8. Cultural Studies and the Commodified Public

1. Gilroy reads Marley in the context of this moment of flux and contradiction.

2. Dub poetry perhaps best manifests the desire seen in chapter 7 to turn the literary field over to subaltern voices, combined with the trend this chapter explores, literature's move toward music as a cultural form produced and consumed by that subaltern public. For that reason, dub poetry has become a focus of critics seeking to disrupt bourgeois, Eurocentric definitions of the literary, as when Brathwaite calls the dub poets "cultural gorillas" ("History" 293). But the tension between wanting to celebrate democratic public cultural forms while still occupying a space of counterpublic critique leads Cooper to state her preference for Jean Binta Breeze and Mikey Smith as "calculating and crafting" (*Noises* 73) and "trained actors" (73), over Benjamin Zephaniah's "pure greeting-card doggerel" (72). Cooper's judgment is tied into the issue of commercial success, even though the ability to refuse to enter the market requires a certain position of privilege. When Cooper expresses concern that "the commercial dub poet can put the audience on, assuming an anger that has not been earned" (70), Brathwaite celebrates precisely what she fears: the triumph of dub poetry is that Mikey Smith "is a pop star" and "the sounds/poems of Linton Kwesi Johnson are on the charts in Great Britain" ("History" 300).

3. I analyze Blades's relationship to anticolonial discourse in the essay "Readings from Aquí y Allá."

4. Many of Rohlehr's contributions to these debates appear in *My Strangled City* and *The Shape of That Hurt*. He describes these collected writings from the 1970s and 1980s as "concerned with the relationship between upheaval and making, the vortex of old worlds going out of and the turmoil of new worlds coming into existence" (*Shape* vii). Rohlehr identifies as the central problematic in his work the question of what this moment of passage, from what I have been calling modern colonialism to postcoloniality, means for Caribbean cultural production.

5. Alongside *Savacou*'s testimonial trend to include poems by Rastafari and Black Power poets like Bongo Jerry and Audvil King, the anthology demonstrates a second trend: the complex interplay between literary intellectuals and popular music. The poems of Morris, Questel, and McNeill explicitly reference music as inspiring literary creation, although each also creates distance from these popular forms. Questel's "Pan Drama" begins with a "pan man / . . . caught (like me)" (147), drawing a connection between pan player and poet and eventually having them switch places as observer and carnival performer. Morris's "Valley Prince," dedicated to ska trombonist Don Drummond, speaks in the first person to describe the poetic process as parallel to the musical, going from "Me one, way out in the crowd, / I blow the sounds, the pain"; entering into this persona allows the poem to eventually move to "Inside here, me one / in the crowd again" (38). This process of learning from the musician also appears

in McNeill's poem about Drummond, not published in *Savacou* but appearing in his 1972 collection *Reel from "The Life Movie"* as "For the D." This poem begins by asking "may I learn the shape of that hurt," requesting of the addressee "teach me to walk through jukeboxes"; the implication is that the poet needs Drummond as a guide to the "dread city" that the literary intellectual is no longer equipped to understand (92).

6. At the same time that Rohlehr champions calypso, reggae, and oral poetry as authentic representations of the subaltern voice, he also hints at the reservations that Wynter expresses. Rohlehr tries to here distinguish between "Bongo Nyah" and other locally made calypsos and reggae songs able to capture and express Caribbean reality (or "soul") as opposed to the "synthetic products of American and Europe" ("West Indian Poetry" 140) functioning only as consumer goods and reproducing colonial forms of cultural imperialism. Even this inside/outside binary becomes troubled as Rohlehr notes the "heavy-handed sponsorship of folk culture" (141) on the part of the Trinidadian state as a means of controlling the local population after the 1970 February Revolution, suggesting how the intellectual move into popular culture can be co-opted not only by international culture industries but also by local political forces.

7. "No creo que en la historia de la literatura puertorriqueña haya habido otra novela tan comentada por sus contemporáneos, en el momento mismo de su aparición, como *La guaracha del Macho Camacho* de Luis Rafael Sánchez" (Barradas 131).

8. "*La guaracha* tuvo inmediata repercusión. . . . Le permitió a un número considerable de puertorriqueños intervenir, desde la literatura y la crítica, en los debates culturales" (Díaz Quiñones 15).

9. Robbins begins *The Phantom Public Sphere* by explaining that he borrows the term from Walter Lippmann's *The Phantom Public*, published in 1925. Robbins begins by invoking Lippmann's lament on the impossibility of a "responsible, well-informed public" (vii) in light of the proliferation of information and the opacity of political, economic, and social reality. At the same time, Robbins insists that even if the public is acknowledged as a fiction, or phantom, it remains essential: "the public has long served as a rallying cry against private greed, a demand for the attention to the general welfare as against propertied interests, an appeal for openness to scrutiny as opposed to corporate and bureaucratic secrecy, an arena in which disenfranchised minorities struggle to express their cultural identity, a code word for socialism" (x).

10. Critics who have joined Sánchez González in emphasizing the libratory potential of popular culture include Aparicio, who reads in the novel "una revolución estilística basada en la poética de lo soez y en la presencia subversiva de los ritmos populares caribeños" (73). On the other hand, critics like Cruz suggest how the novel might be read as an Adornian critique of mass culture as mass deception, emphasizing the deterioration of Puerto Rican identity in light of U.S. cultural domination. Cruz writes that *La guaracha* is "a searing

indictment of Puerto Rico's colonial reality and the role of the American-controlled mass media in maintaining this colonial status" (36).

11. "La novela aspira a crear junto al lector una comunidad intelectual que, aunque contagiados con el vacilón y la cultura de masas, mantengan la distancia necesaria para escribir y leer en puertorriqueña: para asumir la literatura y el arte como resistencia desde la cual fundar y construir la puertorriqueñidad" (Otero Garabís 75).

12. "Sánchez postula 'la literatura puertorriqueña . . . como muro de contención a la insoportable vulgaridad del asimilismo'" (Otero Garabís 55).

13. A number of critics, including Barradas and Otero Garabís, have written about Sánchez's essay "La generación o sea," published in the Puerto Rican cultural supplement *En Rojo* in 1972, presumably the time period that he was working on *La guaracha del Macho Camacho*. In this essay, Sánchez critiques the imprecision in language of Puerto Rican youths, in particular their use of the phrase *o sea* (translated by Rabassa as "what I mean is"), which becomes Benny's catchphrase.

14. In English in the original (Sánchez, *La guaracha* 237).

15. Aimé Césaire writes about the "thingification" of another postcolonial colony, Martinique, in his *Discours sur le colonialisme*: "No human contact, but relations of domination and submission which turn the colonizing man into a classroom monitor, an army sergeant, a prison guard, a slave driver, and the indigenous man into an instrument of production. My turn to state an equation: colonization = 'thingification'" (*Discourse* 21).

16. The *guaracha* is often described as "a guaracha that incites to permanent partying" (Sánchez, *Macho Camacho's Beat* 61).

17. Lovelace discusses his tendency to romanticize the organic wholeness of life in the country in his interview with Thomas: "The whole political structure, the colonialists' stronghold, was in the cities. The country was where the plantations were located, where the colonists didn't live, but where the folk lived. That resulted in two things: one—as you rightly point out—is that it is where the native culture flourishes, and that is why find there a greater support system; and it's not just people sticking together under oppression, it's a togetherness because of the values of the culture" (16).

18. Cooper also connects Fisheye to Ivan in the chapter "Country Come to Town: Michael Thelwell's *The Harder They Come*," from *Noises in the Blood*.

19. Other West Indian novels of the 1970s also depict these futile guerrilla movements. *The Dragon Can't Dance* is somewhat unusual in that the revolutionaries actually appear, if only to be defeated; more typically, as in V. S. Naipaul's *Guerrillas*, the guerrillas keep to the margins of the text, more a spectral threat than a real presence. In *La guaracha del Macho Camacho*, for example, the radical wing of the *independentista* movement, the FUPI (Federación de Universitarios Pro-Independencia), is mentioned numerous times, but the only potentially revolutionary act to take place in the novel, the bomb set off at the

University of Puerto Rico, turns out to have been placed by right-wing terrorists, not by the leftist *macheteros*.

20. In the essay "The Emancipation-Jouvay Tradition and the Almost Loss of Pan," Lovelace notes that the original carnivals of the nineteenth century "were commemorating the celebration of Emancipation" (54).

Conclusion

1. Bongie discusses Glissant's move away from the anticolonial conception of the writer's political role in *Friends and Enemies*, describing Glissant's "faith in 'aesthetic construction' . . . that he now insists has no direct bearing on emancipatory politics" (329). De la Campa provides an insightful reading of Glissant and Benítez-Rojo in relation to their postcolonial, postmodern context in "Resistance and Globalization in Caribbean Discourse."

2. This form of mourning parallels the relationship to past social movements that Derrida discusses in *Specters of Marx*.

3. Critics such as Shohat have pointed to how "as a signifier of a new historical epoch, when compared with *neocolonialism*, the term *postcolonial* comes equipped with little evocation of contemporary power relations" (132). Critics from the Caribbean also point to the "generalizing and homogenizing tendencies of 'Post-Colonial Studies,'" worrying that "the Caribbean, like all other postcolonial cultures, has several unique features which can be erased in this larger conceptual framework" (Donnell and Welch 438). Cooper sees the reemergence of Eurocentrism in the reducing of all of Caribbean history to an aftereffect of European actions: the introduction to *Noises in the Blood* announces her distrust of "totalising literary theories that reduce all 'post-colonial' literatures to the common bond(age) of the great—however deconstructed—European tradition" (15).

4. Gikandi criticizes this "optimistic, celebratory view of globalization" (629) and contrasts it with the deaths of African migrants attempting to travel to Europe in the cargo hold of a plane. Brennan provides another critique of the narrative of globalization as initiating a new utopian world.

5. Said's *Orientalism* was criticized for focusing too much on the overwhelming power of European hegemony at the expense of anticolonial resistance movements by a number of critics; Sivan summarizes these critics in his chapter "Edward Said and His Arab Reviewers." See also Puthak, Sengupta, and Purkayastha; Vaughan; and Ahmad.

Works Cited

Adorno, Theodor. *Adorno: The Stars Down to Earth and Other Essays on the Irrational in Culture*. Ed. Stephen Crook. New York: Routledge, 1994.

Ahmad, Aijaz. *In Theory: Classes, Nations, Literatures*. New York: Verso, 1994.

Alonso, Carlos. "Fiction." In *A History of Literature in the Caribbean*, Vol. 1, ed. James Arnold, 141–154. Philadelphia: John Benjamins, 1994.

Álvarez Cubelo, Silvia. *Un país del porvenir: El afán de modernidad en Puerto Rico*. San Juan: Ediciones Callejón, 2001.

Amin, Samir. *Capitalism in the Age of Globalization: The Management of Contemporary Society*. London: Zed Books, 1997.

Anderson, Benedict. *Imagined Communities: Reflections on the Origin and Spread of Nationalism*. Rev. ed. New York: Verso, 1991.

Andrews, William. Introduction to *Wonderful Adventures of Mrs. Seacole in Many Lands*, by Mary Seacole, xxvii–xxxiv. New York: Oxford University Press, 1988.

Anonymous. "Adolphus, A Tale." [1853]. In *Adolphus, A Tale, and The Slave Son*, ed. Lise Winer, 1–92. Kingston: University of the West Indies Press, 2003.

Aparicio, Frances. "Entre la guaracha y el bolero: Un ciclo de intertextos musicales en la nueva narrativa puertorriqueña." *Revista Iberoamericana* 59, no. 1 (January–June 1993): 73–89.

Apter, Emily. "'Je ne crois pas beaucoup à la littérature comparée': Universal Poetics and Postcolonial Comparatism." In *Comparative Literature in an Age of Globalization*, ed. Haun Saussy, 54–62. Baltimore: Johns Hopkins University Press, 2006.

Arnold, James. *Modernism and Negritude: The Poetry and Poetics of Aimé Césaire*. Cambridge, Mass.: Harvard University Press, 1998.

Ashcroft, Bill. "Globalism, Postcolonialism and African Studies." In *A Companion to Racial and Ethnic Studies*, ed. David Theo Goldberg and John Solomos, 511–520. New York: Blackwell, 2002.

Ashcroft, Bill, Gareth Griffiths, and Helen Tiffin, eds. *The Post-Colonial Studies Reader*. New York: Routledge, 1995.

Baeza Flores, Alberto. "Apasionado destino." *La Poesía Sorprendida* 1 (October 1943). In *Publicaciones y opiniones de La Poesía Sorprendida*, 1. San Pedro de Macorís: Universidad Central del Este, 1988.

Baggett, Paul. "Caught Between Homes: Mary Seacole and the Question of Cultural Identity." *Macomère* 3 (2000): 45–56.

Baker, Houston. "Critical Memory and the Black Public Sphere." *Public Culture* 7, no. 1 (Fall 1994): 3–33.

Barnet, Miguel. *Biografía de un cimarrón*. Havana: Instituto de Etnología y Folklore, 1966.

———. *Biography of a Runaway Slave*. Trans. Nick Hill. East Haven, Conn.: Curbstone Press, 1994.

———. *Canción de Rachel*. Havana: Editorial Letras Cubanas, 1969.

———. "The Documentary Novel." *Cuban Studies* 11, no. 1 (January 1981): 19–32.

———. *La fuente viva*. Havana: Editorial Letras Cubanas, 1983.

———. *La piedra fina y el pavorreal*. Havana: Ediciones Unión, 1963.

———. *Rachel's Song*. Trans. Nick Hill. East Haven, Conn.: Curbstone Press, 1991.

Barradas, Efraín. *Para leer en puertorriqueño: Acercamiento a la obra de Luis Rafael Sánchez*. Río Piedras, Puerto Rico: Editorial Cultural, 1981.

Barratt, Harold. Afterword to *The Man Who Loved Attending Funerals and Other Stories*, by Frank Collymore, 167–178. Portsmouth, N.H.: Heinemann, 1993.

Baugh, Edward. "Frank Collymore." In *Fifty Caribbean Writers: A Bio-bibliographical Critical Sourcebook*, ed. Daryl Cumber Dance, 122–132. New York: Greenwood Press, 1986.

———. "A History of Poetry." In *A History of Literature in the Caribbean*, Vol. 2, ed. James Arnold, 227–282. Philadelphia: John Benjamins, 2001.

Beckford, George, and Michael Witter. *Small Garden, Bitter Weed: The Political Economy of Struggle and Change in Jamaica*. 2nd ed. London: Zed Press, 1982.

Behdad, Ali. "On Globalization, Again!" In *Postcolonial Studies and Beyond*, ed. Ania Loomba, Suvir Kaul, Matti Bunzi, Antoinette Burton, and Jed Esty, 62–79. Durham, N.C.: Duke University Press, 2005.

Bejel, Emilio. "Poetry." In *A History of Literature in the Caribbean*, Vol. 1, ed. James Arnold, 221–238. Philadelphia: John Benjamins, 1994.

Bellegarde-Smith, Patrick. *Haiti: The Breached Citadel*. Toronto: Canadian Scholars' Press, 2004.

Benítez-Rojo, Antonio. *La isla que se repite: El Caribe y la perspectiva posmoderna*. Hanover, N.H.: Ediciones del Norte, 1989.

———. "Power/Sugar/Literature: Toward a Reinterpretation of Cubanness." *Cuban Studies* 16 (1986): 9–31.

Beverley, John. *Against Literature*. Minneapolis: University of Minnesota Press, 1993.

———. "The Margin at the Center: On *Testimonio*." In *The Real Thing*, ed. Georg Gugelberger, 23–41. Durham, N.C.: Duke University Press, 1996.

Beverley, John, José Oviedo, and Michael Aronna, eds. *The Postmodernism Debate in Latin America*. Durham, N.C.: Duke University Press, 1995.

Black Public Sphere Collective. "Editorial Comment: On Thinking the Black Public Sphere." *Public Culture* 7, no. 1 (Fall 1994): xi–xiv.

Blackburn, Robin. *The Overthrow of Colonial Slavery, 1776–1848*. New York: Verso, 1988.

Bongie, Chris. *Friends and Enemies: The Scribal Politics of Post/Colonial Literature*. Liverpool: Liverpool University Press, 2008.

———. *Islands and Exiles: The Creole Identities of Post/Colonial Literature*. Stanford, Calif.: Stanford University Press, 1998.

Bourdieu, Pierre. *The Field of Cultural Production*. Ed. Randal Johnson. New York: Columbia University Press, 1993.

Brand, Dionne. *Bread Out of Stone*. Toronto: Coach House Press, 1994.

———. *Chronicles of the Hostile Sun*. Toronto: Williams-Wallace, 1984.

———. *In Another Place, Not Here*. [1986]. New York: Grove Press, 1996.

Brathwaite, Kamau. *Contradictory Omens: Cultural Diversity and Integration in the Caribbean*. Mona, Jamaica: Savacou Publications, 1974.

———. "Foreward." *Savacou* 3/4 (December 1970–March 1971): 5–9.

———. "History of the Voice." [1981]. In *Roots*, 259–304. Ann Arbor: University of Michigan Press, 1993.

———. "Sir Galahad and the Islands." [1957]. In *Roots*, 1–27. Ann Arbor: University of Michigan Press, 1993.

Breiner, Laurence. "How to Behave on Paper: The *Savacou* Debate." *Journal of West Indian Literature* 6, no. 1 (1993): 1–10.

Brennan, Tim. *At Home in the World: Cosmopolitanism Now*. Cambridge, Mass.: Harvard University Press, 1997.

Brereton, Bridget. *An Introduction to the History of Trinidad and Tobago*. Oxford: Heinemann, 1996.

———. *Race Relations in Colonial Trinidad, 1870–1900*. New York: Cambridge University Press, 2002.

Brickhouse, Anna. *Transamerican Literary Relations and the Nineteenth-Century Public Sphere*. New York: Cambridge University Press, 2004.

Brouillette, Sarah. *Postcolonial Writers in the Global Literary Marketplace*. New York: Palgrave Macmillan, 2007.

Brown, Stewart. Introduction to *All Are Involved: The Art of Martin Carter*, 7–21. Leeds, England: Peepal Tree, 2000.

Brown, Wayne. *Edna Manley: The Private Years, 1900–1938*. London: Andre Deutsch, 1975.

Burton, Julianne. "Individual Fulfillment and Collective Fulfillment: An Interview with Tomás Gutiérrez Alea." In *Memories of Underdevelopment/Inconsolable Memories*, ed. Michael Chanan, 187–198. New Brunswick, N.J.: Rutgers University Press, 1990.

Cain, William. Introduction to *Emmanuel Appadocca*, by Michel Maxwell Philip, xv–lv. Amherst: University of Massachusetts Press, 1997.

Camier, Bernard, and Laurent Dubois. "Voltaire et Zaïre, ou la théatre des Lumières dans l'aire atlantique française." *Revue d'histoire moderne et contemporaine* 54, no. 4 (October–December 2007): 39–69.

Carew, Jan. "Tribute to Martin Carter, 1921–1998." *Race and Class* 40, no. 1 (1998): 105–111.

Carpentier, Alejo. *The Kingdom of This World*. [1949]. Trans. Harriet de Onís. New York: Farrar, Straus and Giroux, 1957.

———. *Los pasos perdidos*. [1953]. New York: Penguin Books, 1998.

Carr, Robert. "A Politics of Change: Sistren, Subalternity, and the Social Pact in the War for Democratic Socialism." In *Black Nationalism in the New World: Reading the African-American and West Indian Experience*, 225–269. Durham, N.C.: Duke University Press, 2002.

Carter, Martin. "A Free Community of Valid Persons." *Kyk-over-al* 44 (May 1993): 30–32.

———. *Poems of Succession*. London: New Beacon Books, 1977.

Césaire, Aimé. *Discourse on Colonialism*. [1955]. Trans. Joan Pinkham. New York: Monthly Review Press, 1972.

———. "Panorama." [1944]. Trans. Michael Richardson and Krzysztof Fijalkowski. In *Refusal of the Shadow: Surrealism and the Caribbean*, ed. Michael Richardson, 79–81. New York: Verso, 1996.

———. "Poetry and Knowledge." [1945]. Trans. Michael Richardson and Krzysztof Fijalkowski. In *Refusal of the Shadow: Surrealism and the Caribbean*, ed. Michael Richardson, 134–146. New York: Verso, 1996.

———. "Presentation." [1941]. Trans. Michael Richardson and Krzysztof Fijalkowski. In *Refusal of the Shadow: Surrealism and the Caribbean*, ed. Michael Richardson, 88. New York: Verso, 1996.

Césaire, Suzanne. "A Civilization's Discontents." [1942]. Trans. Michael Richardson and Krzysztof Fijalkowski. In *Refusal of the Shadow: Surrealism and the Caribbean*, ed. Michael Richardson, 96–100. New York: Verso, 1996.

———. "Leo Frobenius and the Problem of Civilizations." [1941]. Trans. Michael Richardson and Krzysztof Fijalkowski. In *Refusal of the Shadow: Surrealism and the Caribbean*, ed. Michael Richardson, 82–87. New York: Verso, 1996.

———. "1943: Surrealism and Us." [1943]. Trans. Michael Richardson and Krzysztof Fijalkowski. In *Refusal of the Shadow: Surrealism and the Caribbean*, ed. Michael Richardson, 123–126. New York: Verso, 1996.

Cesareo, Mario. "When the Subaltern Travels: Slave Narrative and Testimonial Erasure in the Contact Zone." In *Women at Sea: Travel Writing and the*

Margins of Caribbean Discourse, ed. Lizabeth Paravisini-Gebert and Ivette Romero-Cesareo, 99–134. New York: Palgrave Macmillan, 2001.

Chanan, Michael. *Cuban Cinema.* Minneapolis: University of Minnesota Press, 2004.

Chancy, Myriam. "'No Giraffes in Haiti': Haitian Women and State Terror." In *Ecrire en pays assiégé/Writing Under Siege,* ed. Marie-Agnès Sourieau and Kathleen Balutansky, 303–322. New York: Rodopi, 2004.

Chang-Rodríguez, Raquel. "Colonial Voices of the Hispanic Caribbean." In *A History of Literature in the Caribbean,* Vol. 1, ed. James Arnold, 111–140. Philadelphia: John Benjamins, 1994.

Chartrand, Rene. *British Forces in the West Indies, 1793–1815.* London: Reed International Books, 1996.

Chauvet, Marie. *Dance on the Volcano.* [1957]. Trans. Salvator Attanasio. New York: W. Sloan, 1959.

———. *Love, Anger, Madness.* [1968]. Trans. Rose-Myriam Réjouis and Val Vinokur. New York: Modern Library, 2009.

Cobham, Rhonda. "The Caribbean Voices Programme and the Development of West Indian Short Story Fiction: 1945–1958." In *The Story Must Be Told: Short Narrative Prose in the New English Literatures,* ed. Peter Stummer, 146–160. Würzburg: Königshausen and Neumann, 1986.

———. "Jekyll and Claude: The Erotics of Patronage in Claude McKay's *Banana Bottom.*" In *Queer Diasporas,* ed. Cindy Patton and Benigno Sánchez-Eppler, 122–153. Durham, N.C.: Duke University Press, 2000.

Cobham, Stephen. *Rupert Gray: A Tale in Black and White.* [1907]. Ed. Lise Winer. Kingston: University of the West Indies Press, 2006.

Collins, Loretta. "The Harder They Come: Rougher Version." *Small Axe* 7, no. 1 (March 2003): 46–71.

Cooper, Carolyn. *Noises in the Blood: Orality, Gender and the "Vulgar" Body of Jamaican Popular Culture.* Durham, N.C.: Duke University Press, 1995.

———. "'Only a Nigger Gal!': Race, Gender and the Politics of Education in Claude McKay's *Banana Bottom.*" *Caribbean Quarterly* 38, no. 1 (1992): 40–54.

Cooper, Helen. "'Tracing the Route to England': Nineteenth-Century Caribbean Interventions into English Debates on Race and Slavery." In *The Victorians and Race,* ed. Shearer West, 194–212. Aldershot: Scholar Press, 1996.

Cooper, Wayne. *Claude McKay: Rebel Sojourner in the Harlem Renaissance.* Baton Rouge: Louisiana State University Press, 1987.

Cooppan, Vilashini. "The Ruins of Empire: The National and Global Politics of America's Return to Rome." In *Postcolonial Studies and Beyond,* ed. Ania Loomba, Suvir Kaul, Matti Bunzi, Antoinette Burton, and Jed Esty, 80–100. Durham, N.C.: Duke University Press, 2005.

Corzani, Jack. "Poetry Before Negritude." In *A History of Literature in the Caribbean,* Vol. 1, ed. James Arnold, 465–479. Philadelphia: John Benjamins, 1994.

Costa, Emilia Viotti da. *Crowns of Glory, Tears of Blood: The Demerara Slave Rebellion of 1823.* New York: Oxford University Press, 1994.

Cruz, Arnaldo. "Repetition and the Language of the Mass Media in Luis Rafael Sánchez's *La guaracha del Macho Camacho.*" *Latin American Literary Review* 13, no. 2 (July–December 1985): 35–48.

Cudjoe, Selwyn. Afterword to *Emmanuel Appadocca*, by Michel Maxwell Philip, 249–275. Amherst: University of Massachusetts Press, 1997.

———. *Beyond Boundaries: The Intellectual Tradition of Trinidad and Tobago in the Nineteenth Century.* Amherst: University of Massachusetts Press, 2003.

———, ed. *Eric E. Williams Speaks: Essays on Colonialism and Independence.* Wellesley, Mass.: Calaloux Publications, 1993.

Dalleo, Raphael. "Emplotting Postcoloniality: Usable Pasts, Possible Futures, and the Relentless Present." Review of *Conscripts of Modernity*, by David Scott, in *Diaspora: A Journal of Transnational Studies* 13, no. 1 (Spring 2004): 129–140.

———. "The Public Sphere and Jamaican Anticolonial Politics: *Public Opinion*, *Focus*, and the Place of the Literary." *Small Axe* 14, no. 2 (June 2010): 56–82.

———. "Readings from Aquí y Allá: Music, Commercialism, and the Latino-Caribbean Transnational Imaginary." In *Constructing Vernacular Cultures in the Trans-Caribbean*, ed. Holger Henke and Karl-Heinz Magister, 299–320. Landham, Md.: Lexington Books, 2008.

———. "Shadows, Funerals and the Terrified Consciousness in Frank Collymore's Short Fiction." *Journal of West Indian Literature* 12, nos. 1–2 (November 2004): 184–196.

———. "Ways of Looking: The Global Vision of V. S. Naipaul." *South Asian Review* 26, no. 1 (November 2005): 358–374.

Dalleo, Raphael, and Elena Machado Sáez. *The Latino/a Canon and the Emergence of Post-Sixties Literature.* New York: Palgrave Macmillan, 2007.

Dash, Michael. "Aimé Césaire: The Bearable Lightness of Becoming." *PMLA* 125, no. 3 (May 2010): 737–742.

———. "Blazing Mirrors: The Crisis of the Haitian Intellectual." In *Intellectuals in the Twentieth Century Caribbean*, Vol. 2, ed. Alistair Hennessy, 175–185. London: MacMillan Caribbean, 1992.

———. Introduction to Literary Genres section of *A History of Literature in the Caribbean*, Vol. 1, ed. James Arnold, 407–412. Philadelphia: John Benjamins, 1994.

———. Introduction to *Masters of the Dew*, by Jacques Roumain, 5–21. Oxford: Heinemann, 1978.

———. *Literature and Ideology in Haiti, 1915–1961.* London: Macmillan Press, 1981.

———. *The Other America: Caribbean Literature in a New World Context.* Charlottesville: University of Virginia Press, 1998.

Dayan, Joan. *Haiti, History and the Gods.* Berkeley: University of California Press, 1998.

———. "Reading Women in the Caribbean: Marie Chauvet's *Love, Anger and Madness.*" In *Displacements: Women, Tradition, Literatures in French,* ed. Joan DeJean and Nancy Miller, 228–253. Baltimore: Johns Hopkins University Press, 1991.

de La Campa, Román. *Latin Americanism.* Minneapolis: University of Minnesota Press, 1999.

———. "Resistance and Globalization in Caribbean Discourse." In *A History of Literature in the Caribbean,* Vol. 3, ed. James Arnold, 87–116. Philadelphia: John Benjamins, 1997.

Depestre, René. "André Breton in Port-au-Prince." [1991]. Trans. Michael Richardson and Krzysztof Fijalkowski. In *Refusal of the Shadow: Surrealism and the Caribbean,* ed. Michael Richardson, 229–233. New York: Verso, 1996.

Derrida, Jacques. *Specters of Marx: The State of the Debt, the Work of Mourning, and the New International.* New York: Routledge, 1994.

Di Cenzo, Maria, and Susan Bennett. "Women, Popular Theatre and Social Action: Interviews with Cynthia Grant and the Sistren Theatre Collective." *ARIEL: A Review of International English Literature* 23, no. 1 (January 1992): 73–94.

Díaz Quiñones, Arcadio. Introducción to *La guaracha del Macho Camacho,* by Luis Rafael Sánchez, 11–73. Madrid: Cátedra, 2000.

Donnell, Alison. *Twentieth-Century Caribbean Literature: Critical Moments in Anglophone Literary History.* New York: Routledge, 2006.

Donnell, Alison, and Sarah Lawson Welch, eds. *The Routledge Reader in Caribbean Literature.* New York: Routledge, 1996.

Dubois, Laurent. *Avengers of the New World: The Story of the Haitian Revolution.* Cambridge, Mass.: Harvard University Press, 2004.

Dubois, Laurent, and John Garrigus. *Slave Revolution in the Caribbean, 1789–1804: A Brief History with Documents.* New York: Palgrave Macmillan, 2006.

"Editor's Comeback." *BIM* 1, no. 4 (April 1944): 1.

Edmondson, Belinda. *Making Men: Gender, Literary Authority, and Women's Writing in Caribbean Narrative.* Durham, N.C.: Duke University Press, 1999.

Edwards, Brent Hayes. *The Practice of Diaspora: Literature, Translation, and the Rise of Black Internationalism.* Cambridge, Mass.: Harvard University Press, 2003.

Eudell, Demetrius. *The Political Languages of Emancipation in the British Caribbean and the U.S. South.* Chapel Hill: University of North Carolina Press, 2002.

Fanon, Frantz. *Black Skin, White Mask.* [1952]. Trans. Richard Philcox. New York: Grove Press, 2008.

Fanuzzi, Robert. *Abolition's Public Sphere.* Minneapolis: University of Minnesota Press, 2003.

Ferguson, Moira. "The Hart Sisters: Early Caribbean Educators and the 'Thirst for Knowledge.'" In *Colonialism and Gender Relations from Mary Wollstonecraft to Jamaica Kincaid: East Caribbean Connections,* 34–64. New York: Columbia University Press, 1993.

———. Introduction to *The History of Mary Prince,* by Mary Prince, 1–51. Ann Arbor: University of Michigan Press, 1997.

Fernández Guerra, Ángel Luis. "Cimarrón y Rachel: Un continuum." In *Nuevos Críticos Cubanos,* ed. José Prats Sariol, 529–537. Havana: Editorial Letras Cubanas, 1983.

Fernández Retamar, Roberto. "Calibán." *Casa de las Américas* 68 (September–October 1971): 124–151.

Fernández Spencer, Antonio. "En busca de la realidad literaria ¿Que es *La poesía sorprendida?*" In *Publicaciones y opiniones de La Poesía Sorprendida,* xxviii–xxxii. San Pedro de Macorís: Universidad Central del Este, 1988.

Fick, Carolyn. *The Making of Haiti: The Saint Domingue Revolution from Below.* Knoxville: University of Tennessee Press, 1990.

Fischer, Sibylle. *Modernity Disavowed: Haiti and the Cultures of Slavery in the Age of Revolution.* Durham, N.C.: Duke University Press, 2004.

Flores, Juan. *Divided Borders: Essays on Puerto Rican Identity.* Houston: Arte Público Press, 1993.

———. *From Bomba to Hip-hop: Puerto Rican Culture and Latino Identity.* New York: Columbia University Press, 2000.

Ford-Smith, Honor. "Notes Toward a New Aesthetic." *MELUS* 16, no. 3 (Fall 1989–1990): 27–34.

———. "Sistren Women's Theatre, Organizing, and Conscientization." In *Women of the Caribbean,* ed. Pat Ellis, 122–128. Kingston: Kingston Publishers, 1986.

Forde, A. N. "In All Their Glory." *BIM* 4, no. 1 (December 1950): 26–28.

Fouchard, Jean. *Le théâtre à Saint-Domingue.* Port-au-Prince: Imprimerie de l'Etat, 1955.

Fowler, Carolyn. *A Knot in the Thread: The Life and Work of Jacques Roumain.* Washington, D.C.: Howard University Press, 1980.

Franco, Jean. *Critical Passions: Selected Essays.* Ed. Mary Louise Pratt and Kathleen Newman. Durham, N.C.: Duke University Press, 1999.

Fraser, Nancy. "Rethinking the Public Sphere: A Contribution to the Critique of Actually Existing Democracy." In *Habermas and the Public Sphere,* ed. Craig Calhoun, 109–142. Cambridge, Mass.: MIT Press, 1992.

Friedman, Thomas. *The World Is Flat: A Brief History of the Twenty-first Century.* New York: Farrar, Straus, Giroux, 2005.

Garret, Naomi. *The Renaissance of Haitian Poetry.* Paris: Présence Africaine, 1963.

Garrigus, John. *Before Haiti: Race and Citizenship in French Saint-Domingue.* New York: Palgrave Macmillan, 2006.

Gatón Arce, Freddy. "*La poesía sorprendida*: Números, citas, y etceteras." In *Publicaciones y opiniones de La Poesía Sorprendida*, iii–xiv. San Pedro de Macorís: Universidad Central del Este, 1988.

Gikandi, Simon. "Globalization and the Claims of Postcoloniality." *South Atlantic Quarterly* 100, no. 3 (Summer 2001): 627–658.

Gilbert, Helen, ed. *Postcolonial Plays: An Anthology.* New York: Routledge, 2001.

Giles, James. *Claude McKay.* Boston: G. L. Hall, 1976.

Gilroy, Paul. "Could You Be Loved? Bob Marley, Anti-politics, and Universal Sufferation." *Critical Quarterly* 47, nos. 1–2 (July 2005): 226–245.

Glissant, Edouard. *Le discours antillais.* Paris: Seuil, 1981.

———. *Poetics of Relation.* [1990]. Trans. Betsy Wing. Ann Arbor: University of Michigan Press, 1997.

Glover, Kaiama. "Physical Internment and Creative Freedom: The Spiralist Contribution." In *Ecrire en pays assiégé/Writing Under Siege*, ed. Marie-Agnès Sourieau and Kathleen Balutansky, 231–256. New York: Rodopi, 2004.

González, José Luis. "El país de cuatro pisos." In *El país de cuatro pisos y otros ensayos*, 11–42. Río Piedras, Puerto Rico: Ediciones Huracán, 1980.

González Echevarría, Roberto. *The Voice of the Masters: Writing and Authority in Modern Latin American Literature.* Austin: University of Texas Press, 1985.

Gregg, Veronica. *Jean Rhys's Historical Imagination: Reading and Writing the Creole.* Chapel Hill: University of North Carolina Press, 1995.

Griffith, Glyne. "Deconstructing Nationalisms: Henry Swanzy, *Caribbean Voices* and the Development of West Indian Literature." *Small Axe* 5, no. 2 (September 2001): 1–20.

Grimshaw, Anna. "*Notes on the Life and Work* of C. L. R. James." In *C. L. R. James, His Life and Work*, ed. Paul Buhle, 9–21. London: Allison & Busby, 1986.

Guevara, Ernesto. "Socialism and Man in Cuba." [1965]. In *Che Guevara Reader*, ed. David Deutschmann, 212–228. New York: Ocean Press, 2003.

———. "Speech to Medical Students and Health Workers." [1960]. In *Che Guevara Reader*, ed. David Deutschmann, 112–120. New York: Ocean Press, 2003.

Gugelberger, Georg, ed. *The Real Thing: Testimonial Discourse and Latin America.* Durham, N.C.: Duke University Press, 1996.

Habermas, Jürgen. *The Structural Transformation of the Public Sphere: An Inquiry into a Category of Bourgeois Society.* [1962]. Trans. Thomas Burger with the assistance of Frederick Lawrence. Cambridge, Mass.: MIT Press, 1991.

Hall, Stuart. "What Is This 'Black' in Black Popular Culture?" In *Black Popular Culture*, ed. Gina Dent, 21–33. New York: New Press, 1998.

Hardt, Michael, and Antonio Negri. *Empire*. Cambridge, Mass.: Harvard University Press, 2000.

———. *Multitude: War and Democracy in the Age of Empire*. Cambridge, Mass.: Harvard University Press, 2004.

Harvey, David. *The Condition of Postmodernity: A Inquiry into the Origins of Cultural Change*. Cambridge, Mass.: Blackwell, 1990.

Hassan, Salah Dean Assaf. "Introduction: 'Origins' of Postmodern Cuba." *CR: The New Centennial Review* 2, no. 2 (Summer 2002): 1–17.

Hawthorne, Evelyn. "Self-Writing, Literary Traditions, and Post-Emancipation Identity: The Case of Mary Seacole." *Biography* 23, no. 2 (2000): 309–331.

———. *The Writer in Transition: Roger Mais and the Decolonization of Caribbean Culture*. New York: Peter Lang, 1989.

Hill, Robert, ed. *Walter Rodney Speaks: The Making of an African Intellectual*. Trenton, N.J.: Africa World Press, 1990.

Hoffmann, Léon-François. "Haitian Sensibility." In *A History of Literature in the Caribbean*, Vol. 1, ed. James Arnold, 365–378. Philadelphia: John Benjamins, 1994.

Huggan, Graham. *The Postcolonial Exotic: Marketing the Margins*. New York: Routledge, 2001.

Hulme, Peter. "Beyond the Straits: Postcolonial Allegories of the Globe." In *Postcolonial Studies and Beyond*, ed. Ania Loomba, Suvir Kaul, Matti Bunzi, Antoinette Burton, and Jed Esty, 41–61. Durham, N.C.: Duke University Press, 2005.

———. "Reading from Elsewhere: George Lamming and the Paradox of Exile." In *The Tempest and Its Travels*, ed. Peter Hulme and William Sherman, 220–235. Philadelphia: University of Pennsylvania Press, 2000.

Hurwitz, Edith. *Politics and the Public Conscience: Slave Emancipation and the Abolitionist Movement in Britain*. London: Allen & Unwin, 1973.

James, C. L. R. *The Black Jacobins: Toussaint L'Ouverture and the San Domingo Revolution*. New York: Vintage Books, 1963.

———. *C. L. R. James and Revolutionary Marxism: Selected Writings of C. L. R. James 1939–1949*. Ed. Scott McLemee and Paul LeBlanc. Atlantic Highlands, N.J.: Humanities Press, 1994.

———. *Mariners, Renegades and Castaways: The Story of Herman Melville and the World We Live In*. [1953]. Hanover, N.H.: University Press of New England, 2001.

James, Winston. *A Fierce Hatred of Injustice: Claude McKay's Jamaica and His Poetry of Rebellion*. New York: Verso, 2000.

Jennings, Lawrence. "Cyrille Bissette, Radical Black French Abolitionist." *French History* 9, no. 1 (March 1995): 48–66.

———. *French Anti-Slavery: The Movement for the Abolition of Slavery in France, 1802–1848*. New York: Cambridge University Press, 2000.

King, Sydney. "Foreword to *Poems of Resistance from British Guiana*." In *All*

Are Involved: The Art of Martin Carter, ed. Stewart Brown, 96–97. Leeds, England: Peepal Tree, 2000.

Klein, Naomi. *The Shock Doctrine: The Rise of Disaster Capitalism.* New York: Picador, 2007.

Knight, Franklin. *The Caribbean: The Genesis of a Fragmented Nationalism.* 2nd ed. Oxford: Oxford University Press, 1990.

Kutzinski, Vera. "The Cult of Caliban: Collaboration and Revisionism in Contemporary Caribbean Narrative." In *A History of Literature in the Caribbean*, Vol. 3, ed. James Arnold, 285–302. Amsterdam: John Benjamins, 1997.

Kwayana, Eusi. "The Politics of the Heart." *Anales del Caribe* 4/5 (1984–1985): 362–391.

Lalla, Barbara. "Conceptual Perspectives on Time and Timelessness in Martin Carter's 'University of Hunger.'" In *All Are Involved: The Art of Martin Carter*, ed. Stewart Brown, 106–115. Leeds, England: Peepal Tree, 2000.

Lamming, George. *Coming, Coming Home: Conversations II.* Philipsburg, St. Martin: House of Nehesi, 1995.

———. *Conversations: Essays, Addresses and Interviews, 1953–1990.* London: Karia Press, 1992.

———. *In the Castle of My Skin.* [1953]. New York: Collier Books, 1975.

———, ed. *On the Canvas of the World.* Port of Spain: Trinidad and Tobago Institute of the West Indies, 1999.

———. *The Pleasures of Exile.* [1960]. Ann Arbor: University of Michigan Press, 1992.

Landers, Jane. "African American Women and Their Pursuit of Rights through Eighteenth-Century Spanish Texts." In *Haunted Bodies: Gender and Southern Texts*, ed. Anne Goodwyn Jones and Susan V. Donaldson, 56–76. Charlottesville: University of Virginia Press, 1997.

Lazo, Rodrigo. *Writing to Cuba: Filibustering and Cuban Exiles in the United States.* Chapel Hill: University of North Carolina Press, 2005.

Lean, John, and Trevor Burnard. "Hearing Slave Voices: The Fiscal's Reports of Berbice and Demerara-Essequebo." *Archives* 27, no. 2 (October 2002): 120–133.

"*Légitime défense*: Declaration." [1932]. Trans. Michael Richardson and Krzysztof Fijalkowski. In *Refusal of the Shadow: Surrealism and the Caribbean*, ed. Michael Richardson, 41–43. New York: Verso, 1996.

Leiner, Jacqueline. "Entretien avec Aimé Césaire." In *Tropiques* 1, nos. 1–5 (April 1941–April 1942): v–xxiv. Paris: Éditions Jean-Michel Place, 1978.

Léro, Etienne. "Poverty of a Poetry." [1932]. Trans. Michael Richardson and Krzysztof Fijalkowski. In *Refusal of the Shadow: Surrealism and the Caribbean*, ed. Michael Richardson, 55–58. New York: Verso, 1996.

Levy, Michèle. Introduction to *The Autobiography of Alfred H. Mendes, 1897–1991*, xv–xxxi. Kingston: University of the West Indies Press, 2002.

Lewis, Gordon. *Main Currents in Caribbean Thought: The Historical Evolution of Caribbean Society and Its Ideological Aspects, 1492–1900.* [1983]. Lincoln: University of Nebraska Press, 2004.

Lewis, Linden. "Masculinity and the Dance of the Dragon: Reading Lovelace Discursively." *Feminist Review* 59 (Summer 1998): 164–185.

Lewis, Rupert, and Maureen Lewis. "Claude McKay's Jamaica." *Caribbean Quarterly* 23, nos. 2–3 (June–September 1977): 38–53.

Lewis, Shireen. *Race, Culture, and Identity: Francophone West African and Caribbean Literature and Theory from Négritude to Créolité.* Lanham, Md.: Lexington Books, 2006.

Lomas, Laura. "José Martí between Nation and Empire: Latino Cultural Critique at the Intersection of the Americas." In *The Cuban Republic and José Martí: Reception and Use of a National Symbol,* ed. Mauricio Font and Alfonso Quiroz, 115–127. New York: Lexington Books, 2006.

López, Héctor. *La música caribeña en la literatura de la postmodernidad.* Mérida, Venezuela: Universdad de los Andes, 1998.

Lovelace, Earl. *The Dragon Can't Dance.* Essex, England: Longman, 1979.

———. "The Emancipation-Jouvay Tradition and the Almost Loss of Pan." *Drama Review* 42, no. 3 (Fall 1998): 54–60.

Luis, William. "Exhuming *Lunes de Revolución.*" *CR: The New Centennial Review* 2, no. 2 (Summer 2002): 253–283.

———. *Literary Bondage: Slavery in Cuban Narrative.* Austin: University of Texas Press, 1990.

———. "The Politics of Memory and Miguel Barnet's *The Autobiography of a Run Away Slave.*" *Modern Language Notes* 104, no. 2 (March 1989): 475–492.

Mahabir, Joy. *Miraculous Weapons: Revolutionary Ideology in Caribbean Culture.* New York: Peter Lang, 2003.

Maingot, Anthony. "Politics and Populist Historiography in the Caribbean: Juan Bosch and Eric Williams." In *Intellectuals in the Twentieth-Century Caribbean,* Vol. 2, ed. Alistair Hennessy, 145–174. London: MacMillan Caribbean, 1992.

Manley, Michael. *Jamaica: Struggle in the Periphery.* Oxford: Third World Media, 1982.

Manley, Rachel. *Drumblair: Memories of a Jamaican Childhood.* Toronto: Vintage Canada, 1996.

Martí, José. "Nuestra América." [1891]. In *Páginas Escogidas,* ed. Óscar Montoya, 63–77. Bogotá: Editorial Norma, 1994.

———. "Our America." Appendix 1. Trans. John D. Blanco. In *Divergent Modernities: Culture and Politics in 19th Century Latin America,* by Julio Ramos, 295–303. Durham, N.C.: Duke University Press, 2001.

———. "The Poem of Niagara." [1882]. Trans. Elinor Randall. In *On Art and Literature,* ed. Philip Foner, 308–327. New York: Monthly Review Press, 1982.

———. "The Washington Pan-American Conference." [1890]. Trans. Elinor Randall. In *Inside the Monster*, ed. Philip Foner, 339–367. New York: Monthly Review Press, 1975.

Matthews, Gelien. *Caribbean Slave Revolts and the British Abolitionist Movement*. Baton Rouge: Louisiana State University Press, 2006.

McCutcheon, Mark. "She Skin Black as Water: The Movement of Liquid Imagery in Dionne Brand's *In Another Place, Not Here*." *Post Identity* 3, no. 2 (Winter 2002): 133–152.

McFarlane, J. E. Clare. *The Challenge of Our Time: A Series of Essays and Addresses*. Kingston: New Dawn Press, 1945.

McKay, Claude. *Banana Bottom*. [1933]. London: Pluto Press, 1986.

———. *Collected Poems*. Chicago: University of Illinois Press, 2004.

McKenna, Bernard. "'Fancies of Exclusive Possession': Validation and Dissociation in Mary Seacole's England and Caribbean." *Philological Quarterly* 76, no. 2 (Spring 1997): 219–239.

McNeill, Anthony. "For the D." In *Voiceprint*, ed. Stewart Brown, Mervyn Morris and Gordon Rohlehr, 92. New York: Longman, 1989.

Ménil, René. "Birth of Our Art." [1941]. Trans. Michael Richardson and Krzysztof Fijalkowski. In *Refusal of the Shadow: Surrealism and the Caribbean*, ed. Michael Richardson, 105–111. New York: Verso, 1996.

———. "For a Critical Reading of *Tropiques*." [1973]. Trans. Michael Richardson and Krzysztof Fijalkowski. In *Refusal of the Shadow: Surrealism and the Caribbean*, ed. Michael Richardson, 69–78. New York: Verso, 1996.

———. "Introduction to the Marvellous." [1941]. Trans. Michael Richardson and Krzysztof Fijalkowski. In *Refusal of the Shadow: Surrealism and the Caribbean*, ed. Michael Richardson, 89–95. New York: Verso, 1996.

———. "Lightning Effect." [1941]. Trans. Michael Richardson and Krzysztof Fijalkowski. In *Refusal of the Shadow: Surrealism and the Caribbean*, ed. Michael Richardson, 153–155. New York: Verso, 1996.

———. "The Situation of Poetry in the Caribbean." [1944]. Trans. Michael Richardson and Krzysztof Fijalkowski. In *Refusal of the Shadow: Surrealism and the Caribbean*, ed. Michael Richardson, 127–133. New York: Verso, 1996.

Mignolo, Walter. *Local Histories/Global Designs: Coloniality, Subaltern Knowledges, and Border Thinking*. Princeton, N.J.: Princeton University Press, 2000.

———. "(Post)Occidentalism, (Post)Coloniality, and (Post)Subaltern Rationality." In *The Pre-Occupation of Postcolonial Studies*, ed. Fawzia Afzal-Khan and Kalpana Seshadri-Crooks, 86–118. Durham, N.C.: Duke University Press, 2000.

Miller, Nicola. "Intellectuals and the Cuban Revolution." In *Intellectuals in the Twentieth Century Caribbean*, Vol. 2, ed. Alistair Hennessy, 83–98. London: MacMillan Caribbean, 1992.

Mittelholzer, Edgar. "The Sub-Committee." *BIM* 4, no. 3 (December 1951): 158–162.

Monnerot, Jules-Marcel. "Note Bearing on the Coloured French Bourgeoisie." [1932]. Trans. Michael Richardson and Krzysztof Fijalkowski. In *Refusal of the Shadow: Surrealism and the Caribbean*, ed. Michael Richardson, 44–46. New York: Verso, 1996.

———. "On Certain Common Characteristics of the Civilized Mentality." [1933]. Trans. Michael Richardson and Krzysztof Fijalkowski. In *Refusal of the Shadow: Surrealism and the Caribbean*, ed. Michael Richardson, 59–65. New York: Verso, 1996.

Montes-Huidobro, Matías, ed. *El laúd del desterrado.* [1858]. Houston: Arte Público Press, 1995.

Moraña, Mabel, Enrique Dussel, and Carlos Jáuregui, eds. *Coloniality at Large: Latin America and the Postcolonial Debate.* Durham, N.C.: Duke University Press, 2008.

Morris, Mervyn. "On Reading Louise Bennett, Seriously." *Jamaica Journal* 1, no. 1 (December 1967): 69–74.

———. "Valley Prince." *Savacou* 3/4 (December 1970–October 1971): 38.

Munro, Martin. *Exile and Post-1946 Haitian Literature: Alexis, Depestre, Ollivier, Laferrière, Danticat.* Liverpool: Liverpool University Press, 2007.

Musgrave, Thomas. *Self-determination and National Minorities.* New York: Oxford University Press, 1997.

Nair, Supriya. *Caliban's Curse: George Lamming and the Revisioning of History.* Ann Arbor: University of Michigan Press, 1996.

Nanton, Philip. "What Does Mr. Swanzy Want? Shaping or Reflecting? An Assessment of Henry Swanzy's Contribution to the Development of Caribbean Literature." *Kunapipi* 20, no. 1 (1998): 11–20.

Nesbitt, Nick. *Voicing Memory: History and Subjectivity in the French Caribbean.* Charlottesville: University of Virginia Press, 2003.

Nettleford, Rex. Introduction to *Norman Washington Manley and the New Jamaica: Selected Speeches and Writings, 1938–68*, xi–xciv. New York: Africana Publishing, 1971.

Nicholls, David. *From Dessalines to Duvalier: Race, Colour, and National Independence in Haiti.* New York: Cambridge University Press, 1979.

Nixon, Rob. "Caribbean and African Appropriations of *The Tempest.*" *Critical Inquiry* 13, no. 3 (Spring 1987): 557–578.

N'Zengou-Tayo, Marie-José. "The End of the Committed Intellectual: The Case of Lyonel Trouillot." In *Ecrire en pays assiégé/Writing Under Siege*, ed. Marie-Agnès Sourieau and Kathleen Balutansky, 323–343. New York: Rodopi, 2004.

O'Callaghan, Evelyn. *Woman Version: Theoretical Approaches to West Indian Fiction by Women.* New York: St. Martin's Press, 1993.

———. *Women Writing the West Indies, 1804–1939: "A Hot Place, Belonging to Us."* New York: Routledge, 2004.

Ormerod, Beverley. *An Introduction to the French Caribbean Novel.* London: Heinemann, 1985.

Otero Garabís, Juan. *Nación y ritmo: "Descargas" desde el Caribe.* San Juan: Ediciones Callejón, 2000.

Oxaal, Ivar. *Black Intellectuals Come to Power: The Rise of Creole Nationalism in Trinidad and Tobago.* Cambridge: Schenkman, 1968.

Padilla, Heberto. *Self-Portrait of the Other.* [1989]. Trans. Alexander Coleman. New York: Farrar, Straus, Giroux, 1990.

Paquet, Sandra Pouchet. *Caribbean Autobiography: Cultural Self and Self-Representation.* Madison: University of Wisconsin Press, 2002.

———. "The Enigma of Arrival: *The Wonderful Adventures of Mrs. Seacole in Many Lands.*" *African American Review* 26, no. 4 (Winter 1992): 651–663.

———. "The Heartbeat of a West Indian Slave: *The History of Mary Prince.*" *African American Review* 26, no. 1 (Spring 1992): 131–146.

———. "The Vulnerable Observer: Self-Fashioning in Earl Lovelace's *Growing in the Dark (Selected Essays).*" *Anthurium* 4, no. 2 (Fall 2006), http://anthurium.miami.edu/volume_4/issue_2/paquet-thevulnerable.html.

Paton, Diana. Introduction to *A Narrative of Events, since the First of August, 1834, by James Williams, an Apprenticed Labourer in Jamaica,* xiii–lv. Durham, N.C.: Duke University Press, 2001.

Pellón, Gustavo. "The Caribbean's Contribution to the *Boom.*" In *A History of Literature in the Caribbean,* Vol. 1, ed. James Arnold, 209–220. Philadelphia: John Benjamins, 1994.

Pérez, Louis. *Cuba: Between Reform and Revolution.* 2nd ed. New York: Oxford University Press, 1995.

Philip, Michel Maxwell. *Emmanuel Appadocca, or Blighted Life: A Tale of the Boucaneers.* [1854]. Ed. Selwyn Cudjoe. Amherst: University of Massachusetts Press, 1997.

Plummer, Brenda Gayle. *Haiti and the Great Powers, 1902–1915.* Baton Rouge: Louisiana State University Press, 1988.

Pratt, Mary Louise. *Imperial Eyes: Travel Writing and Transculturation.* New York: Routledge, 1992.

Price-Mars, Jean. *Ainsi parla l'oncle.* [1928]. Quebec: Lemeac, 1973.

Prince, Mary. *The History of Mary Prince, A West Indian Slave, Related by Herself.* [1831]. Ed. Moira Ferguson. Ann Arbor: University of Michigan Press, 1997.

Puri, Shalini. *The Caribbean Postcolonial: Social Equality, Post-Nationalism, and Cultural Hybridity.* New York: Palgrave Macmillan, 2004.

Puthak, Zakia, Saswaki Sengupta, and Sharmila Purkayastha. "The Prisonhouse of Orientalism." *Textual Practice* 5, no. 1 (Spring 1991): 195–218.

Questel, Victor. "Pan Drama." *Savacou* 3/4 (December 1970–March 1971): 147–149.

Quigley, Ellen. "Picking the Deadlock of Legitimacy: Dionne Brand's 'noise like the world cracking.'" *Canadian Literature* 186 (Autumn 2005): 48–68.

Rama, Angel. *The Lettered City*. [1984]. Trans. John Charles Chasteen. Durham, N.C.: Duke University Press, 1996.

Ramchand, Kenneth. *The West Indian Novel and Its Background*. [1970]. 2nd ed. London: Heinemann, 1983.

Ramos, Julio. *Divergent Modernities: Culture and Politics in 19th Century Latin America*. [1989]. Trans. John D. Blanco. Durham, N.C.: Duke University Press, 2001.

Ramraj, Victor. "Short Fiction." In *A History of Literature in the Caribbean*, Vol. 2, ed. James Arnold, 199–226. Philadelphia: John Benjamins, 2001.

Rauwerda, A. M. "Naming, Agency, and 'A Tissue of Falsehoods' in *The History of Mary Prince*." *Victorian Literature and Culture* 29, no. 2 (2001): 397–411.

Read, Alan, ed. *The Fact of Blackness: Frantz Fanon and Visual Representation*. London: Institute of Contemporary Arts, 1996.

Renda, Mary. *Taking Haiti: Military Occupation and the Culture of U.S. Imperialism, 1915–1940*. Chapel Hill: University of North Carolina Press, 2001.

Richard, Nelly. "Cultural Peripheries: Latin America and Postmodernist De-Centering." In *The Postmodernism Debate in Latin America*, ed. John Beverley, José Oviedo, and Michael Aronna, 217–222. Durham, N.C.: Duke University Press, 1995.

Richardson, Michael, ed. *Refusal of the Shadow: Surrealism and the Caribbean*. New York: Verso, 1996.

Roach, Eric. "A Type Not Found in All Generations." *Trinidad Guardian*, July 14, 1971.

Roberts, Peter. *From Oral to Literate Culture: Colonial Experience in the English West Indies*. Kingston: University of the West Indies Press, 1997.

Robbins, Bruce, ed. *The Phantom Public Sphere*. Minneapolis: University of Minnesota Press, 1993.

Robinson, Amy. "Authority and the Public Display of Identity: *Wonderful Adventures of Mrs. Seacole in Many Lands*." *Feminist Studies* 20, no. 3 (Fall 1994): 537–557.

Robinson, Gemma. "'If freedom writes no nappier alphabet': Martin Carter and Poetic Silence." *Small Axe* 8, no. 1 (March 2004): 43–62.

Robinson, Jeffrey. "The Root and the Stone: The Rhetoric of Martin Carter's *Poems of Succession*." *Journal of West Indian Literature* 1, no. 1 (October 1986): 1–12.

Rodriguez Juliá, Edgardo. *Cortijo's Wake/El entierro de Cortijo*. [1983]. Trans. Juan Flores. Durham, N.C.: Duke University Press, 2004.

Rohlehr, Gordon. *Calypso and Society in Pre-Independence Trinidad*. Port of Spain: Gordon Rohlehr, 1990.

———. *My Strangled City and Other Essays.* Port of Spain: Longman Trinidad, 1992.

———. *The Shape of That Hurt and Other Essays.* Port of Spain: Longman Trinidad, 1992.

———. "West Indian Poetry: Some Problems of Assessment (Part Two)." *BIM* 14, no. 3 (July–December 1972): 134–144.

Rosenberg, Leah. *Nationalism and the Formation of Caribbean Literature.* New York: Palgrave Macmillan, 2007.

Roumain, Jacques. *Masters of the Dew.* [1946]. Trans. Langston Hughes and Mercer Cook. Oxford: Heinemann, 1978.

———. *Oeuvres complètes.* Ed. Léon-François Hoffmann. Paris: Collection Archivos, 2003.

Sánchez, Luis Rafael. *La guaracha del Macho Camacho.* [1976]. Madrid: Cátedra, 2000.

———. *Macho Camacho's Beat.* Trans. Gregory Rabassa. New York: Pantheon Books, 1980.

Sánchez González, Lisa. *Boricua Literature: A Literary History of the Puerto Rican Diaspora.* New York: New York University Press, 2001.

Sander, Reinhard. *The Trinidad Awakening: West Indian Literature of the Nineteen-Thirties.* New York: Greenwood Press, 1988.

Sarlo, Beatriz. "Aesthetics and Post-Politics: From Fujimori to the Gulf War." In *The Postmodernism Debate in Latin America,* ed. John Beverley, José Oviedo, and Michael Aronna, 250–263. Durham, N.C.: Duke University Press, 1995.

Saunders, Patricia. *Alien-Nation and Repatriation: Translating Identity in Anglophone Caribbean Literature.* Lanham, Md.: Lexington Books, 2007.

Scarano, Francisco. "Labor and Society in the Nineteenth Century." In *The Modern Caribbean,* ed. Franklin Knight and Colin Palmer, 51–84. Chapel Hill: University of North Carolina Press, 1989.

Scharfman, Ronnie. "Theorizing Terror: The Discourse of Violence in Marie Chauvet's *Amour Colère Folie.*" In *Postcolonial Subjects: Francophone Women Writers,* ed. Mary Green, Karen Gould, Micheline Rice-Maximin, Keith Walker, and Jack Yeager, 229–245. Minneapolis: University of Minnesota Press, 1996.

Schmidt, Hans. *The United States Occupation of Haiti, 1915–1934.* New Brunswick, N.J.: Rutgers University Press, 1995.

Schmidt-Nowara, Christopher. *Empire and Antislavery: Spain, Cuba and Puerto Rico, 1833–1874.* Pittsburgh: University of Pittsburgh Press, 1999.

Schulman, Ivan. Introduction to *The Autobiography of a Slave/Autobiografía de un esclavo,* 5–37. Detroit: Wayne State University Press, 1996.

Scott, David. *Conscripts of Modernity: The Tragedy of Colonial Enlightenment.* Durham, N.C.: Duke University Press, 2004.

———. *Refashioning Futures: Criticism after Postcoloniality.* Princeton, N.J.: Princeton University Press, 1999.

———. "The Sovereignty of the Imagination: An Interview with George Lamming." *Small Axe* 6, no. 2 (September 2002): 72–200.

Seacole, Mary. *Wonderful Adventures of Mrs. Seacole in Many Lands.* [1857]. New York: Oxford University Press, 1988.

Seymour, A. J. "A Commentary on Two Poems." In *All Are Involved: The Art of Martin Carter,* ed. Stewart Brown, 100–105. Leeds, England: Peepal Tree, 2000.

Shannon, Magdaline. *Jean Price-Mars, the Haitian Elite and the American Occupation, 1915–1935.* New York: St. Martin's Press, 1996.

Sharpe, Jenny. "'Something Akin to Freedom': The Case of Mary Prince." *Differences: A Journal of Feminist Cultural Studies* 8, no. 1 (Spring 1996): 31–55.

Shohat, Ella. "Notes on the 'Post-Colonial.'" In *The Pre-Occupation of Postcolonial Studies,* ed. Fawzia Afzal-Khan and Kalpana Seshadri-Crooks, 126–139. Durham, N.C.: Duke University Press, 2000.

Silva Gruesz, Kirsten. *Ambassadors of Culture: The Transamerican Origins of Latino Writing.* Princeton, N.J.: Princeton University Press, 2002.

Simoes da Silva, A. J. *The Luxury of Nationalist Despair: George Lamming's Fiction as Decolonizing Project.* Atlanta: Rodopi, 2000.

Sistren Theatre Collective. "Bellywoman Bangarang." [1978]. In *Contemporary Drama of the Caribbean,* ed. Erika J. Waters and David Edgecombe, 77–131. St. Croix, Virgin Islands: Caribbean Writer, 2001.

———. *Lionheart Gal: Life Stories of Jamaican Women.* London: Women's Press, 1986.

Sivan, Emmanuel. "Edward Said and His Arab Reviewers." In *Interpretations of Islam: Past and Present,* 133–154. Princeton, N.J.: Darwin Press, 1985.

Smith, Faith. *Creole Recitations: John Jacob Thomas and Colonial Formations in the Late Nineteenth-Century Caribbean.* Charlottesville: University of Virginia Press, 2002.

Smith, Matthew. *Red and Black in Haiti: Radicalism, Conflict, and Political Change, 1934–1957.* Chapel Hill: University of North Carolina Press, 2009.

Sommer, Doris. *Foundational Fictions: The National Romances of Latin America.* Berkeley: University of California Press, 1991.

Sourieau, Marie-Agnès, and Kathleen Balutansky. Introduction to *Ecrire en pays assiégé/Writing Under Siege,* 9–38. New York: Rodopi, 2004.

Soyinka, Wole. *Myth, Literature and the African World.* Cambridge: Cambridge University Press, 1976.

Spivak, Gayatri. "Can the Subaltern Speak?" In *Marxism and the Interpreta-*

tion of Culture, ed. Cary Nelson and Lawrence Grossberg, 271–313. Chicago: University of Illinois Press, 1988.

———. "Three Women's Texts and a Critique of Imperialism." *Critical Inquiry* 12, no. 1 (Autumn 1985): 243–261.

Stephens, Michelle. *Black Empire: The Masculine Global Imaginary of Caribbean Intellectuals in the United States, 1914–1962*. Durham, N.C.: Duke University Press, 2005.

Thomas, Nigel. "From 'Freedom' to 'Liberation': An Interview with Earl Lovelace." *World Literature Written in English* 31, no. 1 (1991): 8–20.

Tillery, Tyrone. *Claude McKay: A Black Poet's Struggle for Identity*. Amherst: University of Massachusetts Press, 1992.

Torres-Saillant, Silvio. *Caribbean Poetics*. New York: Cambridge University Press, 1997.

Trouillot, Hénock. *Les origines sociales de la littérature haïtienne*. Port-au-Prince: N. A. Théodore, 1962.

Trouillot, Michel-Rolph. *Haiti, State Against Nation: Origins and Legacy of Duvalierism*. New York: Monthly Review Press, 1990.

Vaughan, Megan. "Colonial Discourse Theory and African History, or Has Postmodernism Passed Us By?" *Social Dynamics* 2 (1994): 1–23.

Veloz Maggiolo, Marcio, et al. *Publicaciones y opiniones de La Poesía Sorprendida*. San Pedro de Macorís: Universidad Central del Este, 1988.

Walcott-Hackshaw, Elizabeth. "My Love Is Like a Rose: Terror, Territoire, and the Poetics of Marie Chauvet." *Small Axe* 9, no. 2 (September 2005): 40–51.

Warner, Michael. *Publics and Counterpublics*. Cambridge: Zone Books, 2002.

"What BIM Requires." *BIM* 1, no. 3 (December 1943): 76.

Whitlock, Gillian. "The Silent Scribe: Susanna and 'Black Mary.'" *International Journal of Canadian Studies/Revue internationale d'études canadiennes* 11 (Spring 1995): 249–260.

Wickham, John. "Colly—A Profile." *Bajan and South Caribbean* (January 1973): 12–17.

———. "Introduction." *BIM: The Literary Magazine of Barbados, 1942–1973*, Vol. 1, iii–viii. Millwood, N.Y.: Kraus Reprint, 1977.

Williams, Eric. *Capitalism and Slavery*. [1944]. Chapel Hill: University of North Carolina Press, 1994.

Winer, Lise, et al. Introduction to *Adolphus: A Tale, and The Slave Son*, ix–lxxix. Mona, Jamaica: University of the West Indies Press, 2003.

———. Introduction to *Rupert Gray*, ix–iv. Kingston: University of the West Indies Press, 2006.

Wynter, Sylvia. "We Must Learn to Sit Down Together and Talk About a Little Culture: Reflections on West Indian Writing and Criticism. Part I." *Jamaica Journal* 2, no. 4 (December 1968): 23–32.

————. "We Must Learn to Sit Down Together and Talk About a Little Culture: Reflections on West Indian Writing and Criticism. Part II." *Jamaica Journal* 3, no. 1 (March 1969): 27–42.

Young, Robert. *Postcolonialism: An Historical Introduction.* Oxford: Blackwell, 2001.

Yow, Laura. "The Essay." In *A History of Literature in the Caribbean*, Vol. 2, ed. James Arnold, 329–355. Philadelphia: John Benjamins, 2001.

Index

Luís Madureira, *Cannibal Modernities: Postcoloniality and the Avant-garde in Caribbean and Brazilian Literature*

Elizabeth M. DeLoughrey, Renée K. Gosson, and George B. Handley, editors, *Caribbean Literature and the Environment: Between Nature and Culture*

Flora González Mandri, *Guarding Cultural Memory: Afro-Cuban Women in Literature and the Arts*

Miguel Arnedo-Gómez, *Writing Rumba: The Afrocubanista Movement in Poetry*

Jessica Adams, Michael P. Bibler, and Cécile Accilien, editors, *Just Below South: Intercultural Performance in the Caribbean and the U.S. South*

Valérie Loichot, *Orphan Narratives: The Postplantation Literature of Faulkner, Glissant, Morrison, and Saint-John Perse*

Sarah Phillips Casteel, *Second Arrivals: Landscape and Belonging in Contemporary Writing of the Americas*

Guillermina De Ferrari, *Vulnerable States: Bodies of Memory in Contemporary Caribbean Fiction*

Claudia Sadowski-Smith, *Border Fictions: Globalization, Empire, and Writing at the Boundaries of the United States*

Doris L. Garraway, editor, *Tree of Liberty: Cultural Legacies of the Haitian Revolution in the Atlantic World*

Dawn Fulton, *Signs of Dissent: Maryse Conde and Postcolonial Criticism*

Nick Nesbitt, *Universal Emancipation: The Haitian Revolution and the Radical Enlightenment*

Michael G. Malouf, *Transatlantic Solidarities: Irish Nationalism and Caribbean Poetics*

Maria Cristina Fumagalli, *Caribbean Perspectives on Modernity: Returning the Gaze*

Vivian Nun Halloran, *Exhibiting Slavery: The Caribbean Postmodern Novel as Museum*

Paul B. Miller, *Elusive Origins: The Enlightenment in the Modern Caribbean Historical Imagination*

Eduardo González, *Cuba and the Fall: Christian Text and Queer Narrative in the Fiction of José Lezama Lima and Reinaldo Arenas*

Jeff Karem, *The Purloined Islands: Caribbean-U.S. Crosscurrents in Literature and Culture, 1880–1959*

Faith Smith, editor, *Sex and the Citizen: Interrogating the Caribbean*

Mark D. Anderson, *Disaster Writing: The Cultural Politics of Catastrophe in Latin America*

Raphael Dalleo, *Caribbean Literature and the Public Sphere: From the Plantation to the Postcolonial*